Van den Broek en Bakema, Faculty of Architecture of Delft University of Technology, 1956-1970 – 2008

EDITORIAL A MAGAZINE OF *NEITHER* / TWENTY-FIVE YEARS OF *OASE*

OASE 75 commemorates the 25th anniversary of *OASE* as a journal for architecture. There is an element of celebration in this initiative. Since its emergence in the early 1980s *OASE* has had the sort of precarious existence that is common to most architecture publications, and most certainly to journals dedicated to critical reflection on the practice and theory of architecture, urban planning and landscape design. This issue is, however, more than a festschrift, a recollection among friends of the particular histories connected to *OASE*. The publication in English of a selection of articles, most of which have only been available in Dutch, also presents an opportunity to reflect on the past 25 years in order to ask some persistent questions about the relationship between design practice, criticism, history and theory, and about the position of architecture journals in general and *OASE* in particular.

OASE RETROSPECTIVE

About 70 issues of *OASE* have appeared since the journal was founded by a group of students at the Faculty of Architecture of Delft University of Technology in 1981. The origin of the journal as part of the fall-out of a period of intense, violent (and certainly in part destructive) debates on what was called the 'democratisation' of education in the 1970s is tangible in both the editorial stance and the organisation of *OASE*. Then, as now, the journal is made by volunteers and relies on the commitment of a large variety of authors, advisers and friends. The role of *OASE* has changed over time; from a *samizdat* publication by a group of Delft students to an autonomous periodical addressing a select yet international audience. *OASE* is a journal of architecture from the Low Countries, but it has followed the emergence of Dutch architecture in the 1990s and its international branding as 'Superdutch' from a fairly studied distance. In fact, the most 'Dutch' aspect of *OASE*, since 1990, has been the consistently outstanding and surprising graphic design by Karel Martens and the Werkplaats Typografie in Arnhem. And, of course, the decision to retain a local European language alongside the English texts.

The origins of *OASE* in the challenging didactic environment of a school of architecture suggest a comparison with publications such as *Perspecta*, *Scroope*, *AA Files*, *Faces*, *Trans* or the *Harvard Design Magazine*, and others with looser connections to academic institutions like *Oppositions* or *Arch+*. Unlike most of these, however, *OASE* was not an initiative of academics but a heroic project of self-education by a generation of students who found the teaching offered to them lacking in rigour and breadth.[1] The first years of *OASE* can probably best be described as the endeavour of a generation to discover architects, architectures and ideas about architecture, which had had no place in the curriculum of the institution where the editors found themselves by default, given the dominant position of Delft among the Dutch schools of architecture at the time. Despite the development of the journal from student magazine to a now peer-reviewed publication for architectural design and reflections, this is still tangible in the thematic focus and the writing. The selection of themes and approaches is predominantly informed by individual interests or 'fascinations', developed by editors who may be practising architects or academics. In one of the first issues of *Perspecta* Henri-Russell Hitchcock wrote about the generic interest in architecture history among architects, adding that 'the aspects, or periods, of history that seem at any given time to merit the closest attention certainly vary with changing sensibilities'.[2] *OASE* is a journal reflecting sensibilities rather than particular disciplines. There are examinations of architecture history or historiography, yet it is not a journal of architecture history. Issues relating to architecture theory may be addressed, but the impulse is not that of an academic discourse confined to theory. Articles that could be described as exercises in architecture criticism take a form, which would be impossible in most professional magazines dedicated to presenting projects to practising architects. And finally there are essays that defy any categorisation; highly personal cultural reflections, which lend the journal a sense of urgency beyond both the professional and academic preoccupations of the discipline of architecture.

A TYPOLOGY OF ARCHITECTURE MAGAZINES

Professional magazines, which in the 1950s and '60s took the role of advocates of particular approaches (one can think of Pevsner's and J.M. Richards' role as advocates of an English picturesque in the *Architectural Review* of the period or the heralding of radically modernist architects in *l'Architecture d'Aujourd'hui*), have increasingly become inventories, journalistically reporting anything happening within the field of architecture that the editors consider relevant. The intention to serve large audiences and to offer a broad perspective on architectural culture has frequently resulted in the recording of the status quo, preferably beautifully illustrated. Academic journals, often set up to emulate the patterns of publishing research long established in other disciplines, notably architecture history and planning, constitute the other end of this field, where there is no place for editorial bias or particular

1 *Trans* (ETH Zürich), *Scroope* (Cambridge School of Architecture) and *Perspecta* (Yale University) are still edited by students of the respective schools.

2 Henri-Russell Hitchcock, 'Food for changing sensibility', *Perspecta 6*, 1960, 2.

interventionist directions. Where a relationship with the practice of architectural design exists in such editorial contexts, it is, at best, indirect. In between there is, or should we say there used to be, a zone where arguments or ideas were put forward in the form of a magazine, often with academic connections, as a recognisable position or tendency, ideologically firm and often supported by graphic experiments. The nature of *OASE* as a 'Magazine of Neither', that does not privilege an exclusive focus – be it architecture history, theory or design – but rather seeks to act as a forum where various disciplinary focuses can interact, means that each issue first of all reflects the interests of its particular editors. Beyond this there is, however, a common thread, which reveals itself when set against the types of available publications on architecture. Within the landscape of architecture magazines the position of *OASE* can only be described as ambiguous, a collective of stubborn and engaged editors pushing ahead, unfettered by the international fashions of academia but also deeply unimpressed by the bravura of celebrity architecture. One could criticise its editorial line as being inconsistent, or marginal, even irrelevant. One thing is for sure, it is precisely its fragile position in between firmly established positions and beyond established management models, this typical 'neither', that distinguishes *OASE*. This 'fragility' has consistently marked the position of the journal over time and its editors have been continuously engaged in protecting this characteristic against outside pressures, be it from publishers, academe, professionals, subsidizing bodies, and even readership.

ARCHITECTURE, CRITICISM AND REFLECTION

Is there still a need for a journal like *OASE*, or indeed architecture journals? Over the last two or so decades, the nature of architectural discourses has changed to such an extent that, by now, *OASE* finds itself in a 'splendid isolation' of sorts. The disappearance of journals such as *Oppositions*, *Assemblage* and *Daidalos*, among others – publications that had an enormous impact and influence on the discourse from the period of, approximately, 1967 to 1999 – cannot be explained by financial reasons only. Instead, much of the discourse has become obsessed with the practical and the pragmatic and developed a significant suspicion to any kind of theoretisation, reflection, even intellectual enquiry. Of course, the very nature of the debate has changed. The preoccupation with the 'critical', obsessively present in the 1980s and '90s, seems to have been replaced by an equally complete predominance of celebrating architects and a select number of buildings. At the same time architecture has entered a phase where spatial experience is only a side effect of its production and reception. In certain milieus – one can think of *Volume* in this respect – architects have been seeking to redefine their role within a broader discursive environment, in an effort to make design operational as an approach and attitude in a wide variety of contexts that no longer necessarily have to lead to spatial or built form. Digital developments have furthermore drastically altered the way that architecture is designed and conceived. Likewise the daily discussion of architecture finds its place not only in conversations between experts, but has extended to easily accessible websites, blogs, inter-forums, and so on. The effacement of the barrier/border to architectural media has not only allowed a broad public to engage in discussions on architecture and the city, but has simultaneously drastically redefined the privileged, but essential role of the informed critic. Meanwhile, the production of texts related to architecture has paradoxically grown exponentially. But where does this leave a publication on architecture?

COMMEMORATING A COLLECTIVE ENTERPRISE

Browsing through 25 years of *OASE* – a task that is now facilitated by an online index made available on the journal's website on the occasion of the publication of this issue – one will be struck, perhaps even puzzled by the variety of themes and fascinations addressed. Issues have covered topics such as the architecture of schools and mass tourism, gentrification, suburban dwelling, the Generic City, 1970s architecture and urbanism, the relationship between architecture and literature, space in cyberfiction, and recent disciplinary positions in historiography, but also eighteenth-century 'architecture parlante', the work of De Stijl and Bauhaus, essays on Paul Valéry, and the *Autobahnen* of Nazi Germany. Even if one could set out on an endeavour to define categories of interests over the years, any attempt to circumscribe a clearly defined, long-term editorial agenda would prove unrewarding. In fact, specific editorial positions are mostly defined at the level of individual issues or a select set of issues, rather than as a consistent project spanning a long period of time. Crucial in that respect is that even while the composition of the editorial board has been continually evolving, the one aspect that has remained constant is the absence of an editor-in-chief. *OASE* has always been a collective project, in which practising architects with an interest in theory, history and criticism sat together with researchers and academics with a strong sensibility for design issues. Editorial boards then have functioned as spaces for internal disciplinary discussions. Of course, at certain moments in time, particular members of the editorial board have impacted more strongly on the position of the journal than others, but in essence every issue of *OASE* is the product of a group rather than an individual. Within such collectivity, internal discussion and conflict have proven as fundamental to the journal as shared interests and fascinations.

Following *OASE*'s slow detachment from a TU Delft student's publication to a peer-reviewed journal, the editorial board is now composed of members who are based in the Netherlands or Flanders but have, in fact, more diverse origins and backgrounds and operate in a variety of international networks. The current composition then, reflects a multifocality of possible positions within the disciplines of architecture and urbanism, which in turn is reflected in the broad variety of topics of the more recent years, even if from an outsiders view, *OASE*'s production might still appear as more consistent than for those who operate within the editorial space of the magazine.

What binds these 25 years of production together is less a shared 'agenda' or 'position' than an *engagement* with architecture as a cultural product and as a discipline with its proper autonomy, integrity and legitimacy – even in conditions that are strongly steered by forces and logics that reach beyond. Issues of *OASE* have often expressed the belief that architecture (from chair to city) is a rich and complex field of cultural production and knowledge that relentlessly redefines itself vis-à-vis spatial, societal and cultural challenges and simultaneously has the intrinsic power to challenge these. Critically reflecting and writing on this intriguing *character* of architecture can be regarded as the engaged project of *OASE* throughout the last 25 years. It is also reflected in the different themes that *OASE* engaged with. Apart from being instigated by the personal fantasies and preoccupations of the editors, these themes often address the perennial questions of architectural culture as they appear and re-appear in a context that is firmly related to the Low Countries but is viewed from a broader, European and even international perspective.

It is precisely this focus on the perennial themes of architecture, on the intrinsic power of architecture to relentlessly challenge its own premises as well as those of the broader social and cultural field that seems to have determined the appeal of *OASE* to a public of academics and students, as well as of practicing architects, landscape architects and urban planners. In an era in which a wide variety of logics influences the development of the built environment, this belief in the cultural strength of architecture seems to be more necessary then ever.

This special issue thus does not seek retroactively to distil a continuous position after 25 years in order to explain its continued existence, a mission impossible given the absence of one clear editorial missive. Instead, it serves as a testimony and a grateful contemplation of the hard unpaid labour of the many diverse editorial constellations and a colourful network of contributors of varying stature, while paying tribute to the generous support of individuals, practices and the foundations constituting the local panorama of subsidised culture. It offers the reader a broad selection of texts, some previously only available in

Dutch. Rather than being a 'best of' of 25 years of *OASE*, the selection, by illustrating the broad scope of themes, issues and fascinations that have occupied those who have made the journal over all these years, also offers insights in the changes within architectural culture in the Low Lands over the last 25 years.

Despite this itinerant nature of *OASE*, which to an extent is also its *raison d'être*, this anniversary issue reveals a periodisation of the review into four rather distinct phases, each with a different significance and audience. For each of these periods of time we have asked an author, each of them respected within the discipline of architecture, to reflect on that timeframe, the role of the architecture magazine in general and *OASE* more specifically. For each period, we have selected a restricted number of important texts that have remained somewhat under-recognised, which are briefly presented by some of the editors at the time. The dedication and commitment, already apparent when reviewing *OASE*'s history itself, has re-emerged through these contributions by former editors, contributions we consider vital to *OASE* 75 as they reflect an ongoing involvement with the discourse. The issue will furthermore present a factual history of *OASE*, a complete index and some aspects of the graphics of the magazine.

The periodisation demonstrates how small and sometimes seemingly insignificant changes can trigger a transformation in content and editorial direction. The periods are organised by specific breaks due to a name change, new graphics, and subsequently a new language. This reveals how practical and external factors can often underlie the traditional understanding of historical continuity. Putting things on the reading table like this, we hope that more reflection on the influences and relevance of *OASE* will follow as a reaction to its anniversary issue. Hopefully, the issue will provoke a discussion inside and outside the audience of *OASE* on what this magazine has been – and, perhaps more importantly, what it should become. More generally, we explicitly hope that it will contribute to a larger discussion on the role of journals of architecture in contemporary architectural culture.

The editorial board, April 2008

'*O*', as *OASE* was first called, referring to Ontwerp, Onderzoek, Onderwijs (Design, Research, Education), was born in an atmosphere of discontent, imbedded in the educational context of the Faculty of Architecture of Delft University of Technology (the then Afdeling Bouwkunde of the Technische Hogeschool Delft). A product of the 'the critical 1970s', it took as its point of departure the international debate on architecture and planning until then seemingly absent in the Netherlands. The founding editorial states that the intention is not to make an in-crowd school paper, but a publication that collaborates with Eindhoven University of Technology, the various architecture academies and the departments of art history in the Netherlands. It aspires to continue the engagement of the student movement that started in 1966, and to offer a platform with the ability to react to current subjects. Issues 1 to 10 collect different articles along a number of simultaneous editorial tracks that are replaced by new ones when exhausted. The virtual absence of a budget was the reason that every issue needed to be sold. After issue 9/10, the last three original editors left, completing the first full replacement of the editorial board. Another factor in ending this embryonic phase is the name change forced upon *O* by the 'Federatie O', the combined organ of the professional organisations of various fields of design in the Netherlands: architecture, interior design, urbanism, landscape architecture and engineering (BNA, BNI, BNS, BNT and ONRI). Regretfully, *O* is compelled to accept the claim to their name by an institution-of-institutions that nobody had ever heard of, appearing from then onwards as *OASE*.

O 1	
O 2	
O 3	
O 4	Jongerenhuisvesting (Youth housing)
O 5	
O 6	
O 7	
O 8	10 jaar stadsvernieuwing Rotterdam (10 years of urban renewal in Rotterdam)
O 9/10	

Period I

FOUNDA-TIONS

A Student Publication and its Name Change 1981–1984

Alexander Tzonis

THE LOST YEARS?

I believe history is a discipline that produces new knowledge grounded on evidence to be found in material things, in texts and in visual records. This implies digging into documents, mining archives, and, if and when needed, using analytical methods and information technology. Last but not least, writing about history must avoid being driven by biases and vested interests in making judgments and drawing conclusions, as well as in indulging in trivia and anecdotes. Alas, life is too complex and full of limitations to satisfy all the above. Working as a historian, one is forced to talk and write about the past, not only looking into documents in a skimpy and inconsistent way but also not being able to avoid a subjective point of view and consequently running the danger of producing texts with very low knowledge value. Hopefully, the following text, although fulfilling too few of the above prescriptions, can still provide some useful information about the interesting period of the first five years of *OASE*, a period which, by accident, coincides with the first five years of my involvement with the School of Architecture (known as 'Bouwkunde') of Delft University (then College) of Technology, a period of major shifts in architecture as well as in world developments.

By way of introduction – mixing two identities, the historian and the witness of the period – I would like to say a few words of about how I became acquainted with Bouwkunde and how this acquaintance led to my long-term involvement with the TUD and subsequently to writing this piece. This appears to be exactly the wrong thing to do if one wants to avoid an anecdotic narrative. Yet, my intention in narrating this story is exactly the opposite, namely to offer through a particular case an entry to the understanding of the situation in the School of Architecture in Delft in the context of broader historical events.

The year was 1968 – a period of major political, cultural and social upheavals in the world and particularly in the USA, where I was teaching at that time, especially among students – when, as a young faculty at Yale, I was asked for advice by a small group of my students responsible for preparing the forthcoming issue of the yearbook *Perspecta* (no. 12). A key person in these discussions was Stuart Wrede, who was reporting on his experience with Indesem, (INternational DEsign SEMinar) a meeting that had taken place the previous year in the School of Architecture in Delft. Indesem was founded in 1962 by a group of architecture students at the TUD in collaboration with Wiek Röling and Jaap Bakema. Aldo van Eyck, Peter Smithson and Herman Hertzberger also participated in this event. The 1962 conference was very much driven by the humanistic ideas that dominated Team 10 and the *Forum* magazine group at that time, anti-functionalist and mildly regionalist-populist. A great number of these European architects were known already in the USA. Smithson had taught at Yale in the 1950s, Bakema in St Louis, and Van Eyck, invited by Jerzy Soltan, was visiting critic at Harvard and I, as a student, had lunched with him in the spring of 1963.

On the other hand, the Indesem meeting that Wrede had taken part in 1967 was not a repeat of the 1962 gathering, and the ideas discussed there had not yet circulated in the USA. Partially influenced by sociopolitical developments of the time – the war in Vietnam, the anti-colonial and peace movements, as well as by the awareness that post-Second-World-War architecture, the architecture of 'reconstruction' or 'urban renewal', whose schemes claimed to be based on the orthodoxy of the Modern Movement, were a failure – the participants of Indesem 1967 were highly polemical and politicized. They disapproved of the established professional architectural practice, mainstream 'functionalist' theories, and, more importantly, blamed the profession and professional education for being subservient to the social and economic 'establishment', the ultimate villain.

Although the names associated mostly with the meeting were those of two Dutch architects, Aldo van Eyck and Herman Herzberger, the names Wrede brought back included those of Walter Benjamin and Herbert Marcusse, whose ideas apparently were very much discussed during the Indesem get-together. Soon after, Wrede met Marcusse. The result of the meeting was a unique contribution by Marcusse in the *Perspecta* issue of 1969. As a result of this meeting, Wrede also conceived, commissioned and installed *Lipstick*, a large-scale sculpture by Claes Oldenburg on Beinecke Plaza, at Yale, a clear monumental statement of cultural protest in the spirit of the nationwide free speech and antiwar movement. Interestingly, behind the Colossal Keepsake Corporation of Connecticut was Philip Johnson, anonymously backing the project, which without doubt was inspired by the debates of the Delft meeting. As for Wrede, he would become, in the 1980s, director of architecture at the Museum of Modern Art in New York.

Delft remained in my mind when I left Yale to move to Harvard and it came back during discussions with Graduate School of Design students. As Yale students were busy at that time with *Perspecta,* the GSD students were busy preparing their 1969 issue of *Connection*, their review of architecture. The architecture Aldo van Eyck and Herzberger was part of their discussions, as their approach to architecture, together with that of Giancarlo de Carlo and Shadrach Woods, was perceived – in contrast to that predominant in the USA, which was seen as mechanistic and formalist – as being humanistic and socially committed. Among those students, the most enthusiastic for Van Eyck and Herzberger was Bob Maltz, an excellent thesis student with whom I had long discussions as co-supervisor of his project. Unsurprisingly, soon after his graduation, Maltz moved to the Netherlands to become a teacher at Delft and assistant to Hertzberger. Soon after his arrival in Delft, I received an invitation to lecture in the School of Architecture there.

The lecture, orchestrated by Maltz, took place in the early summer of 1971. Much to my disappointment, the place was not the old building of the School of Architecture on Oude Delft, where the Indesem meetings took place and, a little more than two years before, on Friday 9 May 1969, the 'democratization' meeting that was to overturn the structure of the School. My lecture, however, happened in the new building, Berlageweg 1, designed by Bakema, where the school had moved in 1970. Given the time of the year, only a handful of people attended (the most vocal among them Henk Engel), enough to fit on one of the balconies of the building. The talk went on for two hours and was followed by a highly inspired discussion with many references to the 9 May meeting, still on the balcony. After that a tour of the building ensued, huge for a school of architecture by American standards of that time and remarkably under-occupied. Later, the discussion continued in the house of Sjirk Haaksma, in a wonderful room overlooking a canal, overcrowded by our group. What was characteristic, and for me impressive, about the discussion was, on one hand, the critical stance towards architectural practice, daring enough to censor even the work of Van Eyck and Herzberger, on the other, the excellent knowledge of the members of the gathering of the European avant-garde movement of the 1920s and '30s, which they approached not as a 'modernist' style but as an architecture 'agent provocateur' dedicated to the cause of a new society, a new way of life.

For many reasons, this kind of approach to modern architecture was not present in the USA at that time. The history of modern architecture was still dominated by the Gideon-Pevsner reductive technophile paradigm, even at Harvard, where the Design School was headed by the formidable Jose Luis Sert, a collaborator of Picasso in 1937. My Delft friends assured me that the School of Architecture of TUD was on its way not only to teach these ideas, but also to teach them through a new pedagogical approach, one free of traditional dogmatic, 'elite' standards, at the same time not 'autonomous', but made relevant through planning action such as Luud Schimmelpenninck's (activist elected in 1967 to the Municipal Council of the City of Amsterdam) and the Provo's *White Bicycle* urban transportation plan. The idea of the university as a 'critical' – referring to the Frankfurt School terminology – institution coupled with that of 'democratization' was no longer a utopia. Because, my company assured me, contrary to what was happening in other European countries, the administration in Delft not only believed in architecture 'in the name of the people' but also possessed the material resources to make it happen.

The story of Bouwkunde of the 1960s and '70s was extreme but not atypical and did not take place in a vacuum. Most schools of architecture suffered from a similar crisis. During this period the Western economy, society, culture and their institutions were undergoing tremendous changes affecting architecture, its practice and its education. The Netherlands was not an exception. By the end of the 1950s, the task of massive post-Second-World-War reconstruction being accomplished, there was an equally massive investment in the so-called welfare state improving the level of social welfare, culture and education. Part of this process was the transformation of TUD from a university of 1000 students, during the first decade of the 1900s, to 5500 by 1950 (13,650, by the 1980s). Bouwkunde, having a handful of students before the war, became a school of about 500 students in the mid 1950s, (2766 by the end of the 1970s). This growth required a different kind of education and administration rules and regulations, and one of the reasons of the furore of the students and young faculty at that time was the failure of the official 'authorities' not only to solve the emerging problems, but even to comprehend the nature of their complexity. Facing this vacuum of leadership, the reaction was very often out of the ordinary and discordant. Such were the attempts of the 'democratic' power of the new administrative structure of the school to control the 'aristocratic' behaviour of the 'elite' faculty, their teaching style and the content of their instruction. An extreme case was the clash that developed between Carel Weeber, as Dean, together with the Board of Directors, and Aldo van Eyck and Herman Hertzberger – who, with Bakema, were the only internationally prestigious members of the faculty at that moment – in 1976. The conflict left deep scares which made cohesion, collaboration and 'cohabitation' impossible, imperative conditions during periods of major institutional change. Members of the stuff did not perceive each other as resources within a win-win game, but as competitors in a fatal zero-sum strife, resembling Frederico Fellini's comic-tragic *Prova d' Orchestra*.

It is unfair to say that the School was not truly struggling to set up a programme of excellence meeting its multifaceted goals, professional quality, cultural worth and social accountability. Towards this end Bouwkunde moved with set of new appointments – Andreas Faludi in 1974, for planning methods, Stanislaus von Moos, at the beginning of the 1980s, for architecture history, and H.M. Höfler, a little later, for design process, Jurgen Rosemann for urban renewal – to fill in positions related to new domains that Bouwkunde did not include before.

Thus, the second Tuesday of September 1981 – ten years after my lecture in the new building of Bouwkunde, I was resting in my hotel room in Delft, watching television with my wife, after a meeting at the School of Architecture of TUD, involving my future tasks as Professor of Design Methodology, a chair formerly occupied by H. Brower, who had died in 1974. Brower had particular interest in developing a systems approach to design, but at the same time he had played an important role in the development of the new direction of studies in social housing during the democratization debates in the School. I was expected to continue in this direction, even more rigorously and on an international platform.

In the room, our attention was drawn by the television programme: Queen Beatrix giving a speech, what we later understood was the speech announcing the plans of the year, in front of the Dutch Parliament. Despite our limited understanding of the language, it became clear that the Queen was outlining a rather grim economic condition of the country announcing a programme of austerity and economic discipline. Indeed, we were witnessing an event signalling the beginning of a new period in the Netherlands, part of a transformation that was occurring in fact around the world at that moment, and an event with major consequences for the future of Bouwkunde.

It took some months for the speech to have an impact on the School of Architecture, which, it seemed to me, was carrying on its lavish, Titanic-style, trip. But when the impact was felt the shock was great. And the agent who transmitted the impact was a politician with special interest in education, W.J. Deetman.

On 11 September 1981, Deetman was appointed Secretary of State for Education and Science and soon after, on 29 May 1982, he was appointed Minister of Education and Science. He was the minister responsible for coordinating scientific policy and he was greatly supported at that time. On 5 November 1982 and again on 14 July 1986, he was reappointed Minister of Education and Science. In his function as Minister he undertook to confront the Bouwkunde challenge, its high cost, its plush style, and – as some people saw it – its eccentric ways. It is not the place here to analyse the efforts of the ministry to reform education of architecture not only in Delft, but all over the Netherlands, including the School of Architecture in Eindhoven and the Academies. Deetman was a conservative, but many of the plans that were discussed and brought out during his tenure were radical, ranging from splitting up and re-concentrating programmes in a small number of centres for building engineering education, to completely terminating architectural programmes and eliminating chairs. These put into question the very existence of Berlageweg 1.

Once more the new crisis of Bouwkunde was severe but not uncommon among the schools of architecture around the Western world and again did not take place out of context. By the end of the 1970s, the welfare state appeared to be running out of money around the world. From the State of California to New York, to the UK and the Netherlands, there were diagnoses of 'fiscal crisis' in most domains of public services and social programmes, followed by remedial acts of massive cuts of welfare-state budgets, and, if not elimination, a shift of such services and programmes from the state to the private domain.

For example, in New York, while federal and state assistance grew between 1962 and 1974 from 25 to 48 per cent every year, by the end of the 1970s it had shrunk dramatically. At the same time, the growth of 'Great Society' intergovernmental funds was reduced from 35 per cent during the period of 1966 to 1969 to 12.4 in the following three years. Paradoxically, as salaries increased during the same period, the real value of income from taxes decreased, assuring the bankruptcy of the city's programmes of architecture and urbanism.

This is not the place to analyse or judge these developments. It is enough to say that they projected not only a different set of priorities for architecture, but also an educational programme drastically different from the one planned during the 1960s and '70s, such as the one dreamt by the young students and teachers in the USA and in Western Europe and in Delft. It was the end of an era, the era of architecture of the welfare state – populist architecture being its last phase – which was characterized to a great extent by public buildings, social housing and mass urban development projects, taught in well-funded schools supported, directly or indirectly, by public money.

But soon after there was also a beginning, the beginning of a period of building driven by private development and private cultural sponsorship, dominated by high-middle-class housing and homes, tourist facilities, headquarters and museums, which required different architectural skills and knowledge from those called for by the welfare state. Thus, the whole curriculum of schools of architecture had to be re-orientated together with the means of their financing.

Once more, Bouwkunde was not prepared. The new administrative structures put in place through the process of democratization were the worse kind of organization to face this kind of crisis. The result was ineffectual confusion combined with activist inaction that dominated during the first five years of the 1980s.

The exhilarating, notorious and tumultuous 1960s were followed by a period of orderly but also depressive cultural reaction in most of the Western world. It is dangerous to match such shifts in *Weltanschauung* with specific architectural products. Buildings appear years after they are commissioned, expressing the aspirations of a client, and it might take years between an architect's sketching of a scheme on the drafting-board that articulates certain desires of the period and its construction on a site that might have imposed constraints at that moment. However, one can safely illustrate the change that occurred between the 1970s and '80s by pointing to the elating *La Mémé* by Lucien Kroll and the exploding *Mummers Theater* by Johansen and Bhavnani and contrasting them to the sedating San Juan Capistrano Library by Michael Graves, the mausoleum-like

Architectural Museum by Oswald Matthias Ungers, and the pharaonic *Les Colonnes de Saint Christophe* by Ricardo Bofill.

If the architecture of the 1960s and '70s was extrovert and dominated by the populist movement, the 'in the name of the people' architecture of the (end of) the 1970s and '80s was one of introversion and professional 'narcissism'.[1]

We employed the term narcissism to portray the architecture of this period not so much to indicate the introversion of architecture of the period, but more in the psychoanalytic sense of the term. Accordingly, narcissism, we wrote, demonstrates 'the confusion between the consciousness of control of the self over the self and of the self over the outside world. This is the state in the development of a child where the self is not yet detached from the things of the external world when the "omnipotence of thoughts" dictates a great deal of his/her acts. A person may regress to this state of denial after facing an acute disaster, such as the death of a loved one, when it is obvious from the outset that no measures can redeem the catastrophe.' In social groups, a professional group for instance, a grave loss or a major frustration can provoke similar symptoms of regression: denial of reality and a take-over of the 'omnipotence of thoughts' in its collective thinking, expressed in the 'preoccupation with formalism, hedonism, graphism', helping practitioners to face up to a 'recent frustration and to deny the separation between reality and desire, turning inward for approval to the closed world of peers or of the drawing board, where everything is possible . . . enabling a feeling of omnipotence to replace the sense of wretchedness.'

1 'The Narcissist Phase in Architecture' (with L. Lefaivre), for the *Harvard Architectural Review*, no. 1, 1980.

Today, one feels that these comments are referring only to one of the aspects of architecture of the 1970s, the other being the shift towards a disciplinarian approach, a 'rappel à l'ordre' – as in the case of the Fellini movie – responding to the need to save architectural knowledge from extinction.

Almost no school of architecture managed to escape this shift, and Bouwkunde was no exception.

In several schools of architecture in the USA, France and West Germany the crisis lead to the production of new design prototypes, new design education paradigms, to research and book products that provided new knowledge for immediate use, but also usable in the long term. By contrast, by the end of the crisis proper, Bouwkunde had very little intellectual output to demonstrate. Why this absence of product?

Pragmatic and severe as most of Deetman's ideas were, they ironically resembled the predominant ideas of the radicals of the previous decade. Both Deetman and Bouwkunde, the school he wanted to reform, paid too much attention to organizational details of architectural education and very little to *design*; design, as knowledge and as a force of-and-for creative innovation, was absent from their vision – which explains the poverty of intellectual yield during this period.

Were these years lost out of the lives of both the students and staff of Bouwkunde?

To some extent I think they were. On the other hand, as the crisis threatening the very existence of Bouwkunde carried on in the first part of the 1980s, the new generation of students that had arrived in the school during these gloomy years began to respond. This was the generation that by the end of the twentieth century would make Dutch architecture once more world famous. But at that time, none of their actions, lacking the drama and bravura of the 1960s and '70s, hinted at such things to come.

Stylos, Bouwkunde's student association, searched for ways to open new discussions about real buildings and cities, beyond the world of committees and their fantasies of administrative diagrams. A driving force in this direction was Peter Loeraker, a unique individual who combined charisma, enthusiasm and great talent in design, as was demonstrated in his graduation design, a real house he built in Almere. In a very short period he initiated and organized a series of events and lectures bringing back the question of design to the Bouwkunde community. In contrast to the intolerant cliquishness and meanness of the previous generation, Loeraker had largess and vision. Within a period of less than five years he worked with the two most notoriously antagonistic personalities of Bouwkunde, undertaking his thesis with Carel Weeber and organizing one of the very best shows of Aldo van Eyck. If not for his tragic death in 1991, he would have had a major influence on Dutch architecture and architectural education and perhaps been an ideal Dean of the School.

One of the student initiatives to bring back design to Bouwkunde was the journal *OASE*. How successful it was and according to what measures is a story and history for another writer, my mission being to provide some kind of contextual framework to understand better these first steps of *OASE*.

The first issue of the journal *O* was published in the spring of 1981. During this period, both the educational and the professional sectors were critical of the outcome of the urban renewal efforts in Rotterdam and Amsterdam.

Education at the Faculty of Architecture in Delft drew on morphological analyses to develop alternative design strategies for housing in old neighbourhoods. At the same time, it explored housing typologies. The education provided by Max Risselada, in particular, was dedicated to analysing plans and developing a theoretical apparatus and set of design instruments. Plan analysis looked at topics such as the access systems and concepts of space in apartment buildings by the Russian constructivists and villas by Le Corbusier and Adolf Loos. Meanwhile, the department of architecture history run by Kees Vollemans studied the concepts of type and model in the development of private homes in Amsterdam designed by the seventeenth-century architects Philip Vingboons and Hendrick de Keyser. Parallel to all of these studies, design studios were examining the typological and morphological structure of the urban fabric by analogy with Saverio Muratori's studies of Venice.

Whereas the practice of urban renewal introduced suburban dwelling types such as the walk-up flat as fremdkörper, or foreign objects, into nineteenth-century neighbourhoods, the analyses conducted at the Faculty of Architecture offered starting points for new creativity. In combination with the typical hierarchy of the street pattern, the typological and architectural features of the nineteenth-century residential home were translated into new dwelling types that became part of the urban fabric. This method was brought to the practice of urban renewal by the graduates who took up posts as designers at the urban development departments in Rotterdam and The Hague. So it happened that the transformation of the city on the basis of its typological and morphological features was applied to nineteenth-century residential neighbourhoods in Rotterdam which were regenerated through demolition and new developments.

The above interaction between plan analysis, morphological and typological research and design, both in education and urban renewal, prompted the theme of the first issue: 'plan analysis and typology'. In his article 'plan analysis and design legitimation', Miel Karthaus outlines the various approaches to and relationship with the design. He argues that plan analysis does not automatically produce a design, but can only serve as a tool for the architect-designer. Alongside this article, we included a translation of a Philippe Panerai article on typologies. The latter initiated a series of articles on the same subject in subsequent issues of *O*.

Roy Bijhouwer
Member of the editorial board
from *OASE* 1 to 7

Translated by Laura Vroomen

Miel Karthaus

PLAN ANALYSIS & DESIGN LEGITIMA-TION

FIRST PUBLISHED IN O 1

In this article I want to take a very broad view of the term 'plan analysis'.

Although it was originally developed as an educational tool, I believe its meaning now covers more than simply learning to read a design. During the past ten years – ever since the democratisation – the term plan analysis has become more prominent in debates on architecture in Delft. So much so, that I would now like to use it as a term to describe a modern view of design and architecture. In this respect I see a link between 'plan analysis' and 'design output'. In doing so, I am giving it a broader meaning than Max Risselada does as a teacher. In his preface to 'Doel en vermaak',[1] he never links 'analysis' and the actual design process. He merely identifies an affinity between the method of plan analysis and the design process. However, especially now that plan analysis has come to be associated with concepts such as 'morphology' and 'typology', there is indeed a reciprocity between analysis and design.

1 Frits Palmboom, *Doel en Vermaak in het Konstruktivisme* (Nijmegen, 1979).

The term 'plan analysis' has its roots in Delft. Although its origins derive in part from the same impulses that, on an international level, are now creating the icons of 'postmodernism', the difference between the two is even more conspicuous: plan analysis has a fundamentally different approach to history. Its methodology may still be underdeveloped, yet plan analysis offers a genuine study of all the tools and material that architecture, as an institution, has generated. This approach is more likely to help the discipline reflect on its own history than all the hype in the illustrated press would have us believe. To preserve this difference, the analyses really ought to develop into a robust set of instruments. Genuinely interested in turning its own history into an 'object' of knowledge instead of merely roaming around in it as if in a nostalgic pleasure

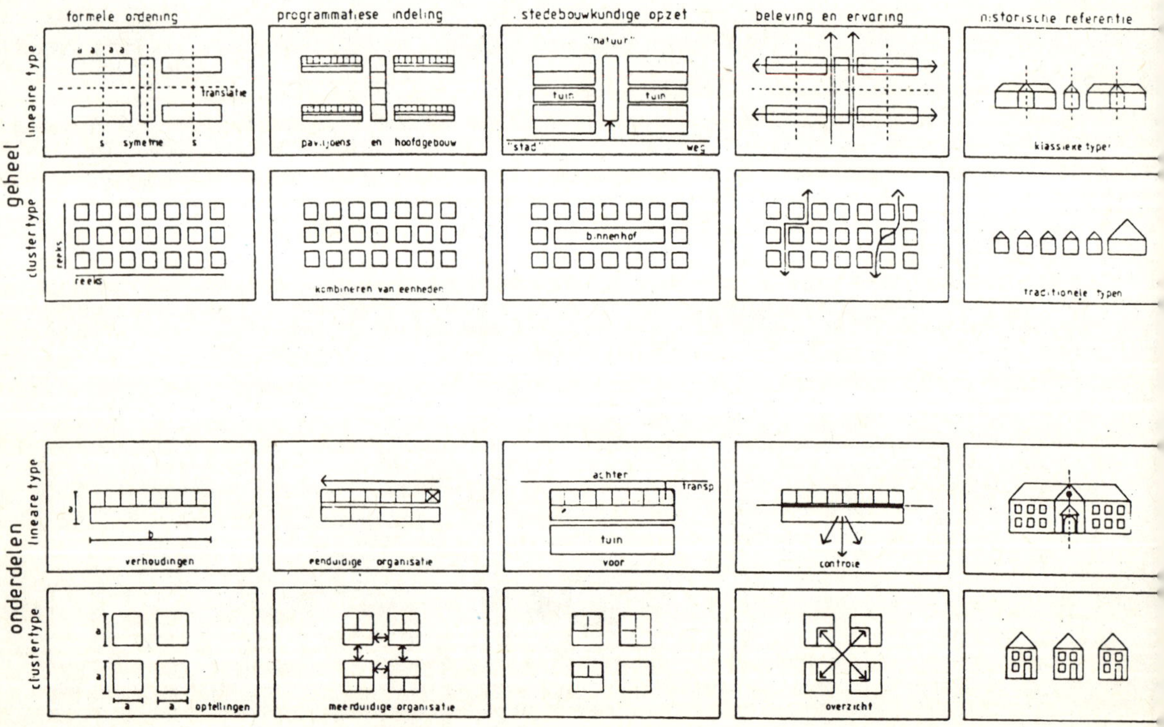

Studies by Jos Louwe & Casper van der Hoeven

garden, it must – as if it were a science – account for its methods. And this is not an easy assignment, as every new theme, every new task that architecture envisages, whether it relates to the city, a particular function or construction, calls for the development of an appropriate method of analysis. The search for real chances to respond to current urban and planning problems continually throws up new questions about the history of architecture, just as it calls for new techniques for deploying that history. It involves continuous debate on those instruments of knowledge. At present, criticism provides the only place for debate on methods of architecture/historical research. But however much a particular form of architecture may benefit from analyses such as those by Wittkower or Colin Rowe, they will never suffice for the simple reason that 'criticism' never leads the way. Whereas architecture may get an idea of its history in a close, reciprocal relationship with criticism, it will still have to pose its own questions, as this is the only trigger for a subsequent development in architectural output.

Initially, 'plan analysis' challenged the then dominant conception of design: that of 'Forum'.[2] Although the approach covered a range of different ideas and methods, it rather limited the precise meaning of the term plan analysis. It found its meaning in the coherence of what it opposed. During the lengthy battle against the so-called ideology of the artist/architect, 'plan analysis' came to mean an approach that covered the method of design as well as its professional practice, the relationship with historical material and design education. In short, it was a completely novel concept of design, a new approach to architecture. The positions that were adopted then, about five years ago, must be retained and reconsidered, as they provide a theoretical foundation for the further development of the 'instruments of knowledge'.

Over the years the term plan analysis has been associated with such a diverse range of aspirations and movements in architecture that the term now circulates too widely. A great deal of international work, such as that of the five Americans, Stirling, Rossi's typological work, and so on, has also left its mark on those studios that draw on plan analysis. As a consequence, the term has become rather imprecise. Right now, it refers to a certain approach to design rather than a clearly defined method. A single method among many.

This imprecision need not be a barrier to the concept's effectiveness at all. Something that is difficult to define in any detail can still be extremely effective in a wide range of areas. This is particularly pertinent to matters governing human behaviour. And to some extent it also applies to 'plan analysis' as an 'approach'. It actually managed to establish itself fairly easily in education, and I suspect that the current generation of students cannot quite understand what we were struggling with at the time of the reappointments of Van Eyck and Hardy.[3]

Certainly enough to not pursue it any further. Yet this fosters a number of misunderstandings. One such misunderstanding is the notion that you can use 'plan analysis' to design. Another is the idea that a typological study is indispensable if you are commissioned to build a library or psychiatric institution. After all Jos Louwe,[4] in his explanatory notes to the competition entry for a psychiatric institution, wrote: 'The type. The concept of type plays an important role in our *understanding of form*. In general terms one might say that the type is a fundamental principle that

2 The name 'Forum' refers to a magazine in which architects Herzberger, Van Eyck, Apon, Bakema and art historian Hardy published work between July 1959 and May 1963.

3 For those who are interested, the debate surrounding history education provides a good entry point. In Delft, too, there was a struggle to establish historical materialism in education. One might say that this laid the foundation for the 'plan analysis' that would emerge later. See the reports *Historie Nu* (June 1973) and *Historie Nou En* (October 1973).

4 Jos Louwe was long associated with the working group of C. Weeber and L. van Duin, one of the studios that developed plan analysis in education. Last year he and C. van de Hoeven submitted a design called 'März, no. 223' to a competition for a psychiatric institution. Quote: illustration, 1.

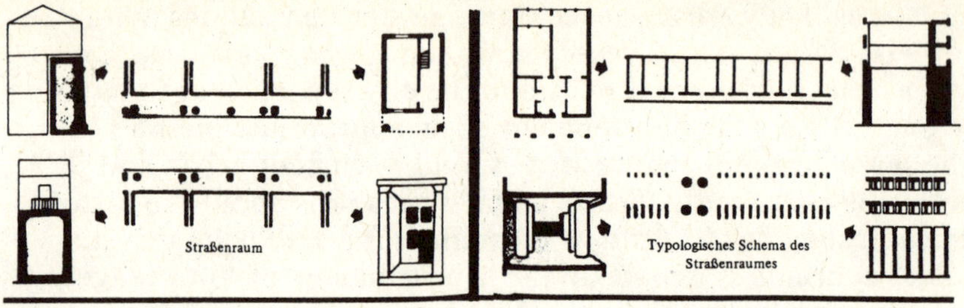

Aldo Rossi

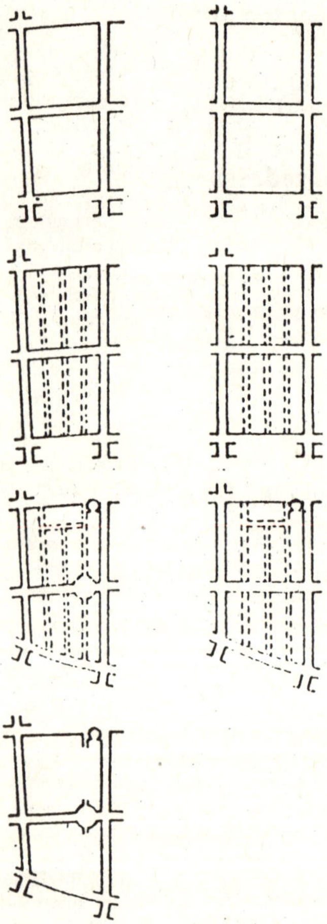

Aldo Rossi

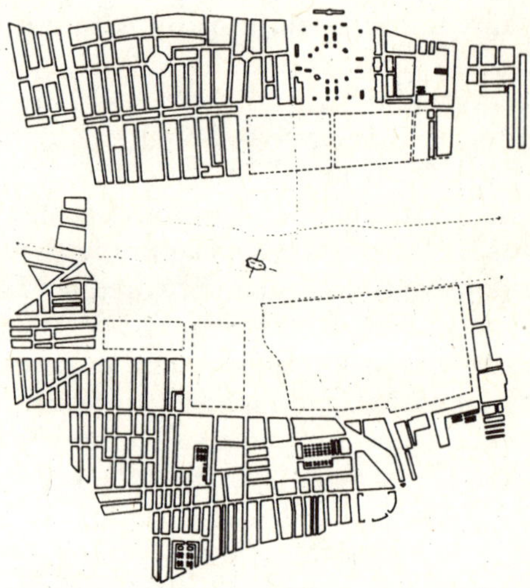

'Witte nota' (white paper)

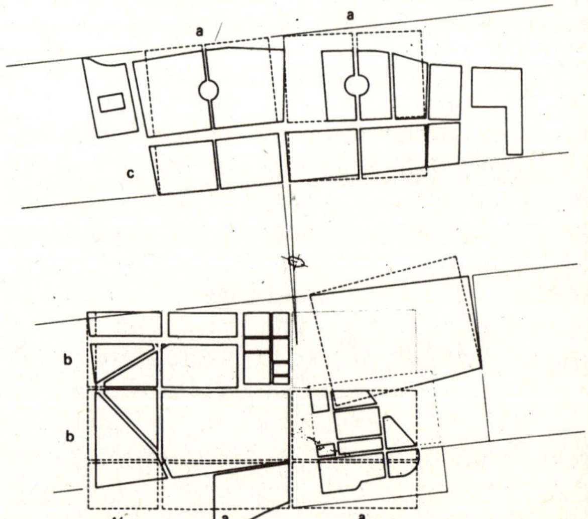

'Witte nota' (white paper)

governs the construction of buildings. Because a type has crystallised over the years it offers the guarantee of satisfying certain practical requirements and finds itself embedded in the experience and collective memory of users. It thus offers the designer a starting point from which to interpret the type and arrive at a 'good' design.'

Following Rossi, a great deal of modern, so-called formal work is characterised by 'typological clarity'. These designs present themselves 'as' type, and not as concrete, temporal and spatial *interpretations* within a typological series. In these instances an analytical tool, the typological, is instantly assimilated in the design. Type becomes Form. Strictly speaking, any reference to a type to legitimise a particular form is based on a misunderstanding of the role of analysis in design. Of course, a design touches upon the *reasons* why a type transforms or survives. It's those reasons that legitimise a design, not the analysis itself. This kind of misunderstanding is to be expected at a time when architecture wants to show an interest in its history. At that point plan analysis is in fact its opposite, because it is not used as an instrument of knowledge but as a design tool. There is no one-to-one relationship between analysis and design. No more than form ever followed function, does form follow type.

Now that the word is starting to crop up in job descriptions for new lecturers, it is threatening to become a magic word that can be deployed anywhere, anytime. Architects have always had a predilection for magic words to help them flog their designs. If we want to be able to discuss plan analysis as a collection of methods we must first make a clear distinction between the many purposes it serves.

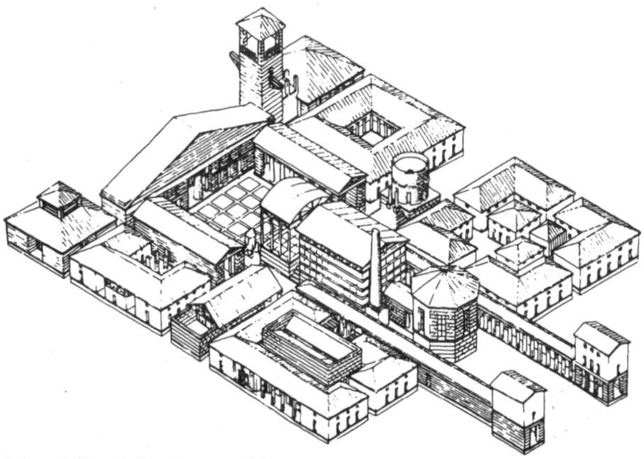

Léon Krier, School ensemble

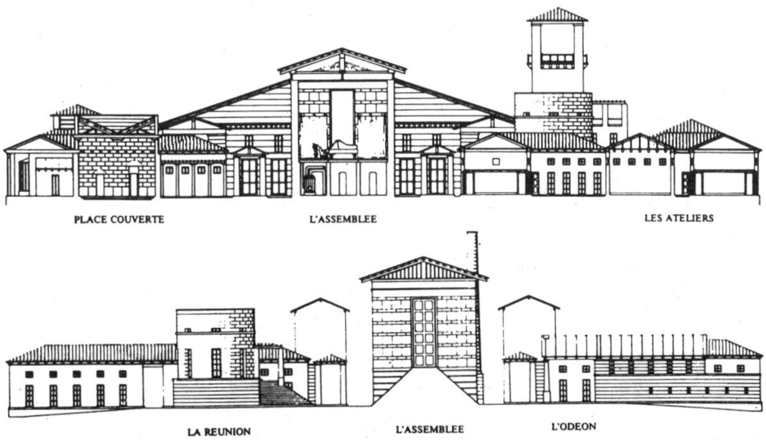

For instance, is the analysis in question quite distinct from a design commission or is it directly linked to a particular design process? Are we dealing with a study that transcends a mere ideological critique? Is it a checklist? These questions can be put to every single design with the aim of quickly obtaining similar sets of information. Or are we trying to identify the specific qualities of a piece? Is it a single piece or an entire oeuvre? Does the analysis consider the piece as a whole or is it trying to find meaning in its constituent parts? Is the key focus on urban planning or on the buildings themselves? Sometimes things become confused: in his analysis of urban morphology, in favour of squares and streets, Léon Krier harks back to a very distinct, almost allegorical historicism of monumentality.

He needs this exaggerated monumentality and its 'historical value' to come up with a compelling design for these public spaces. This architecture serves his urban-planning analysis and is subordinate to it. (Unfortunately, he extends this analysis of the European city into a critique of industrial society as a whole.) A truly perceptive analysis of specific monuments within the historical context of the city and their effect amid the modernist onslaught would distract from his strategy! It would sap the power of his exaggeration. He needs the 'image' of history rather than history itself.

Our best option, if we were prepared to take people like the Kriers seriously, would be to develop, with painstaking accuracy, instruments and drawing techniques that will tell us about certain types of buildings, façades, blocks and site layouts and their relationship to the urban space. In this respect the analysis of Amsterdam neighbourhood Dapperbuurt by Engel and Hobus as well as Louwe and Louët's graduation project continue rather than contradict the Kriers' approach.[5] I should also mention

5 These two studies have never been published, but do have a place within education. The morphological study of Amsterdam by J. Louwe and Louët can be found in the architecture library; this study will soon be published by SUN.

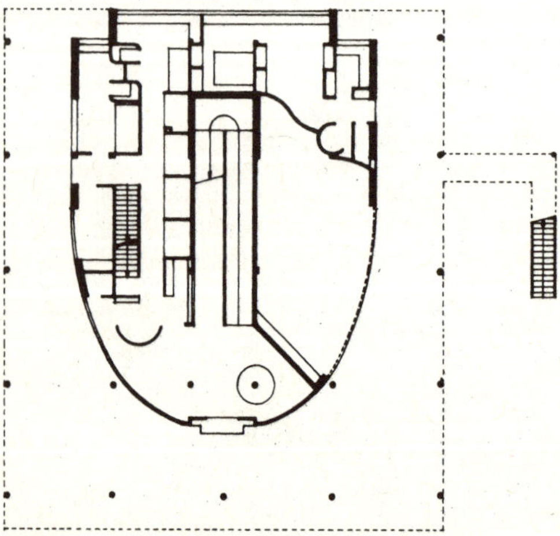

Le Corbusier, Villa Savoye, October 1928

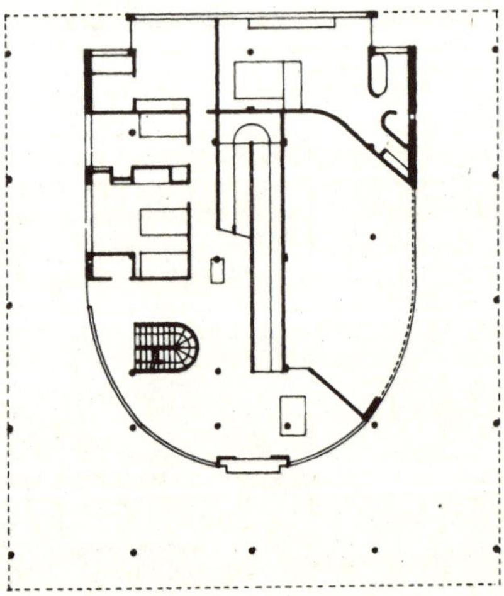

Villa Savoye, April 1929

the so-called 'Witte Nota' (White Paper), a morphological study carried out for The Hague, because it was the first time a city council (its urban development department) made use of such an analysis.[6]

The case of the Kriers demonstrates that a particular form of architecture can be used to explain something else. Rather than seeking its own perfection or balance, it focuses on a particular theme that it would like to know more about. This, of course, is the normal state of affairs. However, it places the plans in a position parallel to the analysis of design. Although using different tools, both methods can aim for similar things. If Rossi had not had any specific intentions, he might as well have excluded typology from his design and included it in his analysis. This interchangeability hampers our ability to distinguish between their potential. Before addressing the constantly changing relationship between plan analysis and design, I want to look at some of the general characteristics to come out of the polemic with the 'Forum' architects.

6 Urban Development Department, *The inner city layout, an urban planning approach to the problem of crossroads* (The Hague, August 1980). The morphological study was done by R. Van Genderen and J. Hoffman.

PLAN ANALYSIS AND THE CONCEPT OF HISTORY

Back in the day when everyone who wanted to familiarise himself with the world of architecture did so 'at his master's feet'; back in the day when architecture in its 'counterform' had to uphold the reality of human civilization against a deceitful, bureaucratic society; back in the day when a design could only be created by a highly personal and independent imagination and only acquired its meaning in 'experience'; back in that day, 'plan analysis' started questioning the neurotic wranglings of a discipline that had lost its function. It posed simple questions such as: 'What are the

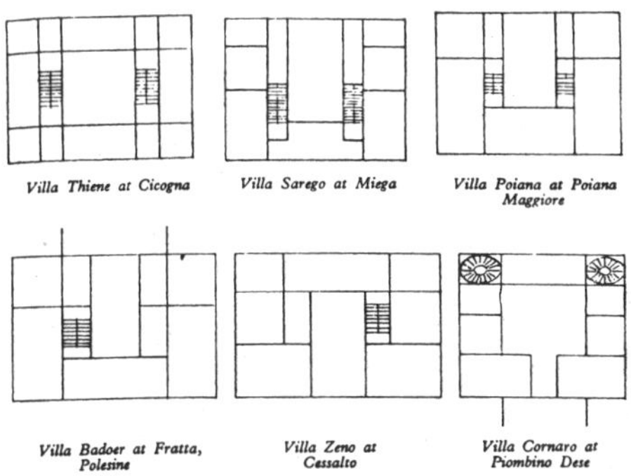

Palladio's geometry: the villas

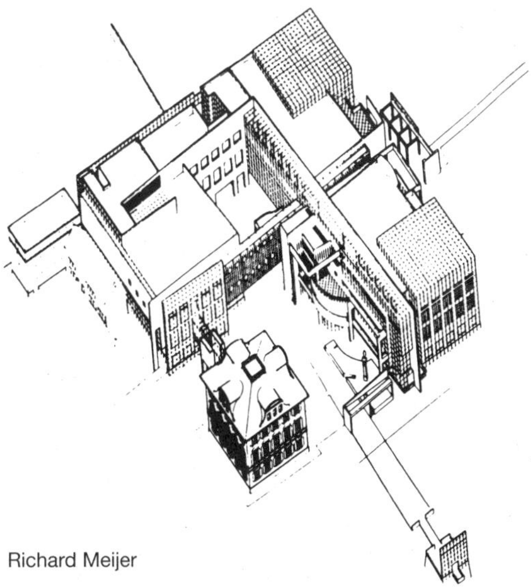

Richard Meijer

building blocks used here?' and 'What are we actually looking at?'

With this down-to-earth stance, plan analysis put itself up against a complex, but very cohesive system of ideas. The idea of a creative personality, who places his immaculate reputation against the political establishment, was confronted with his powerlessness in planning. The 'autonomy' of an independent intellect had to face up to the frustrations it was creating for itself. The individual creative process, the arena of the conscious and subconscious, the 'image' as the source of the design, came up against the historicity of the material. The idea of progress in history, with each subsequent design shouldering the expectation of 'deliverance' from an old contradiction; an architecture heading for freedom . . . The notion of the perfect, eternal work of art. Suddenly all this could be undermined. Plan analysis made us realise that the totality of a work of art or a design can be taken apart, dissected into constituent parts that, from an objective point of view, are found to be effective in the work as a whole. This realisation then provides the basis for taking the material further – further in what is ultimately a random direction.

The realisation that an analysis need not target the whole, the unique synthesis of the individual components, was liberating in the sense that the next step in the narrative need not be taken by a struggling individual, the tormented artist, who is forced to try and understand the essence of the phenomena surrounding him. It brought to an end the holy quest for a new Unity.

The optimistic conclusion that *partial* knowledge suffices may not enable us to get an immediate sense of what makes a work of art unique, but it is enough to allow us to objectively supply material for subsequent interpretations – interpretations that may be experimental, whose direction

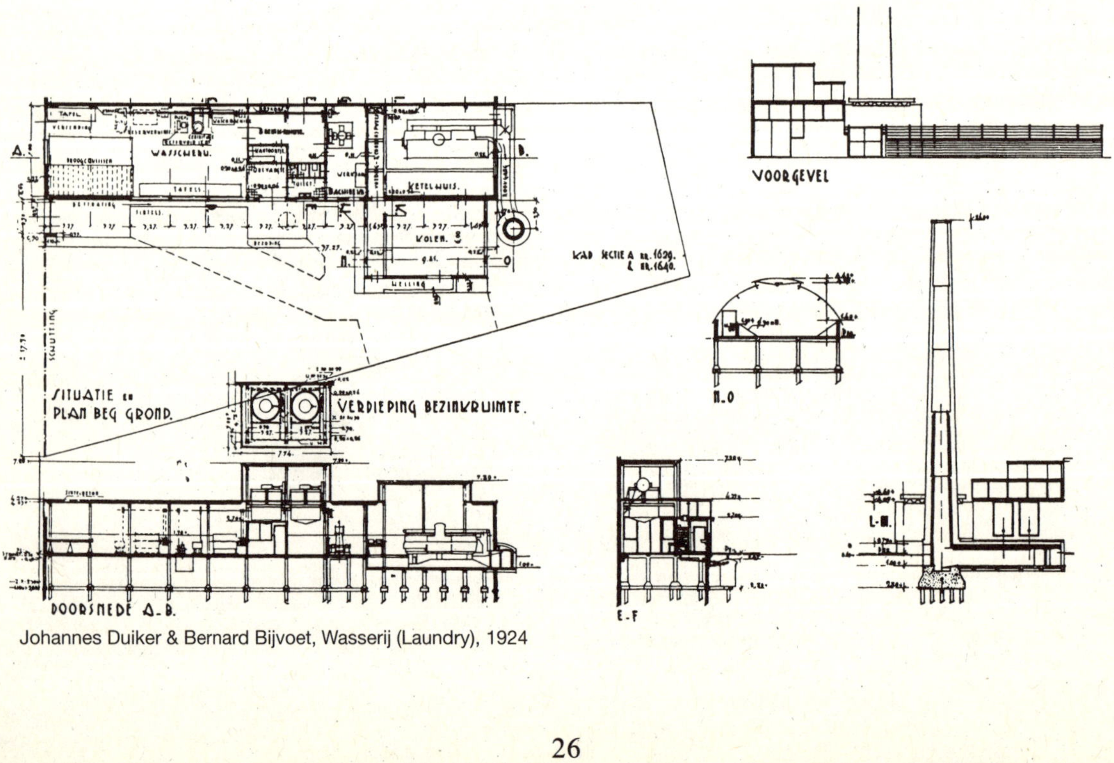

Johannes Duiker & Bernard Bijvoet, Wasserij (Laundry), 1924

is determined by minor, practical considerations. Service-driven.

This view of history, which is implied by the term 'plan analysis', took quite a bit of weight off our shoulders. Suddenly, many of our struggles proved futile. The futility of architecture as 'fruitless effort': the effort to implement a certain form as quality and truth against the constraints of regulations and across the communication quagmire of multidisciplinary planning. New prospects were opened up because the built product was no longer required to meet strong, a-priori expectations as *form*; because the built product was no longer compared with the original intentions, the idealising 'image' of the artist; and because the work of art was no longer competing with its creator's original intentions. From now on, the design could incorporate bureaucratic stipulations just as easily as it had always taken its cue from natural constraints. Just as the whole area of spatial planning draws on 'dialogue', the team-based design process was opened up. It was now possible to 'discuss' the design, because its constituent parts could be named. This facilitated a new, pragmatic approach, without the risk of lapsing into opportunism.

Plan analysis as a form of historical research allowed architects to obtain design principles from a *fragmented* historical study. Gone was the need to travel like tourists through time and space, looking for lost modes of existence. And gone, too, the need to become a historian. After all, an architect need not identify a structure in history. He needs to see his commission in its historical context – not to derive it from that historical context. After all, history does not tell us what needs doing. At any moment in time, history is open to renewed interpretation. At any moment in time, you can identify new links between current commissions and what

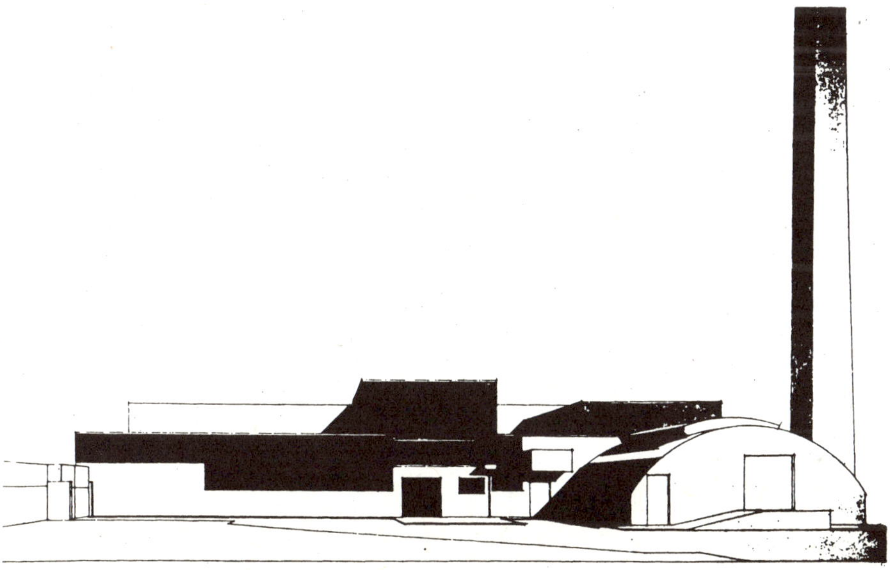

Johannes Duiker & Bernard Bijvoet, Wasserij (Laundry), 1924

has gone before. Plan analysis stands for an instrument that, in contrast to the subjective experiences of the 'tourist' travelling through time and space, can obtain an 'objective' knowledge from the history of architecture. Objective because it objectifies this history: examines its constituent parts and their effect. It never 'subjectifies' by trying to find the answer or the solution to its own problems in history.

Plan analysis as an instrument of historical research also stands for a 'fragmented' knowledge, because it never organises history or attributes an underlying plan to history; instead it names and examines fragments thereof. It makes history available to us as material that can be interpreted. Nothing more and nothing less. 'The way things were' is of secondary importance. What matters most is the question which elements, which fragments are most evident in history. This is where it differs from a plan analysis at the service of historiography. The question of which historical elements are objectified – and thus isolated and turned into material – is an extremely practical one. Deciding which questions to ask of the historical material, into which constituent parts to deconstruct the work, and which levels to distinguish: in a word, the analytical methodology need no longer legitimate itself in terms of historical accuracy. The method can be directed by the practical problems posed by the present commission. For instance, the method of plan analysis could be built on the products of Wittkower's historiography. In 'Architectural Principles'[7] he demonstrates how architects such as Alberti and Palladio based their designs on archaeological research into the ruins of their illustrious past. Using detailed analysis, Wittkower shows us how they experimented with these 'archaeological fragments' in brand new commissions. I mention this text

7 Rudolf Wittkower, *Architectural Principles in the Age of Humanism* (London, 1974).

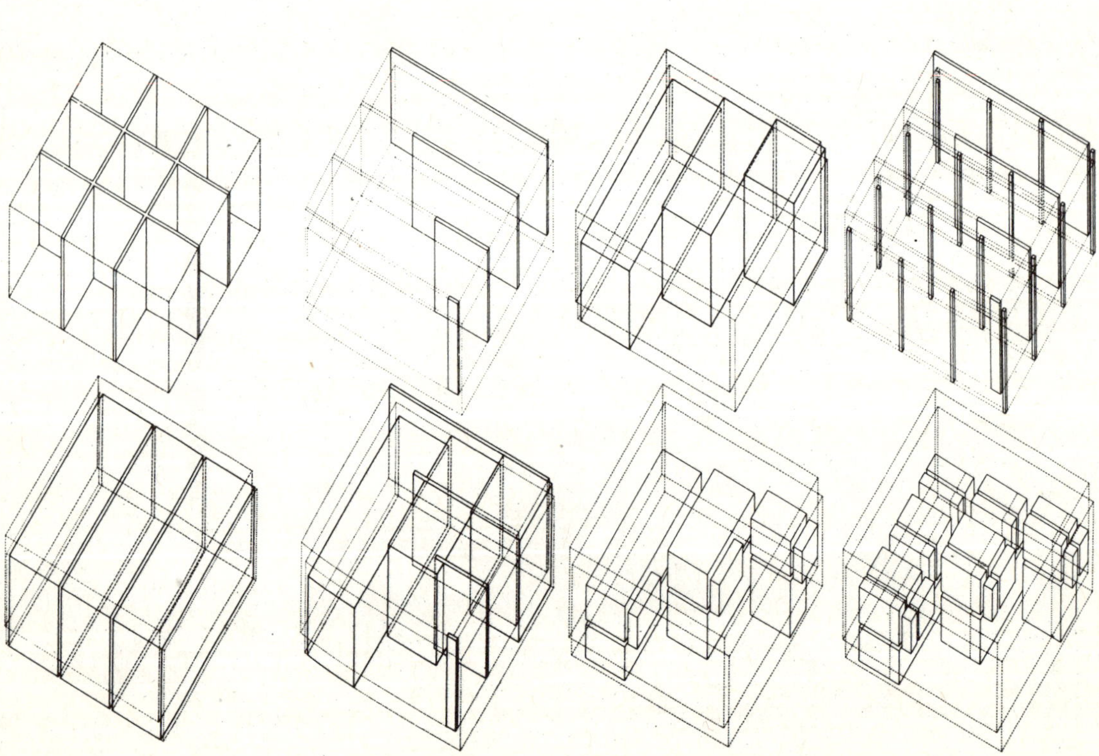

Peter Eisenman

at the roots of 'plan analysis' because this reading of Palladio's work was once the subject of a polemic with Van Eyck, who stressed that Palladio's mannerism achieved a new relativist unity. Whereas Van Eyck seeks a new balance, a new synthesis, unity, Wittkower exposes the montage technique that uses fragments of form. Plan analysis is more of an archaeological task than a form of historiography. Frits Palmboom notes something similar when he describes the work needed for 'Doel en Vermaak'. What it shares with archaeology is an interest in the actual material being dug up. This material does not serve primarily as a means of reconstructing history, but as an end in itself. It does not seek to tell the story of the historic city and support this with examples of ancient morphologies, but tries time and again to unearth new forms from the city, and to differentiate them amid the noise of the developed city. Every form that can be differentiated by a suitable drawing is one. We can determine, quite objectively, that the form exists and is therefore effective. It is then up to the designer to determine the consequences. It is this view of history that gave rise to the major 'relief' brought by plan analysis. A culture that neither progresses, as was planned, nor fails to do so, no longer requires the kind of intellect that wants to fathom, let alone control, the overall picture.

So instead of the world becoming ever more complicated, because everything became exponentially tangled up, it became simpler. The neurotic urge to keep explaining the part in relation to the overall picture and seeing this whole in every part was replaced by the possibility of a pragmatic approach: the possibility to isolate a form from history and to explore the potential of individual aspects. Just as Foucault's words want to merge with the flow of words, architecture can now enter history and in so doing probably also the city.

This also means that architecture need not pose *as* history. *Architecture* is the last guise in which architecture will make its presence felt.

ARCHITECTURE IN THE GUISE OF ARCHITECTURE

This obviously paraphrases Tafuri, when he stresses architecture's will to survive. But what can we expect of an architecture that delves into history? So far I have been talking about plan analysis as a tool to enter history. As a technique this analysis is *separate* from the design process. The analysis objectifies the historical material and makes it available to us as an object; the design then works with it, interprets it.

Through analysis, the design develops a certain distance from history. Simply by keeping this moment of deconstruction separate from the design process does the design come to occupy a certain relationship vis-à-vis history. And it is *not necessarily* completely 'devoured' by history, which is, generally speaking, what happens in postmodernism. The latter gets completely caught up in the abundance of past forms. Without any degree of distance it flaunts itself by saying 'I look like architecture so I must be architecture'.

Such distance can be the strength of plan analysis as well as its weakness. Let's compare it briefly with the design process that keeps its relationship with the historical material within the design itself.

Now that a rational formulation of function and production criteria appear to have lost their edge as a foundation for a design output, we need to develop another source of information. If this information must come from within the discipline, and from the way this discipline fulfilled its potential in the city, it means an examination of our own tools . . . and an understanding of their historicity.

And we need to view these tools objectively, because if we don't we run the risk not of a subjective method of design, but of a tautological design output. A design may materialise, and even be beautiful, but it will only ever be self-referential (or reference its creator). Precisely because a design is not just aspiration or a sign but also always involves output, because it always (trans)forms something outside itself, it must be rooted in something external, objective to itself. This is the first meaning of objectification.

What matters is that this need for objectification also applies to an architecture that wants to root itself within itself, that is to say within its method.

We can now formulate the problem facing all post-functionalist architecture as follows: how can a design discipline isolate something from itself to objectify it, detach it from its own output, so that it can serve as a foundation, so that it can be interrogated and (trans)formed within that very same output? And what does an architecture that must objectify itself look like? To meet this challenge, today's architecture is developing as many tools as there are movements identified in the journals. These include all sorts of techniques to bring about alienation through traditional architectural means: bricolage, reversal, scale adaptations, and so forth, and so on. These can all bring about objectification. What may be confusing, however, is that it is often extremely difficult, especially for the designer, to determine whether the targeted objectification has been achieved. There is a difference between an architecture that produces a patchwork of historical quotations and keeps echoing these and one that is genuinely transformative and productive, and seems to have successfully defined an 'object'. And this object can be as literal as Hejduk's wall, Eisenman's structure, or Graves' 'referential' fragment. We can only gauge the success of these kinds of architecture if either the design itself or an explanatory note accounts for the *relationship* between the objectification and its interpretation in the design.

Things were simpler for the avant-gardes. Their declared a-historical stance complemented the fact that their object lay outside architecture, that is, modern life. This is, in fact, an exception in the history of architecture. It was possible to radically alter form by basing it on knowledge of something completely separate from the design. In that sense, the maxim *form follows function* marked the greatest possible differentiation between the two. Both throughout the entire classicist period and in our time we need to turn something from our arsenal of tools into the object of interpretation, which can give rise to a new design output capable of meeting new demands.

Architecture is similar to science in that both must always ascertain how practicable, verifiable and manageable the theoretical and practical instruments are that they have developed in order to define and map out an object. And this brings us to a second meaning of objectification: one relating to verifiability, to whether architecture will keep its tools available for some kind of assessment or debate. This is the difference between an architecture that is merely eclectic and one that is genuinely analytical. The work of someone like Eisenman meets the latter requirement.

This example of Eisenman, especially, could inadvertently create the impression that the verifiability requirement calls for a particular kind of objective 'looking' tools. Rationalistic ones, for instance. (Eisenman himself is extremely doubtful about whether his architecture can be seen as 'rationalistic'.) Nothing is further from the truth. The objectification in question is perfectly well achievable with extremely subjective resources. What matters is that these tools can be criticised. The many neo-classicist image-boosting designs cannot. Pretty illustrations for a story that calls for change. Mere rhetoric.

We can single out two distinct moments in self-reflective architecture: a moment of analysis, that is, a moment of distancing, and a moment of output, the interpretation of the 'object' acquired through distance. Both are found simultaneously within a single design. The relationship between the two, which presents a permanent problem for architecture, must be established anew every time. If not, the design becomes tautological, capable of connecting with external social forces at an ideological level only.

Another method used to manage the relationship and distinction between objectification and output is separation. The moment of objectification is taken out of the design. And this brings us to plan analysis. Like any method, it has both advantages and disadvantages. Viewing this method as another variant allows us to compare it to other methods of objectification. Assessment of the method will be easier with a comparison than without. Such assessment, the critique of the method's validity, is necessary, as without one it would be impossible to determine the relationship with the design output. The case of a plan analysis that, as a methodology, is taken out of the design, brings with it the distinct risk that this relationship is no longer centre-stage. The reciprocity between design output and analysis will disappear from view amid the semblance of objectivity created by a separate plan analysis. Plan analysis then becomes a prefix or suffix to a design and turns into a legitimation.

The primary advantage of plan analysis is obvious. The targeted objectification, the distance vis-à-vis the interpretation, is indeed achieved by taking it from the design medium, by granting it a position of autonomy. Separating the moment of analysis, however, does not remove it from the design! It occupies a parallel position. Within the design, the relationship between analysis and design keeps calling for further definition.

A plan analysis is often seen as a preliminary study, with the design as its logical outcome; the design is the elaboration of an external learning process. In other words, you conduct a typological study and integrate its results in the design. The design analytical study is then added to the design as 'DATA'. The analysis takes on a purely legitimising function, like someone defending the form of his design by saying it has properly integrated the programmatic requirements.

The objectification achieved in the parallel analysis must also be achieved *within* the design itself, where it must be seen in relation to the interpretation. The objectification within the design will also look completely different. An analytical drawing is not a design drawing. Plan analysis thus assumes a position as an auxiliary science, in the same way that a design can utilise research by historians and anthropologists.

With this difference: plan analysis has the advantage of being more familiar with typical design questions. It is a tool for Architects.

Translated by Laura Vroomen

Two trends had a decisive effect on the development of the journal *O*, later *OASE*: the re-establishment of the autonomy of architecture at Delft University of Technology, on the one hand, and the economic recession of the 1980s on the other. For a decade after the student protests of 1968, social rather than architectural questions had the upper hand in Delft. The architecture from that period, especially within the process of urban renewal, may have been a critique of the modernism of the earlier period, but yielded few architectural statements and was not very evocative. The subsequent generation struggled to define a relationship to its predecessors and therefore had little choice but to hark back to the heroic, modernist period.

The 1984 article 'Stadsbeeld en massawoningbouw' (Cityscape and Mass Housing) by architect Henk Engel and researcher Jan de Heer does not just epitomize Delft's response to this situation, but also long shaped editorial developments at *OASE*. The professional response can be summed up with the words 'academic depth' and 'detachment'.

At the time, writing about architecture was not expected to offer direct criticism on other people's work or propaganda for one's own work, as in the writing of Loos or Le Corbusier; instead it was seen as a quest for the architecture that drew the right conclusions from history. Never before had young architects immersed themselves so deeply in the formal, but above all ideological motivations of earlier generations. It is not surprising, therefore, that we see the footnote forcing its way into these texts.

Such architects' studies, however, should be explicit about their objectives. Their focus can vary from a more applied and critical-historical question, an autonomous architectural question or the clarification of one's design motives, or the architectural analysis itself can be the study's focus. Unless their focus is outlined clearly, these studies may easily degenerate into articles aimed at a small group of insiders and hence slide into academism. Readers are left with the impression that these studies promise more than they deliver, that they fail to cross a certain barrier or continue a certain line. To their credit, these studies provoke readers' curiosity, such as Engel and De Heer's study into the schism between the romantic and rationalistic approach to urban planning. But the study of architecture wants more, its scope extends beyond curiosity. Its ultimate aim is to find arguments for arranging stones in a particular way during a particular era here on earth.

Arjan Hebly
Member of the editorial board
from *OASE* 5 to 9/10

Translated by Laura Vroomen

Henk Engel and Jan de Heer

CITYSCAPE AND MASS HOUSING

FIRST PUBLISHED IN *O 7*

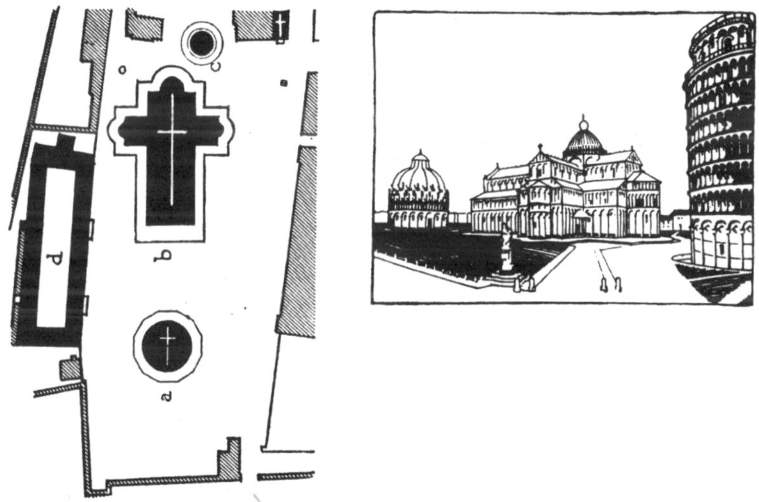

Camillo Sitte, Pisa, Piazza del Duomo

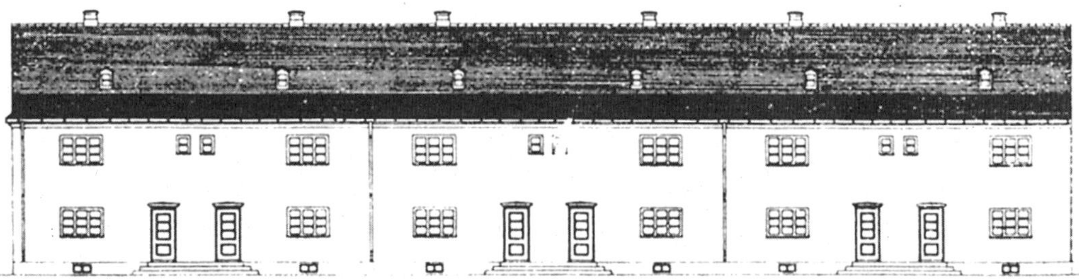

Ernst May, homes for *Das Schlesisches Heim*, 1921

Stadtebauen heisst mit dem Hausmaterial Raum gestalten.[1]

In these few words, Albert Erich Brinckmann captures the leading architectural paradigm of the twentieth century. Within architecture and urban planning, mass housing is the field in which the contrasting schools of architectural thought have sought to demonstrate their distinctiveness. Among these schools, the modernists hold a special position. In the challenge of mass housing, they see the foundation of a new architecture.

During the economic crisis of the First World War, private construction of housing came to a complete standstill. The production of housing could only be maintained through government subsidies. Ernst May claims that this fact was of historic significance for the architectural development of cities: 'For the first time in a hundred years, he [the city architect – H.E.] can truly hope to bring about a new age of architectural harmony through deliberate action.'

May considered city governments, in their roles as clients, financiers, and supervisors of the construction of public housing, to be the pillars of the *Neues Bauen*, the new international style: 'Gone are the days when spiritual and secular rulers who aspired to imperial power could build magnificent private buildings, districts and even entire cities, practically overnight. In our democratic age, city governments have replaced these leaders. They are the great commissioning authorities whose commissions will set the tone for the development of the *Neues Bauen*.'[2]

Unlike in the nineteenth century, the construction of mass housing is no longer seen as a practical matter, a variety of ordinary building, but as one of the greatest cultural challenges of the modern era. After the First World War, the concentration of housing production in the hands of local governments opened up new prospects for the pursuit of a contemporary style and a harmonious cityscape, concepts which had been central to architectural debate around the turn of the century. For more than 20 years, theoretical debate had centred on the same fundamental themes, first among them the integration of mass housing into the field of architectural challenges. This trend led, first of all, to the breakdown of the conventional artistic view of architecture as a visual art. Mass housing fell outside the definition of the architectural work in idealistic aesthetics, which involved the concept of the autonomous work of art.

As Theodor Fischer put it in his book *Stadterweiterungsfragen*: 'The rented home will always remain unsatisfactory as an independent work of architecture. Architectural works only have an individual character when they are not tossed onto the market like merchandise, but designed for a specific goal with a personal quality. In contrast, mass products such as rental homes produced before there is a known user must, in architectural terms, be treated as masses.'[3]

The individual dwellings in mass housing have no individual identity; they are anonymous products on the market and, from an architectural point of view, only of interest as a basis for a higher-level task: grouping dwellings into blocks and cities. Elevating the city as a whole to the status of an art object salvages the idea of the self-contained work of art and leads to the emergence of an aesthetic object into which the phenomena of capitalist rationalization can be integrated. Individual initiatives must be aimed at a common goal. In his studies of the history of urban planning, the art historian Albert Erich Brinckmann attempts to show how this is possible.[4]

1 Albert Erich Brinckmann, *Platz und Monument, Untersuchungen zur Geschichte und Aesthetik der Stadtbaukunst in neuerer Zeit* (Berlin, 1908), 170.

2 Ernst May, 'Organisation der Bautatigkeit der Stadt Frankfurt a.M.', *Der Baumeister,* vol. 27, no. 4, 98-104.

3 Theodor Fischer, *Stadterweiterungsfragen* (Stuttgart, 1903). Cited in Walter Curt Behrendt, *Die Einheitliche Blockfront als Raumelement im Stadtebau* (Berlin, 1911), 77.

4 Albert Erich Brinckmann, *Deutsche Stadtbaukunst in der Vergangenheit* (Frankfurt, 1911); *Stadtbaukunst, Geschichtliche Querschnitte und Neuzeitliche Ziele* (Berlin, 1920).

Brinckmann considers himself above all an art scholar. His findings have strong general applicability and practical relevance to current issues. In his writings, he formulates architectural problems through comparison with similar situations in the past. Take, for instance, the conclusion of *Deutsche Stadtbaukunst in der Vergangenheit*: 'There is mounting evidence that private architecture, too, will play a more modest role in the streetscape. It will not be long before people abandon their pointless attempts, so wasteful of money and artistic energy, to give rented homes a personal look. The rented home must once again become a mere part of the cohesive wall, so that it derives its aesthetic appeal precisely from that wall.'[5]

5
Brinckmann, *Deutsche Stadtbaukunst*, op. cit. (note 4), 159.

This same train of thought forms the basis for Walter Curt Behrendt's study of the housing block. In *Die einheitliche Blockfront als Raumelement im Stadtbau*, Behrendt examines the development of uniform housing blocks through the lens of their historical antecedents.[6] In architectural terms, seventeenth and eighteenth-century blocks are especially relevant to the present day, precisely because of the economic and organizational conditions under which they came into being. According to Behrendt, urban planning's greatest achievements came in periods when a central governmental authority was able to ensure compliance with particular architectural guidelines by means of subsidies. The regimes of Enlightenment monarchs were exemplary in this respect. In their works, Brinckmann and Behrendt develop the urban aesthetics of Camillo Sitte in a significant way. In *Der Stadtebau nach seinen künstlerischen Grundsatzen*, Sitte laid the groundwork for the modern spatial, architectural approach in urban planning.[7] According to Sitte, urban planning should no longer be the domain of surveyors and engineers, but should be approached as a work of architecture. Urban development plans, he argues, must go beyond two-dimensional indications of building lines, which are no more than outlines, formal abstractions that attempt to capture the cubical, three-dimensional appearance of the cityscape.

6
Walter Curt Behrendt, *Die Einheitliche Blockfront als Raumelement im Städtebau* (Berlin, 1911).

7
Camillo Sitte, *Der Städtebau nach seine künstlerische Grundsätzen* (Vienna, 1889). See also George R. Collins and Christiane Crasemann Collins, *Camillo Sitte and the Birth of Modern City Planning* (New York, 1965).

Only architects have the ability to design city plans based on the spatial image of the cityscape – in other words, as representations of the spatial sequence of streets and squares that will be formed by buildings. Sitte suggests that architects should strengthen this capacity for spatial design by studying the historic centres of Europe's cities.

Sitte's studies focus primarily on aesthetic issues in the design of squares and the placement of monumental buildings. He strives for painterly, 'Mahlerian' variation in the cityscape. Unlike Sitte, Brinckmann and Behrendt concentrate on the great mass of dwellings forming the neutral background to the city's special places. Behrendt identifies the mass production of housing as a critical factor in the modern cityscape: 'The appearance of the city, especially that of the recent expansion sites, is not greatly influenced by the architecture of independent buildings. Grouping grand monumental buildings for public or commercial purposes will never yield more than a few highlights, though conspicuous ones, within the city as a whole.

'Having learned this lesson from experience, we know that the cityscape is shaped primarily by the products of private building companies meeting the general public's demand for housing. The systematic organization and management of this mass production must therefore be regarded as a challenge for urban planners, and ought to be one of the main tasks of local authorities today.'[8]

8
Behrendt, *Die Einheitliche Blockfront*, op. cit. (note 6), 12.

Sitte's wish was for the discipline of architecture to have the opportunity to design special places in the city, as an artistic counterbalance to the rationalization and commercialization which had seized hold of urban life.[9] Brinckmann, and Behrendt along with him, rejected this type of eclecticism. 'Now that the tradition has been destroyed, the art of urban planning cannot be cobbled together from our studies of past periods. It must be developed out of our own practice of residential building.'

Brinckmann claims that housing provides a living basis for the development of architectural forms: 'The architectural styles of residential building and urban planning are very closely connected. The nature and style of residential life affect the form of the urban complex, which is therefore subject to constant change. Every step forward in public housing entails the transformation of the cityscape. It follows that, though we may admire the appearance of an older city, we can never truly take it as a model.'

Brinckmann concluded from this that the study of historical forms should not be guided by the particular modes of expression linked to the particular circumstances in which those forms came into being, but should focus on general laws of form: 'The ephemeral mode of expression changes; the laws of form remain. One must observe those laws and yet find new forms of beauty. And the earlier they appear, the less people will cling to special modes of expression, to motifs.'[10]

Brinckmann and Behrendt's aim is not so much painterly variety in the cityscape, which can only result from an accumulation of accidents, but the rhythmic articulation of the body of the city. In Sitte's framework, the architectural object is formed by the closed image of a separate space, such as a square or street bounded by buildings. As an alternative to that closed image and its characteristic mode of reception, Brinckmann proposes the *Raumprinzip*, which is intended to make possible a comprehensive image of the city. Because the city as a whole cannot be experienced, however, a time dimension is introduced. Rhythmic articulation makes the continuity in the great body of the city palpable. In opposition to the here-and-now experience of separate, self-contained images, Brinckmann proposes the rhythmic succession of regular units, producing an abstract experience of the whole: 'Rhythm requires a certain regularity, or in any case a prior intention . . . Rhythm is the artistic rule of well-considered work in urban planning; this working method will not, like "picturesque design", wage a continual, frenzied battle between design and implementation. If urban planning has been well thought through, a restrained style of management is sufficient to achieve the objectives of the development plan.'[11]

One of the primary elements of urban planning is the plastic structure of the development plan, the relationship between the open spaces and the built masses. In this context, the development of the regular housing block can become the point of departure for the composition of the cityscape. The features of the façade are then no longer a romp through the history of style, alluding to a magnificent past with its more grandiose projects; instead, they are a structural element, mediating between the internal articulation of the housing block and the three-dimensional bordering of the street and square areas: 'Turning a housing block's frontage into a coherent whole through architectural design is not a matter of superficial decoration to satisfy a desire for representation. The use of such means would inevitably lead to destructive measures. If what is at stake, however, is the development of the architectural form of mass housing with typically repetitive floor plans, then the uniform frontage of a housing block is a social consequence which is, as it were, demanded by aesthetic necessity.

9 Carl E. Schorske, *Fin-de-siècle Vienna* (New York, 1961), 62 ff.

10 Brinckmann, *Deutsche Stadtbaukunst*, op. cit. (note 4), 23 and 159.

11 Ibid., 81.

‘Furthermore, in the historical art of urban planning, merging multiple houses into a greater whole is a deliberate technique for giving form to space, because the street space is easier to control with a self-contained mass resulting from such merging than with a junmble of small, insignificant parts.’[12]

After the First World War, Herbert Boehm, a close colleague of May’s, built on these ideas, speaking of a new ‘will to form’. Boehm tells us that after a period of experimentation with mixed results, urban planning began heading in a more sustainable direction. This new turn was closely related to contemporary tendencies in other areas of cultural life, such as architecture, painting, clothing, and norms of social interaction. From this vantage point, he traces a half century of urban planning, culminating in the cubic approach of the 1920s: ‘The age of schematism, in which cityscapes were constructed on the drawing board with a ruler and compasses in a misguided attempt to emulate the great traditions of classicism, was followed by a period of romanticism. In an overzealous and, again, misguided imitation of their master Camillo Sitte, urban planners would ideally have liked to create countless little Nurembergs, and they hoped to build cityscapes of enduring value out of twisty roads and picturesque nooks.

‘This period was followed in turn by an exaggerated naturalism, which came to full flower in combination with *Siedlungsbau* and is rational in the sense that it limits itself to the objective. This naturalism initially took the orientation and characteristics of the building site as the sole basis for a design. In doing so, it lost sight of formal concerns about the whole. What was forgotten was that, unless it limits itself strictly to ensuring an adequate supply of housing, urban planning is always a form of architecture. In other words, it is plasticism (*beelding*), design, which takes individual dwellings and groups of dwellings as its building blocks and creates large cubic and spatial wholes.’[13]

Boehm contends that only the use of formal rules brings architectural cohesion to the city plan. This does not mean that the main criterion for harmony in the cityscape is to be found in a generally accepted formal vocabulary. The many attempts to introduce a collective architectural style had led only to a chaotic cityscape, composed of as many individual styles as there were architects. According to Boehm, coherence in the cityscape can only be the result of spatial plasticism, the tectonics of the development plan. One’s attention should not be focused on ornamental details, but on the formative powers that generate a style.

In *Typ und Stil*, May criticizes the misconception that a style can be introduced through agreements between the organizations involved: a style cannot be made. ‘Only gradual development arising from progressive expansion of our understanding of the nature of architecture can lead to change.’

May thus regards the continued tendency towards creating typologies in public housing, during the crisis following the First World War, as a groundbreaking step: ‘It is above all when one builds small dwellings that the identical or related requirements which apply in each case form the first, rudimentary foundations for agreement on the general principles of building. The standardization of residential floor plans, which has been going on for decades, has been accelerated enormously by post-war conditions. Necessity has brought about what rational reflection could not.’[14]

In the development of new types of building, May sees a common basis for a future style. Behrendt shares this view. In *Zum Bauproblem der*

12 Behrendt, *Die Einheitliche Blockfront*, op. cit. (note 6), 13.

13 H. Boehm, ‘Besiedlungsplane’, *Das Schlesisches Heim*, 1922 no. 9.

14 Ernst May, ‘Typ und Stil’, *Das Schlesisches Heim*, 1924 no. 2

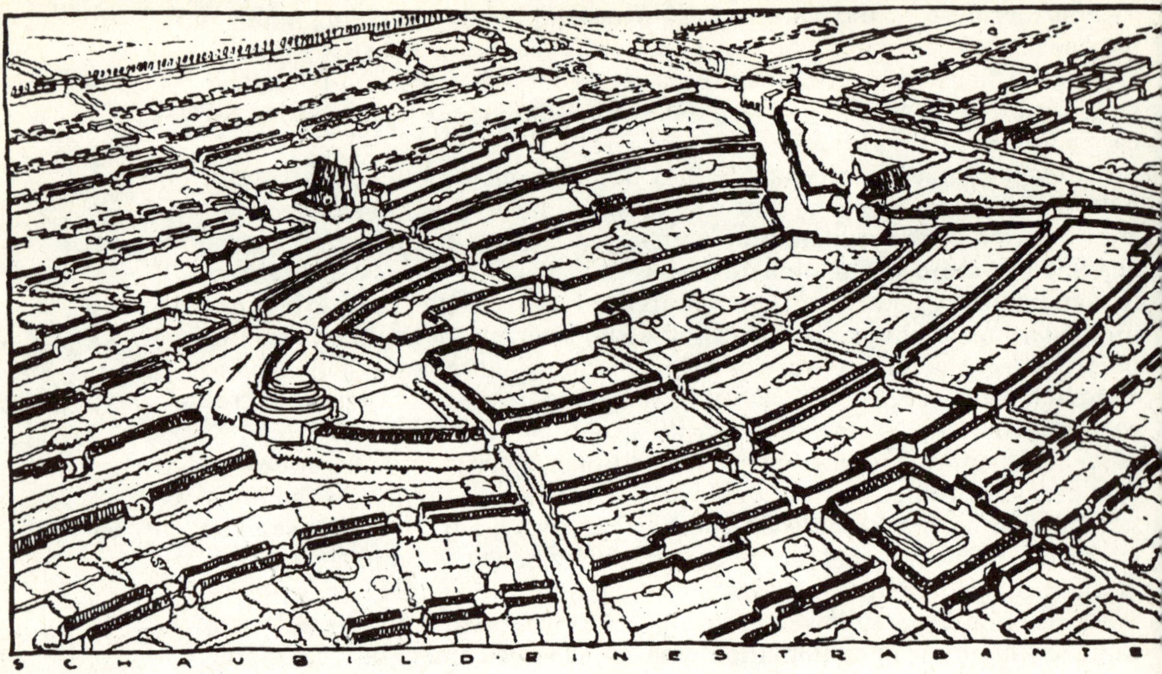

Ernst May and Herbert Boehm, satellite town from the expansion plan for Breslau, competition, 1922

J.J.P. Oud, Tusschendijken, 1921

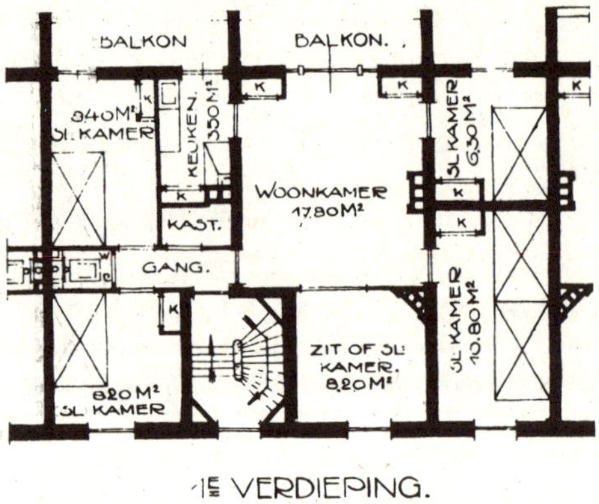

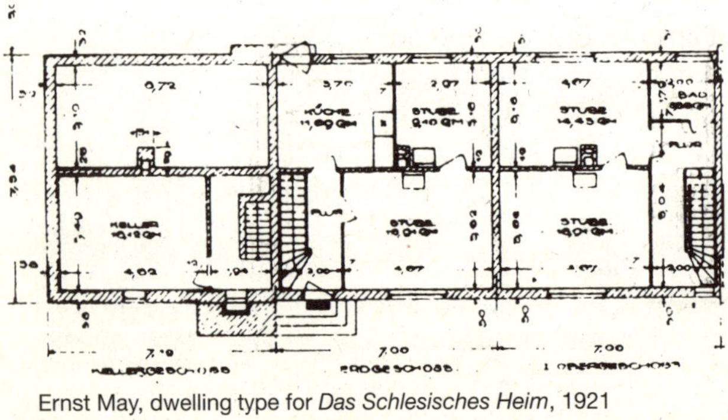

Ernst May, dwelling type for *Das Schlesisches Heim*, 1921

Zeit, he writes, 'The problem of architecture is the problem of plasticism, a formal issue. But how can architecture arrive at forms of its own – and thus develop a style of its own – in this day and age, when no new fixed forms of labour and work have yet developed anywhere? For example, how can one speak of a formal problem of the city when there is hardly any consensus about the most basic questions, about habitation and the settlement?'

In his discussion of modern building, Behrendt raises the issue of architecture's relationship to social stability. His text emphasizes the fragility of the functionalist theory of form. We can see that where functions are unclear and inconstant, form eludes the grasp of functionalist architects. In such cases, the determination of form becomes deeply problematic. Behrendt, too, sees types of building as the first general ideas of form, an essential basis for further development of the differentiated formal vocabulary of an architectural style. He regards the problems that face architecture because of technological, economic and social development primarily as constructive problems.

Before we can speak of a modern building style, we will need new types of building that provide a stable basis for it: 'The only way to accomplish anything is by focusing our attention more on the essential than on the superfluous and incidental, more on the generally applicable than on the individual, more on the type than on the detail. We will need all our strength to bring the new typology into existence, and we will have reason for joy and satisfaction if we manage it. We can leave concerns about the details for future times.'[15] For the time being, we will have to make do with an elementary, pared-down conception of form.

In general, 'habitation' is referred to as the living basis on which a new style can be founded. It is the point at which architectural style and lifestyle merge. This opens the way to a fundamental transformation of the form of the city based on the requirements of interior design, but that is not to say that the problem of form can be directly reduced to a problem of multiplying an organic kernel, the housing unit.

New forms of spatial organization, such as single and double rows of housing, make it possible to meet the requirements posed from within individual dwellings. May discusses such forms in this sense, as a correction of the flaws in the traditional building method, namely closed-off housing blocks without open spaces at their centres.[16]

The abstract, anonymous fact of mass housing cannot, however, give shape to the city on its own. The problem of the modern city is in fact projected onto the mass reproduction of housing units, which threaten to become an excrescence destroying the city, choking its heart and blurring the boundary with its surroundings.[17]

Alongside sound principles for the interior design and spatial organization of the dwellings, we need an architectural model that brings order to unbridled growth: 'We must study not only the parts of a city plan and its realization, but also its construction and borders, so that instead of spreading over the surrounding area like a rising tide, the city develops along predetermined lines and in accordance with predetermined principles.'[18]

The experience of historical cities plays an especially dominant role in the development of expansion models. In all models, alongside the internal articulation of the buildings, the relationship between the city centre and the periphery is seen as crucial to the cohesion of the cityscape.

15 Walter Curt Behrendt, 'Zum Bauproblem der Zeit', *Der Neubau,* 1925 no. 1.

16 Ernst May, 'Fünf Jahre Wohnungsbautatigkeit in Frankfurt a.M., *Das Neue Frankfurt,* 1930 no. 2/3.

17 Ernst May, 'Stadterweiterung mittels Trabauten', *Der Städtebau,* 1922, 41. See also *Das Schlesisches Heim,* 1922 no. 11; H. Boehm, 'Die Stadtebauliche Planung', *Das Schlesisches Heim,* 1925 no. 1.

18 Raymond Unwin, in a lecture given in Amsterdam in 1922 for the Nederlands Instituut voor Volkshuisvesting (Dutch Public Housing Institute). See F. Smit, 'Van tuinstedebouw tot stedelijke uitwaaiering', *Wonen-TA/BK,* 1975 no. 13.

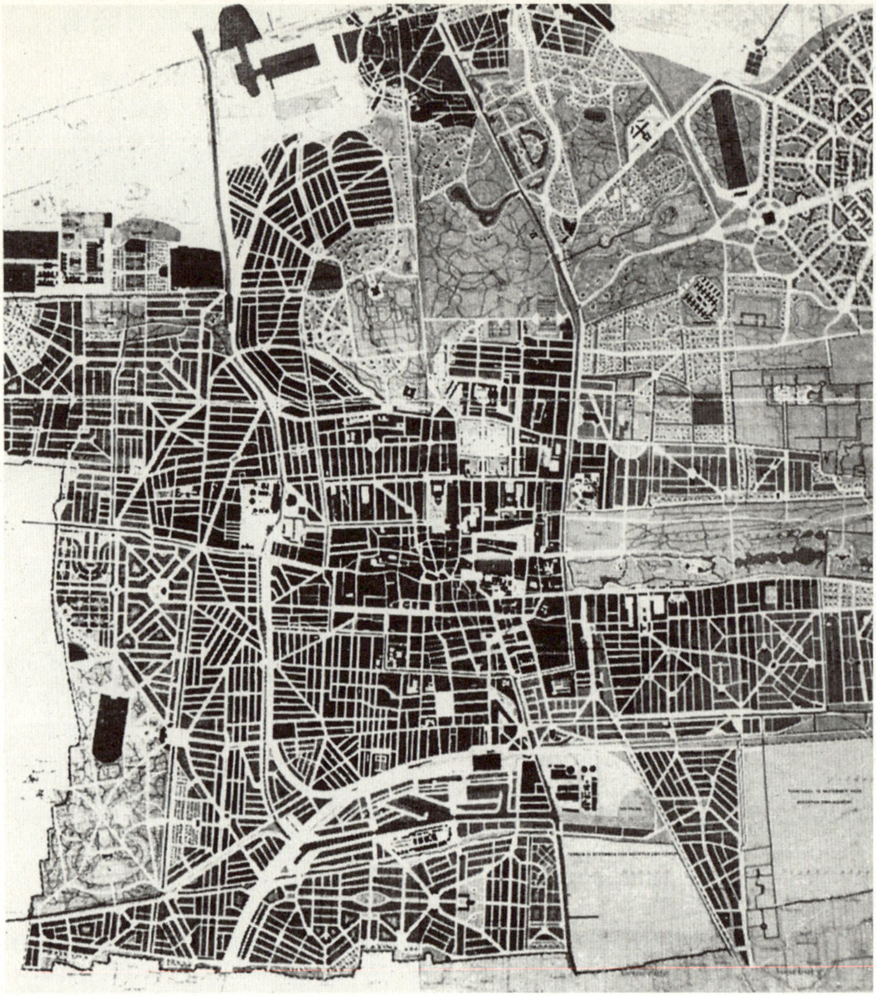

H.P. Berlage, The Hague expansion plan, 1908

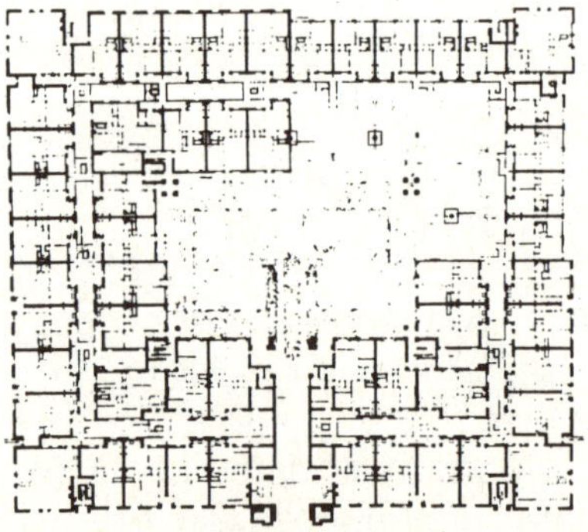

Frank Lloyd Wright, Lexington Terraces, 1909

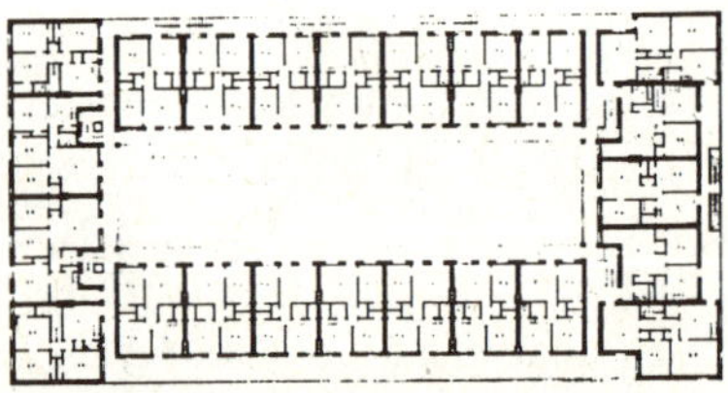

Frank Lloyd Wright, Francisco Terrace, court with access galleries, 1885

BERLAGE, OUD, VAN DOESBURG AND VAN EESTEREN

The Dutch architects Hendrik Petrus Berlage, and later J.J.P. Oud and Cornelis van Eesteren, developed positions stemming from the German theoretical tradition in architecture and mass housing, and these positions were of critical importance in the Dutch *Nieuwe Bouwen* movement, the counterpart of the German *Neues Bauen*. Berlage took issue with Sitte and Brinckmann's ideas, steering an independent course. Oud drew on Berlage's thinking and, in his period as a member of De Stijl, elaborated on the relationship between the housing block and mass housing. This provides the context in which German architects' admiration for Oud's work should be understood.[19] Ideas about the regular housing block, such as those espoused in Germany by Brinckmann and Behrendt, played a pivotal role in Oud's experiments.

In the first issue of the journal *De Stijl*, Oud calls the housing block the greatest challenge facing modern architects: 'Architecture is a plastic art, the art of defining space and thus expressing the most general truths in the cityscape: in individual buildings and in the combination and juxtaposition of buildings.'[20] In a later article, Oud describes the characteristics of modernism in greater detail, explaining that the modern spirit 'is not defined in terms of the individual (inside: the house), but in terms of the crowd (outside: the street – the city). In the streetscape, a unique house is contraband to him, even if it is aesthetically pleasing, and spatial continuity is essential.'[21] As a result, Oud says, 'the architecture of the block [will] profoundly influence the character of modern aesthetics in Architecture'.[22]

Unlike the German purists, Oud's objective is not to simplify the traditional forms and return to the essence of the house and the city. He sees

19 See, for instance, H. Boehm, 'Blick über die Grenzen, Reiseeindrücke aus Holland und England', *Das Schlesisches Heim,* 1925 no. 9.

20 J.J.P. Oud, 'Het monumentale stadsbeeld', *De Stijl,* 1917 no. 1.

21 J.J.P. Oud, 'Architectonische Beschouwingen. A. Massabouw en Straatarchitectuur', *De Stijl,* 1919 no. 7.

22 J.J.P. Oud, 'Het monumentale stadsbeeld', op. cit. (note 20).

H.P. Berlage, Amsterdam-Zuid expansion plan, 1917

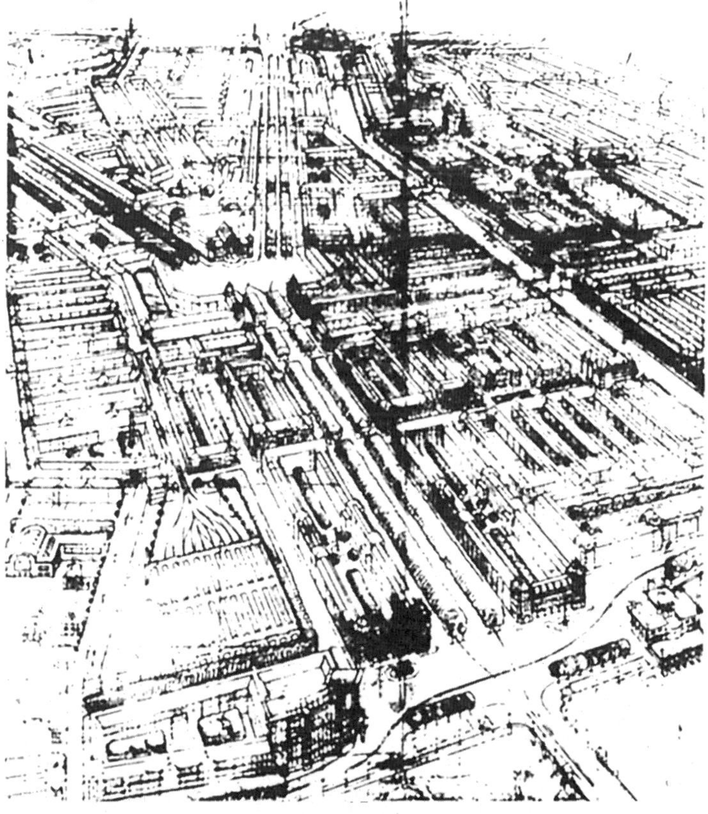

mass housing and the big city as entirely novel phenomena. Oud takes the perfected nineteenth-century block as his point of departure, offering a thorough reconstruction of it in his work.

Van Doesburg, who at first sympathized with Oud's approach, took a radical turn with his experiments in the early years of De Stijl. During his time in Weimar, Van Doesburg wrote, 'Putting residential boxes and housing units next to each other or on top of each other according to a particular typology or standard is not all there is to plastic (*beeldend*) building either. That makes the activity of building mechanical, repetitive, comparable to the work of a photographer or the use of historical building styles. The (apparent) spatial economy (of normalization), organized at the level of the town or city, forms an obstacle to plasticism in building.'[23]

And a year later, in the manifesto 'Tot een beeldende architectuur' [later published in English translation as 'Towards plastic architecture'] that accompanied the exhibition of his Parisian models, Van Doesburg aimed to move beyond all concepts of form, in the sense of predetermined typologies: 'Unlike all previous style, the new architectural method has no fixed typology, no fundamental form.'[24]

23 Theo van Doesburg, 'Von der neuen Aesthetik zur materiellen Verwirklichung', *De Stijl,* 1923 no. 1.

24 Theo van Doesburg, 'Tot een beeldende architectuur', *De Stijl,* 1924 no. 6/7.

Van Doesburg rejects not only any notion of form as a reflection of content, but also the elementary composition techniques to which German purists preferred to restrict themselves: symmetry and repetition. In his General Expansion Plan for Amsterdam, Van Eesteren then seems to extend the consequences of Oud's elaboration on Berlage's proposals to their utmost limits.

As early as 1883, in his essay 'Amsterdam-Venetië' (Amsterdam-Venice),[25] Berlage had used the categories of the picturesque and the monumental in his urban-planning assessment of the city of Amsterdam. Forty years later, he was still using them. Both categories are rooted in Hegelian philosophy and form the systematic polarity in Berlage's urban designs. Initially, they are equal in value and represent two different fundamental artistic concepts. The picturesque is synonymous with emotion, whimsy, Gothic style, and the beauty of nature, while the monumental stands for reason, geometry, classicism and composition based on motifs from nature.

In his book review of Sitte's *Städtebau* (City Planning),[26] he maintained the equilibrium between the two approaches, concurring with Sitte's views and, in particular, his conclusions about the aesthetic function of squares, namely to create a self-contained architectural whole. In the essay 'Bouwkunst en Impressionisme' (Architecture and Impressionism),[27] however, he pointedly distanced himself from the Romantic approach to urban planning, which he associated mainly with Sitte and described as seeking to add a picturesque effect to the rational street plan for the city. 'That sort of Romantic art has had its day,' Berlage said.

25 Hendrik Petrus Berlage, 'Amsterdam en Venetie, schets in verband met de tegenwoordige veranderingen van Amsterdam', *Bouwkundig Weekblad,* 1883.

26 Hendrik Petrus Berlage, 'De kunst in stedebouw', *Bouwkundig Weekblad,* XII, 1892.

27 Hendrik Petrus Berlage, 'Bouwkunst en Impressionisme', *Architectura,* II, 1894.

Like Sitte and Brinckmann, Berlage was interested in the aesthetic aspects of urban planning and kept his distance from the legal and civil-engineering sides. Nevertheless, he believed that the aesthetic elements of a new approach to urban planning would have to come from the technical-rational plan for the city, which is based on practical requirements. Consequently, he considered monumental urban architecture superior to the Romantic variety: 'The great monuments, and/or the distribution of mass – crucial! . . . modern perspectives on time and money force this on us. First and foremost, those modern perspectives have more to do with urban planning in general, ordaining long, perfectly straight streets that intersect at right angles and the inviolability of the public road. This approach to urban planning, which differs from those that preceded it in literally every way, always inherently suggests a general tendency towards both simplification of residential building en masse and a mass view of housing blocks. Instead of a speculative housing block that can be interpreted as a whole, each dwelling is now turned into a traditional Dutch house, according to a complete programme based on avoiding monotony.'[28]

Architecture must become impressionistic, restricting detail with the utmost austerity in order to create a distinctive silhouette. Berlage worked out the implications of this monumental approach to urban planning in his expansion plan for The Hague and the accompanying essay, 'Stedebouw' (Urban Planning), which opens with Brinckmann's pithy remark, *Städtebauen heisst mit dem Hausmaterial Raum gestalten*.[29]

When trying to solve the problems of the modern city, of traffic and hygiene, Berlage says, one is pushed towards the greatest possible simplicity, including aesthetic simplicity. This naturally leads to the classical preference for a simple delineation of the street grid. Urban construction and architecture must be brought into harmony with each other, he argues, and the design must therefore proceed from the square around which the main buildings are located and strive to create a self-contained visual whole. Berlage also warns of the great danger of the geometry of the traditional approach, the danger of monotony.

To stave off that threat, Berlage introduces the principle of pleasant accident, corresponding to the romantic spirit, which is intended to allow a transition from strict geometric standards to an urban plan with a rhythmic pattern of geometrically structured districts, the spatial structure of which is based on the city squares: 'And the fact that in the present day one must look far ahead – one is forced, in other words, to make an urban plan long in advance – pushes one naturally towards regularity. This measure, if it comes about through artistic insight in the spirit of the classical masters, in fact represents a higher beauty. That is why I believe that local sections should be designed according to a regular plan, as long as no natural obstacles stand in the way. On the other hand, all the natural features of the landscape, such as bodies of water, hills, stands of trees, and so forth, should not be removed but incorporated into the plan. If they are connected to regular features in an artful way, they will provide the pleasant variation needed to dispel the monotony of a regular plan that is extended to its furthest implications. Furthermore, this guarantees that the separate, regular sections will differ from one another, because the basis for each one is different.'[30]

In a series of lectures delivered to the Vereniging Praktische Studie in 1913 and 1914, entitled 'Het aesthetische gedeelte van Stedebouw' (The aesthetic component of urban planning), Berlage again espouses this view.[31] But, largely under the influence of Karl Scheffler's book *Die Architektur der Großstadt* (The Architecture of the Metropolis), he expands the scope of his attention to cover the entire territory of the city, rather than just the expansion areas. He proposes to view the city as the result of modern science – in particular, he has Langer's graphical statistics in mind – and of modern art: 'The modern urban plan should be a whole composed of a group of regular plan components, a chain of cells, each of which in turn is subdivided in a regular manner.'

The architectural nucleus of each unit, or cell, is the city square, the architectural space to which the streets (as autonomous plastic spaces,

28 Ibid., 105.

29 Hendrik Petrus Berlage, 'Stedebouw', in: *Beschouwingen over bouwkunst en hare ontwikkeling* (Rotterdam, 1911).

30 Ibid., 62.

31 C. W. Schwagermann, 'Het aesthetische gedeelte van Stedebouw, Verslag van lezingen door H.P. Berlage voor het Civiel- en Bouwkundige Studentengezelschap "Practische Studie" te Delft', *Bouwkundig Weekblad*, 1914.

beeldruimten) are oriented. The cells are connected in a 'natural' way. The spirit of the modern city is the idea of democracy: 'The character of the modern city is the plastic representation of that idea.' Berlage's views form the framework in which Oud developed his housing projects. In his essay 'Het monumentale stadsbeeld' (The monumental cityscape), he repeats Berlage's words.[32] But his experiments focus much more on the architectural control of *Hausmaterial* than on *Städtebauen*.

32
Ibid.

Oud's interpretation of the housing block relinquishes the individual form of the Dutch house entirely. The house in all its components is transformed into a figuration that serves as a motif guiding the composition of the housing block.[33] This composition technique, which Oud further developed in his housing projects, may have been inspired by Frank Lloyd Wright's early housing complexes, such as Francisco Terrace and Lexington Terrace, but it also shows striking similarities to Van Doesburg's decorative art from the early years of De Stijl.

33
H. Engel, 'Van Huis tot Woning, een typologische analyse van enkele woningbouwontwerpen van J.J. Oud', *Plan*, no. 9 1981.

COMPOSITION AND THE CREATION OF MOTIFS

The concepts of composition and the creation of motifs characterize the working method that Van Doesburg used from 1917 to his Elementarist period. Almost all works are originally inspired by nature. Forms derived from nature are abstracted into an aesthetic image, and in the process the natural forms dissolve into purely visual elements. In 'Grondbegrippen van de nieuwe beeldende kunst' (Fundamentals of neo-plastic art), Van Doesburg describes this process of aesthetic reconstruction in detail.

Through the transfiguration of a cow, he demonstrates the stages in the process, which leads from the 'accentuation of relationships linked to form' and the 'annihilation of form' to an abstract painting of rectangular fields of colour drifting over a white background.[34]

34
Th. van Doesburg, *Grondbegrippen van de nieuwe beeldende kunst* (Nijmegen, 1982).

In the stained-glass *Compositions II* and *III*, the work is not completed through the aesthetic reconstruction of the natural object. The pared-down image, a seated figure in *Composition II* and a skater in *Composition III*, forms the basis for a new construct. The composition is an extension of the process of creating motifs. In *Composition III*, Van Doesburg uses various forms of repetition, in which the motif is reflected, rotated, or simply reiterated. Because the motif (which remains constant) changes its position, a rhythmic pattern of two-dimensional forms emerges, in which the original motif can be recognized only with difficulty, yet retains its identity thanks to the colour pattern, which is always identical.

Van Doesburg soon rejected the composition technique that he had developed in his first windows as being too simple. His ideal was the compositions of Bach. In a letter, he wrote, 'Still, there is a great gap in my work, of which I am fortunately aware. Once I have a motif, I hold it together too much in my manipulation of it. In music, especially Bach's music, the motif is constantly being manipulated in a new way.'[35]

35
C. Blotkamp, *De beginjaren van De Stijl* (Utrecht, 1982), 27.

In *Composition IV*, Van Doesburg does not take a natural object as his point of departure. Instead, he deforms two parts of the motif from *Composition II* and varies them using not only the above-mentioned principles of reflection and rotation, but also by making the colour independent of the motif.

This independent use of colour releases the individual elements from their interdependence within the formal motif, and they can enter into

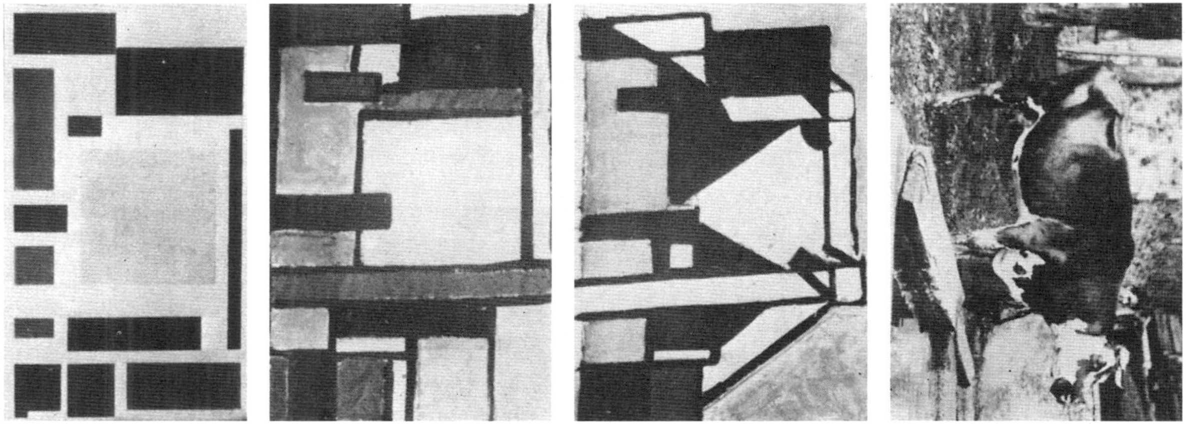

Theo van Doesburg, transfiguration of the cow, 1916-1925

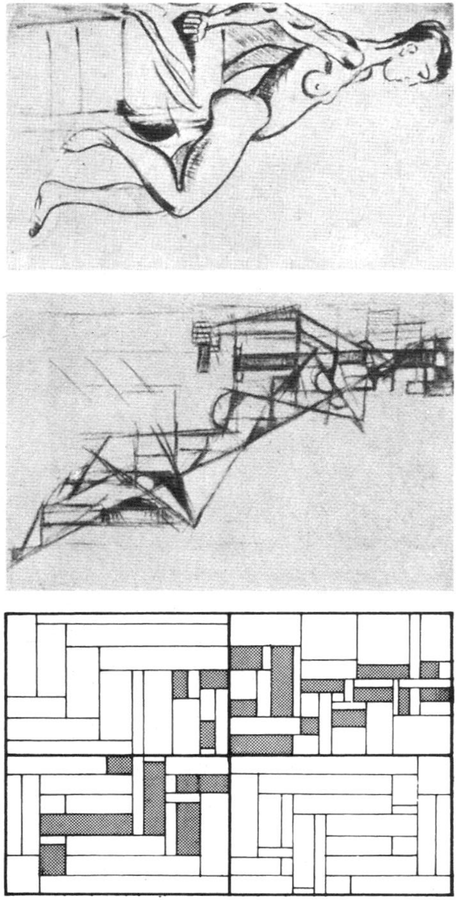

Derived from design for *Composition II*

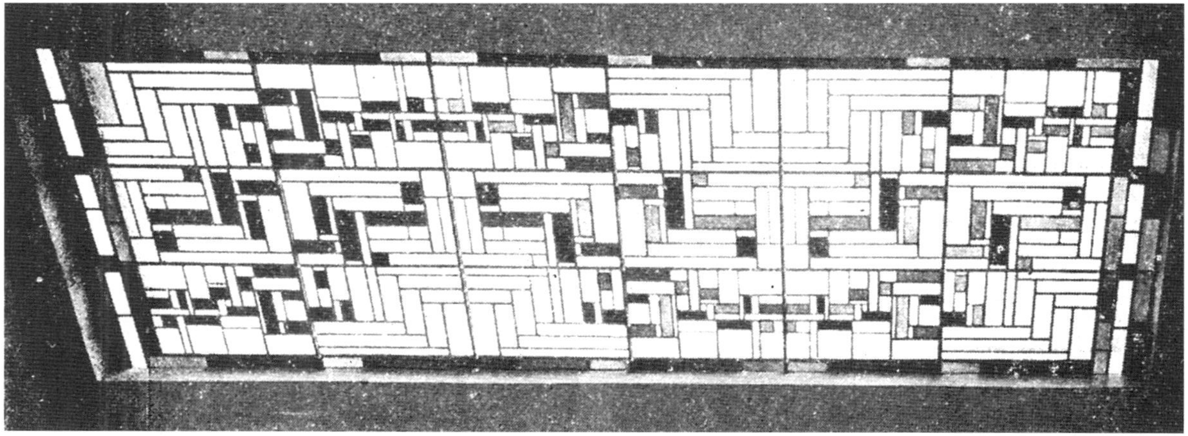

Theo van Doesburg, stained glass, *Composition II*, 1917

Theo van Doesburg, stained glass, *Composition III*, 1917

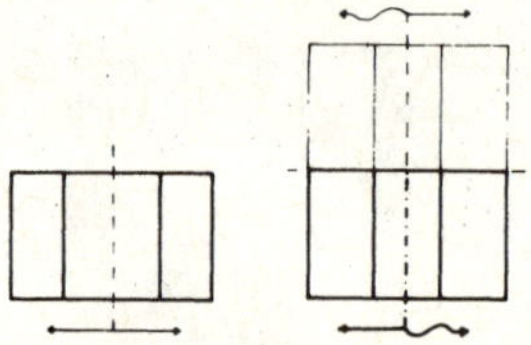

Theo van Doesburg, stained glass, *Composition IV*, 1917

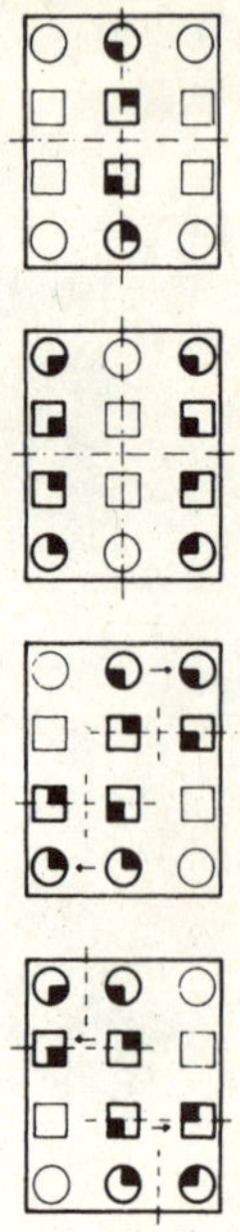

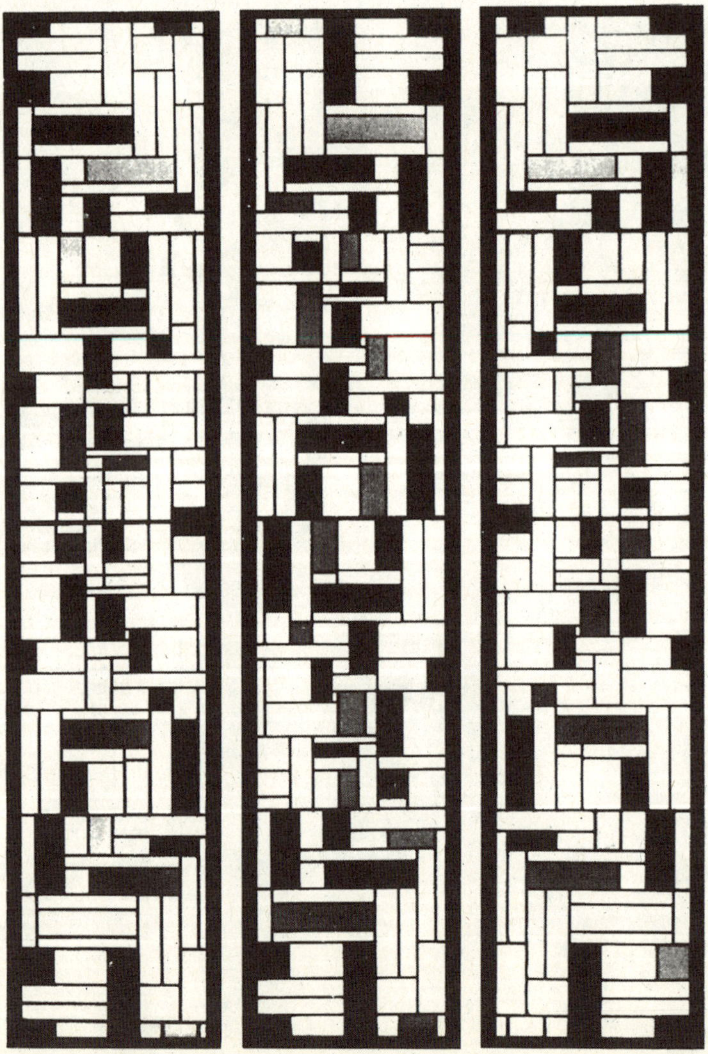

Theo van Doesburg, stained glass, *Composition IV*, 1917

new relationships throughout the picture plane. This led to a technique of free composition, not derived from anything in the natural world, composition based purely on formal relationships, articulated through colour. Van Doesburg not only frequently draws a connection between the development of this technique and similar working methods in painting and music, but also sees affinities with architecture, Oud's work in particular. In 'Aantekeningen over de nieuwe muziek' (Notes on new music), Van Doesburg writes, 'The destruction of naturally appearing forms in painting is analogous to the destruction of melody in new music. That is not to say that in the new conception of music the melodic element is wholly eliminated. That is impossible in a mode of expression that manifests itself in time (1 dim.). Because temporal progression (one thing after another) is the identifying characteristic of music, music is always tied to a melodic rhythm . . .' In a footnote he adds, 'In this respect, it displays a fundamental similarity to architecture, particularly Oud's architecture of the street, and his idea that harmonious balance can be attained only in the cityscape as a whole is therefore very logical.'[36]

Street architecture is also based on accentuating the moment in time, the sense of one-thing-after-another (*het na-elkaar*), by reiterating a particular motif. In earlier notes on Oud's design for the promenade at the beach resort of Scheveningen, Van Doesburg says, 'Because an artist, in the design process, concentrates all his attention on what takes place within, and because he has grasped the unity of function in all houses, he can repeat a particular motif, both the inner and outer aspects of it. We see this motif dominate the entire work – not monotonously, but with great animation and expression – in the tension of horizontal and vertical relationships.'[37]

One can regard Oud's housing projects as an exploration of the possibilities afforded by this composition technique. The identical function of each dwelling in mass housing provides the motif, which determines the form of the housing block and the street frontage through repetition and stacking. In this respect, the 'street composition' published in De Stijl is one of the most interesting experiments. A rhythmic pattern is developed on the basis of point reflection of the house plans around two intertwined stairwells.

Here, the process of creating motifs and of composition is linked to the total destruction of the natural form of the Dutch house. The row of dwellings in Hoek van Holland goes much further still. There, the repeated motif frees itself from the individual dwelling. The housing unit is a variable unit. The enduring elements of the composition are the components of the dwelling, rather than the dwelling in its entirety. Through the straightforward repetition of architectural elements, a variety of dwellings are created, with two, three and four rooms.

Thanks to this method, Oud sees no obstacle whatever to the development of architecture in the demand for standardization and normalization in construction work: 'If the standard types are well executed, in aesthetic terms, then they can be used to create a stylishly sculpted street (*stijlvolle straatplastiek*) of great monumentality, and then it will be possible, in future, to enjoy not only the dwelling in itself, but also the street as a whole. For then the standard types will bring the proportions and the rhythm that the cityscape now lacks.' Oud believes that the anarchy in the building sector can in fact be *reined in* by giving an aesthetic form to the output of mass production: 'The architect then acts as a director, stage-managing mass products into an architectural whole.'[38]

36 Theo van Doesburg, 'Aantekeningen over de nieuwe muziek', *De Stijl,* 1919 no. 1.

37 Theo van Doesburg, 'Bij de bijlagen', *De Stijl,* 1917 no. 1.

38 J.J.P. Oud, 'Bouwkunst en Normalisatie bij den Massabouw', *De Stijl,* 1918 no. 7.

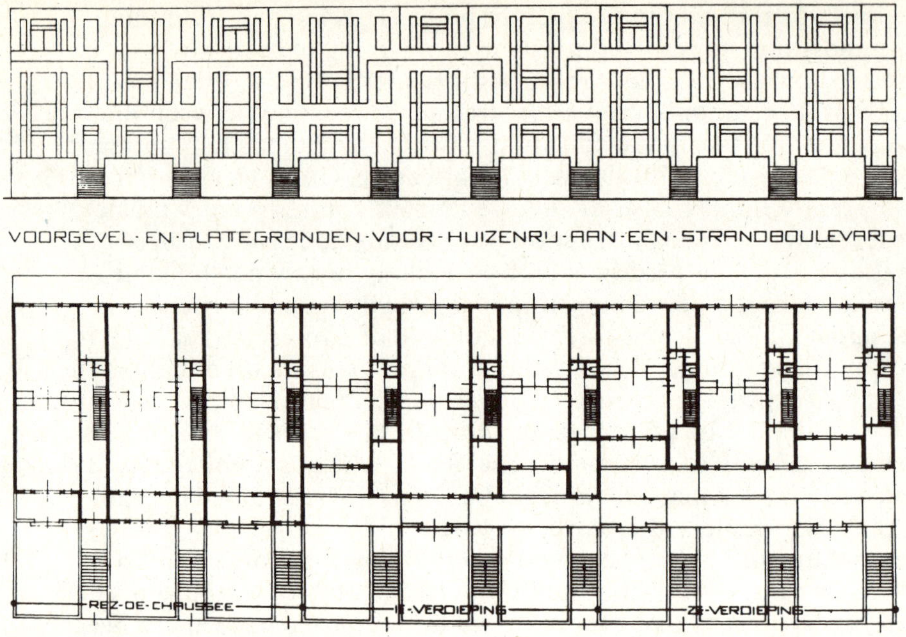

J.J.P. Oud, Promenade, 1917

J.J.P. Oud, row of working-class homes, 1919

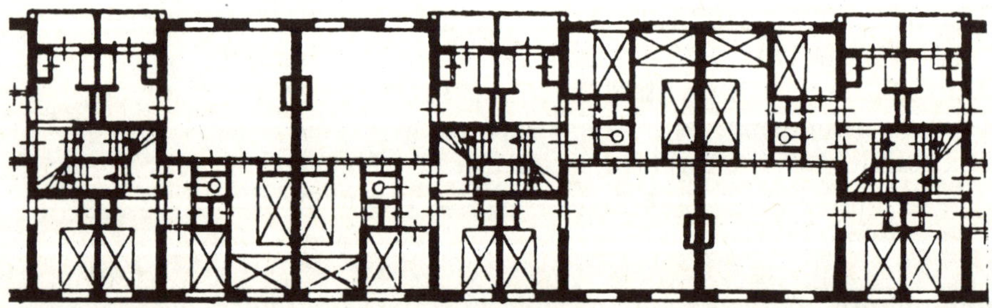

J.J.P. Oud, row of working-class homes, 1919

J.P. Oud, Hoek van Holland, 1924-1927

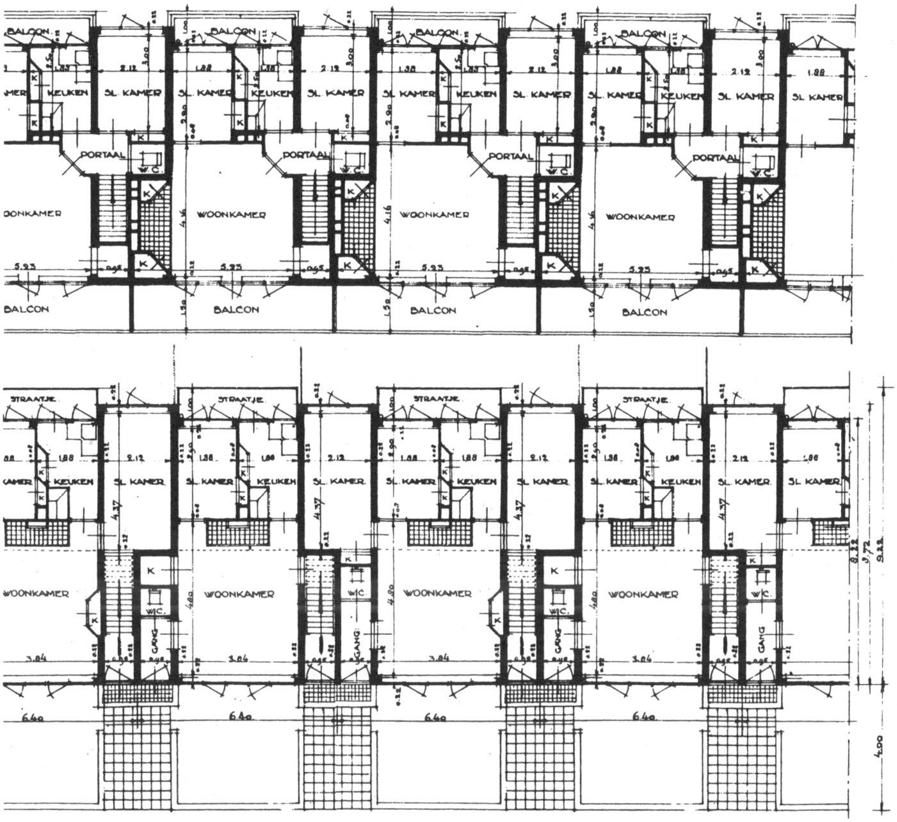

J.J.P. Oud, Hoek van Holland, 1924-1927

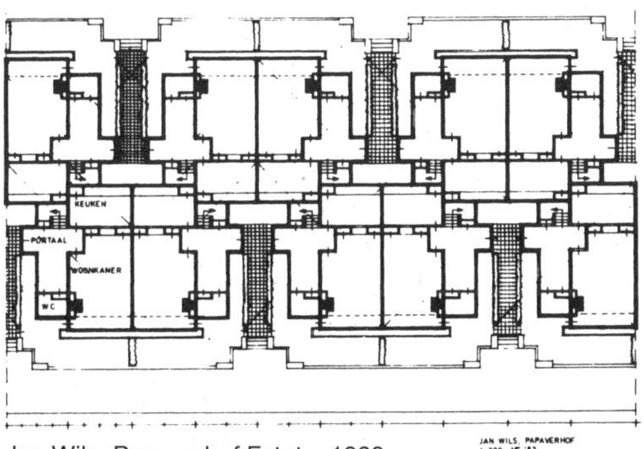

Jan Wils, Papaverhof Estate, 1922

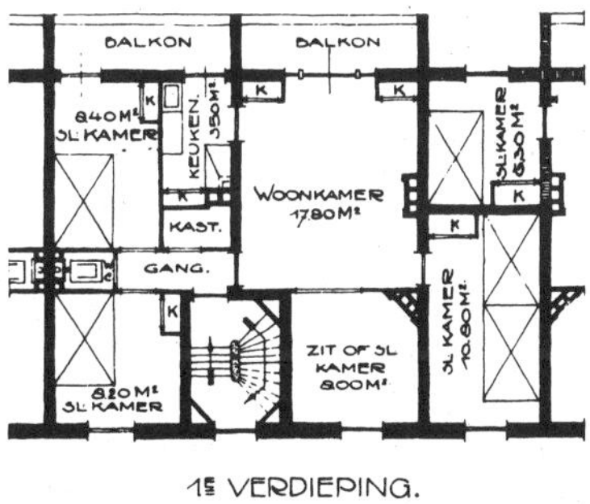

J.J.P. Oud, Tusschendijken housing plan with transitions, 1921

Oud's experiments remain scrupulously within the bounds of modern culture, as Kracauer described it in *Das Ornament der Masse*.[39] The composition of the mass elements can be manipulated in an entirely rational way, but never crosses the line into self-satisfied mechanism. Their serial nature cannot become a senseless game, because it is always dominated by the meaning attached to the transformation of received forms. For instance, 'natural transformation, which emerges from consistent normalization, [has] an inherently "ornamental" effect. But complete, harmonically balanced plasticism will only be possible in the cityscape as a whole . . . if the forward motion of the street, a result of the predominantly horizontal tendency, is interrupted by highly emphatic vertical elements, in the form of major corner solutions or detached buildings.'[40]

39 Siegfried Kracauer, *Das Ornament der Masse* (Frankfurt, 1977), 50.

Even in Oud's last housing projects, for the Weissenhofsiedlung and for Blijdorp, in which he adopted the row housing principle and swept aside the framework of streets and squares put forward by Berlage, the spaces are described as transformations of the traditional street and courtyard spaces.[41]

40 Oud, 'Architectonische Beschouwing', op. cit. (note 21).

41 H. Engel, 'Het strenge onderzoek naar de woning', in: *Architectuur van J.J.P. Oud* (Rotterdam, 1981).

Starting from a free style of composition, Van Doesburg's experiments led in an entirely different direction.

MAISON PARTICULIÈRE, MAISON D'ARTISTE

In Van Doesburg's work, repetition of the motif in the picture plane can take the form of a system of symmetry axes or, as in *Composition III*, rotation around a point; in sculpture, rotation around an axis; and in architecture, stacking, repetition and reflection, either around an axis or from an orthogonal midpoint, as in the model Van Doesburg called the Tesseract.

Theo van Doesburg, room for Bart de Ligt, 1919

Theo van Doesburg, elementary forms of expression in art: painting, sculpture, architecture

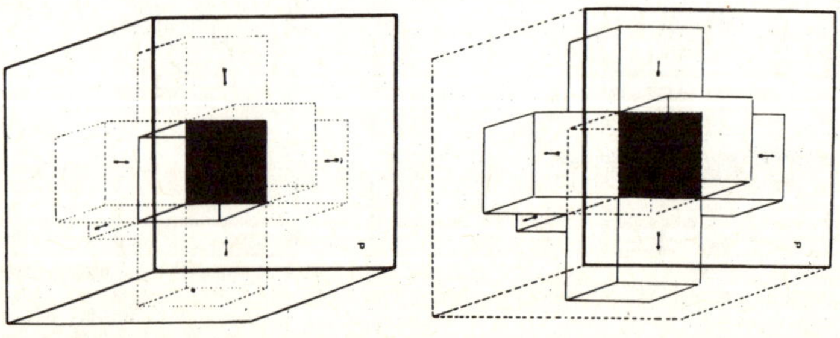

Theo van Doesburg, Tesseract, ca. 1922

In each case, this mode of 'repetition' of the motif is intended to bring the sense of one-thing-after-another into rhythmic harmony, to organize a simultaneous image of the object.

The colour scheme that Van Doesburg developed for his interiors and exteriors should be seen as the same kind of repetition of motifs, in which the *natural* form of the architecture is the formal object under attack. The geometric accentuation of the ceiling and the individual walls, in combination with the use of colour, is intended to make spatial relationships apparent in a single glance. In these colour schemes, straightforward repetition of the motif has been abandoned. Instead, they are based on variation and adaptation of motifs whose fundamental geometry is derived from the architecture itself, and on the independent use of colour. This working method is roughly equivalent to the free composition technique in the stained-glass *Compositions IV* and *V*.

The highly distinctive style in which the interiors are drawn in the design drawings – folded out upside-down and mirror-reversed – suggests that what mattered was not the actual situation, but the relationships between motifs.

The transition from this creation of motifs and composition to Van Doesburg's Elementarism is more or less marked by the models that he made with Van Eesteren in Paris in 1923. Let us crudely sketch that transition. With regard to the relationship between colour and architecture, we will examine the *maison particulière* in the light of the composition style discussed above, and contrast it with Elementarism and the *maison d'artiste*.

In the very first issue of *De Stijl*, Bart van der Leck defined the relationship between modern painting and architecture:

1 Modern painting is the destruction of the plastically natural, in contrast to the plastically-natural construction found in architecture.
2 Modern painting is open, in contrast to the connective, closed quality of architecture.
3 Modern painting creates colour and space, in contrast to the colourless, flat quality of architecture.
4 Modern painting is plasticism in spatial flatness: expansion, in contrast to the spatially limiting flatness of architecture.
5 Modern painting is plastically balanced, in contrast to the constructively balanced supporting and burdening found in architecture.[42]

Colour is used, as it was in the stained glass windows, to represent relationships (in this case, three-dimensional ones). Colour is the counterpoint to architectural form. Although the *maison particulière* does not have a frontal structure, but is oriented towards all sides equally, the anatomy of the house is closely connected to that of the traditional country estate, with a service wing and private quarters. Inside and out, this house shows a high degree of *secondary* plasticism, through *arbitrary* dislocation of interior and exterior walls.

It has a full 11 external canopies. Some cover entrances and patios, while others are awnings over the window openings to keep out the sun. Along with the overhanging upper storey, they give the house a pronounced horizontal character, reinforced by the enormous canopy adjoining the *salle commune*, which detaches the house from the ground there. The vertical accent in the house is provided by the central hall, which is bordered by the two chimneys and the staircases.

42 Bart van der Leck, 'De plaats van het moderne schilderen in de architectuur', *De Stijl*, 1917 no. 1.

Theo van Doesburg and Cor van Eesteren: *Maison Particulière*, 1923
Reconstruction of the floor plan (C. Maas, 1984)

Projection of counter construction onto house

Grisaille and colour scheme; counter construction

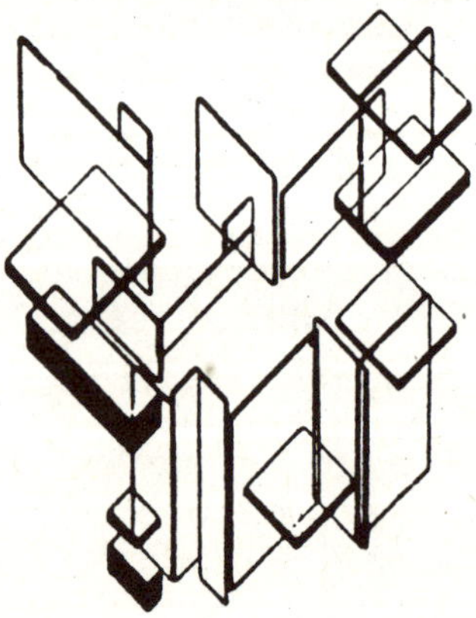

Counter construction; geometric abstraction of the outer surfaces

The floor plans by Van Eesteren and Van Doesburg do not provide clear-cut and adequate information allowing us to construct the building. In conjunction with the counter construction, they may be seen as conceptual memos.

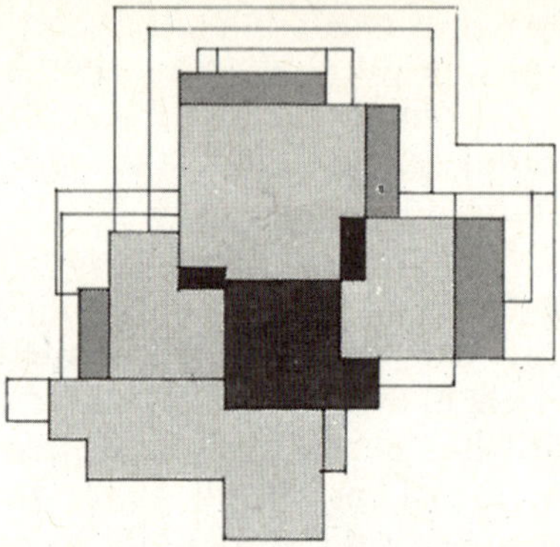

Projection of the floor slabs: ground floor to roof, light to dark

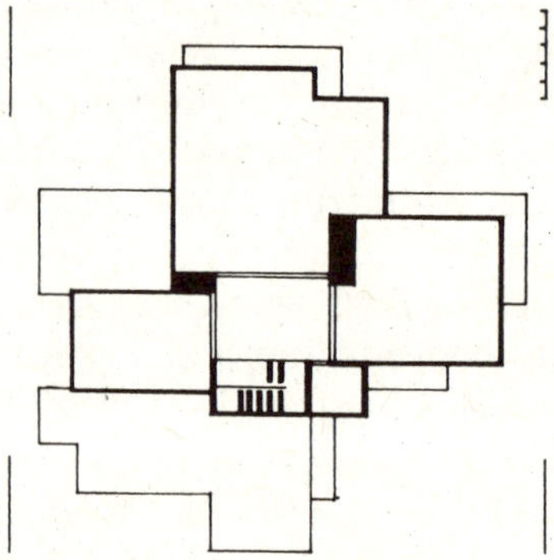

2nd floor and roof

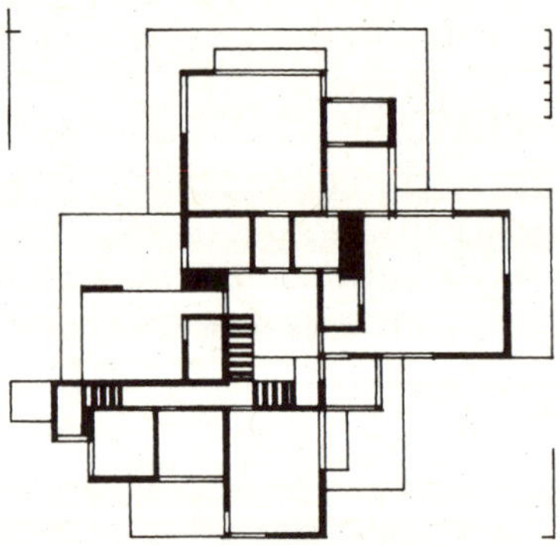

1st floor

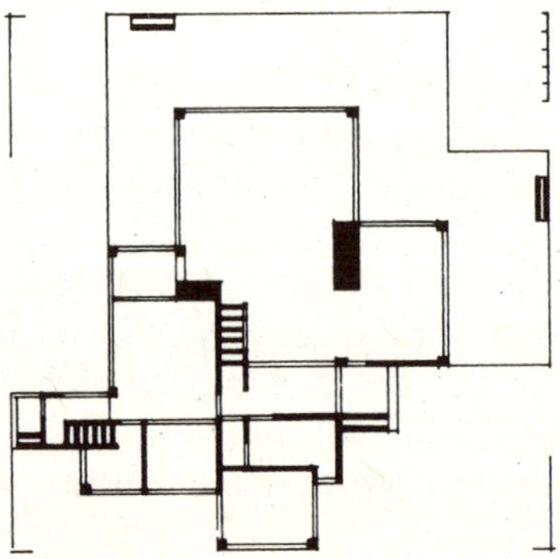

Ground floor

The verticality is visible solely in the upward motion and the position of the chimneys. It should be added that there is a strict division between the lower and upper levels. From the exterior, one sees the vertical accent: the elevation of the central section and the towering chimneys. The window openings in the house front are defined from the inside out. From the exterior, they are *arbitrary* gaps, which will (at the next stage of design) form the borders of the areas of colour on the outer walls.

For the painterly plasticism of the house, Van Doesburg develops what he calls a contra-construction. He begins with an axonometric representation of the exterior of the house, displaying its plastic structure. Then he makes a drawing that abstracts away from the axonometry, showing only the exterior walls and canopies. The drawing displays a transparent interplay of rectangular horizontal and vertical planes, in which balconies and chimneys are indicated as opaque massive blocks contrasting with the transparent planes.

After that, he makes a grisaille showing this spatial interplay of geometric relationships, in which the non-colours white, grey and black are used for the transparent planes, accentuating their relationships in space. The next step is an axonometric colour design based on the grisaille. This axonometric abstraction is then projected onto the architecture again, and a final correction is made to the colour proposal based on the geometry of the wall openings.

There is a widespread misconception about this contra-construction. One might interpret it in a Mondrianesque way, thinking that it represents a manifesto for a new architecture, in which the mutual interpenetration of interior and exterior, of universal space, is achieved through an architecture of horizontal and vertical planes. But the interior of the house of which these drawings are an abstraction plays no role whatever.

Van Doesburg reduces the plastic structure of the exterior of the house to colourless flatness, so that he can create a sculptural harmony (*beeldende harmonie*) with the aid of colour. The contra-construction is a *spatial* representation of geometric abstraction, which we also find in the stained-glass windows and the paintings.

To illustrate this Elementarist procedure, let us now turn to the analysis of the *maison d'artiste*, by way of a quote from Van Eesteren and Van Doesburg's above-mentioned 1924 manifesto 'Tot een beeldende architectuur':

'14. *Colour*. The new architecture has done away with painting as a distinct, imaginary expression of harmony, whether secondarily through representation or primarily through areas of colour. The new architecture incorporates colour organically, as a direct expression of its relationships in time and space. Without colour, these relationships have no living reality; *they are not visible*.'

And from the manifesto '–□+ = R4', by the same two authors: 'VIII. L'époque de la destruction est totalement finie. Il commence une nouvelle époque. La grande époque de la construction.'[43]

The *maison d'artiste* lacks *arbitrary* plasticism. Each room is conceived as a simple geometric form. This form also plays a predominant role in the external plasticism. Vertical areas indicate where one can enter the house; above them are horizontal canopies. A canopy is also used two other times, but less 'accidentally' than in the case of the *maison particulière*.

The stacking of box-shaped rooms around the central, transparent stairwell and the solid chimney, the use of overhanging architectural

43 Theo van Doesburg and Cornelis van Eesteren, '–□+ = R4', *De Stijl*, 1924 no. 6 & 7.

Theo van Doesburg and Cor van Eesteren: *Maison d'Artiste*, 1923

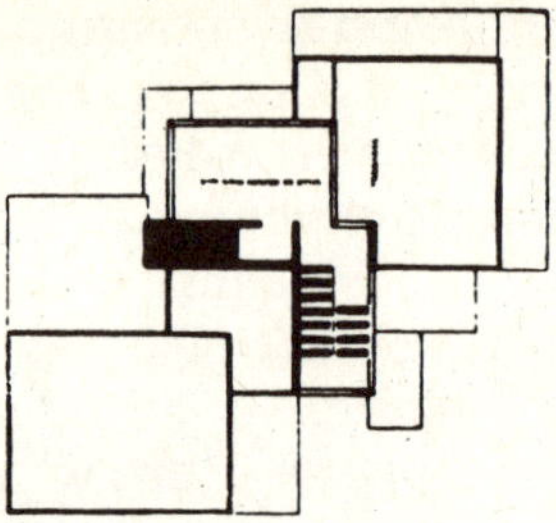

3rd floor and roof

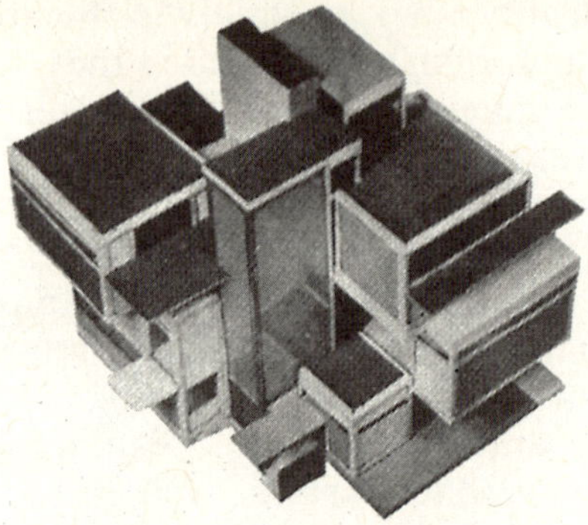

Model

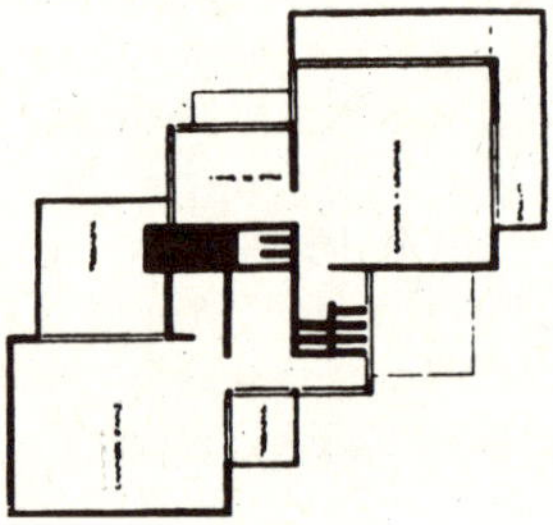

2nd floor

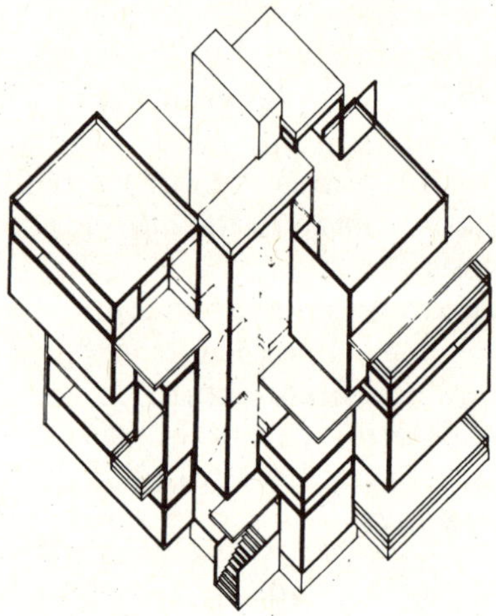

Axonometric projection

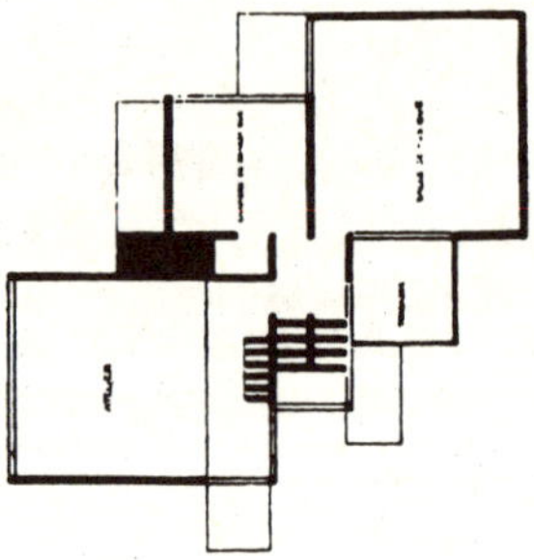

1st floor

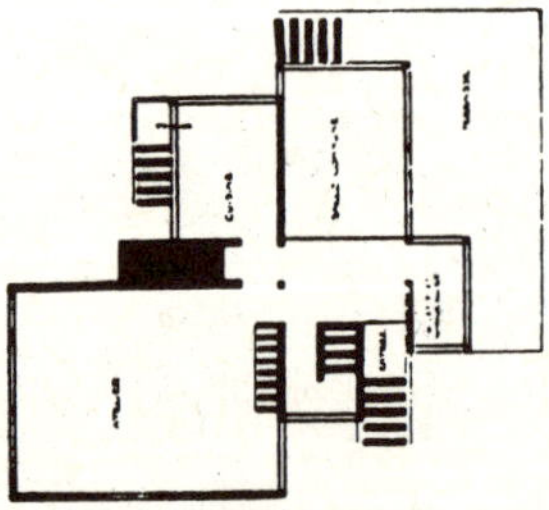

Ground floor

Grisaille and colour scheme: counter construction

volumes, the interplay of the canopies and patios, the strange overlap between boxes – all this ultimately creates an appearance of extremely mobile, unstable, geometric plasticity. In this house, almost no use is made of 'accidental' openings in the outer walls, which are thought of as a panel construction, filled with glass or an opaque material. The opaque division of the panel filling in the construction coincides with the division of the colour areas.

The procedure of contra-construction was not used for this house. The painting was done directly on the axonometric projection of the house, with its geometric arrangement of outer walls.

The colour solution for the architecture, the reduction of the architectural form to a geometric relationship, and the destruction of the natural plasticism of the architecture are, in other words, no longer a part of the conceptual universe that underlies the *maison d'artiste.*

L'époque de la destruction est totalement finie. In the creation of motifs, natural form disappears amid a geometry of relationships. Then, in free composition, all reference to natural form disappears and colour is liberated to depict the balance of those relationships. The contrapuntal relationship between painting and architecture is also relinquished at this stage.

The Elementarist working method is not limited to painting and architecture.[44] Van Doesburg and Van Eesteren write in 'Tot een beeldende architectuur' that the creation and repetition of motifs in street architecture is no longer the right way to form a cityscape:

'(12) Symmetry and repetition – The new architecture has done away with both monotonous repetition and the rigid identity of two halves, the mirror image, symmetry. It has neither place for repetition in time, nor for continuous street frontage or normalization. A complex is just as much a whole as a detached house is. The same laws apply to both the complex of the city and the individual dwelling. In contrast to the symmetrical, the new architecture proposes the balanced *relationship of unequal parts*, that is, parts that differ in their position, measurements, proportion and placement because of differences in their functional nature.'[45]

Urban planning therefore does not have to be based on cells combined from within to form complex entities, any more than street architecture does. This view has profound ramifications for the transformation of Berlage's ideas about urban design, since he sees urban planning primarily in the light of the expansion of the metropolis, which he achieves mainly by adding units.

44 Jan de Heer, 'AUP + AUB(ette)', in: *Raderwerk* (Delft, 1981).

45 Van Doesburg, 'Tot een Beeldende Architectuur', op. cit. (note 24).

VAN EESTEREN AND THE GENERAL EXPANSION PLAN

The 1934 General Expansion Plan for Amsterdam is in many ways consistent with Berlage's views on the modern city, the result of modern science and modern art. The differences between this plan and Berlage's are instructive.

The plan drafted by Van Eesteren is also based on a system of cells, attached like lobes to the body of the existing city. The internal structure of the cells – the geometric street pattern emanating from the square, which is meant to form the architectural highlight of each cell – is absent. No indication of the architecture of the cell is given anywhere. Oud's systematization of the composition of the housing block within

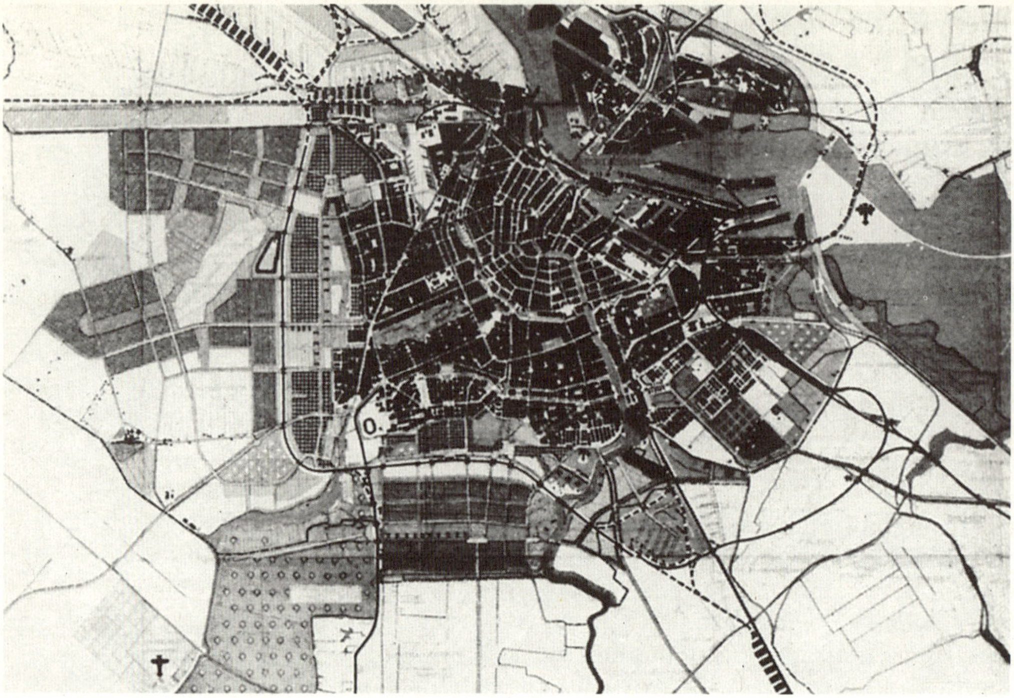

Cor van Eesteren – General Expansion Plan Amsterdam, 1934

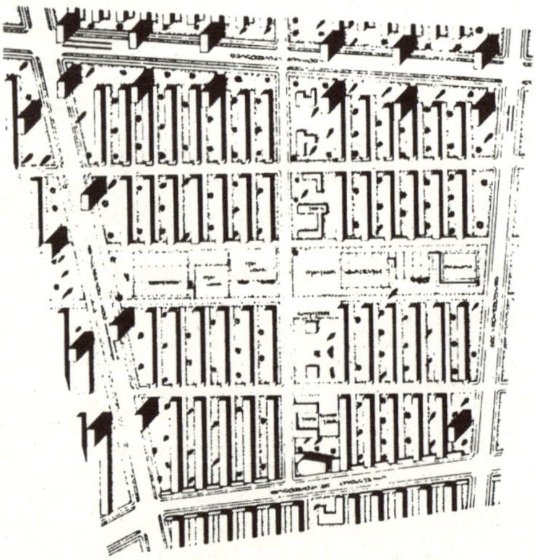

B. Merckelbach, Plan for an organic housing estate in open planning, 1932

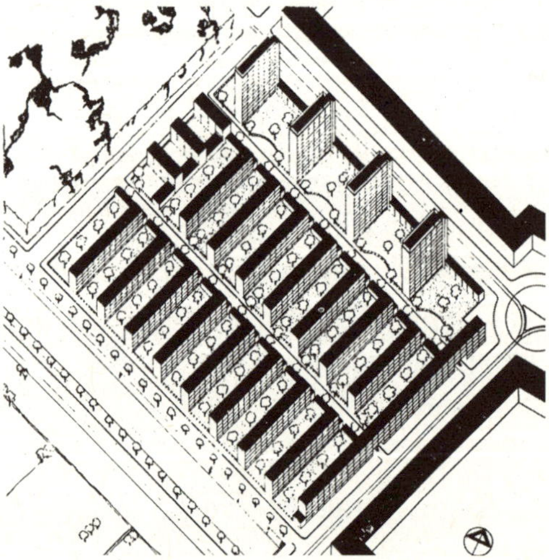

J.H. van den Broek, Competition entry for 'Cheap working-class homes' with the motto 'Optimum', 1934

the formal urban plan provided by Berlage had, since his project for the Weissenhofsiedlung and the plan for Blijdorp, led to the breakdown of that recipe for urban space.

The use of row housing as an organizing principle eliminated some of the polarity between the street and the courtyard that is characteristic of the closed housing block.

It remained unclear what should replace that old framework. 'The organic residential district with low-density construction' also strongly resembles Berlage's cells.[46] The housing blocks are replaced with rows, and the street pattern is adapted accordingly. The most important buildings are not placed around a central square, but in a specified zone. In the most provocative entries to the 1933-1934 competition to design inexpensive working-class housing, such squares had disappeared entirely. What remained were the geometry of the housing and the accentuation of the peripheral buildings.

46 De 8 en Opbouw, 'De organische woonwijk in open bebouwing', *De 8 en Opbouw,* 1932.

A second difference from Berlage's cell system was the *natural* connections between the cells. Berlage made use of natural obstacles in the landscape to dispel the monotony of geometry. The elements used to link the individual lobes in Van Eesteren's plan, however, are designed in a much more independent way. It is only there that the plan includes architectural specifications. The Sloterplas, the Nieuwe Meer with the adjoining Amsterdamse Bos, the Amstel, and the park, together with the parks on the west and south of the pre-existing city, form the *natural* border of the built-up area. In some places, this border is accentuated by tall buildings, while elsewhere – for instance, where new and pre-existing buildings meet – the edge is first carefully finished.

What Berlage saw, within his system of cells, as monumental architectural highlights of the urban plan, take on a new dimension in Van Eesteren's proposal, which is no longer based on street architecture that culminates in the symbolic centre of the cell. The geometry of the housing remains intact, though in a system of rows rather than blocks, and without any centre towards which it is oriented. The architectural accent has shifted from the centre to the borders. The reason these edges are important is, however, not primarily that they demarcate the district, but that they form the architectural borders of the city parks.

Translated by David McKay

The double issue 9/10 of the journal *O* includes Luuk Boelens' article 'Naar een onverkorte stedenbouw' (Towards an Uncompromised Urbanism) and marks the end of the pioneer phase. *O* 9/10, published in spring 1985, was the final issue I was involved with as a member of the editorial team. The magazine then changed its name and from issue 11 onwards continued as *OASE*.

The editorial in *O* 9/10 notes: 'Recent years have seen a widespread interest in the work of the "generation of young architects". . . . Dissatisfaction with the architectural output from the past few decades is boosting the demand for "young designers with fresh ideas".' With hindsight, this is an understatement: the architecture from that period was indeed the most dismal since the introduction of the housing act in 1901. The reaction against modernism led to an uninspiring architecture and an impoverished vocabulary of forms. A new generation of young architects began practising, exploring new ways and receiving (international) recognition. The architectural output in the Netherlands has since become much more varied and attractive. The double issue *O* 9/10 presented, whether or not coincidentally, this rich diversity, thus reflecting the work of the pioneer phase: different contours and categories, seemingly unconnected yet also complementing each other.

Luuk Boelens' article contributed to the discussion about urbanism and thus formed part of the debate on the relationship between urbanism and architectural design – two completely distinct disciplines at that time. Back in 1979 Carel Weeber, in his article 'Formele objectiviteit in stedebouw en architectuur als onderdeel van rationele planning' (Formal objectivity in urbanism and architecture as an element of rational planning), had tried to remove the discussion about urbanism and architecture from its ideological context and to regard it more objectively. In Italy and France especially, earlier attempts had been made to objectify the professional dimension.

Boelens restricts his outline of autonomy and synthesis to the development of urbanism by the avant-garde in the twentieth century. Via the Deutsche Werkbund (1907-1914) and the Bauhaus (1919-1927) we end up at the Weissenhofsiedlung (1927) and via the CIAM we arrive at the Hansa Viertel (1953). After that, the development lost its consistency: the jump to postmodernism and the current debate on urbanism, of which the IBA Berlin (1987) is an example, simply proved too big. At the same time, the article demonstrates the degree to which the debate on urbanism and architecture was, at that time, unable to free itself from the shackles of the legacy of the Modern Movement of the twentieth century.

Henk Döll
Member of the editorial board
from *OASE* 1 to 9/10

Translated by Laura Vroomen

Luuk Boelens

TOWARDS AN UNCOMPROMISED URBANISM

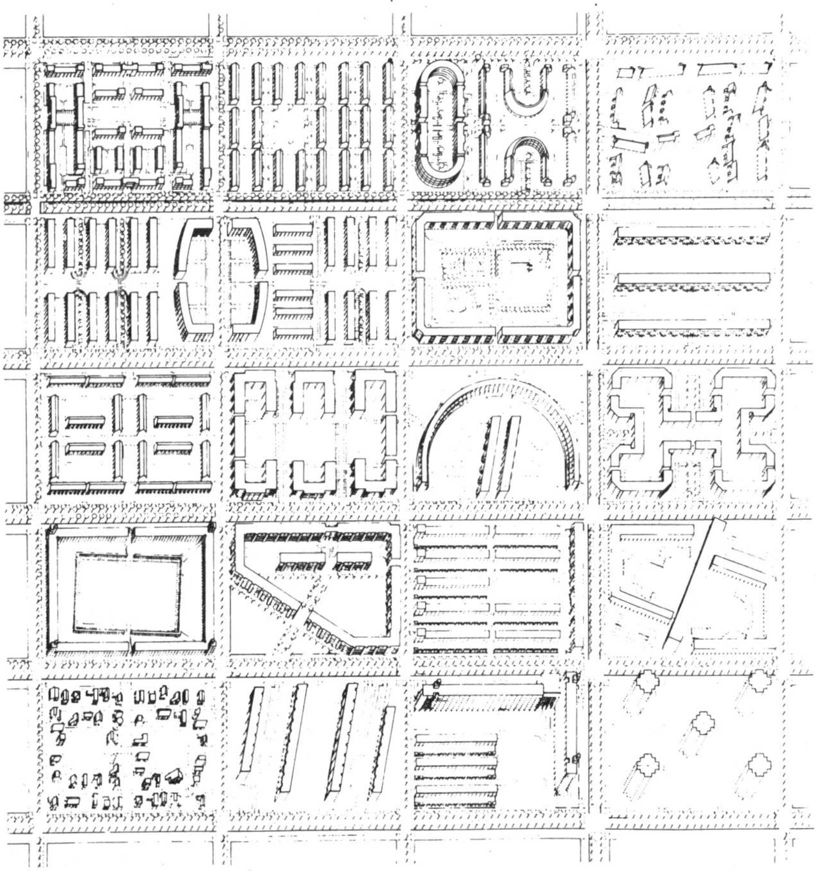

The 'grid' city, based on a final academic project by Gerard Fischert and Han de Kluyer focussing on the Weeberian delineation of the interfaces between architecture and urban design

FIRST PUBLISHED IN O 9/10

AUTONOMY-SYNTHESIS

The recently initiated, broadly defined debate on urbanism seems definitively to ignore the social relevance of the labour of the urban planner. With the ad hoc objective of filling an observed gap in thinking about form in urban design, this debate has re-emphasised the autonomy of the discipline and the individual artist. The fact that urbanism is drawing on an option which emphasises that the social origins of the formal are unknowable – and thus deliberately and voluntarily retreats as far as possible from reality – has its roots not least in the formalist approach developed by the postmoderns in the 1970s. In 1979 Carel Weeber, one of the Dutch representatives of this school, pointed out that the discipline of urbanism should be encouraged to shed the mask of other disciplines, in order for it to focus exclusively on designing formal structures on an urban scale. Alongside the autonomy of urbanism as a discipline, he advocated re-introducing urban design as an independent, formal level of planning, and thereby restoring the artistically motivated organisation of individual architectural projects to its rightful place. Urban design would then relate not only to the problem of the borders and limits of disciplinary design practices, but also to that of opting for an indissoluble link between urbanism and architecture. Because even though urban planners were no longer supposed to speculate about the visual qualities of the built environment, and even though architects, for their part, were no longer supposed to dream of cities that were actually buildings, it was still thought to be only through urbanism that architecture could flourish, and only through architecture that urbanism could be elevated to the status of a three-dimensional reality.[1]

On account of the fundamental malaise in which urban design work had become bogged down in the early 1980s, Weeber's half-formed, one-sided formal approach swiftly gained currency (in the Netherlands) in thinking about urbanism, and so, to a large degree, has come to dominate the current debate on urbanism. Increasingly, the contributions to that debate neglect the inherent social and political message of urban design activities, even though studies by Manfredo Tafuri, Bolte & Meijer and others have shown that architects and urban planners simply cannot afford the luxury of being apolitical.[2] Debate and research on the visual structures still possible at the urban level are thus degenerating into a highly neurotic formalism, which as such is no longer able or willing to advance and articulate its own practice within other, non-aesthetic practices. This becomes even more painfully apparent as we see separate, individual architectural projects succeeding one another faster and faster, driven by the winds of fashion, and as this fixation on form, without reference to actual content, is accompanied by growing independence and fragmentation in spatial design practice(s). When urban planners retreat into an ultimate autonomy and give their own specific field of knowledge a central role, the link – so crucial

1
See Carel Weeber, 'Formele objectiviteit in stedebouw en architectuur als onderdeel van rationele planning', *Plan* no. 11, November 1979; 27-35. My impression is that Weeber's preference for an urban 'grid' is a reference to Habraken's concept of urban 'carriers'. But while Habraken is referring to the mass of the city itself, in which the architect's role is limited to the constructive development of the carriers, for Weeber urban design remains no more than a two-dimensional grid, which is supposed to be indifferent to future patterns of use.

2
Manfredo Tanfuri, *Ontwerp en Utopie* (orig. title: *Progetto e Utopia*; Rome/Bari, 1973); Sunschrift 117 (Nijmegen, 1978). Wouter Bolte and Johan Mijer, *Van Berlage tot Bijlmer: architektuur en stedelijke politiek*, Sunschrift 167 (Nijmegen, 1981).

for contemporary projects – between architectural and urban-planning practice and its dialectical relationship to the social configuration of time and place can no longer take concrete form. From now on, the practice of spatial design will thus unapologetically disintegrate into its separate components – planning, urbanism and architecture – which, on the basis of a kind of closed learning and feedback loop, can each develop in a unique, idiosyncratic way. This parting of ways at the level of spatial action systems has, however, made it obvious that no part of current design practice is self-evident any longer; even its right to exist is no longer self-evident, according to Jürgen Habermas.[3] Because of the crisis of the multi- and interdisciplinary approach that is the inevitable result of this, and because of the more complex field of urban integration in which the discipline of urbanism has traditionally operated, this situation is, for the time being, most clearly visible in the domain of urban design.

Against this background, it seems to me that the above-mentioned restriction of personal responsibility to purely formal questions of urban design becomes somewhat problematic at the moment that the discipline of urbanism, as such, aspires to bring about spatial cohesion between the components of the (urban) plan, which have become isolated and autonomous, and thereby to make the city 'legible'. This is because the 'expression of unity' in any cultural concept – or, as Weeber puts it, the consensus effect of the objective, formal approach to design – is doomed to fail as long as the discipline of urbanism has not developed a position on the social significance of its design activities, and as long as this spatial consistency can, accordingly, be traced solely from the (relatively) autonomous discipline. In itself, this pursuit of both the formal autonomy of urbanism and the demarcation of one's own field of knowledge in relation to the other cultural action systems is diametrically opposed to the pursuit of the coherent and spatial synthesis of separate, individual architectural projects.[4] Given that under present conditions these design practices refer to nothing but themselves, one is much more likely to achieve just the opposite of what one hopes.

This duality between autonomy and synthesis, which informs the current debate on urbanism, is the focus of this article. As a contribution to what was conceived as a formalist debate, it attempts to locate the social nature of the 'expression of unity' in the history of three avant-gardes and their *Bauausstellungen*. In doing so, rather than focusing primarily on the political conditions and implications of urbanism, it tends to complement this political aspect, since it calls into question the inherent dialectics of the aesthetic interpretation of urban design and tries to present its conditions, possibilities and impossibilities, with the aim of clarifying the nature of design work in the field of urbanism. It thus seems sensible to begin by returning to that practice, which made the heuristic search for unity within architectural style(s) – for the

3
Jürgen Habermas, 'Het moderne – een onvoltooid project', lecture delivered upon receiving the Adorno Prize, translated into Dutch by Cyrille Offermans, in *Raster* no. 19, 1981, 137; the opening words of Adorno's *Ästhetische Theorie* are quoted, see Theodor W. Adorno, *Ästhetische Theorie* (Frankfurt am Main, 1970), 9.

4
See also Jürgen Habermas, 'Moderne und Postmoderne Architektur', *Arch+* no. 61, February 1982; 54-59.

formal order within urban chaos – its central theme. This design code was adopted from the nineteenth-century Arts and Crafts Movement by the Deutscher Werkbund and, via the Bauhaus, eventually led to the Modern Movement. The subsequent developments within Team 10, Forum and postmodernism showed an increasing tendency towards autonomising artistic design practices, thus exacerbating the identity crisis within the field of urbanism, despite what were probably good intentions. This aesthetic falsification, which pushed ahead forcefully along the same lines in the 1970s, has arrived at its logical continuation in the current debate on urbanism: disregard for the practical content of form, so that the discipline of urban design now produces its own indecisions.

THE DEUTSCHER WERKBUND (1907-1914)

In the early years of the twentieth century – the period of the 'second industrial revolution' – the need to return to formal questions of urban design and rethink architecture's identity became the central theme of debate for the Deutscher Werkbund, an association of artists and architects. In a survey of the first five years of the Deutscher Werkbund (*Jahrbuch 1912*), Hermann Muthesius observed that while the Werkbund had helped to improve the quality of German industrial production – especially in the technical and material senses – this did not mean that it had achieved its goal. From the

Herman Muthesius: the factory floor at the Michiels & Cie silk mill

Werkbund's perspective, industrially manufactured goods had a conceptual value above and beyond their immediate practical value. Not only was it thought to be possible and essential for the new style of art to express this value, but it was in fact seen as the prior condition for all modern forms of design work.[5] The Werkbund code cannot, therefore, be characterised as a one-sided formal approach. It is much more accurate to call it a direct aesthetic confrontation between the ideal of individual freedom of artistic *Gestaltung* and the general economic laws of industrial utilitarianism. All forms of design work, as defined within the Werkbund's ideologies, were predicated on the creed that they could not be practiced as separate, individual projects, but could only succeed if the design process was inseparably linked to the social and economic circumstances from which it emerged. 'For art was not, after all, just an aesthetic force, but also a social one, which two together were meant to lead not least to the most important force of all, the economic one'.[6]

This contrasted with the 'negative thinking' of individuals such as Adolf Loos, who developed his 'compositions' from the inherent contradictions within the capitalist social formation. The Deutsche Werkbund thus tried to build bridges between art and industry, while Loos's theories envisaged vast gulfs.[7] This made the notion that was propagated of a relationship between individual artistic endeavours and scientistic economic practice – between artistic creation and the generation of norms – a political one, in the sense that it involved a new alliance between productive and spiritual forces, an alternative cultural and social use of mechanical means of production, which was ultimately expected to lead to social and artistic 'liberation'. But given that the political awareness of the prewar Werkbund was inadequate to achieve this goal and still at a formative stage, the association could not maintain any kind of conceptual unity. It splintered into separate projects, which were either characterised by unreflective artistic utopianism (*Wiederherstellung des reinen Lebens durch die Schönheit*) or entirely dominated by the productive promise of the capitalist social formation (*Wirtschaft als Selbstzweck*). The debate between Van de Velde, Muthesius and Naumann at the 'Werkbund-Ausstellung' in Cologne (1914) is especially revealing of this clear inner contradiction within the Werkbund's ideologies.[8]

THE BAUHAUS (1919-1927)

After the First World War, the pursuit of not only the relationship between art and industry, but also of 'unity among the various languages of composition and views on art' was the central theme of the *Bauhauslehren*. Founded in 1919 by Walter Gropius and serving (at least initially) as a pedagogical complement to the Werkbund, it strove for the coordination of all creative work – for unification in art and design – in order to arrive at a progressive synthesis between and within architec-

5
'Much more important than the material is the spiritual; above the goal, materials and technique stands the form . . . That is why the revival of an architectural culture is a requirement for all the arts and an absolute necessity for the general process of artistic renewal that we should expect to take place.' Hermann Muthesius, 'Wo stehen wir?, Vortrag gehalten auf der Jahresversammlung des Deutschen Werkbundes in Dresden 1911', in: *Das Jahrbuch des Deutschen Werkbundes* (Jena, 1912), 19-25.

6
Julius Posener, 'Der Deutschen Werkbund (1907-1914), Vorlesung gehalten auf das Fachbereich Architektur der T.U. Berlin', *Arch+* no. 59, October 1981; 24; quote from Schumacher's 'Gründungsrede des Deutschen Werkbundes' (Munich, October 1907).

7
See, for instance, Massimo Cacciari, 'Loos-Wien', in *Oikos: van Loos tot Wittgenstein* (orig. title: *Oikos da Loos a Wittgenstein*, Rome, 1975), Sunschrift 196 (Nijmegen, 1982), 20. A review responding to this article of Cacciari's was published in *O* no. 7 (Geert Hovingh, 'Loos-Wien; cultuurkritiek en architectuur; een bespreking', *O: ontwerp, onderzoek en onderwijs* no. 7, spring 1984, 28-36.

8
See, for instance, Julius Posener, ibid., 19-20; Niels L. Prak, 'Art and Industry: notes on their relations between 1750-1914', in: *Avantgarde und Industrie* (Delft, 1983), 8/9; Ludwig Hilberseimer, *Berliner Architektur der 20er Jahren: neue Bauhausbücher* (Mainz/Berlin, 1967), 8-9.

ture and society.[9] Accordingly, the Bauhaus ideology was based on a dual design code, at two complementary levels: the level of the *Gesamtkunstwerk* (that of the unity of all arts in the vision of an all-encompassing architectural *style* of the future) and the level of *machine art* (the connection between the artistic and industrial production processes). Although the separate components of this two-part ideology had been developed earlier, the former within the Arts and Crafts Movement and the latter by the Werkbund, the Bauhaus, in bringing them together, gave them a specific social content and meaning.

9
See Walter Gropius, *Idee und Aufbau des Staatlichen Bauhauses* (Munich, 1923), 24.

In response to the social tendency that promoted growing specialisation and fragmentation of the various cultural action systems, and in response to the contradiction still present within the Werkbund between artistic dilettantism and economic determinism, the Bauhaus postulated the fundamental unity of all artistic expression as a necessary condition for any type of modern design work. Walter Gropius considered social and cultural theory necessary for this purpose. He reasoned that the progressive synthesis of modern architecture, collective construction, which involved communication both among artists and between art and society as a whole, could only be brought about if it was also the logical product of the intellectual, social and technical conditions of the 'modern era'.[10] Particularly with the arrival of Theo van Doesburg and Lazló Moholy Nagy and, later, its move to Dessau, the Bauhaus thus propagated the unity of all artistic work by virtue of its relationship to life itself, and from

10
Gilbert Herbert, *The Synthetic Vision of Walter Gropius* (Johannesburg, 1959), 11-21.

Walter Gropius, Bauhaus buildings in Dessau

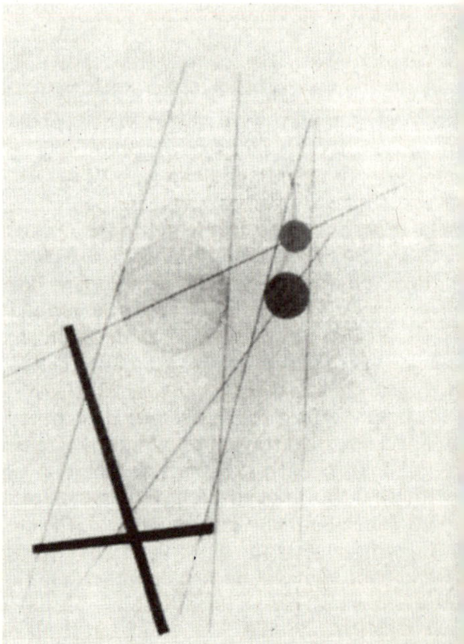
Lazlo Moholy Nagy, *Z III*, a 1922 painting

1923 to 1927, it thereby laid the groundwork for a collectively shaped, intersubjectively oriented *Maschinenstil*.

The problematic contradiction between art and industry, between design and technology, was then resolved by mediating between the artistic potential of art and the processing potential of mechanical means of production at a particular stage in the design process. This stage was the traditional, artisanal development of the prototype, the standard, which – as both the artistic result of laboratory experiments and the foundation for mass production – made the art-industry fusion a logical one. The prototype, it was thought, would be the best possible representation of what the discipline could produce at a given moment; it would eliminate the incidental and individual while emphasising what was formally essential and intersubjective. In this respect, the tendency towards standardisation and prefabrication in Bauhaus thinking was not a step backward, but one of the most important artistic conditions – in both a cultural and economic sense – for moving forward with social development.[11]

This postulate of cultural development was a philosophical borrowing from Hegel's definition of progress in terms of the dialectical sequence of thesis-antithesis-synthesis. Not only was the educational programme known as *Bauhauslehren* divided into the three separate stages of *Vorkurs*, *Fachstudium* and *Gestaltstudium*, but the Bauhaus code itself could also be characterised by an analogous series: art-technology-style. Alongside its above-mentioned views about the unity of all artistic views and compositional idioms, as well as those about the unity of the artistic and industrial production processes, the Bauhaus opted for 'multiplicity within this unity', for variation in the size and composition of the parts, in an attempt to avoid a looming sterility and uniformity in social and cultural development. The key concepts of the Bauhaus ideology (unity, prototype and style) were thus rooted in the paradox of variation (in reference to art) versus standardisation (in reference to industry), a seeming contradiction which was regarded not as a forced choice between two options, but rather as a productive 'conflict' that could lead to reconciliation (synthesis) and thus to a new and better architectural style. Under the protection of the intersubjectively created artistic codex and of industry, it was thought that it would be possible to safeguard the unity of the formal while also – in the other, sociocultural domain – leaving enough scope for personal, individual taste and the creative/intuitive approach. 'The final result would thus be a successful combination of consistent standardisation and far-reaching potential for variation,' Walter Gropius concluded.[12]

WEISSENHOFSIEDLUNG (1927)

These modern formal principles, developed by the Bauhaus and others, formed the basis of the Werkbund exhibition *Die Wohnung*, which took place in the summer of 1927 in

11
Walter Gropius, foreword to *The Synthetic Vision of Walter Gropius*, ibid., VII.

12
Walter Gropius, *Die neue Architektur und das Bauhaus: Grundzüge und Entwicklung einer Konzeption (Neue Bauhausbücher)* (Mainz/Berlin, 1965 [1935]), 12-18.

Building model, Weissenhofsiedlung, Stuttgart 1927

Aerial photo, Weissenhofsiedlung at the time of the exhibition

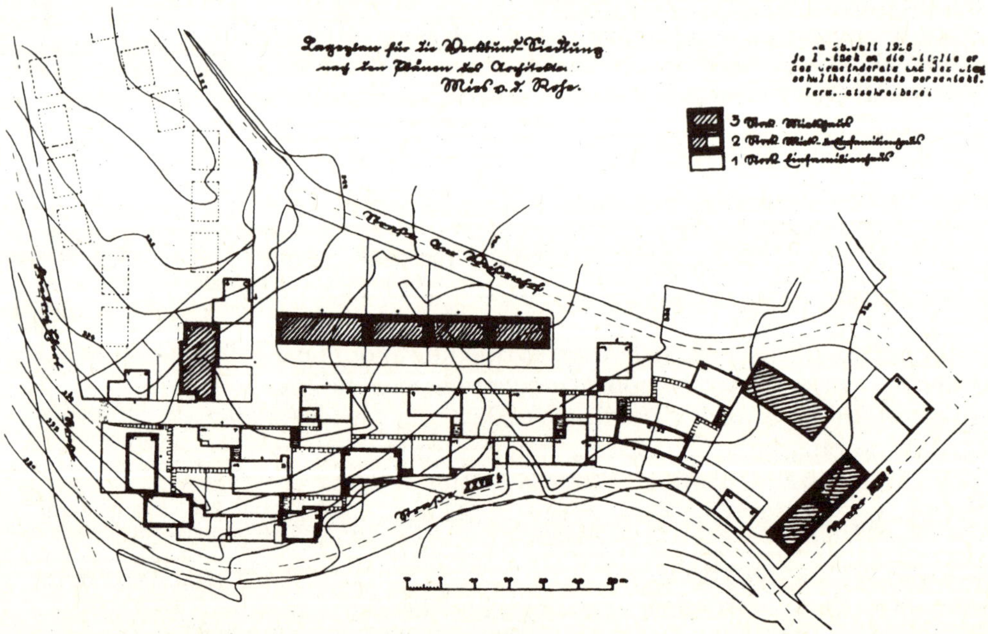

Ludwig Mies van der Rohe, building plan, Weissenhofsiedlung, 1926

Weissenhof, a suburb of Stuttgart. The Weissenhofsiedlung, as this model housing estate came to be known, departed in the following three fundamental respects from the Berlin Wohnsiedlungen, which had been developed in the preceding years:

1 its programmatic aspect;
2 its conception of urban development; and
3 its status as the first clearly international cooperative endeavour by the Central European avant-garde.

1 In 1926, Ludwig Mies van der Rohe became the general director of the Weissenhofproject, for which he designed both the urban plan and the first housing block. He described the problem of the 'new housing', and thus the programme of the Weissenhofsiedlung, as follows: 'The postulate of "rationalisation and standardisation", as well as the pursuit of profitability in housing production, are merely facets of the problem, which are very important, to be sure, but can only become truly significant when placed in the proper perspective. Alongside or, more accurately, above and beyond them is the spatial problem, which can only be solved by means of "creative force" and not by rational or organisational means.'[13] This principle thus highlighted the pursuit of rationalisation and standardisation in architecture, but also emphasised that this pursuit was only a means of getting at the modern formal aspects of the 'housing question'. On its own, the Weissenhof programme provided an open (or half-open) method, which gave individual architects the greatest possible artistic freedom, despite the modern requirement that the building process be unified and unequivocal.[14] Nevertheless, the avant-garde participants, who had previously worked in relative isolation, managed to jointly produce an astounding degree of formal unity. Through the intermediary of the socioeconomic conditions of modernity, the international avant-garde seems ultimately to have succeeded in finding a single artistic code and thereby rallying around a single collective style.

2 The unity shown at the architectural level was not, however, reflected in the overall plan. Although Mies van der Rohe attempted to create a free, organic and thoroughly green housing estate according to 'modern planning principles', and although, with the aid of his own project and the housing blocks designed by Le Corbusier and Peter Behrens, he aimed to make the intended organisation of the estate apparent to the eye,[15] these proposals could not undo the impression that the individual villas followed the contours of the Killesberg only in a haphazard way, and hence that, in urban planning terms, the Weissenhofsiedlung disintegrated into its architectural parts. This was because Mies van der Rohe's design initiatives were only meaningful at the level of reception, and thus did not conform to the newly introduced scientific methods, which made it increasingly clear that the problem of

13
Ludwig Mies van der Rohe, 'Vorbemerkungen zum ersten Sonderheft "Werkbundausstellung die Wohnung Stuttgart 1927"', orig. published in *Die Form*, Heft 9/1927; reprinted in *Die Form: Stimme des Deutschen Werkbundes 1925-1934* (Güthersloh, 1969); 132-133. In this article Mies van der Rohe comes close to the option expressed 15 years earlier by Hermann Muthesius (see note 5).

14
See Jürgen Joedicke and Christian Plath, *Die Weissenhofsiedlung Stuttgart* (Stuttgart, 1968/1977), 16-41.

15
Ibid., 9-11.

urban design involved not only formal, but also organisational and political coherence. Contemplating the initial results of the exhibition, Walter Gropius wrote, 'The Werkbundsiedlung thus clearly demonstrated the new potential of modern building and the possibilities of its architectural style, but at the same time, it clearly revealed the urban-design failure of Weissenhof and the urban problems that the avant-garde had yet to solve. . . . Instead, the new role of the architect-urbanist should be that of organiser, and thus oriented in multiple directions; it should be linked to research on biological, social, technical and aesthetic problems, which should be merged into an independent and more complex whole.'[16]

16
Walter Gropius, 'Wege zur fabrikatorischen Hausherstellung', in ibid., 32.

3 Given, however, that both the French and the Dutch avant-gardes had already come to a conclusion similar to that of Gropius, it was felt that the international nature of the Weissenhofsiedlung presented excellent prospects for this approach. Sixteen members of the avant-garde from five Central European countries,[17] working in collaboration, had not only produced an 'international style' – clearly demonstrated for the first time at the Weissenhofsiedlung – but had also taken the first step towards a follow-up at the Congrès International d'Architecture Moderne (known as CIAM; La Sarraz, 1928), which provided the Modern Movement with an authoritative institution at a political level that was capable of linking its architectural programme to urban planning. As soon as Bauhaus

17
The countries and architects represented were: Germany: Ludwig Mies van der Rohe, Walter Gropius, Peter Behrens, Adolf Schneck, Adolf Rading, Richard Döcker, Ludwig Hilberseimer, Hans Poelzig, Hans Scharoun and Bruno and Max Taut; the Netherlands:

Le Corbusier, *La Ville Radieuse: une réponse à Moscou*, 1929-1930

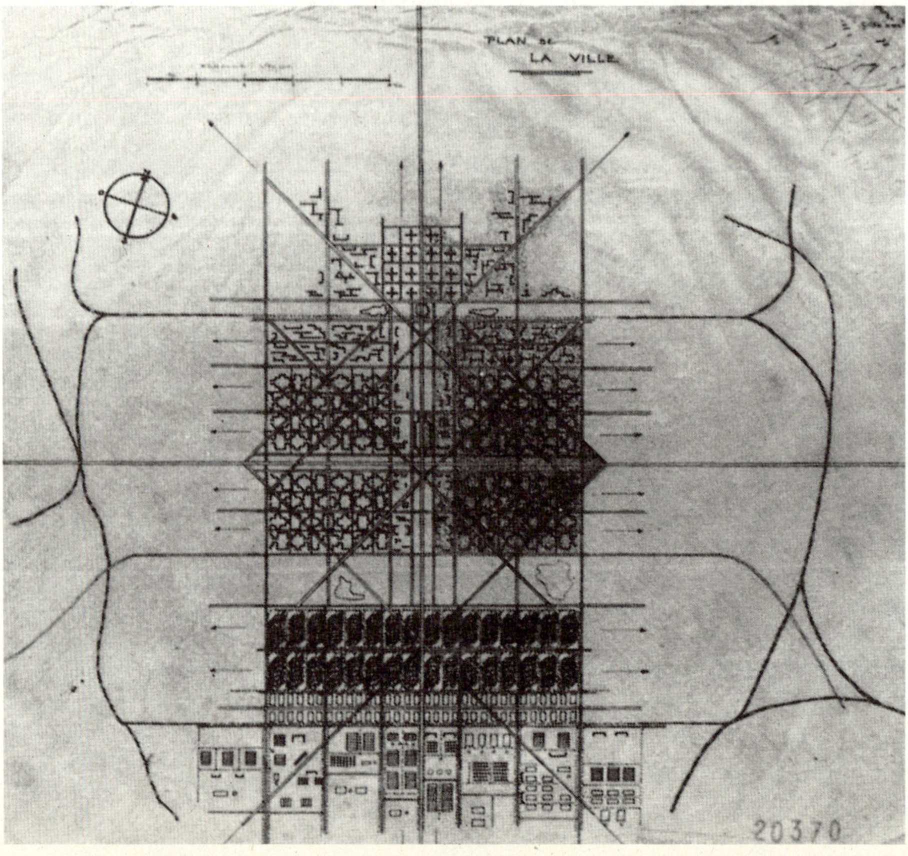

ideology became political and the Modern Movement began to present itself internationally as the vanguard of an alternative, liberated society, it could take a stand against the reactionary criticism of the national socialists and the Deutsche Heimatschutz and thus prevent the impending schism, 14 years after a similar schism had struck the Werkbund-Ausstellung in Cologne. At the same time, the ideal of unity could thereby extend beyond the borders of architecture and, as a progressive synthesis at the architectural level, culminate in a more complex urban organism, which in turn created the conditions for comprehensive regional and national planning. That led to the emergence – starting from the prototype (developed in the Bauhaus laboratory), and by way of serial architecture and the international style (the Weissenhofsiedlung) – of the functional approach to urban planning and design (the CIAM code), which conversely influenced the design of individual houses and rooms and the relationships between architectural 'cells'. The first CIAM conferences, in the period from 1929 to 1933, are especially clear illustrations of this artistic postulate of visual continuity in the production chain from 'sofa cushion to metropolis'.[18]

THE PERIOD OF CRISIS AND RECONSTRUCTION (1929-1957)

The promise of this approach to urbanism, which CIAM believed it could promulgate on the basis of its social and

J.J.P. Oud and Mart Stam; France: Le Corbusier; Austria: Josef Frank; Belgium: Victor Bourgeois. The Weissenhofsiedlung also served as the model for a number of other model estates organised along similar lines. Examples include the Werkbund exhibition in Breslau (1929), the Neubühl estate in Zürich (1930-1932) and the Czechoslovakian experiments Brno (1928) and Baba (1932).

18
After the initial meeting in La Sarraz (1928), the following three CIAM conferences dealt with the themes of housing for people at the subsistence level (Frankfurt am Main, 1929), the functional housing estate (Brussels, 1930) and the functional city (Athens, 1933). In 1942, even before the Second World War ended, Le Corbusier established the Assemblee de constructions pour une rénovation architectural (l'Ascoral), which can be regarded as a first attempt to introduce 'a comprehensive architectural doctrine for spatial planning' at the national and even international level.

Walter Gropius, Dammerstocksiedlung, Karlsruhe, 1928

political message, was never realised. The international reorganisation of capital and labour resulting from the Stock Market Crash of 1929 made it impossible to sustain the formal ideology of the 1920s, whether in the Soviet Union with its five-year plans, Hitler's fascist dictatorship in Germany, or even the social-democratic West of the New Deal. Precisely as it reached its apotheosis, precisely in the first five years of CIAM, the period when the Modern Movement achieved public recognition and appeared to reach its apex at the Athens conference (1933), it became clear that it would have to revise its theories of planning substantially. Confronted with polyfunctionality, multiplicity and the disorganic character of modern society, urban design could no longer be viewed as the transformation of social forms envisaged in the artistic laboratory into new metropolitan spaces, but rather as a form of instrumental and programmatic consistency, of an entirely different nature from that which was taking shape in the unified architectural code. Given that the synthesising approach of Bauhaus philosophy referred directly to 'productive dialogue' between the individual and the collective, to the power-free dialectic between collective order and personal freedom, which characterised the ideal prehistory of civil society (that is, the ideal democracy),[19] it was by its very nature incapable of adapting to the new forms of state interventionism in the free-market economy that derived from Keynes' 'General Theory'. Its political and ideological message, along with its

19
'Democracy is shaped by two contrasting manifestations. On the one hand, it is founded on the diversity of the spirit, which results from an intense and individual action; on the other hand, it is based on a common denominator of regional expressions which, drawing on the cumulative experience of successive generations, gradually become able to distinguish the more arbitrary from the characteristic and essential. Although these two manifestations appear irreconcilable, I believe a merger will have to take place; otherwise, we will end up as robots.' Walter Gropius, *Scope of Total Architecture* (New York, 1935), XIV, as quoted in Herbert, *The Synthetic Vision of Walter Gropius*, op. cit. (note 10), 19.

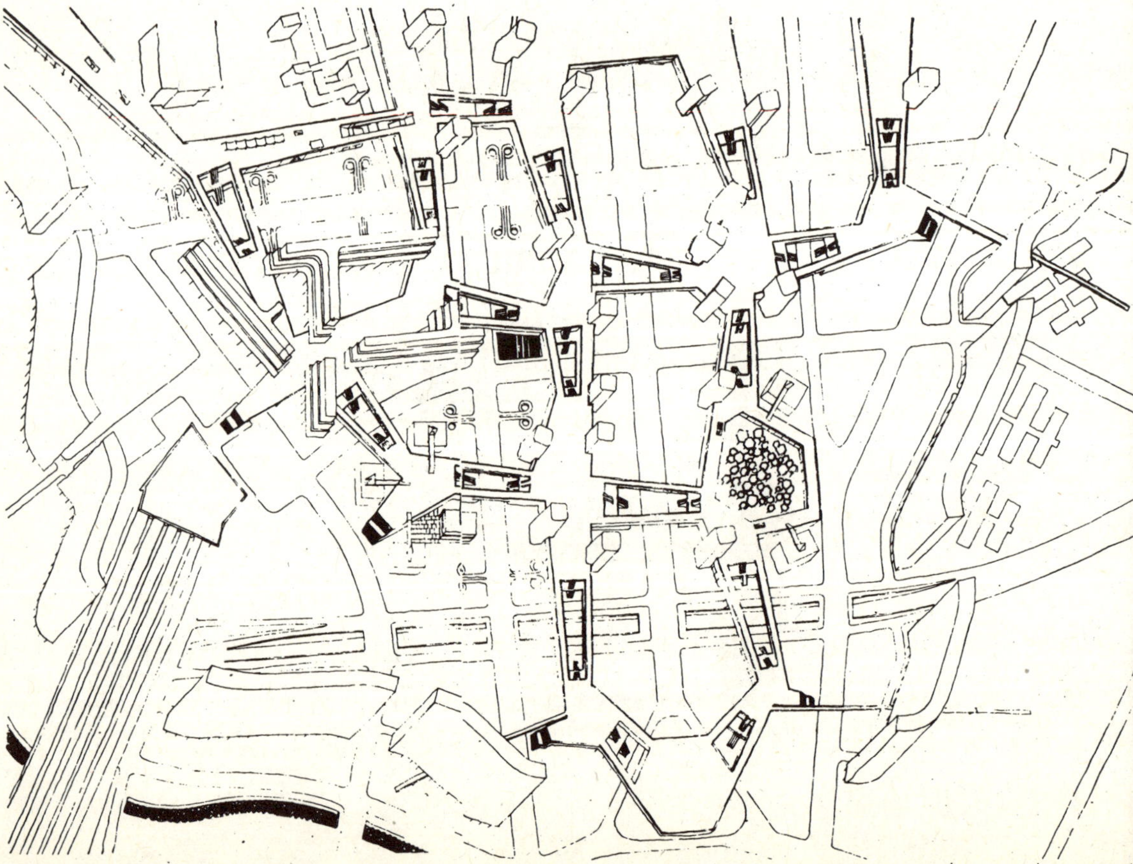

ideal of unity, thus rapidly lost its relevance, and the Modern Movement found that it could only sustain itself on the basis of technological and economic considerations, which allowed no more than minimal attention to aesthetic principles.

This inadequacy of the architectural thinking of the 'old modern masters' prompted the post-Second World War generation to rethink the formal tasks of the spatial design disciplines. Opposing the CIAM approach, which had become rigid and doctrinaire, they criticised the view of urbanism presented in the Athens Charter, arguing that it was spatially sterile and socially outdated, because it seemed to overlook something valuable, namely the existential and absolute values of human life. 'They [the old modern masters, ed.] cheated society by neglecting the essence of the contemporary age. No one can truly live in what they concoct, although they themselves think otherwise.'[20] Following the 1953 CIAM conference in Aix-en-Provence, in the firm belief that the Modern Movement's technological determinism was an anachronism, these 'angry young men' formed a relatively loose-knit group known as Team 10, which placed new emphasis on individual ideas and opinions – if necessary, even at the cost of the ideal of unity, which they saw as an unhealthy obsession. In its stead, they proposed interdisciplinarity, voluntary collaboration, which could make urban complexity manageable by marshalling greater expertise, and hence lead the way to the urban design of the future. No longer would any abstract 'master plan' stand between the spatial designer and the architectural object of his work, and no longer would any general, formal codex be permitted to organise the form and content of separate, individual architectural creations, because urbanism would be based on the 'core', that is, that which forms a community within the settlement (and the architectural discipline). The field of urban development was thus sidelined by 'an overgrowth of proportionally determined architectural, urban, and planning elements'.[21] Architecture was given the central role and expected to generate urban design from the bottom up.

This same approach, with its individualist tendency, not only surfaced in Team 10's programme of work, but also informed its neo-humanistic approach to design work, which centred not on theorising, but on actual building.[22] Especially after the disintegration of the CIAM (Dubrovnik, 1956), it became possible for this 'pragmatic account of another way of thinking', this architectural urbanism that made reference to the core, the habitat and the kasbah, to become the dominant design code of the Modern Movement and thus dominate international architectural thinking during the revival that took place in the post-war reconstruction period.

20
Aldo van Eyck, address given at the Team 10 meeting in Otterlo, September 1959, in: Alison Smithson (ed.), *Team 10 Primer* (London, 1974), 20.

21
Umberto Barbieri and Cees Boekraad, *Kritiek en Ontwerp. Proeven van architectuurkritiek*, Sunschrift 169 (Nijmegen, 1982), 50.

22
See Smithson, *Team 10 Primer*, op. cit. (note 20), 3-24.

HANSAVIERTEL (1953)

The fragmentation that inevitably resulted, however, could not express any message, social or otherwise, for an alternative future practice of urban design. All too rapidly, the Team 10 code became capricious and arbitrary, and therefore antithetical to urbanism.

Less than a year after the CIAM became permanently inactive, the Hansaviertel in Berlin – a model estate intended as a euphoric example of the *Wirtschaftswunder* – once again clearly demonstrated this inability to make good, after 30 years, on the promise of the Weissenhofsiedlung for the field of urbanism. This project – which claimed to offer the 'architecture of freedom' and the 'planning of the city of tomorrow' and involved 48 architects from 13 countries[23] – was meant to win the world over to the progressive, modern spirit of Western democratism, as opposed to the purportedly conformist social realism of East Berlin in the reconstruction period.[24] On balance, however, it was a adverse development for architecture and urbanism, because the event overlooked the field's duties to society. Despite the propagandistic and pathetically demagogic pretensions of this excessively personalised architecture, there was little cultural substance behind its haughty exterior, and instead it seemed as though the avant-garde had turned their clock back to the earliest stage of the Modern Movement. Whereas the Weissenhof project had at least presented a single, international architectural style, the Hansaviertel exhibition had nothing to show but an uncoordinated, idiosyncratic collection of individual architectural personalities. True, they proposed intriguing solutions to particular problems, but

23
Including Alvar Aalto, Walter Gropius, Oscar Niemeyer and Van den Broek and Bakema.

24
See, for instance, Harm Tilman's article on Berlin, 'Berlijn, veranderende stad: De wederopbouw van de hoofdstad van de D.D.R.', *Wonen TA/BK* 6/7 1984, 41-53.

the district's green spaces were not enough to tie their work together into a coherent urban whole. 'What was intended to be a cultural prototype of Western society became, at best, an artistic exception, legitimated in ideological terms.'[25] The ideal of unity, the dialectic approach to art and society, appeared to have been utterly defeated, and the avant-garde as such could no longer take a stand against the impending unconditional surrender to the contradictions, imbalances and chaos that characterised the modern metropolis. In response to this alarming prospect, architecture and urbanism tried to regain their cultural significance through the semantic and procedural approaches, respectively, by retreating into a lasting autonomy. The fact that, in the process, they not only scrapped the social programme of the Modern Movement, but also exacerbated the growing division of labour and fragmentation of cultural action systems, was seen not merely as a banality, but as one of the greatest feats of modern architecture, accomplished with great difficulty after the rigid straitjacket of CIAM's functionalism. Now that 'practical content' had been dispensed with, once again anything seemed possible in design work, which could make its highest priority the pursuit of constant novelty and an ever-changing variety of forms and symbols.

25 Vittorio Lampugnani, 'The Berlin tradition of architectural exhibitions', *Architectural Design* 53, 1/2 1983, 14.

POSTMODERNISM AND THE CURRENT DEBATE ON URBANISM

In highly simplified terms, this growing independence – and, consequently, the increasing specialisation of individual design practices – has characterised the last 20 years of the architectural and urbanist disciplines. While Team 10 and Forum were still trying to maintain some degree of connection to the social context of their design activities, the introduction of the linguistic method in the design process firmly categorised the spatial object of manipulation as a formal, independent, autonomous knowledge complex, which therefore went beyond the domain of everyday ideological, political and economic reality. In contrast to both the functional and the humanist approach to design, which attributed a message (social or otherwise) to architecture, the postmoderns showed an increasing tendency to distance themselves from the cultural and political ideas associated with traditional approaches to design, ideas which seemed overblown to them, and instead posited that modern (and postmodern) architecture was a 'formal language'. The focus was no longer on direct engagement with social and functional conditions, but on a 'theoretical discourse' relating exclusively to what the postmoderns claimed was the only objective subject matter at architecture's disposal: the architectural form itself. By concentrating solely on the communicative relationship between individual images and signs, between the form and the receptacle, they believed that they could transcend the functional meaning of form, instead ascribing an intrinsic value to architectural concepts.[26]

26 See, for instance, Peter Eisenman, *House X* (New York, 1982).

This obsessive quest for the ontology of architecture was, by its nature, drawn to the internal organisation and aesthetic proportions of the architectural object, to a closed and purely self-referential formal system which no longer had any serious connection to reality whatsoever. In this process, the means of design and techniques of production also became aesthetic objects in their own right, and thus no longer amenable to any functional or organisational interpretation.

This definitive sequestration of postmodern architectural thinking into autonomous spheres, cut off from the real world, thus became more painful for two reasons: first, the impending impoverishment of the avant-garde significance of traditional modernism and, second, the increasing specialisation and fragmentation of aesthetic thinking at the level of cultural systems. With the return of a practice espousing *l'art pour l'art* and the accompanying undialectical application of, and reference to, the history of architectural design practices, the postmoderns adopted 'the present of the past' as their principal theme, thereby betraying both their neo-conservatism and their unequivocal antimodernism.[27] The architect's position, the realisation of the past in the solidified present, is no longer the central issue; instead, a new type of formal historicism is emphasised, one which detaches the aesthetic effect of the historical plan from its original context and introduces this fact as new material in current design practice. Cutting across periods in this way may seem to restore the architectural continuity

27
See Habermas, 'Het moderne – een onvoltooid project', op. cit. (note 3), 126. It was this position that led Habermas to investigate the nature of the consciousness of the moderns. Arie Graafland, too, tried to use this as the starting point for a theoretical understanding of the postmodern conception of architecture, see Arie Graafland, 'Kritiek & Ontwerp; ontwerp-onderwijs', *0* no. 5, summer 1983, 19-32.

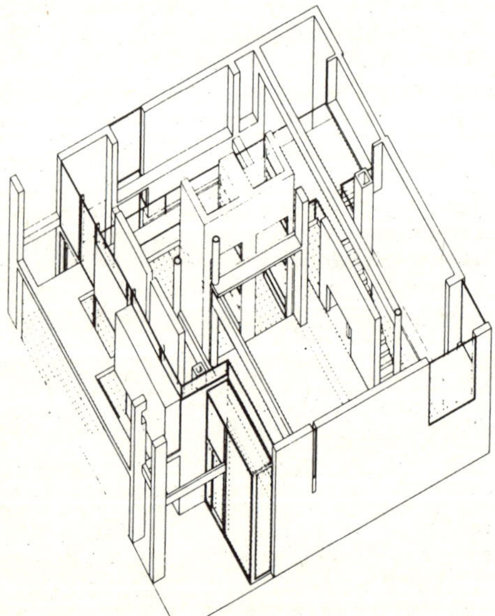

Peter Eisenman, House I, 1968

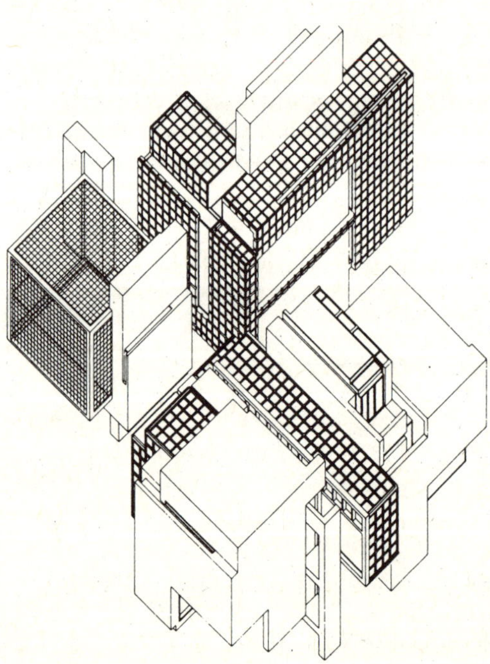

2

Peter Eisenman, House X, 1976

of modern building, but by disregarding the specific character of the knowledge involved, it also accelerates the process by which the practice of spatial planning and design disintegrates into its separate components, each of which can only define a value orientation in relation to one knowledge complex. While architects have gotten away with this exclusivity so far (because it is the built object itself, rather than the theorising, that legitimates social acceptance, the postmodernists tell us), because the discipline of urban design is directly linked to a more complex field with a *sui generis* unity, the tendency towards specialisation and autonomy has played a fundamental role in the recently generally acknowledged debacle in urban design work. The attempts now being made to preserve a degree of 'unity' in modern architecture, to preserve the integration of individual components, are problematic by definition within the framework of formalist thinking. In this context, Jürgen Habermas makes an interesting point in his Adorno lecture. Habermas, too, sees a direct link between the increasing segmentation of cultural spheres of value – the growing differentiation of science, morality and art – and the autonomisation of sectors adapted to specialised tasks, which have branched off from a path that has continued in everyday practice as if its rightness were self-evident. In this process of ever-greater autonomisation of individual practices with respect to those of the broad public, the aesthetic aspect, instead of being a means to an end, can become an end in itself. As a result, architecture may from now on have its own internal history, which shuts out social and other extrinsic criteria that could conceivably bring about communicative rationality and interaction between specialisms. This is because in the autonomous and specialised handling of specific problems, one only ever draws one's own intellectual positions and the knowledge belonging to one's own field, without recourse to other action systems or to social practice. Therefore, for Habermas, artistic deviation from everyday practice is not only the problem at the root of the fragmentation of the range of cultural action systems, but also, as such, forms the basis for the doomed attempts to do away, at this late stage, with the cultures of these groups of experts.[28]

28 Habermas, ibid., 133/1.

It is precisely because the current debate on urbanism seems to have associated itself with the formalistic design approach of the postmoderns, thus demanding its own autonomy, that the discipline of urban design – viewed against this epistemological background – is farther removed than ever from its proclaimed objective of bridging the gap between the planning process and architecture. While in the 1920s and '30s urban design could take a socially engaged form, drawing on the intersubjectively created codex and mediating between art and industry, and as soon as it became political could, likewise, indicate the programmatic and spatial conditions required for national and regional measures, the return to pure elitist formalism seems to have ruled out any such communicative practice by definition. Because the current debate on urbanism dispenses with the practical content, social integration and formal interaction that should characterise the artistically successful and socially responsible practice of urban design, it will, in all probability, also fail to mediate between the architectural fragments within the scope of a single code, let alone safeguard an aesthetic conception of urban design. The discipline as such is now producing its own aporias and can no longer hold any position with authority.

DIE INTERNATIONALE BAUAUSSTELLUNG BERLIN (1987)

The Internationale Bauausstellung (IBA) in Berlin, the end date of which has already been shifted to 1987, does not seem to present good prospects. Despite the central programme of this building exhibition, which emphatically faces up to the problem that individual architectural works and the city need to be brought into a positive, constructive relationship with one another, and despite the fact that the IBA – unlike the above-mentioned *Bauausstellungen* – is deliberately and voluntarily confronting existing urban structures, in this *Berichtsjahr* it seems reasonable to conclude that the IBA will achieve no more than the expansion of a few excellent works of architecture.[29] Given its exorbitant solutions and the differences between individual projects – a few fragments, such as Krier's project in Ritterstrasse and Baller's residences on the

29
See, for instance, Collin Rowe, 'Comments on the I.B.A. proposals', *Architectural Design 53*, 1/2 1983, 121-127. See also Maarten Kloos, 'Berlijn, stad van brede allees en straten die van niets naar niets leiden', *De Volkskrant*, 12 October 1984; 13/19. Furthermore, the special issue of *Arch+* gives a clear overview of the types of reservations one might have about the IBA, *Arch+*, no. 66, 'I.B.A. – Halbzeit', December 1982.

Rob Krier, housing block in Ritterstrasse, 1980-1982

Inke and Heinrich Baller, construction against a firewall of a tenement block

Fraenkel-ufer have already been completed – it appears more likely that the avant-garde aspirations of the IBA – which has also been called the Internationale Bluff Aktion – will result in the fetishisation of the formally incidental than that it will gradually set in motion a process that can turn the city back into an integrated whole. Because it focuses directly on the 'great masters' whose stars are currently rising,[30] and thus often relies almost exclusively on the one-sided, half-formed formal approach to design, the IBA escapade stands almost no chance of contributing meaningfully to Berlin's urban reorganisation. In my opinion, this impotence of the practice of urban design says a great deal about not only this particular international exhibition, but *the entire Western approach to design.*

30
Including John Hejduk, Aldo Rossi, Rob Krier, Peter Eisenman, Oriol Bohigas and Oswald Mathias Ungers.

Instead, this article has suggested the following conclusion about the problem of urbanism: *As long as the disciplines of architecture and urbanism do not formulate positions on the social message of their design activities, as long as they refuse to take up the practical content inherent in form, the avant-garde significance of the modern will progressively diminish and – by following fashionable trends and developing specialised working methods – inevitably disintegrate into its incidental fragments.* Against this backdrop, the future prospects for urban designers are anything but rosy. In contrast, however, a socially engaged approach – which takes architecture and urbanism to be two distinct but inseparable parts of a single spatial practice – still generates polemic. The right approach does not locate the link between form and content in a linear dimension, in which one follows logically from the other ('form follows function' or 'function follows form'), but rather in a dialectical relationship which shows that the fields of operation of form and content are inseparable – joined by an elastic cord, as it were. Once the content of spatial design relates not only to technical design issues, but also to social content, the form can absorb the historical and social postulates so essential to modern-day projects and make them inherent to itself. The more productive approach thus provides direct mediation between design and criticism, between artistic creation and the formulation of norms, and thereby operates in both the domain of the aesthetic and expressive, and that of moral and practical knowledge complexes. To arrive at a two-part design production process of this kind, however, it seems we must return to square one – that is, if we ever really moved beyond it.

Translated by David McKay

The editorial board of *OASE* evolves over time and begins to include people from outside the school in Delft. The period from 1985 to 1989 is characterised by the regular inclusion of translations of seminal texts deemed interesting to a Dutch-speaking audience, making them available to students in their mother tongue. These texts are revealing testimonies of what was becoming relevant at the time: texts by Jorge Luis Borges and Adolfo Bioy Casares, Christian Devillers, Friedrich Hölderlin, Francesco Dal Co, Michel Raynaud, Helmut Färber, Bernard Tschumi, Paul Virilio, Franco Rella, Henri-Pierre Jeudy, and Bernard Huet are translated into Dutch and so become a part of the architecture culture of the Low Countries. The journal is accompanied by various items, such as a cahier with Martin Heidegger's 'Bouwen Wonen Denken' (Building Living Thinking), an architecture map of the town of Heerlen, and even a piece of aluminium foil. The period ends, in the winter of 1990, with the double issue 26/27, dedicated to the work of Aldo van Eyck, which attempts to address his celebrated oeuvre from a distance that is rare in Delft.

OASE 11
OASE 12
OASE 13
OASE 14 Het Witte Dorp (J.J.P. Oud's 'Witte Dorp' housing project)
OASE 15
OASE 16
OASE 17
OASE 18 Film en architectuur (Film and architecture)
OASE 19
OASE 20 Bloemen van het kwaad (Flowers of evil)
OASE 21
OASE 22
OASE 23
OASE 24 Stedelijke identiteit en collectief geheugen (Urban identity and collective memory)
OASE 25
OASE 26/27 Aldo van Eyck

Period II

MATURING 1985–1989

Bernard Colenbrander

ON THE EVE OF SOME-THING BIG AND NEW

Originally in virtual symbiosis with the architecture programme at Delft University of Technology, *OASE*'s editorial staff began to distance itself from the school and make room for outsiders in the mid-1980s. This greater openness to the outside world was expressed in the contents of the journal, whose diversity began to accelerate to the point that the precise motivation for the periodical begins to blur. What exactly is *OASE* about in the latter half of the 1980s? Theoretical discussions about movements like postmodernism or mannerism alternate with monographic discussions (not always devoted to architects whose reputations have stood the test of time); there are studies in historical urban typology, usually with Amsterdam or Rotterdam cases as pretext; there is architectural philosophy and there are many more genres. Above all, in the issues spanning the period between 1985 to 1990, there is room for free-wheeling literary impressionism, for instance in regard to the peculiarities of the landscape garden throughout history or placing the reputation of an established legend such as Aldo van Eyck in a completely other light than usual. The free-thinking tenor of the content was also a free-thinking tenor in editorial style; leafing through the issues, one gets the feeling the editors demonstrated blind tolerance for all manner of explorations of the limits of the architectural discourse. Such tolerance is fitting to an architectural culture that was subconsciously, but no less fundamentally, redefining itself. This redefinition concerned the ideology of the profession, but also the pragmatic aspects of day-to-day practice; it related to philosophical foundations, but in equal measure to contextual conditions. This contribution focuses on the interpretation of what, for the most part, was unfolding beyond the columns of *OASE* and would gradually come to alter the character of the journal as well.

When Herman Hertzberger was commissioned to design the new Dutch Ministry of Social Affairs in The Hague in 1979, he was asked for 'an open building for an open organisation'.[1] By the time it was completed, 11 years later, little of this had come to pass. The new edifice was clearly a Hertzberger, to be sure. The programme called for extensive floor space, but the inevitable dominance of the volume this entailed was mitigated by the finely articulated grammar that has always typified Hertzberger's compositions. However, his intention to have the offices gradually merge, on all sides, into the public space of the surrounding city had lost out, in the construction climate of the 1980s, to concerns about easily monitored spatial organisation and security. No matter how passionately Hertzberger argued about the execution of his design, entrance to the building had to be restricted. As a result, the edifice displayed all the characteristics of what has come to be known as structuralism, even as it presented the aspect of an impregnable fortress. The longed-for interweaving of spaces and functions had become merely a feature of its interior.

1
Hans van Dijk, 'The retreat of the public domain', in: Ruud Brouwers et al., *Architecture in the Netherlands Yearbook 1990-1991* (Rotterdam, 1991), 87-90.

The sort of ambivalence that characterises the Social Affairs building can be identified in a project completed five years earlier in Amsterdam's inner city: the Faculty of Letters of the University of Amsterdam. Its design is the work of a kindred spirit of Hertzberger's, Theo Bosch, and its completion entailed an equally lengthy process. Bosch initially carried out the commission in collaboration with his then-partner, Aldo van Eyck. The two men strived to produce a building with a structure that would enable it to fit comfortably into its setting. In Van Eyck's case, his dedication to the city was such that he wanted to give it 'something meaningful' in return for the space the building volume would consume, in the form of a number of urban functions that would introduce nuance into the transition between building and public space.[2] This intention failed, just as Hertzberger was unable to extend the indentations in his edifice in The Hague to the level of the street. In both Amsterdam and The Hague, the end products were structures that referred, externally as well as internally, to the structuralist ideals of the Dutch contingent of Team 10, yet came up short in their interlacing of city and building.

2
Francis Strauven, *Aldo van Eyck: Relativiteit en verbeelding* (Amsterdam, 1994), 576.

Deeply disappointed by the implementation of the design for the Faculty of Letters, Van Eyck eventually ended his partnership with Bosch, who had apparently shown himself more accommodating than he in regard to the demands of the university and the city authorities to rigidly segregate, rather than interlace, the building's inside and outside. The indentations in the façade were confined to the upper storeys and left the building line undisturbed at street level. Critic Hans van Dijk, in his discussion of Theo Bosch's achievement in Amsterdam, indeed came to the conclusion that the Faculty of Letters displayed more than simply structuralist characteristics.[3] Because of the autonomous architectural order Bosch applied, the building's conceptual premise was a city composed of separate fragments: therefore, Van Dijk claimed, the faculty was also contextual in nature. He even argued that the Faculty of Letters, in the respect shown for the building line, had a rationalist foundation. Van Eyck must have seethed with sorrow and rage upon reading such qualifications, for he shared at most one-and-a-half of the three references attributed.

3
Hans van Dijk, 'Structuren en hun relativering: de Faculteit der Letteren van Theo Bosch', *Wonen TA/BK* 1 (1985), 8-17.

The fact that the Social Affairs ministry was ambivalent in character and that the Faculty of Letters was a hodgepodge typifies the sea change that took place in architecture during the 1980s. This change signified the end of a tradition, an end described by Hans van Dijk in a different context and with appropriate solemnity as 'the demise of structuralism'[4]. By the time the Social Affairs edifice was completed in 1990, not only were the practical difficulties of structuralist design condemned, but its underlying ideology – which had seemed incontestable in Dutch architectural culture for so long – was also now under attack. In retrospect, a symposium held in Delft in the same year and entitled 'How modern is Dutch architecture?' stands out as the final episode in the dethroning of the Dutch Team 10 and

4
Hans van Dijk, 'The demise of structuralism', in: Ruud Brouwers et al., *Architecture in the Netherlands Yearbook 1988-1989* (Rotterdam, 1989), 6-10.

the corresponding group centred round the editors of *Forum* circa 1960, led by Van Eyck. The symposium was held to mark the end (remarkably enough not the *start*) of Rem Koolhaas's brief tenure as a professor at Delft University of Technology's architecture faculty. In his address, Koolhaas himself attacked the emancipatory pretensions of the Dutch version of modernism, including the interpretation given it by Van Eyck and his cohorts. He found it all suffocating and was not shy about saying so. 'Locking down, identifying, proclaiming grand intentions, being unable or unwilling to leave anything empty – these are all characteristics of Dutch modernism, be it Rietveld, Van Eyck or Van Velsen.'[5] This modernism contained 'not one iota of futurism', nor 'one iota of constructivism' and certainly 'not one iota of materialism . . . as in America with all its dangerous things like capitalist exploitation'.

5 Rem Koolhaas, introduction in: *Hoe modern is de Nederlandse architectuur?* (Rotterdam, 1990), 11-20.

In the next address at the symposium, contributed by Ed Taverne, it was the supposed anti-urban character of *Forum* and the Dutch Team 10 that was particularly denounced.[6] Van Eyck's Amsterdam Orphanage may have been a radiant and fresh building, but it was still a 'fairy tale in the city', not equipped to deal with the complex reality of that city. Because post-war Dutch modernists were unable to respond to the concrete morphology of the city and got mired in abstract configurations, the contribution of Van Eyck and his fellow travellers had resulted in nothing better than 'the provisional retirement of Dutch architecture from the international scene', Taverne argued.

6 Ed Taverne, 'Towards an open aesthetic: Ambities in de Nederlandse architectuur 1948-1959', in: ibid., 23-59.

Finally, this Delft symposium featured a third address, which followed on perfectly from the previous contribution and was of course given by Hans van Dijk, surely the most productive Dutch architecture critic of the 1980s. In his address Van Dijk reviewed the ideological remnants of an architecture that had declared its own modernist inspiration null and void. The term Van Dijk used was 'schoolmaster modernism', alluding to a craft passed on academically, especially in Delft, in which modernism had been reduced to a 'tradition of form . . . as a totality of knowledge, skills and norms that was identical to architecture as a profession, as a *métier*.'[7] This *métier*, contrasted in particular by Carel Weeber – displaying a considerable talent for polemics – with the blessings of the modernism of the past, was the end point of a process of erosion that had been dramatically made clear, for the attentive observer, in the drawn-out design and construction process of both the new Social Affairs ministry in The Hague and the Faculty of Letters in Amsterdam.

7 Hans van Dijk, 'Het onderwijzersmodernisme', in: ibid., 173-191.

This end point, reached between 1985 and 1990, was an architecture that could only be understood in terms of form, that distanced itself from the edifying, emancipatory intentions that used to cling to the avant-garde and that presented itself as a purely architectonic interpretation of the programme, without any pretensions beyond the craft. The profession had adopted a more passive, more pliant position than it had throughout the entire history of modernism that preceded it – in order to achieve, paradoxically enough, a long-forgotten autonomy and freedom of action.

In terms of ideology, this conclusion coincided with the coming into fashion of postmodern philosophy. This philosophy should be seen not so much as a complete overhaul of all norms and values but rather as a continuation of the modern project under crisis conditions.[8] Frequently represented, then and now, by dissonances and negatives, postmodern analyses mainly seemed to describe the decline of a worldview that, throughout the first several decades after the Second World War, had been able to rely, with little resistance, on a general faith in the ability of planning to construct a society understood as an integral entity.

8
See Bernard Colenbrander, *De verstrooide stad* (Rotterdam, 1990), 34; René Boomkens, *Een drempelwereld: Moderne ervaringen en stedelijke openbaarheid* (1998), 35; Nan Ellin, *Postmodern Urbanism* (Cambridge/Oxford, 1996), 182-201.

The rejection of the idea of constructing society towards the end of the twentieth century affected not only the social order, but also, in the material world, the design of landscapes and cities. The movements of people and capital gradually broke free of the formal structures of the city, most recently adapted on a large scale during post-war reconstruction. Increasingly, the spatial order bore the brunt of this uprooted behaviour. Yet the fundamental premises of a modernism launched in the mid-nineteenth century continued to be fully applicable even at this new juncture. At first glance, postmodernism may have seemed to entail a revival of the past, yet its relationship with tradition was in fact just as complicated and twisted as before: the organic connection with an unbroken tradition had been abandoned long before the transition from the nineteenth century to the twentieth. Similarly, the two great sociocultural trends of social individualisation and massification remained active in parallel. The deeper reality of modernity, that existence was based on the transitory, the ephemeral and the coincidental, retained the validity it had acquired in the late nineteenth century.[9]

9
See Michael Müller, 'Over de "schone schijn" van de postmoderne architectuur', *OASE* 13 (1986), 2-16.

On the other hand, the norms and values of the service economy that established itself in the West, as they spread far and wide, did bring about an acceleration of the process of globalisation. It helped that a 'substantial cross-fertilisation' in the cultural discourse had been taking place across the Atlantic Ocean since the 1960s, including in regard to the status quo of the city.[10] The differences between Europe and America were increasingly blurred. The 1980s saw the launch of an intensively shared discourse, not least in relation to the spatial order. As though the American model were contagious, on the European side too the city began to drift from the ideal of a harmonious social organisation of society, right down to the level of spatial morphology. Two movements became particularly manifest in this respect during the 1980s. The first concerned the retrenchment of state authorities from public housing. Overseas, the Reagan administration slashing government spending in this social sector by 80 per cent over

10
Nan Ellin, *Postmodern Urbanism*, op. cit. (note 8), 44.

seven years was in keeping with a detachment on the issue that is virtually anchored in the Constitution of the USA. But the fact that major European countries like France and Britain joined this trend, after almost a century of intensive involvement, was definitely something new.[11] Even the Netherlands followed suit. 'In the last five years there has been a marked shift in the Netherlands from idealistically inspired town planning and public housing, sometimes with a tinge of state control, to a policy which adopts a subservient and flirtatious position with regard to investors and project developers,' Ruud Brouwers wrote in 1989. 'The "bodily and spiritual elevation of the population" as it used to be called, has had to make way for a pragmatism motivated by financial considerations alone.'[12] Henceforth, residents would have to make it on their own in the housing market, with as little support as possible from the powers that be. 'At the moment, the cities are being presented as enticing opportunities for investors,' Brouwers also noted. 'But it is precisely the socially inspired urban renewal undertaken by the government in the years 1975-1985 which has made this possible.'

In the place of the state and the traditional social middle, another prime mover had indeed appeared on the urban stage: the project developer.[13] This advent changed the public domain of the city from something that is essentially an indivisible whole into a collection of fragments, most of them marketable. Accordingly, the role of the urban planner changed: in the final decades of the twentieth century, this dwindled to supplying a form of 'applied architecture', sneered London planning professor Peter Hall.[14]

In the 1980s, the environment of the city was exposed more openly than in the past to the invisible, organising hand of the market, even in Europe. This did not mean that the intervening influence of the state ceased to operate; it was simply handled in a different way. In France, architecture became one of the instruments used to lend the culture of the state a personalist face. François Mitterrand marked the years of his presidency with an impressive series of *Grands Projets*, having made it clear immediately upon taking office that he intended to expand the Louvre.[15] Paris was given a number of striking new focal points. In other countries, a similar surge of interest could be detected and the organisations of such events as a World's Fair or the Olympics (in Spain) were used to launch a large-scale infrastructure-building campaign, led by the government.

In this tableau of continued state ambitions, the Netherlands also featured a clearly identifiable profile, because the culture of design was given free rein on several fronts. Even the modernist idea of social engineering remained partially intact. Abroad, the construction of the new town of Almere was considered an amazing project.[16] This was not simply because a city was conjured out of nothing in a few decades of accelerated building fever, but also because in Almere, spatial

11
Deyan Sudjic, *The 100 Mile City* (London, 1992), 181.

12
Ruud Brouwers, 'Ideals and one-off projects', in: Brouwers et al., *Yearbook 1988-1989*, op. cit. (note 4), 25-28.

13
Sudjic, *The 100 Mile City*, op. cit. (note 10), 44.

14
Peter Hall, 'The strange case of the new city', *Blueprint* 5 (1992), 35-36.

15
Erica Winterbourne, 'Architecture and the politics of culture in Mitterrand's France', *Architectural Design* 114 (1995), 24-29.

16
Diane Ghirardo, *Architecture after Modernism* (London, 1996), 26.

design was put to intensive use in mediating the segregation of classes and incomes prevalent elsewhere. The state, even in the Netherlands, may have pulled out of the positions it had once occupied in public housing and urban planning, but in the exceptional circumstances of the construction of a new town in the polder, an equally exceptional administrative dynamism was evidently *de rigueur*.

In addition to being the country in which, late into the postmodern era, a new town could be created from the top down, the Netherlands was also the land in which 'architecture policy' was invented: the definition of a full-fledged policy domain for the state, focused on the creative exercise of architecture, officially positioned alongside a building and monument preservation policy 100 years its senior. The first government report on architecture, 'Space for Architecture', was issued in 1991 and described the interest in architectural issues in the official practice of various governments in recent times. Ironically, this interest was at odds with the tendency of the state, in view of supposed cost efficiencies, to distance itself from its traditional responsibilities as a commissioning client. Public buildings, for instance, should now preferably be rented from the private market rather than built on the government's initiative: this would even be more profitable in the long run, the office holders involved incorrectly assumed. The subjugation of the state's commissioning capacity to the norms of the market especially surprised the Government Architect in office during the latter half of the 1980s, Frans van Gool. Van Gool observed that his government agency was virtually bankrupt and there was little credit to be gained anymore in the commercialised construction of public buildings, going on to note that his minister nonetheless 'was full of edifying stories about architecture'.[17]

17
Bernard Colenbrander, *Frans van Gool: Leven en werk* (Rotterdam, 2005), 234.

Under such circumstances, the government report on architecture was the document that camouflaged the decline in self-evident administrative power by identifying and positioning the autonomy of architecture as a separate area of interest. As such, 'Space for Architecture' is a fitting official counterpart to 'schoolmaster modernism' in the architectural discourse. In both instances, these were phenomena that were the result of a process of inflation and erosion that, miraculously, nevertheless produces a residue that can be deemed fortunate: autonomous architecture as a laudable cultural craft.

The first Dutch government report on architecture was a more specifically noteworthy achievement because it furnished the policy domain of architecture with an impressive array of stimulus measures that were to be found in no other country. Its implementation was entrusted to several institutions, the most significant of which were established immediately before and immediately after 1990. The Berlage Institute was a new institution intended to give the teaching of architecture a post-doctoral international impulse; the commercial survival of this initiative was made possible by the state. The Netherlands

Architecture Institute became a new museum centre with monumental aspirations and a landmark presence in the city, supported by a government subsidy budget unthinkable anywhere else in the world. The Netherlands Architecture Fund complemented the existing subsidy infrastructure with a funding source able to support the culture of design with a considerable budget, again without equal abroad.

When all these institutions were established in Rotterdam around 1990, this accentuated that city's new status as a major nucleus in the architectural discourse. This status had been prepared with clear political control by the work of the architecture section of the Rotterdam Art Foundation and also, although unintentionally, by Rem Koolhaas locating his agency in Rotterdam – if only because the latter turned the city, in the course of the 1980s, into a pilgrimage site for architecture connoisseurs with a preference for the cutting edge.

The way the government marketed its architecture policy in the Netherlands circa 1990 and Rotterdam began to promote itself as an architecture city was hardly in synch with the reality on the construction site. The rhetorically evangelical architecture policy concealed an anemic public commissioning role in an era of ideologically drained modernism. This period (starting in 1988) saw the start of the series of *Architecture in the Netherlands* Yearbooks, and what was published in these accurately reflects this ambivalent reality. Among the buildings featured, *tour de forces* by gifted architects in all shapes and sizes predominated. From the very beginning, the new generation is pervasively represented, and its early work more often than not bore the marks of schoolmaster modernism. However, the cheerfulness of these buildings is immediately put in perspective in the discussions published alongside about the state of public housing, urban planning and public space: this is architecture of high formal quality but with a weak cultural foundation – that is to say, one that is shifting towards a new paradigm – which would only take on a more enduring form in the course of the 1990s. The mutation of the programme, context and commissioning of the building in the 1990s would launch an architectural movement that displays little remaining affinity with the phantom pains of structuralism and the flare-ups of modernist nostalgia of the preceding decade. After 1990, architecture and architects as a profession reinvented themselves. The extensive reliance on market mechanisms in developing the Vinex housing programme during this decade was a major incentive to this. By increasingly adapting the design of the most prominent building locations, even beyond Vinex housing estates, more explicitly to the criteria of the public-private partnership, architecture was subjected, to the fullest extent, to the interaction of often highly explosive social forces.

In their landmark history of modern architecture published in 1976, Manfredo Tafuri and Francesco Dal Co describe the architecture of the time as an architecture of alienation. 'Often, in fact, architecture speaks very much more fluently precisely of that in which it has no part,' they write, 'The production of the 1960s and 1970s is much more a demonstration by negatives than by positives.'[18] In this latter decade, the alienation to which they allude still bore the traits of the negative, because designers were unable to make a meaningful contribution to the societal sea change that was taking place, from the late-modern welfare state to the globalised network society. In relative isolation, they did their thing – which did not mean that a movement like schoolmaster modernism was not in fact able to draw strength from the denial of the ideological aspirations that had been handed down. The autonomous craft, cured of its illusions about ideals of social engineering now proven unfeasible, recovering from its addiction to an impossibly symbiotic longing to pay back the weather-beaten old city with new architecture, made multiple leaps of pure vitality in the 1980s. Peter Eisenman, for instance, found in the harsh dismissal of three putative 'fictions' in classical thinking about architecture the appealing starting point for a new, unfettered beginning.[19] The three fictions were representation (the idea that architecture is the expression of something else, of reality for instance), reason (that architecture is somehow 'true') and history (that architecture expresses the spirit of the age). Against this Eisenman proposed an architecture that expresses itself not in fictions, but that is *itself* fiction: 'it is merely different from or other than. A "not classical" architecture is no longer a certification of experience or a simulation of history, reason, or reality in the present. Instead, it may more appropriately be described as an *other* manifestation, an architecture as is, now as a fiction. It is a representation of itself, of its own values and internal experience.' Self-assured arguments such as this cannot have failed to be instrumental in freeing architectural criticism from an ideological pattern that had become unworkable. Aldo van Eyck had to contend for the first – and not for the last – time with free interpretations of his work. A discussion of Aldo van Eyck's houses by Joost Meuwissen published in *OASE*, 'Aldo in Wonderland', was replete with lavishly poetic interpretations that offered a welcome change from the established tendency of architectural criticism to elucidate 'twin phenomena' and the like more as a profoundly human gesture than as a formal architectonic quality.[20] 'Wonderland is defined here as the place where things become bigger or smaller gradually, and not in fits and starts as in our world.' Just as conventions of architectural criticism were redefined in the latter half of the 1980s, so was it with the call made upon history. Oddly enough, the stage in this regard remained, for the moment, filled with the same main characters. Virtually all of the figures who had personified the historic avant-garde of the period between the world wars were given a new interpretation, better informed by historical sources and more nuanced: this was the case for Mies; it was the case for Le Corbusier; it was the case for Loos; it was the

18
Manfredo Tafuri and Francesco Dal Co, *Modern Architecture* (New York, 1979 [1976]), 391.

19
Peter Eisenman, 'The End of the Classical: The End of the Beginning, the End of the End', in: Kate Nesbitt, *Theorizing a New Agenda for Architecture: An Anthology of Architectural Theory 1965-1995* (New York, 1996), 219-220.

20
Joost Meuwissen, 'Aldo in Wonderland: opmerkingen bij de woonhuizen van Aldo van Eyck', *OASE* 26/27 (1990), 64-77.

case for Gropius; it was the case for Oud. Diverse international studies lent the historical tableau of leading characters a psychological texture that had grown noticeably more layered in comparison to the first decades after the Second World War.

Spatial research did not concentrate merely on individuals. The 1980s also witnessed a wealth of geographic urban explorations. A random selection out of several volumes of *Archis*, for example, offers a range of generally academically grounded studies on cities like Paris, Rome and Venice. Usually these combined a morphological reading with an examination of aspects of culture, socioeconomics and political governance.

In terms of methodology, urban research in particular underwent a great leap forward. For the Dutch-speaking world, the 1987 publication of Frits Palmboom's compact study, *Rotterdam, verstedelijkt landschap* (Rotterdam, urbanised landscape), was a landmark event. This study was a painstaking attempt to 'drill through time' and provide insight into the city's evolutionary strata. The study of this evolutionary process makes it possible to diagnose the nature of interventions in the city's autonomous morphology, providing an overture for a sequel by means of spatial design.[21] In this regard, even Palmboom, fascinated as he was by precise morphology, did not lose sight of the issue of fiction raised by Eisenman. For the evolution of the city cannot be summed up in simple objective terms. Palmboom got himself out of this bind by evoking the way Van Eyck, of all people, had placed the analysis of the city in the context of the interpretation of dreams. 'Just like dreams, Van Eyck argues, cities are "kaleidoscopic, chaotic and constantly subject to metamorphosis". Just as in dreams, experiences from all time periods leave their traces, apparently thrown together at random, always changing, popping up unexpectedly and influencing one another. Just as in dreams, time and space lose their defined edges and events unfold largely outside any conscious control.'[22]

From these words it is clear Palmboom was ready for what awaited architecture in the 1990s. It would become the decade of Rem Koolhaas, whose global launch in the 1980s had been carefully prepared and whose status in Dutch culture had already been discussed in detail when he was awarded the Maaskant Prize in 1986. 'So I'm a sort of poltergeist,' he announced in his hilarious acceptance speech, going on to plead, in this capacity, for 'a reconstruction programme . . . for the mythology of the architect'.[23] 'It is also in your interest that the time comes back when the architect, like a Rumpelstilskin, perhaps stamping his feet, can say, "I want it, because I want it!" And in compensation he can astound you with the never-beforeseen, the impossible, with new horizons.' Admittedly these horizons, for the most part, lay far from the European continent, but armed with their own mythologies and those of others, an elite of gifted designers did indeed manage to astound the world.

Translated by Pierre Bouvier

21
Frits Palmboom, *Rotterdam, verstedelijkt landschap* (Rotterdam, 1987), 11.

22
Ibid.

23
Rem Koolhaas, 'De wereld is rijp voor de architect als visionair', *Archis* 8 (1986), 45-47.

The article 'Come una Ola di Fuerza y Luz' (Like a wave of energy and light), written by Frans Sturkenboom, was published in *OASE* 20, some 20 years ago. The year was not mentioned, but it must have been 1988. For *OASE* and its editorial team the period from 1986 to 1990 was, in many ways, a period of transition. The direct links with Delft University of Technology were being relaxed, heralding the tentative start of an independent existence. Moreover, from *OASE* 17 onwards, the award of a government subsidy fostered the journal's 'professionalisation' in both form and content. One of the ways in which this professionalisation manifested itself was the decision to pursue a thematic approach, thus allowing *OASE* to develop into a programmatic journal.

OASE 20, which focused on the theme of the baroque, was one of the first programmatic issues to highlight the experience of architecture in a broad sense of the word. As a member of the editorial team, Frans Sturkenboom was one of the brains behind and writers of this issue. The issue was entitled 'flowers of evil' and its cover showed two anamorphic images. These peculiar, flattened and elongated images revealed their 'true' nature only when viewed through a rolled-up piece of reflecting paper that came with the issue. Six texts focused on the construction of images and illusions in and by architecture. The same is true of Sturkenboom's article on the architecture of Borromini. Its composition played a key role in the way Sturkenboom fostered our understanding of this architecture. Its lyrical sentences slowly tied the different strands of the arguments into a central point, namely that Borromini, 'beyond classicism' and without nostalgia, 'perhaps against his better judgment and certainly with great reservations, has once again explored the synthesis, architecture as a synthetic product'. Along with other allusions in this issue, this phrase briefly illuminates the issue's objective: the baroque as a 'countermove', as a potential strategy in a postmodern time.

In the late 1980s, the search for an answer to the present condition was highly topical. It was also an important question in architecture (and its relationship with urban planning processes). However, the editorial team of architects spent little time addressing this debate explicitly. Rather, it dedicated itself to exploring and establishing architecture as the outcome of experience and expertise, as a discipline. Frans Sturkenboom's statement in the editorial of *OASE* 21 epitomises this approach: 'Design and theory: beyond the dichotomy that presupposes a distinction . . . the design should be read as a form of expertise and theory as an architectural design. This not only reflects Grassi's proposition that the design is part of the analysis of architecture (of its theoretical tradition) . . . rather it reflects the idea that every single design, whether it draws on the *theoria*, *techné* or poiesis, incorporates a body of knowledge and therefore carries authority: either hypothetically in the assumption of a secret or the positing of a question, or synthetically in the offer of an answer.'

Endry van Velzen
Member of the editorial board
from *OASE* 14 to 36

Translated by Laura Vroomen

Frans Sturkenboom

COME UNA OLA DE FUERZA Y LUZ*

* The title is taken from a musical composition by Luigi Nono, *Como una ola de fuerza y luz*, based on the homonymous poem by Julio Huasi.

On Borromini's Naturalism

FIRST PUBLISHED IN *OASE* 20

Bell tower of the monastery of the Filippini

San Ivo della Sapienza

San Carlo alle Quattro Fontane, entablature, arches and arched roof (All pictures by Paolo Portoghesi. He has captured Borromini's architecture beautifully . . .)

'Like a wave of power and light . . .' That is how we experience Borromini's architecture, and how we are inclined to describe it. In its animation is a sense of vitalism, like an ode to nature and its elements. Luminous, powerful, undulating, florid. But there is yet more significance in this line of music, namely the notion of a simile. In the manner of, *like* a wave. An analogous motion, perhaps a metaphor, a turn of phrase, maybe even sleight of hand. That, then, is the question: what are we to make of this liveliness? This naturalism? This blossoming decoration: colossal sunflowers, bees the size of a fist, lavish garlands and a shower of pomegranates? Vital, all too vital! An almost showy imitation of nature, a summer of surrealist proportions. And amid all that foliage, we even find the head of a winged cherub giving us an ironic smile . . . What knowledge, then, is concealed in this ironic gesticulation, in this mimoseous mime? What leads Borromini to overload architecture with flowers? What will is it that inspires these *fleurs du mal* to open their petals? This, already, is nearly a *hypothesis.*

The *task*, then, is to blaze a trail through this obtrusively naturalistic idiom, to establish a genealogy, with the aim of tracking down that will and capturing it in the tapestry of time. The tapestry of time? Yes, where Renaissance and baroque, classicism and Gothic, pre-, pleni-, and post-modernism, warp and weft, still industriously weave away at that image of the word, that countenance, called architecture . . .

THE LIGHT

One of the loveliest passages in Vitruvius' ten books tells of the birth of architecture from light, the light of the sun. This passage describes how to determine the cardinal directions, in order to plan a city in accordance with them. For this purpose, Vitruvius recommends a bronze gnomon or 'shadow tracker'. He instructs the reader to mark the end of the shadow cast by the gnomon at the fifth hour of the morning. Then draw a circle using a compass, with the supporting leg at the centre of the sundial and the drawing leg passing through the marked point. In the afternoon, when the shadow once again touches the circle, make a second mark, and draw two semicircles of equal diameter with the two points at their centres. The points of intersection of these semicircles, and the straight lines passing through those points and the centre, give us the septentrional and meridional quarters.

We are not concerned here with how Vitruvius attempts to capture the health of the corresponding winds, the north and south winds, or those of the east and west, Favonius and Solanus, in order to connect them to human well-being. What interests us most is the sunlight that either touches earth directly or, in failing to do so, draws a shadow, a dark line. This dialectic of full and empty, black and white, for once and for all gives shape to Classicistic light-writing: architecture is the place where heaven kisses earth. The light is as white as the sun, the shadow as black as ink, and it is with this graphic sensibility that Vitruvius, Palladio, Jones and, yes, even Rossi write their treatises. The second aspect of interest to us is that the city and its architecture are founded from light as well as from the order of the day; from the cycle of the sun – in short, from precisely measured time. The fifth hour in the morning and hour x in the afternoon give us a compass. Here, in its forms, architecture sets itself up as a strict geometer and a precise chronometer. The success of the kiss, the cosmic happiness of architecture, is now contained in the perfection of this contract between earthly space and the time of the sun's path.

It is not entirely clear whether Borromini's library included the handbooks of the Roman author Vitruvius or the Vicentine Palladio, though it very probably did include Palladio's. Borromini's early years betray a Palladian inspiration, manifest in the courtyard of the monastery of S. Carlo. The columns there are surmounted by the same alternating arches and rectangular sections that characterise a Palladian window. But what is more important is the graphics of light and dark, which establish the surface as a play of fullness and emptiness. Still, it must be said that precisely that classical light makes this an exceptional work in Borromini's oeuvre. The first and last of its kind, you might say, because Borromini's architecture is not this type of object, measurable by the sun. His architecture might be cosmic, but in the sense of a falling star. For Borromini, architecture shines a light of its own, a light that detaches it from the earth, a light that isolates it from its surroundings. Borromini's architecture is an architecture that illuminates. The time this architecture inhabits is not the space from morning to afternoon; no, it is the immeasurable moment when architecture gets up, arises, as light that differentiates itself, as colourism. To achieve this effect, Borromini has to construct a light machine with which to lead and mislead the sunlight, the natural light, forcing it to bend its rays and no longer fall directly on the earth. The light will sweep and skim, and even send its shafts skywards!

At S. Giovanni in Laterano, Borromini divides the now diffuse light into two components: regular light in the central nave and light that alternates bay by bay in the first aisle. He then differentiates the surfaces of the pillars in between, into straight and concave ones. The 'interference' between these two forms of light – each with its own rhythm – and the alternating contact with receding and flat surfaces gives rise to a very complex sequence of light-dark gradations. Rhythmically, the architecture begins to sing, to resound, in and with its own light, a purely architectural material.

This light evolves even further at S. Ivo della Sapienza. An exceedingly slow snowfall of light descends from the chapel , its tones so high that the last remnants of classical composition (columns reduced to thin pilasters, the tambour diminished to the laughable proportions of an attic) dissolves and the tonal play now brings out only the slow rhythm of the moulding, and the organism vanishes in a luminous cadence. Hear Argan sing the praises of this supremely subtle play of light, and its effects in the façade of the Oratory of S. Filippo Neri: 'For the front of the monastery of S. Filippo Neri, the artist had envisaged a frontal view, but precisely there, where the space was more open and accommodating [than at the Collegio di Propaganda Fide, F.S.], the relief flattens out and empty areas appear on the surface; the light effects are kept within a more moderate range; the rhythm is more restless and fluid. The entire façade moves in a soft curve, almost seeming to draw back from the space that faces it. The strongest dark accent is found at the bottom, in the niches of the first order, which are positioned further back than the windows above them, while both are embedded in a coffered pattern created by the threefold iteration of the order. This thrusts the empty surfaces of the windows forward and upward, beyond the capitals and against the central cornice. All the dynamic accents merge, here, like waves breaking against the shore, and in an act of unbelievable liberty, the window-frames are placed above the capitals, where they break the static coherence of the façade irrevocably. Higher above, in the second order, the rhythm resumes, in a more relaxed passage that is more open to the light, ending above the final cornice in the 'capriccio' of the crowning section. The difference in the rhythmic development of the two orders is mediated by the central axis; below, a narrow, convex area serves as a hinge for the two wings of the façade, and above, the flattened concha of the niche opens the lighter areas and makes them stand out.'[1]

A complex interplay, thus, that finally departs from the dark-light balance of classicism. But what are the forces at work in this light? We have seen that in classicism, architecture appears as a place where heavenly light and earthly matter kiss, in a contract of perfection. It was thus inevitable that this architecture would be possessed by ideal forces, that the compass would become a compass for humanity, that the site of the kiss would also become a site for their reconciliation of divine sky and human place, that at this site, architecture would be tied to the fate of the world. That the time of the sun's course would be the time of the course of human lives, and that architecture would function as the ideal mirror between them, as an ideal sign and the sign of an ideal. The triangle of the pediment thus became the human forehead, and the mirror-game of heliography no longer wrote any stories but human ones. Classicistic architecture intended itself to be a peace offering, sacrificing itself for the happiness of the world. The forces of the earth triumphed over the light *of* architecture.

In Borromini's case, the opposite happened. He could appear only after (alongside) classicism, and began with the remnants of that happiness, began overloading architecture with symbols that refer to the fate of the world, in the religious, political and moral realms. What is more, he misled the light of

1
Giulio Carlo Argan, in his article 'Borromini'. The quoted passage clearly shows the affinity and accuracy with which Argan approached Borromini's architecture. He is the greatest of Borromini's many biographers and historiographers. Everything he wrote about Borromini is now available in the collection *Opere di Giulio Carlo Argan*, vol. 2, *Immagine e persusasione: saggi sul Barocco* (Milan, 1986). Other studies that had a significant influence on this essay are: Hans Sedlmayr, *Die Architektur Borrominis* (Munich, 1939); Christian Norberg-Schulz, *Architettura barocca* (Milan, 1979). Let me also mention Tafuri's articles in various publications, which are quite simply some of the best ever written about the baroque Borromini. In contrast to almost the entire body of literature on Borromini, Tafuri does not see Borromini's architectures as homogeneous objects or rounded organisms but as a universe of fractures. See e.g. *Studi sul Borromini* (Rome, 1967).

nature, turning it into a demiurgic machine, an architectural artefact. He thereby melted down symbolism – the language of the ideal and the idealistic language – and transformed it into a luminous relief. And through this alchemy, he gave architecture a sun of its own. Like a true Phosphorus (morning star), he wanted to ignite architecture into a *will to shine*.

Now come, O fire!

STRENGTH

Like the morning star, he wanted to liberate architecture from the ground. But that requires consummate technique! After all, doesn't it entail contradicting the force of gravity? What refinement this must demand, you will undoubtedly say. True, but even so, Borromini's proposed solution is simper than we would think.

If we take matter as the starting point, then we must say that architecture is an art of challenging and defeating gravity. The classically minded turned to nature as a model. Sturdy buildings that aspire to carry the heavens should stand like trees. An acanthus, for instance, whose leaves remain recognisable in the Corinthian capital. Its power also lay in having the right proportions: to carry x times as much foliage and sunlight, it grew a trunk x times as thick. We will never know whether the classical column in fact derived its power from material with suitable dimensions, or from its harmonious proportions. We can, however, see in Vitruvius' treatise how the problem of natural strength is submerged and dissolved in exquisite mythical images of the origin of the orders, in an anthropomorphic image: Doric is strong and masculine, Corinthian slender and feminine. Ionic comes from Ion, a young warrior. And the Caryatids bear their punishment nobly, heads held high. All these bodies are oriented towards the sun, like heliotropic flowers, their feet firmly planted on the ground, neatly topically divided into form and substance, light and matter, image and strength. Yes, strenght may be real and material, but more than that, strength is an evocative image, a question of figurative language, of metaphor!

The seventeenth century aimed to see through this metaphor, to treat it as a figure of speech. As a natural scientist, one can of course take a hard line, rejecting this image of proportional strength as a fallacy.

That was what Galileo did (in the famous passage about the two bones).[2] But one can also devise a much more refined natural science that reveals nature's mirror-game to be an unreal play of forces, and can use technology as a real means to this revelation. This affirms the distinction between image and reality, and tackles both problems head on. In the case of the image, that problem lies in its metaphorical nature. For if architecture is more truly an image of beautiful natural force than an image of real scientific force, then it would be better to search for the genesis of beauty, for the beauti-

2
Galileo Galilei, *Discorsi e dimostrazioni matemetiche intorno à due nuove scienze* (1638). The passage in question can also be found in Liane Lefaivre and Alexander Tzonis, *Theorieën van het architektonies ontwerpen* (Nijmegen, 1984).

ful thing, than for the accurate depiction of proportioned power. Of course, one should not forget how to lay bricks and construct an arch – on the contrary – but doesn't the refinement of beauty lie in the subtlety of the stucco? It is thus *crucial* to acknowledge that action is reaction, of course! But the two do not form a couple in the architectural sense. It is even more crucial to acknowledge that imagination is active, and therefore not reactive. This may be less natural, but it is nonetheless a reason not to approach the image of a naturally painted power with resentment. The masterly thing, at this point, is to say, let us wear this natural mask and truly exaggerate, raise the power, force the issue – yes, a *tour de force*, a show of power, because only then is there a chance that the balance of strength will shift, that we will disempower the natural idiom and that something will bud there, that the budding power of beauty, of architecture will come to us and triumph. It is masterly to say this because it is *disinterested*, for that arrival cannot be measured in terms of interest.

To see this, let us travel to S. Carlo alle Quattro Fontane, the small church in the heart of Rome where Borromini began his career as an independent architect. In the interior, the image of nature is visible not only in the decoration but, most importantly, in the verticality of the columns, like an imagined triumph over gravity. They stand firmly, these tree-columns. Alongside this classical motif, Borromini introduces a horizontal, placing the columns in overlapping groups so that they generate a decelerating and accelerating rhythm. He then crowns them with one continuous entablature, thus disrupting the logic of the arches, which should rest directly on the columns (for continuity in the conveyance of force). In particular places, selected for planimetric and perspectival reasons, he has the entablature recede and balloon the walls. This builds on the idea of dilating and contracting forces. The image of a supporting framework is eroded by the elliptical experiments, and with arches that twist where they bear the heaviest load, the ideal image of gravity appears to have been conquered. The power of matter makes way for the power of space: centripetal and centrifugal space, evasion and invasion. Diastole, systole . . . aha! The image of *nature* has not yet been conquered. In fact, what emerges is a vital, multidimensionally pulsating organism. A beating heart. But more important than this organic space is the type of observation it demands. The idea of an organism creates the impression – reinforced by the compactness of the dome's oval – that the space can be surveyed in a single glance. Nothing could be further from the truth! This impression goes back to the idea of the oval as a perspectival space in which everything flees our gaze to converge at the vanishing point. S. Carlo does not work like that at all. Along with the longitudinal axis of the oval, which can be detected in the ground area as well, the lateral and vertical axes are emphasised. The lateral axis is reinforced by the two concave altar niches, in which the arrangement of the elements and the disappearance of the receding coffers of the concha behind the pediment create a perspectival illusion. The longitudinal and lateral directions now begin to modify each other. In both cases, the perspective is more radial than central. The eye itself is subjected to centripetal and centrifugal forces, forced to keep moving, and it grows disoriented among the frames, supports and arches that light up like lines of force. The potential for the gaze to draw a conclusion – a potential that could be taken for granted only because of central perspective and the consequent closure of the organism – ceases to exist, as does the possibility of taking in the overall distribution of the space. Even the balanced play of masses is sacrificed to the edgy suggestiveness of the structure. In following the lines, the eye takes pleasure in antics and tumbles, half-curves and arabesques that constantly turn back on themselves and thereby circle something else, a simple motif, a single organ, as it were, the organic quality of which has however been lost in our astonishment at the motif as a beautiful thing in itself, *una bella cosa*![3]

Before the wandering eye, the astonished eye, the play of veins and muscles thus loses its depth, the organism becomes ornament, a collection of lines and objects of which only the beautiful forms matter. How powerful, this will to seize architecture away from nature's profundity and transform it into surface, this will to make the architectural eye, after all that turbulence, end in the stasis of the gaze, to swallow it up in the absurdity of seeing. But it is sublime too, the start of this degeneration in the ambiguity of the lines of force as a natural motif, a motif that is stripped of its nature by strong, rapid oscillation. And all this so that it will come, that beautiful thing, architecture.

Three ideas then play with the strength: (1) It is real, it is real gravity, and can be taken on by real, technical methods. (2) It is an image of natural forces. These can be taken on with a special technique: the further imagination of the entire organic arsenal. (3) Only in this hypertrophy of the organism does the eye degenerate into the absurdity of seeing. This is where the third force comes to light, a vital, rising force: making architecture lighter by stripping it of the weight of its natural content. The consummate technique that this seemed to require is therefore as simple as it is ingenious: intensifying the image of the force until it is lost in the multiplicity and velocity of lines. The will to deprive the viewer of his overview, a folly of the eye, a *will to see*.

3
A body without organs, one might say, echoing Deleuze and Guattari. In their joint studies, these authors made the organic the theme of their research. For them, the organism is a question of the organisation of the earth. To take on this question, they propose the art of 'unearthing' (deterritorialisation) and thereby attaining a 'body without organs'. This art does not target the organs as much as it does the organic. The art is to trace a convergence line out of it, a line of 'inorganisation'. The problem is not that of order and chaos, but that of the 'plane of consistency' that one must draw with these convergence lines, a cosmically composed chaos or Joycean chaosmos. See Gilles Deleuze and Felix Guattari, *Capitalisme & Schizophrénie I & II, l'Anti-Oedipe* (Paris, 1972), and *Mille Plateaux* (Paris, 1980).

WAVE

What mark does this desire leave on the façade, the outside? And what is the relationship between that outside and the inside, the interior? Two questions, and Borromini addressed both of them through the idea of the wave. A wave can die away romantically or froth up expressionistically. In both cases, it is subject to the idea of an origin, whether dying or, on the contrary, making one last appearance in all its intensity. There are 'neutral' waves too, however, in which other forces are at play, not those of the interior as origin but those of the surface as neuter, an undulation, *Schwung* or swing. But in this case, again, the natural resemblance remains, and we write in nature's idiom – of a rippling stream, for instance.

How are we to characterise Borromini's waves? Many authors have sought a prefiguration of modern architecture in his façades, and above all in their relationship to his interiors, seeing the undulation on the outside as an expression of the movements within. This might put one in mind of Mendelsohn's expressionistic buildings, in which expressiveness does create continuity between the inside and outside, as if in the façade, we see the intimate nature of the interior, the intimacy of the human, sloshing outside for one last moment, to remain standing in the artificial domain of the city. This movement does not greatly differ from that other modernism in which the interior and exterior become entirely homogeneous and the façade effaces itself, becoming a transparent medium.[4] The same continuity could lie at the basis of Borromini's undulating façades: convex and concave movements could refer to the vitality of the organism within, in a homogeneous spatial concept. Brandi and Norberg-Schulz even speak of causality: a centrifugal spatial force on the inside gives us a bulge on the outside. The baroque space then becomes a *res extensa*, homogeneous, without a crack or cranny.

For ordinary visitors, however, the moment of cause and effect is never observable. To be sure, the image of a similarity imposes itself upon us, but if we trace the planimetric movement of the internal and external contours, we see that there is no continuity whatever, no linear relationship. The movement of the façade is never necessitated by spatial or constructive requirements of the 'organism'. This causality is a kind of mime, an art of the simulacrum.

What is more interesting than the bare fact of this rupture, however, is the architectural problem to which it points us, namely the independence of two undulating components as a reference to their own *space*. The interior points us to the question of typology: is there a formal concept belonging to a type of building? The exterior points us to the city, less a morphological problem than a question of the silhouette and rhythm of the wall. At S. Agnese, he plays a clever game with the component of the wall and profile.[5] He incorporates the church into the fabric of the city with two linking sections, thereby reinforcing the wall, but then makes the façade recede so that the cupola protrudes outward and enters into a rhythmic play of verticals with its own campaniles and the belvederes of the adjacent Palazzo Pamphili, pointing towards the sky and at the same time adding strength to the wall.

The urban and typological factors thus reinforce the independence of the interior and exterior. As we see below, the undulations dissolve into the typological fixation of the

4
It is therefore not so strange that Mendelsohn managed, almost soundlessly, to take the step from a sloshing continuity to a more regular one.

5
At least in the drawings that Borromini made for this purpose. This urban game has been reconstructed by Manfredo Tafuri (see note 2).

baroque era; in the genesis of the formal concept of a plan, they develop a swinging typology. On the outside, the wave gives the city more *Schwung*. This says very little, however, about the natural appearance that both undulations retain. That raises the issue of the genesis of form. This problem is more complex than that of the city or the typology; it is precisely here that the resemblance between the interior and the exterior comes into being. As noted, this resemblance can be striking (as it is at S. Carlo and S. Maria dei Sette Dolori), and perhaps even a fortuitous accident, but never a necessity. It arises from the fact that the façade and the interior have the same type of planimetric origin. The problem that arises here, however, is quite different from that of a possible formal resemblance between the interior and exterior; specifically, it is that of the convergence of nature and science. For Borromini sets himself the task of extracting a natural and naturalistic image from mathematics. He achieves this by superimposing the geometric figures – diamonds, circles, ovals – that serve as the basis for the floor plan, or embedding them in one another, until they form a natural motif, whether it is a frenetic line or the regularity of a flower. Then geometry is no longer an ideal figure of nature, and nature no longer the content or idea of an ideal geometry. Nature emerges as the product of mathematics. The relation between science and nature is then as follows. Science is besotted with nature, but its cruel fate is that it is forced to pervert and metamorphose its own ideal laws if it wishes to obtain nature's beautiful features: a wave requires endless circling from a variety of points, a flower the endless rotation of squares. Nature lures geometry into this game, encouraging it by producing ideal figures in the course of its own metamorphoses: crystals, shells. And hence triangles and stars, waves and circles form mutual convergence lines. This art is perfectly reserved, however. Nowhere do we find the excesses of rococo. Architecture searches for the untraceable moment when geometry and nature come closest to convergence, searches for the *slightest* difference, the moment at which one cuts off flower-nature as a motif that is no longer real but linguistic, a product, an artefact. The slightest difference, but *ineradicable* – a question of restrained gardening.

Detail of one of the lateral chapels at San Giovanni in Laterano

San Giovanni, pillars of the central nave, detail. Brightening the architect

San Giovanni, pillars of the central nave. Rhythm of light

Let us return to S. Carlo to look at all of this in combination. This little church cannot be approached from the front; it stands on a corner at the intersection of two narrow streets. From the two streets, two different urban design motifs were developed. Approaching from one of the two, we see the corner tower, confirming the status of the little church as a monumental moment, a pivot of the city. In the other street, from a distance, the façade looks like a luminous motif and a slight rippling of the wall. When we come closer, this manipulation of the urban accent metamorphoses into swinging architecture. As we approach, the dynamism of the wave increases. On a sunny day, the chiaroscuro enhances the effect; light and shade are not artfully balanced but used to expand the amplitude. And when we finally arrive in front of the façade, our gaze shoots upward along the rising columns, encounters this stone undulation along the way, and ends where the silhouette, with a stray cloud alongside it, looks like a veil blown by the wind. There it dissolves in a tactile wave of light.

When we enter the elongated space of the interior, a striking resemblance washes over us. But above all, the interior raises the typological question of the baroque era: is an elongated plan best suited to the new requirements imposed on church architecture by the liturgy? (Masses had to unite ritual with spectacle.) In other words, does the formal concept have to fall halfway between the temple and the basilica? No, Borromini says, and he places the oval that the baroque selected as the ideal answer to this typological problem atop the dome of this small church, instead of using it as the floor plan. The question of the elongated plan is irrelevant; it is much more interesting to put typology to the test in the genetic game of nature and geometry, thus attaining flexibility and the atypical. Within this approach, the planimetric figure of the wave is a welcome one.

We now know that the correspondence between the wave on the outside and the wave on the inside is a simulacrum. The exterior is no longer a product of the interior, or vice versa (as is confirmed by their planimetric genesis: the interior is a product of right angles and ellipses, the exterior of pure circles). Both waves are informed by the idea of severing the image from its origins, preferably as close as possible to the source, the continuing recession into the intersection of geometry and nature. The will to see is thus a *will to sever*. The interior is severed and separated from the exterior; the image is severed and separated from its nature. And it is precisely in this cutting technique, in this sharp art, in their confirmation, that one says to architecture,

'You must come . . .'

GARLAND AND STAR

Like a wave of strength and light, then. Light and strength belong to the surface, as a language of architecture. The wave gives us an idea of the genesis of this language in a desire to sever. Power was not only the image of the power of gravity or contraction, but also the germinative power of the image, a will to see. Light was not only sunlight or side-light, but also the illumination of architecture, like a desire to shine, a craving to seem.[6] In each case, we can see naturalism, as a linguistic moment, a moment of luminous seeming, in which the natural habitat of architecture is lost. But this loss contains a potential point of arrival for architecture, an architecture that seems to sing of its own accord . . . *como una ola de fuerza y luz*. The future of architectural life is at play here. But in this idea of the future, the idea of history is also at play, the idea of architectural life's faculty of memory.

6
Translator's note: In this passage, the author plays on the ambiguity of the Dutch verb 'schijnen', which means both 'shine' and 'seem, appear'. Author's note: The concept of the earth as a battleground of earthly and 'unearthing' or degenerative forces comes from Nietzsche-Deleuze. See Gilles Deleuze, *Nietzsche et la philosophie* (Paris, 1962). The will always germinates in a relationship between two forces. Bachelard has developed a typology of the will for representing this battleground of forces: *La terre et les rêveries de la volonté* (Paris, 1947). An exceptional will germinates when earth no longer resists imagination and a rising psychic force emerges, a will to fly. Bachelard sees this force in all the 'Manichaeistic flowers', as he calls them: Shelley, Poe, Nietzsche, Baudelaire, Novalis, Rimbaud (*L'aire et les songes*, Paris, 1943). Borromini should be counted among this family.

What is their relationship? We can find the answer in the art of decoration as Borromini practices it. Borromini reveres and adores history. He does so with humour, in which the powers of error play a part. Let us look at the structure of the order in the interior of S. Carlo, for example. A concave architrave – unimaginable, impossible. The pediment is crooked in places, truly laughable. And decorating the sunken quarter-vault of the concha with square coffering, that's asking for misshapen lines. But to frame this entire grimace with a twisted arch like a sarcastic aureole is to summon the devil and curse in his face. Pure heresy, as Bernini remarked, betraying a poor sense of humour. For it is truly hilarious to see how Borromini deprives this structure, this old code, of its reality. Likewise, in the courtyard of the Oratory of S. Filippo Neri, for instance, the syntax of the elements is intensely ironic; the classical entablature of architrave, frieze and cornice, which should not be separated from the capital by anything more than an abacus, is lifted up, the distance between the two monstrously increased, so that the remainder, a light cornice with a heavy Attic, simply hovers. *Vergogna*!

Yet not only the classical code, but also the mannerism and Gothic, that drift in this ether of gently mocking or mocked signs. The gesticulation of laughter: what was once structure is now grimacing memory; what was once syntax is now a decoration, a smile; what was once a forbidden past, is now a Gothic quip. O, that hallucinating memory.

The same is true of all those other languages: the symbolic, the allegorical, and that of the icon. S. Ivo is freighted with them, inside and out. Take the star in the plan, for example. Is it really a star? A flower, perhaps. In any case, a double triangle, a double trinity. Father, Son and Holy Spirit, twice! But it is also a papal emblem and, allegorically, a star of salvation. And it pays homage to geometry as a clever science (S. Ivo della Sapienza is the Roman university church of the baroque period, dedicated to the patron saint of science). Allegorical, emblematic and symbolic voices jockey for possession of a single motif. And so it goes, every time: mountains of loaves, oak leaves or palms, it is unclear whether the reference is to nature or religion, or both. What multiplicity of meaning, what polysemy! But – and this is the ultimate of ironies – isn't S. Ivo dedicated to unity, to science's victory over the confusion of tongues? Isn't that the Tower of Babel crowning its roof? Indeed it is, but even the Babel allegory can be interpreted in at least two ways. So we have lost them, those beautiful signs, round or flat, the Gothic triangle – Father referent, Son signifier and the Holy Spirit as the messenger meaning – or the Renaissance realm of analogies. But what is even more beautiful is anticipating the lost future of all full signs, of signs that by inner necessity refer to their reality. This stirring of the future, for instance, in the flora and the fauna, the flowers and the foliage, the fruit and festoons. The galleria of the Accademia di San Luca: it is as if the cornucopia has spilled its contents

Academia di San Luca, the galleria

for the last time, to compensate for the lost nature of the sign. What hangs down like a wreath of joy, a festive gesture, rises to a winged but flesh-eating medusa head. And note the columns with their ultra-vital capitals, the volutes veiling the overflowing abacus-fruit dish, the apples, bunches of grapes and pinecones, and so much more. It is all much too much, much too real, much too lively. It is as if this excess of stucco wished to proclaim its opposite: death, nature's cadaver, an image once and for all.[7] *Vivat, crescat, floreat*, but only as a *natura morte*! Furthermore, it is not even decorum, wreathes no value and confers no dignity. Or yes, its own emptiness. Garlands coil and curl around themselves like their own funeral wreaths. Take another look in back, against the wall there: upwards coiling, downwards hanging, both light, with a semicircular black surface between them. Almost Piranesi's famous altar. In any case, death . . . and darkness, void . . . and light; something is dawning there, perhaps architecture. *Architecture?* You have to cut the flower before you can enjoy it, and hold it up to the light to see its beauty. You have to cut even more flowers to get used to the idea of cutting, to learn architecture *as* a technique and embrace it *as* an artefact. But the basket of flowers strewn for the purpose of concealment must be infinitely rich, to mislead the eye like a *will to deceive*. There is nothing at all negative about that: infinite quantities of foliage are needed to cover up architecture when it no longer speaks in the immediate proximity of nature, under nature's protection, and at the same time to honour and commemorate the grave of this lost reality of architecture. So much foliage to conceal the naked, blinding secret of architecture, because now there is a chance that it will come, architecture, burning like that original fire, burning up space and consuming itself and wiping out all difference, an answer that will drain space dry once and for all. The art is to respect that secret then, to cover the blinding riddle, a rain of pomegranates to douse the proximity.

7 See Jean Baudrillard, *L'échange symbolique et la mort* (Paris, 1976), 79-82.

It can be even more direct, making the flames recede, by representing them, see high above on the campaniles and Borrominiesque magic caps, and by reiterating the flames representationally, and departing in that reiteration from the original flame, the archi-flame, differing in *techné*, in tectonics, and hence in archi-*techné*, architectonics. So that it will not come, will not come . . .

'And it does not come, it does not drain us dry . . .'

CRYSTAL

And so it was questioning the impossible, to return architecture to its origin and originality, the inherent meaning of tectonics; it was an impossible question and an unsatisfiable demand. For what is architecture? If we knew that, we would not build, would never build again . . . That is why we must cover up that riddle, so that it does not solve itself; we must surround it with stone, with architecture. Dal Co aptly remarks

San Carlo, the façade viewed from below, a deluge of light

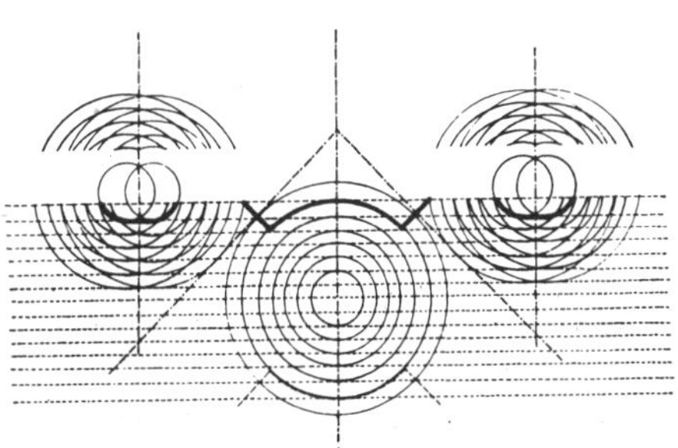

Planimetric plan of the exterior of Santa Maria dei Sette Dolori

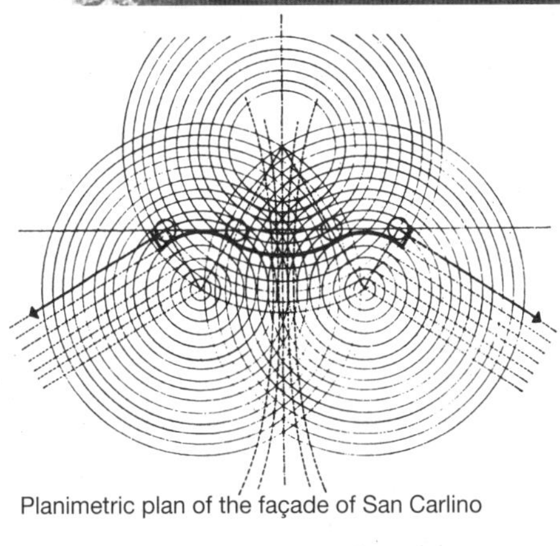

Planimetric plan of the façade of San Carlino

that architecture is a construction for concealing itself. And so it remains a question and a sign, a mark, a question mark in the tapestry of time, an ephemeral moment in the endless conversation of and with architecture, in the tapestry of time where it becomes tangled up with other lines of thought and questions, Borrominian architecture, a constellation.

What other lines of thought, for example?

With *classicism*. Classicism is an architecture devoted to the earth. That is where it traces a true history, an origin and continuation. In this framework, the origin of architecture is an ideal object: a Platonic idea or an earthly *noema*. This idealisation relates to time as history (Greek architecture as an archetype), space as nature (ideal proportions as harmonic physics) or technology as primitive (Laugier's hut of branches as natural technology). This ideal idea is supposed to be reinscribed, and approached as closely as possible, in every architectural object. That object must be a mirror or imprint of it, preferably a faithful copy. Any classicism measures history by the success of this venture. For Vasari, thus, Michelangelo was a hero; he rivalled and *outdid* even the ancients. For the neo-classicist Winckelmann, he was an object of degeneration and decline for that very reason. And so, in the eyes of classicism, Borromini – who revered Michelangelo as the grandfather of his architecture – must have looked like an aberration and an error, a bizarre and capricious degeneration, turning the world and his roots on their head.

Even so, the baroque Borromini never did anything but draw the utmost consequences from what was already taking place in the Renaissance and Mannerist periods – what was, in fact, already occurring in the heart of classicism. He saw that if the archetypal, earthly noema of architecture contained so many notable phenomena, so far removed from one another and so diverse, so many interpretations and so many imitations, that equally many origins just might reveal themselves in those images, equally many fragments of the origin.
Ora questo è perduto . . . But even then, it already was!

These fragments were Borromini's building blocks. And that is a second line of thought, not anti-classicist but *beyond classicism*; the fragment that links Borromini to Piranesi, cartographer and cataloguer of a lost but imagined Rome and Egypt, and with Soane, that archaeologist of the frivolous for whom it is not enough to gather up the fragments, for whom even the four cardinal directions, once involved in the birth certificate of a great deal of classical beauty, grace the walls like empty labels. The baroque Borromini was not a classicist, but nor was he an anti-classicist. When he mocked classicism, it was not out of resentment, but because it was an object of affection, just as he mocked nature with his frenzied reverence, to confront both with their senseless beauty. The baroque Borromini; but was he truly *baroque*? This question is difficult to answer; it requires a baroque yardstick. Architecture does not have such a thing. All we can say is that compared with Bernini, Cortona and Rainaldi, he was the most baroque of all, that is to say the least classicistic. Not only stylistically; for Bernini, the truth of history was still at stake. Borromini strayed farthest from the path. Even so, this was not pure excess. For unlike rococo, which is often seen as the legitimate heir to the baroque, rococo, for which excess was merely excess, unlike this wilderness, Borromini saw excess rise out of emptiness. And so he did not practice an art, like rococo, of maximal departure from an already distant truth of nature, but an art of minimal difference with the still-intimate illusion of nature. He sensed that cutting the flower would bring not only the joy and perversity of the game, but also the separation and the farewell, the scar and the wound.

And he bears them without nostalgia.[8] His lack of nostalgia may have been the most baroque thing about him. So much so that – possibly against his better judgment and, in any case, very hesitantly – he returned to the practice of synthesis, architecture as a synthetic product. This, then, is what links him to Guarini and Vittone, those other chemists of future material (Giedion and Argan, those advocates of the modern, they recognised them!).

It was Borromini, Guarini and Vittone who started to become aware of the intermediary, of the technique of architecture, of architecture *as* a technique. Even before neo-classicism, Borromini saw that even an architecture that mimicked nature would need a technique, the technique of pantomime. All three of them then said: if the technique, the instrument, the machine is necessary, surely it is finer and more beautiful for it no longer to invoke nature, but to evoke architecture, utter deracination, transcendental technique. Acrobatic domes, a trapeze of vaulting, an athletics of architecture was what they placed there in the machina-mecano-metamorpho-sphere. Borromini, Guarini, Vittone, they lived the baroque architectural life, in them a cosmonautic space flight began and a fallen star ended. With their domes, those magic caps, they fittingly covered up the riddle, honoured the star.

A star, a crystal, then, a diadem, because there the imaginary values of heaven and earth are interchanged, because the crystal, perfectly inorganic, still invisibly preserves the memory of organic time. But also because it opens the time of polishing, a technical time, yes, but as a mathesis of midnight figures. In nature's crystal farewell, a constellating dream is also at play, one which must stake earthly thoughts in order to heave, to dare, to devise an ethereal future.[9] What knowledge we have asked for, what knowing conceals itself in this naturalism. It is the knowledge of the evening and the knowing of the wound, not without a smile or quip. A feigned reality, a mined crystal, a *desire to sparkle*. Loss and gain, nature lost, fire regained, even if it does not come, does not come, for it dies like all nature. Then it is a fine thing to say with furore, like Borromini:

'To die a diadem . . .'

Translated by David McKay

8
The baroque is often seen as the era of melancholy. Walter Benjamin sees it as the era of the *Trauerspiel*. The melancholy is then allegorical (see Henk Hoeks, 'Trouw aan de dingen'). When melancholy rids itself of allegory, lost time triumphs, and the concept of a 'Malinconia felix' takes shape, as Pieter Jan Gijsberts describes in his work on the paintings of Adriaen Coorte (see 'Het in zijn nu verblijvend hier'). Both of these articles can be found in the superb issue of *Museumjournaal* (no. 5/6) devoted entirely to 'nostalgia for seeing'. It is well known that Borromini was a very melancholy person; his architecture, however, is devoid of nostalgia; after all, the idea of a house or home lost in history is incompatible with his hallucinatory art of memory. In fact, nostalgia is probably a phenomenon characteristic of the twentieth century.

9
Borromini lived in the age of doubt. Not only because the heliocentrism of Copernicus and Galileo threatened to do away with the earth as a fixed point of reference, and this in its turn was outdone by Giordano Bruno's infinite space with infinitely many suns, but more generally because the possibility had been called into question of the existence of any fixed point at all, for being and seeing, morality and thought. Pascal, Descartes and Leibniz came up with dubious responses to this (see Michel Serres, *L'interference*, Paris, 1972, 137 ff.). Borromini's version of this doubt could be expressed as follows: Is an architecture that transcends earth, nature and humanity possible? Is there any point at all to which architecture can be fixed? After writing down this question, he shot it into the heavens, where it still sparkles, architecture's foolish question mark. Then he weighed his options, wondered . . . and went to work to give life to that architecture.

In 1981, when I started my architecture degree at Delft University of Technology, Dutch architecture was in a very sorry state. The number of first-year students barely reached 200, and even this small number of first-years were told that less than half of them could expect to actually find work as architects. After all, the Netherlands was completely built up and the only area with any kind of future was urban renewal – that is, replacing the existing collection of buildings. Whereas the international scene was experiencing a postmodernist wave (reaching its peak with the first Architecture Biennale in Venice in 1980), this was given little chance in the Netherlands. Both the older Forum generation, spearheaded by angry old man Aldo van Eyck ('Rats, Posts and other Pests'), and the younger, politically minded public housing proponents saw a plea for such a populist architecture as evidence of a despicable flippancy.

1988 – the year this interview was published – saw a glimmer of hope. Student numbers were on the increase. Slowly but surely, Dutch architecture was climbing out of its deep well of self-chastisement and slowly building a new self-confidence. And postmodernism managed to make an impact after all. Weeber and Meeuwissen are important players in this development: Meeuwissen as a representative of the Eindhoven School, which sought to put architecture back on the map by incorporating auteurism within a cultural-historical context, and Weeber as a representative of a postmodernism that argues in favour of an autonomous architecture that does not revolve around originality but around the application of architectural rules and regulations derived from the history of architecture. For this reason the handbook – the interview's central theme – means different things to the two men: Weeber sees it as a collection of recipes capable, at least on paper, of solving any problem, while Meeuwissen views it as a product of history which – like other forms of culture – can be used as a source of inspiration during the design process. This difference, incidentally, is never clearly articulated in the interview. The two men may be discussing the same theme, but they are also talking at cross-purposes. But they certainly agree on their common enemy – the Delft functionalism and its thirst for originality.

It is worth noting that in the year this interview was published, Rem Koolhaas was appointed visiting professor at the Faculty of Architecture. The enormous success Koolhaas and his followers were to enjoy in the 1990s meant that even before it really got off the ground, postmodernism in the Netherlands was overtaken by the supermodernism of Koolhaas and co. This supermodernism was particularly adept at dealing with the media boom: not just the proliferation of books and magazines on architecture and the development of the Internet, but even more so the need for non-stop presentation: every architect is a participant in a never-ending competition that determines his or her success or failure. As with the presentation of any other product, the innovation decried by Meeuwissen and Weeber is decisive in this respect. While the grumpy old men are talking handbooks, the modern student is preparing for this endless struggle for survival. And an architectural handbook here will be just as ineffectual as the soldier's handbook in a cyber war.

Bart Goldhoorn
Member of the editorial board
from *OASE* 18 to 32

Translated by Laura Vroomen

Endry van Velzen and Pieter van Wesemael

EXERCISES A Discussion about Architectural Education with Joost Meuwissen and Carel Weeber*

FIRST PUBLISHED IN *OASE* 22

*
This interview took place at the offices of the ArchitectenCie in Amsterdam, 10 October 1988. Joost Meuwissen is an architect, theoretician and lecturer in architecture at Eindhoven University of Technology and several other schools and editor of *Wiederhall* magazine. Meuwissen obtained his doctorate in architecture with a thesis on 'Architecture as Ancient Science'. Carel Weeber is an architect, professor in architectural design at Delft University of Technology and the man behind the Durand institute.

CW In my opinion, architects in the Netherlands are incapable of building on any kind of architectural tradition. Building is in constant flux. Everything is extremely dynamic, with a new big thing coming around every ten years. Elsewhere in the world you see a huge output of buildings that are simply buildings. They do not feature in any publications – they're simply there. At the same time, you see the kind of output that we will be looking at. In the Netherlands everything at the more experimental reaches of architecture is often quickly channelled into mainstream output. It is strange to see no more trace of an architectural tradition with its roots in the nineteenth century, such as we see in the work of Van der Steur or Evers. It has been ousted by the Delft School on the one hand and the Modern Movement on the other. The latter usually sees the Rietveld-Schröder house – a piece of furniture rather than a building – as its apogee. An unusual experiment is seen as architecture. I believe this is a worrying trend. We are lurching from one movement to the next, with scant opportunity, indeed scant appreciation, for simply producing buildings. In other countries, modern architecture is rooted in both architectural output *and* in design. This is something that never really got off the ground here. The Netherlands has no nineteenth century and that is why Delft has proven an unstable course. Instead of teaching students how to build we expect them to experiment.

I suspect that virtually every student of architecture grapples with the question of 'how to become famous'. But that is a stupid question. Still, this is the kind of environment that our students are taught in. Artistry is an issue until the very last, even though it is largely irrelevant to most of our students. Of course it is good to be familiar with the cultural context of architecture, but if you are learning how to design buildings it should be little more than a side issue, not the main focus. The emphasis on artistry gets in the way of learning a skill, of designing buildings. Students feel frustrated because they cannot draw what they want to draw.

I am surprised to see the curriculum attach such prominence to buildings that I consider, from a construction point of view, to be bad buildings. There is this strange predilection for collapsing buildings. Duiker's sanatorium and Van Eyck's orphanage are a case in point. I suspect that for most students this is all rather unproductive, unless these buildings are looked at within a contemporary and even older context. Show students the significance of a Duiker building compared to a building by his contemporary De Bazel; explain their architectural qualities, the architectural themes and their different social contexts.

The element of stability is extremely important for education at the big schools. The smaller schools, the ones providing post-graduate training for instance, could then offer a more informed and comprehensive approach to the experimental. That is what I had in mind for the Durand Institute, now the Berlage Institute.

EDUCATIONAL MODELS: TWEAKING REALITY

OASE While preparing this issue we were struck to find elements of different approaches, both practical and cultural, exist side by side in education. It seems important to us that the differences between these approaches are clearly outlined and that the theories underlying these approaches are understood. A course taking these differences as its starting point would be an option.

JM Yes, but what I find problematic is that often the practical aspects of building immediately find their way into education, whereas the development of concepts, the theory, is seen as something quite distinct, as a form of embellishment. I, on the other hand, believe that theory generated in practice is important. Theory does not provide some kind of added value. What is important is the rate of recurrence of problems and the way these problems are formulated. This is what I would call a problematising approach. It raises questions about the context in which the architect creates a design for a building and about the interpretation of this context. Modern architecture only needed a few words to describe this context, thanks to the presence of groups of architects united around a collective programme, legislation and a clear view of urbanism. This kind of contextual information is what is missing now. In order to achieve some level of success, architects are now forced to define their context on a case-by-case basis. What's more, the context must cover a broader area. The design is expected to deal with more problems than it did back in the 1950s.

CW But this is all based on the current situation. Surely you cannot use that as a foundation for education?

JM But the current situation is important. In the past you could explain the concept of council housing to someone by referring to so-called *Wenken en Voorschriften* (Rules and Suggestions). It allowed you to take a more limited approach to housing design. It was unnecessary to explore the housing programme, since it was already in place.

CW I believe there is a much more implicit set of regulations. And that set seems to me to be of greater importance than the legislation targeting local issues, such as the Rules and Suggestions. The design process remains essentially the same, whether you're designing council housing in the Netherlands or in the south of Italy. What's more, I believe that the design brief is largely irrelevant to the design process. However, in Delft functionalism has become so entrenched that everybody is convinced that a brief is indispensable for design. The upshot of all this is that Delft has no theory of architecture.

JM Architectural education is almost always based on simulation – the simulation of a hypothetical situation. Yet this is never made explicit.

CW Yet strangely enough, such simulation models rarely feature the cost of construction, the Rules and Suggestions, the building regulations, and so forth. The word in Delft is that these elements inhibit creativity. So you end up simulating nothing other than the free interpretation of a practical commission.

As I was saying, the design brief is really crucial in Delft, even though the brief in itself does not produce a design. There seems to be a kind of knowledge that allows you to predict, as it were, that such-and-such a form of spatial planning will be suitable for such-and-such a brief. The resulting spatial planning then becomes a variation on familiar spatial planning. For instance, everyone automatically draws corridors with rooms or stairwells with levels, even when the brief does not specify this. In other words, certain schematic plans lend themselves to dealing with certain briefs. But the number of suitable schematic plans turns out to be limited. All in all there may be ten schematic plans that are capable of dealing with any number of design briefs. You need to know these schematic plans inside-out. They form the foundation for your designs. In my view, this is receiving nowhere near enough attention in Delft. At the start of their course, especially, students must be made aware of these schematic plans, quite independently of any briefs. Question: how do you organise a building? You can turn this around: the floor plan of a building does not tell you what the building is like. Archaeologists usually cannot determine the purpose of a building until they have located the pots and pans.

The current educational system does little to teach knowledge of buildings. Students are expected to invent the wheel all over again. In the end it is usually less difficult than anticipated, because there seems to be a kind of intuitive sense of buildings. But because this intuitive knowledge is not properly structured, the whole design process becomes rather laborious. At present, the emphasis is mainly on visual aids. Students are being bombarded with pictures of architecture, but these do not tell them how a building was actually made.

OASE Visual aids form part of the knowledge of buildings. The vertical elevations, the use of materials, etcetera, can be described and analysed. The book *Kleur en Architectuur* (Colour and architecture)[1] is a good example. This kind of structured knowledge is conspicuous by its absence in our educational system. It surprises me that the debate around typology and morphology has been adopted from other countries, but the debate around elevations has not.

1 Jan de Heer (ed.), *Kleur en Architectuur* (Rotterdam, 1986).

CW: Yes, theory is an extremely tricky issue in the Netherlands. Before you know it, theory has turned into theology, with everything taking on an ideological hue. Other parties knock it down immediately, and that puts a stop to any further development. In that sense, the Netherlands does not offer very fertile soil.

JM But these kinds of debates are essential to architectural education. I like the fact that theory is seen as something that comes after the buildings and not as something that precedes them. As such, the process no longer revolves solely around the design but also around the way in which architectural material is structured. This has been covered by so many theories. I believe that education is less about making a selection from a certain typological set of architectural material, and more about explaining the consequences of that selection and the composition of that set. This applies to the elevations, the colours, the floor plan and the relationship between the building and its environment.

Everybody must know the old schematic plans of architectural material inside-out and much of our education should be geared towards this. It is possible to explore the nature of these schematic plans. Typological sets are often characterised by similar floor plan solutions. The solutions can still be adjusted at this mental level. A hallway, for instance, can be 2 or 3 m wide. It is also important to bear in mind that the design process no longer follows the usual sketch-to-working-drawing route. Students must be taught to render their ideas clearly at the level of the schematic plans. At the moment there is no sign of this whatsoever. Drawings are virtually non-existent in the design process, while the schematic plan, which could be drawn up in advance, is usually drawn up in retrospect. Theory plays a crucial role in all of this.

Evaluation poses a significant problem within architecture. We see this in practice in the case of new commissions or the judging of competitions, and in education when a teacher is marking. The evaluation process is a highly underdeveloped area. For a long time after the implicit evaluation that characterised functionalism we were told that anything goes. That is not true. Some buildings are better than others. The significance of theory lies in this, namely that when you describe something as good, you can explain why. This can be done both within education and within architectural criticism. And the schematic plans play a major role in this process.

So what education needs is the formulation of certain extra-educational objectives. Objectives are quantifiable. For instance, it is not inconceivable that an objective is not achieved, which can be significant in itself.

CW One option would be to expose the premise of a certain design by analysing the existing architectural material. In education these premises could be translated into objectives. All exercises ought to have such objectives. For instance, an assignment with a particular brief may focus on the problems associated with the asymmetrical axis. This should then be worked out in the design. That is how you build up the requisite knowledge.

After a while, the students will have processed all this architectural knowledge, enabling them to select their own combination of premises. Familiar with the premises, the problems and the material, they can then use that knowledge to pursue their own interpretations. And perhaps one day they will identify a premise themselves.

JM I believe that the way the commission is interpreted in practice is important too. The design objectives will be far more dependent on the context. If you are commissioned to design a museum of architecture the objective extends beyond the architectural material to include the body that selects the architect. It is not just your interpretation of the design brief that matters, but also how you expect the board of such an institution to interpret this brief. You might decide against a single large space, and opt instead to house the institution's various functions in a number of different types of building. The end result will be a different kind of architecture.

It is about the will of the individual architect, about how far someone is prepared to take his work. Once I was involved in a second-year project at the academy in Rotterdam. They had initially approached John Körmeling to act as a supervisor, but he refused, describing the project objective as disgraceful. The objective was: 'How can I become just as famous as Le Corbusier.' I quite liked the objective, because it really opened things up. It enables you to draw up a brief and actually assess afterwards whether or not your students have been successful. Not at that particular moment in time of course, but whether or not they would in theory. In other words, the objective need not necessarily derive from the architectural material. It can have a social dimension as well.

The course teaches students to work with the tools of the trade. Yet the architect's role in society receives very little attention. Students have no idea what to do after graduation. I see this at the Individuele Subsidie Commissie Bouwkunst (Architectural Commission for Individual Subsidies), which processes grant applications from new architects. The applicants often aspire to little more than buying a computer and preparing a pamphlet to showcase their work. There is absolutely no sign of an objective. As soon as the educational safety net is removed, this giant no-man's land appears to open up. However, this no-man's land is full of professional architects and a constant flow of commissions. Education ought to address the way you conduct yourself within this environment. There is no need to learn about business management, but the ability to clearly formulate objectives on a project-by-project basis – which problems can be identified? – would be a start. Such an approach would make it a lot easier to undertake a new study.

CW We were confronted with a similar deficiency when we were preparing to set up the Durand institute. We launched five different subjects, one of which we labelled 'design management', the role of design in society. This is where the client and user come in. It is not about the way the BNA (the Royal Institute of Dutch Architects) works or the fact that there are contractors, but about how you explain your designs to the public. Delft does not do this. We are made to believe that you create a genuine simulation, with due emphasis on the social aspects. But this is not the case, as the school is simply too hermetic.

JM What it boils down to is that you may be offering simulations – still the best approach – but that within these simulations you create artificial conditions that call for the formulation of objectives. For instance, you may set an assignment and omit the design brief or the urban planning simulation or only emphasise the cost dimension. By tweaking the reality of the simulation, by slightly shifting the emphasis in your role as a supervisor, you force the students to formulate objectives. That is exactly what happens in practice. And architecture theory plays a role in this process, because it is necessary to reflect on what details remain unchanged, what architectural material you are dealing with, how it is currently organised and how you might like to change this.

When I was teaching in Eindhoven, my initial approach to this was quite extreme. To give you an example: I would ask students to design Rietveld's red-and-blue chair. This turned out to be a terribly difficult assignment. It did not work on a didactic level. All the students would make improved versions, while that was not really the point.

CW Tweaking the assignment, as you would in practice, often challenges your ideas about architecture. But that never happens in Delft. The assignments always follow on from ideas that are already circulating at the school. Too much is taken for granted. You are discouraged from interpreting the theory because the practical example is usually quite workable. On a programmatic level things are equally tame: a school here, a town hall there, some council housing, and so on. In my view, asking students to come up with a completely absurd programme would be quite a fruitful exercise.

OASE What it boils down to then is that the simulation model, because of its tendency to take things for granted, does not encourage people to articulate their deliberations and decisions and is therefore incapable of generating theory. This can be avoided by tweaking the reality of the simulation. Moving away from a design project to an analytical project, the focus shifts from the architectural material itself to your interpretation of that material. For education, this would mean a shift towards research.

CW That's right, but a special kind of research. As a matter of fact, plan analysis shouldn't really be seen as research. Research proper is the next stage, the so-called architectural study: how do you interpret the brief with the knowledge at your disposal? People working on their graduation projects often start with typological, morphological and historical research. Six months on they produce the results and think they're done, whereas nothing has actually happened yet. They are unable to link the results of the research to their own design capacities. They don't see the point; they think it is just an exercise. In short, they are unable to formulate objectives that may generate research results that are useful to the design process.

JM What's worse, they often identify stipulations in order to achieve some kind of link between research and design. So they might say that the urban environment stipulates a particular building height. You end up with the most peculiar choices.

CW The research ends up legitimising the solution. Because the objectives are not made explicit, the research becomes normative. A contrast within the urban planning context, for instance, is always valued less than a perfect fit.

THEORY: INDIVIDUALISM AND HANDBOOKS

OASE We have talked about knowledge of buildings and the significance of theory. We are talking here about the way architectural material is organised in handbooks. Looking at the tradition of handbooks now it seems fair to say that the past 50 years have not produced any new handbooks, unless you would want to describe books such as Neufert[2] and the *New Metric Handbook*[3] as such.

JM No, excellent as they are, they are certainly not handbooks. Handbooks are about more than just data and measures. But what I do see as an architectural handbook is something like *Architecturalia* by Oud.[4] It does not feature a single drawing. The account sort of ambles from one detail to the next. Oud identifies the important issues and the level at which he makes decisions. A good example would be the staggered cornice at the curve in his housing project in Hoek van Holland. In his book, Oud describes the reasons for this staggered feature in very precise terms.

It is significant that Oud uses language rather than a drawing to explain such an architectural feature. It is the problem of individuality. Lacking the requisite resources, he cannot generalise the solution at that point. However, a detailed study of the old handbooks would provide plenty of formal resources. Explanation need not be verbal, as in Oud's case.

Modern architecture has done little to develop a terminology. For instance, Oud himself does not speak of a 'cornice' but of 'eaves'. When all you have are verbal resources you can only describe things literally. The word cornice opens up more possibilities. As a concept, independent of its historical connotations, it can offer a range of solutions.

This, then, is the importance of theory: the right word at the right time, allowing a solution to be seen in a wider context, as

2 Ernst Neufert, *Architects' Data* (London, 1970), originally published as *Bauentwurfslehre. Handbuch für den Baufachmann, Bauherren, Lehrenden und Lernenden* in 1936.

3 David Adler (ed.), *New Metric Handbook: Planning and Design Data* (Burlington, MA, 1979).

4 J.J.P. Oud, *Architecturalia voor bouwheren en architecten* (The Hague, 1963).

more than a particular solution at a particular time. Otherwise you end up with the problem that a design by Oud is considered to be important, without anyone knowing why. People will end up seeing it as an individual solution, which of course it is not.

CW It is indeed peculiar that modern architecture has failed to develop a higher level of abstraction. Insofar as there are any modern architecture handbooks they refer to solutions by individual architects. So you might say: I made a Dudok door or Duiker eaves.

But the old handbooks do use terminology. There are different names for rows of five columns and rows of six. Such terminology is lacking in modern architecture, forcing us to resort to descriptions. Talking about architecture has thus become quite a laborious process.

The situation is different in music. You have the same terminology at your disposal whether you are discussing a piece by Stockhausen or one by Strauss.

Likewise, the absence of a conceptual framework is a serious problem in education.

JM Modern architecture refused to use the term cornice for eaves. All the old concepts were originally conceived and introduced because people were aiming for a single style, with set rules. Modern architecture abandoned this practice, which created a greater degree of individuality, and hence more freedom of choice. That is what Oud came up against. In my opinion, however, Oud's eaves can definitely be described as a cornice.

CW In education, the absence of a conceptual framework results in a kind of Montessori system. But I do not see why we cannot have a regular approach, you know, one that uses books.

JM And in that case it is not about reading one book and applying it. If you did that, any random book would do. There are so many different architectural theories that it would be much more interesting to teach why a particular book is significant. Schinkel's *Lehrbuch* is significant because it indicates, using a particular style of drawing, why a solution is or isn't good. When you are thinking about a particular architectural element – a column, say – you need to know it was Schinkel who formulated this particular approach to the problem. And that he did so in words as well as in drawings.

The style book is important, since it organises the architectural material in a particular way. It is not a question of applying all of these styles. That would be impossible, because far too expensive. So architecture theory is not just any old book, it is a whole series of books and their documentation of schematic plans and principles of organisation. But there is no need to start with Vitrivius, before moving on to Alberti and Palladio, and so on. That would be rather demoralising, I think. You need to understand the underlying ideas in all of these books, so you can extend the sequence to *Delirious New York*. It is disgraceful that these books are not used in education. Tzonis uses some, but he takes a formalist approach.

CW There is no tradition of using handbooks – that is the problem. Before you know it, you stand accused of plagiarism. A lack of proper understanding also encourages copying. One of my final-year students is interested in Loos but is incapable of moving beyond Loos. Students often find it difficult to digest other architects' work.

OASE So the crux is an understanding of the architectural material, defined as the sum total of drawn, written and constructed material. The next step is adopting a particular position vis-à-vis that material.

JM . . . being able to determine.

OASE Of course there is always a certain implicit relationship vis-à-vis the architectural material. But it looks as if you reject such subconscious position-taking.

CW In education, yes, where it is not very productive because you cannot talk about it. If you cannot identify relationships with other things – whose merits we know – it becomes virtually impossible to talk about the work. You end up talking bullshit about whether the room is too big or too small. In fact, that is how most designs are explained. Here's the entrance, there's the exit. We are not presented with a story about the design, about the illustrations.

OASE So this is the big gaping hole?

JM / CW Absolutely. The huge gaping hole.

OASE Does this answer the question 'how do you learn to build'?

JM You learn to build from being able to use handbooks.

ARCHITECTURE: THE CURRENT SITUATION

OASE Does this also answer the question 'how do you learn about architecture'?

CW Joost once said that architecture is not a qualitative concept. Architecture constitutes the cultural dimension of buildings. You can teach someone how to construct buildings. Architecture is a continuation of this process.

JM I see architecture, first and foremost, as a discipline that is taught and practiced at an academic institution. Delft is not the only such institution, there are many more. In that respect the situation is not dissimilar to other disciplines. You know what others, such as Colin Rowe, Peter Eisenman and John Hedjuk, are doing. Taking this as your starting point, you put together a programme. And – coming back to the current situation – this programme could or should then make a contribution to the field as a whole.

Delft is of course not the only place providing architectural education. There is the Cooper Union, the Staedelschule, the AA. You must aspire for your institution to have a certain standing among these as well. I believe it is fair to assume a certain degree of competition with other institutions. I think it should not be taken for granted that someone living in Rotterdam and wanting to study architecture will go to Delft. Why not Karlsruhe?

OASE The design school is one of a range of institutions that shape our architectural culture. The same happens in the media. How much influence do the media have?

JM I believe the schools still have the edge. At the end of the day this is where it all happens. The schools are extremely important for the evolution of ideas within the culture of architecture. And this process is not just driven by students, but also by lecturers. The media cannot show something unless it has actually been made. It was the same in the visual arts five years ago. All the innovative material came from the schools. It was plucked from the schools and displayed in the galleries, thus sidestepping the established arts institutions. Things have never been quite so extreme in architecture, but it comes close.

And then there is the issue of long-term opinion; the problem of oeuvre. The media have no say in this. It only emerges retrospectively. The process is so much slower. Initially, Oud received little appreciation, then a bit more, and now his star is slowly waning again, with Dudok the up-and-coming man. It results in a kind of constantly changing top ten. It all takes a really long time to crystallise. But that is not something you need to worry about now.

OASE If you are capable of clearly formulating objectives and one of those objectives is participating in architectural culture, then you should also be able to tackle the relevant problems and come up with the right designs.

JM Yes, but it is extremely difficult to get a proper sense of all of these aspects of architecture at the same time. A common experience in Eindhoven is that someone may be coming up with a new kind of architecture, but because he is unable to draw, it cannot be published. Everything must be in the right place.

Translated by Laura Vroomen

The somewhat overdramatic title 'Modernisme, catastrofe en openbaarheid' (Modernism, Catastrophe and the Public Realm) of René Boomkens' article in *OASE* 24 epitomises the brand of late twentieth-century social critique that analysed the relationships between urban settings, urban culture and politics. It was suffused with the critical ethos of the 1970s and turned its back on the urban politics of the 1980s and 1990s. These decades also gave rise to the much-talked-of postmodernism; a palette of positions that broke away from the supremacy of the CIAM doctrine. Robert Venturi's *Learning from Las Vegas* (1966) and Aldo Rossi's *L'architettura della città* (1972), offering a viable alternative cultural construction to modernism, were groundbreaking in this respect.

The public nature of the urban space formed the central theme of critical urban analysis. Much of the writing drew on the sociological theories of Hanna Arendt, Richard Sennet, Jane Jacobs and Alexander Mitscherlich and revolved around attempts to fathom and explain the function and effects of the social processes of group formation, identification, urban integration and segregation. It saw urban space as first and foremost a product of social practice and mental maps, resulting in a broad, overlapping palette of urban domains, occupying a space somewhere between public and private. While enabling personal and group identification, it also provides the basis for potential conflict.

During the 1970s, the debate on the influence of the built environment on human behaviour nearly triggered an existential crisis in the design disciplines – which were being 'eroded' by the social sciences. This was the context that prompted the urban policies of the 1980s and 1990s with their growing awareness of the competitive economic climate. The urban realm came to be defined in terms of investment, management, control and city marketing.

Boomkens' text epitomised the interventions championed by the critical intelligentsia with their debate on the course of urban politics. The article is scholarly, but strongly politicised. Both modernism and the CIAM legacy are put in the dock for having caused the alleged 'catastrophe' of the public nature of the urban realm and the heavily monitored city, stemming from a deep-rooted fear of the chaos of an everyday, urban reality. Under the headline of 'the new metropolitanism', the phenomenon of global city marketing is condemned, levelling particularly fierce criticism at the redevelopment of Kop van Zuid in Rotterdam.

However, the urban policies of those days effectively observed the unmistakable logic *behind* the cultural expression of modernism: the inevitable globalisation that modernism had merely provided with a fresh and distinct identity. The text is thus typical of a period in which modernism was written off in an audacious attempt to use this theoretical position to also regard the underlying cause of progressive globalisation as a political choice. However, in so doing it failed to consider the inevitability of the *experience of modernization*, in which – to quote Marshall Berman – *All That Is Solid Melts into Air.*

Willem Sulsters
Member of the editorial board
from *OASE* 22 to 43

Translated by Laura Vroomen

René Boomkens

MODERNISM, CATASTROPHE AND THE PUBLIC REALM

FIRST PUBLISHED IN *OASE* 24

During a visit to New York in the summer of 1988 I witnessed, both in person and through the media, the spectacular effect of two diametrically opposed forms of 'public life'. In the New York suburb of Yonkers, one of the countless, largely homogeneous communities that surround American cities, the predominantly white residents rose up en masse *in protest of a decision by the state of New York to build low-income housing in their community. The planned apartment complex was sure to attract poorer (read: black) tenants. Tensions were running high and eventually the courts had to be called in to settle the dispute. If I understood correctly, the city council and the municipal officials were slapped with an injunction.*

In his 1977 book The Fall of Public Man *the American theoretician Richard Sennett describes a similar case of a deeply homogeneous suburban community revealing itself to be a defensive, inward-looking mechanism, bent on excluding 'strange blood' from its midst. 'Community becomes uncivilised' is the unambiguous title of the relevant chapter. In a situation like the one in question, public life in these kinds of suburban communities takes on a highly destructive character or, to put it differently: the public realm is turned against its own laws and rules.*

The other manifestation of public life occurred in the heart of Manhattan, in and around Tompkins Square in the East Village, a small park that doubled as a refuge for many of the city's homeless. In the middle of the hot summer of 1988, Mayor Ed Koch decided to close the park at night – except, oddly enough, for the homeless, who 'belonged' there. The park had become a meeting place for anarchist punks, heavy metal enthusiasts and neighbourhood activists who disturbed the slumber of the people living in the surrounding area. The latter group, which was relatively new to the area, consisted mainly of young professionals who were paying a great deal of money to rent recently restored apartments that had previously been occupied by junkies, squatters and vagrants. In other words, the East Village was undergoing a process of gentrification. Koch's decision led to a brutal police crack-down and outright urban warfare. And since several yuppies were on hand with sophisticated video cameras to record the event for posterity, the rest of the city could watch the battle between the punks and the police from the privacy of their homes. After that tumultuous night Koch rescinded his decision for the remainder of the summer.

Whatever one may think of the controversy, the situation in Tompkins Square is fundamentally different from the one in Yonkers. The former was a complex public sphere in which a wide variety of interests and needs were at stake. There were upper middle class yuppies, artists, the homeless, anarchists, poor blacks, young white activists, students, Hispanic groups, Asian shopkeepers and tourists: every one of them was involved in some way in both the decision-making process and the dispute about who should have access to the park. In contrast to the conflict in Yonkers, the situation in downtown Manhattan was far from predictable. In Yonkers it was a community pitted against the state and the courts, while in the East Village, by contrast, the controversy centred on a highly unpredictable, variable and diverse public sphere, in which a riotous police operation ended up backfiring on the authorities. It is questionable who the real winners were and what that victory was worth.

This article is about the public realm in an urban context. This public realm includes more than just public spaces, as I hope should be clear. And yet, as I will argue, those urban public spaces form an indispensable element of the structure and viability of the public realm as such. The question before us now is how the urban public realm has evolved over the past century. I will attempt to answer that question by way of a critique of the twentieth century modernist attitude towards urban development and urbanism. The concept of catastrophe will play a prominent part in that critique. At the conclusion of the article, my arguments will be applied to a commentary on the new metropolitanism that seems to have captured the imagination of municipal officials and urban planners in Amsterdam and Rotterdam, and elsewhere.

My central thesis is as follows: twentieth-century modernism conceives of itself as a response to a global catastrophe, but over the decades it is modernism itself that has proven to be a catastrophe. Or, to put it in different terms, modernism sees itself as a movement of universal communication, as a universalised public realm. Yet it revealed itself to be one of the greatest enemies of that realm.

CATASTROPHE

The myth of modernity confronts its audience with the idea they have somehow passed a point of no return. Modern people are confined within a linear model of time in which every human action only points in one direction: forward. Every relationship with the past seems to be either non-existent or disrupted. There are no traditions that can be experienced as meaningful aspects of present-day life. Modernity appears to be the result of a comprehensive, global break with not only traditional values, but also with the traditional concepts of time and space.

Tenacious though it may be, this myth is clearly ripe for demystification, if for no other reason than because it has long since lost the ability to give meaning to the practices and experiences of 'modern' individuals. Of course, this process of demystification has been going on for decades in the form of various debates on the crisis or deficit of avant-gardism in politics and the arts. But instead of revisiting the well-worn polemics directed against modernism or the Avant-Garde as such, I would like to address the diverse roots of the modernist tradition. Or, in the words of Walter Benjamin, the 'prehistory' of modernism, its infancy as it were.

The turn of the nineteenth century is often regarded as the start of modernity, with the French Revolution as its glorious opening salvo. But in that same nineteenth century we find highly divergent interpretations of the roots of modern life. Running counter to the triumphant image of enlightenment and revolution is a current of thought that distrusts the very triumphalism that had accompanied the break with tradition: Romanticism, a modernist movement par excellence. Not in the glorious sense of the myth of modernity, but as a movement preoccupied with what might be termed problematic individuality or, alternatively, the problem of the individual. One of its chief preoccupations is the inner processes of the psyche of a lost, isolated and guilty subject. It focuses on the patterns of a private discourse which, in many respects, supersedes the safe and familiar discourse of the traditional community. In that sense Romanticism can be seen as the first artistic and philosophical reflection on the modern individual's experience as an inhabitant of the modern town or city.

This is even more true of the decadent movement of the second half of the nineteenth century, which in many respects pursues and radicalises themes that had first been brought to the fore by the Romantics. As with the Romantics, the attitude towards the city espoused by the decadent poets and writers was at best ambivalent and occasionally downright antagonistic. More so than during the Romantic period, an attempt was being made to accept the new conditions of urban life and examine them as opportunities for a new, 'modern' way of life. The latter issue – the question of what form this new way of life should take – should be seen as the central problem of the decadent poets. Their literary experiments were also lifestyle experiments. This is plainly the case with a figure like Baudelaire, whose definition of modernity as 'the transient, the fleeting and the contingent' has since become classic. Here we also see the roots of the ambivalence mentioned above: the question was how a modern, urban individual could capture and maintain an identity in the light of the realisation that everything that could serve that end was, by definition, fleeting and contingent. Ambivalence: the state of being adrift among the modern masses, reliant on one's own deeply private thoughts and experiences, an enduring social and psychological instability.

The typical nineteenth-century themes, such as the problematic individual, the transience of social and private identity, the isolation in the midst of the modern, urban crowds, resonate well into the 1980s. Nineteenth-century modernism has remained current. But in order to understand 'our' late twentieth-century modernity, we are missing one experience that would change the face of twentieth-century modernism: the experience (or myth) of catastrophe.

Jürgen Habermas defined modernity (and with it modernism) as the condition or movement that is compelled to derive its standards and values from itself, from the process of modernisation and modernity. Under such a system, an appeal to any form of tradition becomes impossible. Habermas neglected to say where this compulsion originated. One is struck by the crucial difference between the nineteenth-century modernists and their twentieth-century successors on this question. Marshall Berman has already pointed out this disjuncture in his *All That Is Solid Melts into Air*. The nineteenth-century ambivalence betrays a still vital contact with premodern ways of life and with 'tradition' as such. The twentieth-century modernist avant-garde, by contrast, seems to derive its self-image from the belief that it bears the responsibility for designing and building an entirely new world after the old one has met a catastrophic end. Any productive ties to traditional ways of life and experiences seem to have been severed. Ambivalence has been supplanted by schizophrenia. To paraphrase Berman, modernism has split into two: on the one hand pessimism and the apocalyptic undertones of much of modernist philosophy and litera-

ture (from the German expressionists to Adorno) and, on the other, optimism and constructivism – in film, in the International Style in architecture, in the work of the futurists, etcetera.

Similarly, factors like industrialisation, capitalism and the First World War played a role in the process by which the notion (and the experience) of catastrophe – a disastrous, but more importantly, irrevocable break with the past – is given a central and constitutive place in the development of the modernist avant-garde. In a sense this concept of catastrophe destroys the empathetic character of modernity: we are no longer part of it. Rather, it manifests itself as an autonomous process, an anonymous destiny. From that point on, the modernist presented himself as someone whose task was to point the way to the future, riding the waves of fate and not looking back. There is still only one direction open to us: forward, but this time without the spontaneous commitment that typified nineteenth-century modernism. Rather, there is a tendency among some to resign themselves to a destiny of permanent change, modernisation and revolution. And if we can speak of optimism, of the variety that permeates the manifestoes of Bauhaus and CIAM, it is an austere, strict, Calvinistic brand of optimism. Charles Jencks described the modernist movement in architecture as a Protestant revolution, which abandoned the ornamentation, symbolism and the narrative force of traditional forms. They were all replaced by a rigorously formal and functionalist brand of architecture and urban planning, which was essentially already a blueprint for an entirely new, modern social order. This new order envisioned a society that would be built on rational foundations, with the help of the latest technology, and ruled by a political system rooted in scientific principles.

That society was not to be, but its architecture took hold and eventually became dominant. No longer as a social blueprint, but primarily as a formula, a cheap way of building, a cheap way of creating a stir: anonymous, inward-looking and arrogant. And thus functionalism, formalism and prefabrication became goals in themselves, especially during the massive reconstruction necessitated by the next catastrophe.

THE PUBLIC REALM AND PUBLIC SPACE

Let me begin by reiterating what might be called the ideal definition of the public realm, courtesy of Hannah Arendt in her book, *The Human Condition*. The 'ideal' public realm and the 'ideal' public space could be found, in Arendt's view, in the ancient Greek *polis* (city-state). The activities of the

polis existed in opposition to the practices of the private sphere, the latter being dominated by matters like (economic) necessity, self-preservation, and the need to care for and feed one's family and humanity as such. In the public realm of the polis, by contrast, everything revolved around 'speech as a way of persuasion' (page 26). 'To be political, to live in a polis, meant that everything was decided through words and persuasion and not through force and violence' (Ibid.). The public realm was preoccupied with issues that lay outside the sphere of material necessities. Here a citizen could form his opinions without the pressure of brute necessity.

Arendt's definition is important because it embraces four different elements, which have remained crucial to the modern history of the public realm:

- first of all, the thesis that the public sphere exists in opposition to the private sphere as the domain of free will (voluntarism) exists in opposition to the domain of (economic) necessity;
- secondly, the emphasis on the essentially *practical* character of the public sphere (with speech as a central feature);
- thirdly, the fundamentally *open* character of the public realm, which is not bound to any system. The public realm is certainly not coterminous with the world of organised politics or that of the State (whether democratic or otherwise), and it has nothing to do with formalised notions of freedom or equality;
- fourthly, the spatial aspect of the public sphere. This last point is critical. Only in highly concentrated and diversified spatial situations is it possible to achieve the kind of communication that is the hallmark of modern, pluralist societies.

Berlin, Anhalter Bahnhof

The agora, the marketplace, the major town squares, the coffeehouses, the parks – these were the traditional urban spaces in which public life was acted out. With the rise of new means of communication the situation changed dramatically. Newspapers, the telephone, radio and television did not only affect the quantity and availability of information, they also implied a change in the subject of the public discourse. It is even conceivable that the new media blocked the public realm as such. Yet this means that the media are not identical to the public realm; they remain media: resources that exist for the use of the public realm, or resources that ultimately turn against it. They cannot replace it.

In the aforementioned book, *The Fall of Public Man*, Richard Sennett examines the development of the public sphere in modern European cities from the eighteenth century onward. Like Arendt, Sennett regards the urban public realm as a central feature of and a prerequisite for democratic, pluralist societies. More than that, it is the prerequisite for an open and experimental lifestyle. The urban and practical dimensions of the public sphere are fundamentally important to Sennett as well. As it is used here, 'urbanity' signifies a concentrated, diverse and even somewhat anarchistic and dangerous lifestyle, while the 'practical dimension' denotes a public realm that exists as an unlimited series of acts (especially linguistic acts), lifestyles and cultures. Sennett describes eighteenth-century urbanity as the stage of a theatre: the public sphere offered the opportunity to put on a refined and civilised 'performance' with various masks and roles. Public life was a play of *presentations* in which masks and roles liberated the individual from the world of necessity and 'nature', which formed the heart of the private sphere. Public, urban life played a civilising role with respect to the 'lower' sphere of private life.

The story of *The Fall of the Public Man* is the story of the decline of this theatrical and 'civilised' urban public life. In the nineteenth century Sennett discerns the advent of a new culture of intimacy. Together, capitalism and secularism fostered the belief that individuals could derive their identities from (and manifest those identities in) the world of material objects with which they surrounded themselves. The belief in a transcendent order gave way to an immanent order, which centred on the inner emotions of the individual. Earlier, I referred to the Romantic movement as an example of this concentration on the problematic inner self of the modern individual. From Sennett's perspective the Romantic movement is a good example of the transition from an era of the public man – who was outward-looking and proud of his refined manners – to that of a new, inward-looking private man, who became immersed in the turmoil of his intimate life. Public life became the arena where the *re-presentation* of the personality's inner essence was played out; all manner of external traits – objects, clothing, make-up – suddenly became psychological symbols.

It was not until the present century that this new culture of intimacy began to spread in earnest, eventually becoming – in Sennett's view – the greatest enemy of public life: an entire society permanently tyrannised by a mad quest for a deeper essence, for true passions, for the hidden secrets of the navel-gazing, 'authentic' individual.

Sennett's historical criticism of nineteenth- and twentieth-century urban culture should be seen as a polemic attack on prevailing notions of urbanity and urban planning. On occasion he exaggerates the level of the intimist tyranny for the sake of argument. More important for our purposes here is

New York, 42nd Street

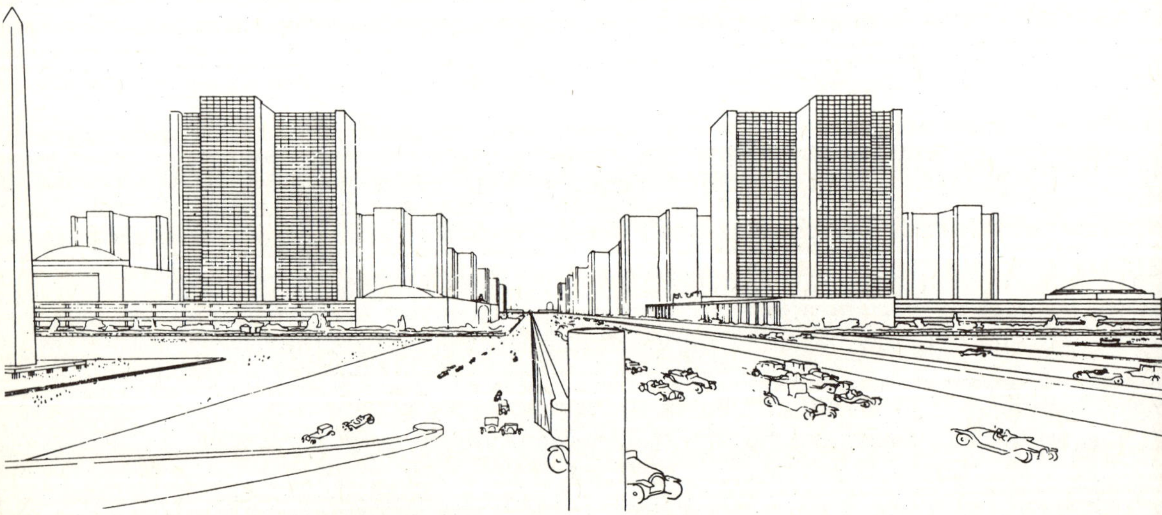

Le Corbusier, city for three million inhabitants, 1922

the fact that the urban planning and modernist architecture of the twentieth century can indeed be analysed (and criticised) quite adequately. They are shown to be an instrument for the defence of an inward-looking culture of intimacy against the dangers and shocks of the urban public realm.

This becomes all the more clear when we combine Sennett's analysis with the research done by the British-Israeli criminologist Stanley Cohen. In his *Visions of Social Control*, Cohen puts a radical spin on Sennetts' thesis of the anti-urban attitude of modern urban development and urban planning in his fascinating overview of the significance of the 'city' as metaphor. Cohen, too, identifies the fundamental anxiety about urban life as the most important source of inspiration for the projects of the nineteenth- and twentieth-century urban planners and developers. In their eyes, cities were places dominated by the rationality of the market, where impersonal relationships, segmentation, deprivation and above all disorder reigned supreme. The answer to this put forward by the modern urban planners was less modern than expected. The views on urbanity held by the modernists and their contemporaries were anything but an absolute break with the past. On the contrary, they consisted of a combination of pre-modern, traditional social ideas with a deep-seated belief in the problem-solving power of modern technology and modern materials. From the theories of Ebenezer Howard to the grand visions of Le Corbusier we can observe an infusion of a pre-modern ideal of agrarian community life into the disarray of urban public life. It is plainly not a struggle against tradition, though it is a fight against the dangers and the unpredictability of public life in the city streets. Vertical construction reduced the dangers of the street while simultaneously providing a solution for the shortage of space. Zoning laws aimed to functionalise the various urban activities, stimulating a clearer organisation and control of urban life as such. Suburbanisation achieved the dream of a safe and intimate community life of isolated monads, at once close to and far away from the dangers of the inner city. Crowning this urban blueprint is the creation of 'zones of neglect', areas of the inner city that were deliberately abandoned, thereby giving rise to a home for the homeless and a semi-legal netherworld where drug dealers and petty criminals can ply their trade. The Zeedijk in Amsterdam is an example of just such a zone.

In the outskirts of the city or suburbs Cohen suggests that we can see an afterimage of the cleansed community, the model that was used in the fight against leprosy in the Middle Ages. It is his contention that the zoning of urban life grew out of strategies that had been employed against the

St. Louis, demolition of Pruit-Igoe, 1971

plague. Segmentation, diffusion, classification and various forms of statistical and social research all helped control this lethal epidemic. Together, these measures form the ideal of a disciplined, mechanically organised and monitored society that is supposed to be capable of holding the plague of the urban public realm in check and keeping its lepers at a distance.

In early twentieth-century modernism, these notions of a cleansed community and disciplined society were still subordinate to an overarching vision of social progress or indeed of utopia. After the Second World War, by contrast, this politics which drew its motivation from a fear of the city became imbued with an air of crisis and decay. This laid the foundation for a politics centred on societal blueprints that aimed to achieve a systematised social order. While the critique of the countless blind spots of modernist functionalism is already some 30 years old, few attempts are made, even now, to cure the ill by seeking out its causes. I think we need to seek the virus in the intellectual heritage of modernistic planning and urban development itself: the permanent fear of the uncontrollable effects of urban public life as such.

AN URBAN ROMANTICISM

The mechanistic models and theories of our modernistic predecessors and contemporaries are now the history of *our* present day. But were the modernists cognizant of *their* own history? I don't think so. The modernists took catastrophe (whether real or metaphorical) as their starting point. Their politics aimed to build a 'future' out of nothing; to create, in other words, an utterly new, perfectly homogeneous, modern space. What was forgotten in the process was the anxiety that lay at the foundation of those politics. On the other side of the catastrophe we recognise the ambivalent roots of modernism in the Romantic and decadent movements. Romanticism articulated a non-rationalist view of the newborn modern individual. It offered a fresh and typically modern take on the relationship between man and nature, expressing for the first time the modern city-dweller's 'alienation' from the natural world. Typically modern and urban themes like the isolation of the individual and the ironic distance of the intellect play an important role in the work of authors like Goethe, Schlegel and Schiller.

And then came the decadents who integrated isolation and irony into a conscious politics within the urban domain: the dandy and the *flaneur* form new urban identities in which the problematic individual is combined with the public personality who puts himself 'on display' and thus wants to be seen (while simultaneously remaining part of the anonymous urban crowd). In their public strategies we encounter an experimental politics of lifestyles, a politics concerned with shaping the new, urban identities into new modes of living with the open and disorienting character of modern urban life. Without a doubt, these are strategies that refine Sennett's one-sided representation of an urbanity that is falling ever more under the sway of intimacy. Perhaps it is in the decadent movement (and principally in the work of Baudelaire) that we first come across the realisation that the foundation of 'modern life' and the 'modern identity' lies in the knowledge that there can be no such foundation. A true measure of progress would be to succeed in translating this realisation into a politics that sees nothing catastrophic about it. History is crucial to this type of vision. Not as a supplier of a forgotten origin or essence but as a Nietzschean wardrobe: history as a collection of costumes, from which modern individuals can draw inspiration for new articles of clothing. Maybe none of those costumes will fit us, as Nietzsche thought, and we will look even more ridiculous in them than we do already. But at the end of the day, this is no reason to stay undressed. Yet in the view of twentieth-century modernism, this was not only possible but also necessary: the time for dressing up was over. We needed to get back to reality. But what that reality might be – apart from a 'naked reality' – has remained unclear to the present day.

Am I then trying to suggest that a new Romanticism or a revitalised *décadence* could undo 60 years spent denying the public space and the public sphere? No. In pointing out the significance of Romanticism and *décadence*, I am merely trying to point out that our views on urbanity and the public realm, and indeed on the modern identity, cannot be complete if we are unable to see beyond twentieth-century modernism. What is more, such a limited frame of reference severely distorts these views. Over the course of the twentieth century, the public sphere came to be understood increasingly as the effect of a planned system of urban order. Conversely, in the Romantic philosophy and under influence of the decadents, the public sphere was seen as a *practice*, as a network of heterogeneous activities, possibly as a series of conflicts and fights. In this connection I would refer to my earlier remarks about Arendt's notion of the public realm. The relationship between the individual (as a consumer, an intellect, a creator) and his or her surroundings was also defined differently in the nineteenth century than it was by the twentieth-century modernists. For the latter group, those surroundings were little more than the material upon which rational and creative intellects could project their blueprints. For the nineteenth-century modernist (whether Romantic or decadent), those surroundings were something with which to cultivate an internal relationship. The question of whether or not an individual felt at home there was crucial for his or her creative or intellectual attitude to those surroundings. In my view it is this very notion of the creative intellect *as a participant in* the urban public sphere that is indispensable when we attempt to take a position on the current debates on urban renewal, urban development and the use and organisation of public space.

THE NEW METROPOLITANISM

Finally, I would like to take a brief look at some recent trends in urban development, in the light of the foregoing. For the past several years it has been possible to speak of a reassessment of the city, a revival of the metropolis. In the stories told by the new enthusiasts of big-city life, we hear the first echoes of a new voluntarism: we can change, we should change, we have the will to do things differently. It would seem as if we're out to rediscover the city! But a glance at the plans and projects, the background to this re-advertised urban space, suggests otherwise.

A few years ago the municipality of Amsterdam launched a promotional campaign explicitly aimed at the city's own residents. The main slogan was *Amsterdam heeft 't* (Amsterdam's got it). The poster designed to go with this slogan is well-known: the second 'a' of Amsterdam has been replaced by a smiley-face in the shape of a step-gabled house. This banal and self-congratulatory approach was greeted almost immediately by ironic commentary from a variety of quarters. Some 'distorted' the slogan to call

New York, South Street Seaport

Teun Koolhaas, Kop van Zuid, 1987

attention to a range of urban ills. The slogan was also used to spotlight certain urban lifestyles that the municipality may not have been so keen to advertise, such as the city's lively gay subculture (which has actually been quite beneficial, from an economic perspective). With thinly disguised jealousy, Rotterdam countered with *Amsterdam heeft 't, Rotterdam maakt 't* (Amsterdam's got it, Rotterdam makes it), a nod to its own identity as a working-class town. The smiling house should have warned us. It can be seen as the essence of the new metropolitan attitude: the city as *façade*, as merchandise on display.

In one respect we can speak of a step forward with respect to the functionalist notion of the modernist city-dwellers: people are apparently coming to the realisation that the urban space is actually being used, and not merely as a route from building A to building B, or from function X to function Y. But the community of users or consumers is a different one from what had been suggested. This reveals the more germane interpretation of the grinning façade. The new metropolitanism attempts to create scope for a growing tourist market and, in more general terms, for a community of 'temporary' and highly selective users. This applies to all those cities that have lost their original economic functions, particularly ports like New York, London, Baltimore, Amsterdam and Rotterdam. All those cities are discovering new possibilities for their waterfronts, and along all those waterfronts the same three-masters will complete the picture of the metropolitan appeal of these cities.

Behind the new voluntarism of the urban planners, a pattern can be discerned in the plans and programmes they devise. In the various programmes for Rotterdam, we read about economic necessity and inevitable choices. But inevitable choices are not choices at all. In other words we find ourselves shunted back to the domain of the catastrophe. If we can't agree to do the following, then . . . and so forth. This 'inevitable choice' in favour of a new urban economy is connected to two other elements.

First of all there is the overriding preoccupation with the visual dimension of the urban space, which we encounter time and again. It's about giving the 'old' urban centres a new status, a new face. This is not meant as a historic reappraisal of the facelessness of modernistic architecture, or as an ironic commentary on the movement to redesign those centres, but rather as a deadly serious affirmation of midtown Manhattan as the *nec plus ultra* of urban development. 'A city should look like a city' appears to be the underlying thinking, and what else could this signify but a skyline?

Behind the magnificent skyline, however, is the everyday reality of those who live and work in the centre. We now know that new buildings in the 'City' must be attractive and high-grade, that the city should offer a 'metropolitan ambiance' and an 'alluring' public space for the millions of tourists and businesspeople. The plans also have something to offer for the city-dwellers themselves. Metropolitanism should be combined with 'hospitability' (the term is not mine). In the case of Rotterdam, this means 'attractive' residential building in a beautiful setting, for old and new categories of residents alike. Small households end up in the city centre, while new suburbs are built for middle class families (since that was where they were living already). And just to be a bit daring, we mix those two groups together in the area called *Kop van Zuid* (see *Vernieuwing van Rotterdam* [Renewing Rotterdam]).

The metropolitanism of the 1980s consists of three elements: tourist appeal, visual presentation, hospitability ('there's no place like home').

In Rotterdam these concepts go hand in hand with the unavoidable idea of the city's forward-thinking dynamism. 'The future has a future in Rotterdam,' to quote the ironic commentary of poet Jules Deelder in a book on urban renewal in that city. But that classic dynamism will vanish with the disappearance of traditional economic functions, a fact that is only emphasised in the plans for a railway tunnel. The new dynamism will be much less visible.

The new metropolitanism is neither a rethinking of the role and significance of the urban public realm, nor a refusal to prolong a failing modernism in architecture and urban planning. Rotterdam was rebuilt after a genuine catastrophe, and there are few who would regard that reconstruction project as a success. Yet the dynamism remains. It pains me to say so, but the current plans to give Rotterdam a new, metropolitan look are suspiciously similar to comparable plans for the centre of Amsterdam. They include a museum for the twenty-first century, 'high-grade' housing and offices, a greater 'density', a greater appeal . . . all of which is doubtless both necessary and inevitable. Yet when politicians or urban planners talk of necessity and inevitability, you can bet that at least one inevitability will always be overlooked. If we momentarily forget the façade of an excessively cautious, accommodating and occasionally dowdy ('hospitable') metropolis the size of Amsterdam or Rotterdam, we are faced with a very different kind of inevitability. Without optimism or voluntarism, I would like to point out the inevitably *practical* character of all urbanity: practices engaged in by city-dwellers and 'users' of the urban space. Tourists are consumers of urban space; they are not city-dwellers. Indeed, their practices are oriented towards the façade of the city, its visual qualities, its appeal.

The practices of the residents, by contrast, are directed at more than just the visual dimension of the city (though the visual aspects do form an obvious background, in a sense). Walter Benjamin once referred to the tactile qualities of architecture, of one's surroundings as such. These qualities do not require a conscious, intentional gaze; rather, they exist for the casual glance of people who use 'their' city day in, day out – qualities that evoke a sense of being at home without the explicit need to feel at home.

The soft-focus advertisement and the story of the happy city deny the inevitability of another aspect of the 'appeal' of city life: its *true* public sphere. In the movements and activities that take place in that public realm, in that space, traces can be found of the ongoing catastrophe of urban planning and urban social control. This sphere contains what could be called the 'sense of the possibility' (Robert Musil's *Möglishkeitssin*) of urban life. Here we find 'the impossibility' of urban policy, that which is permanently disclaimed by the façadism and the colour advertisements: an urban underclass, the homeless of New York, the junkies and long-term unemployed of Amsterdam or Rotterdam. But what is also overlooked is the unpredictable diversity of an 'open' urban realm. Politicians and planners regard all these things as problems, because they are resistant to control. But it goes beyond that: the original sin of modernism has returned, like a form of cancer, especially among planners, real estate developers and municipal administrators. The policy of order and control is becoming increasingly contaminated by the fear of an *internal* catastrophe, the fear that a surfeit of complexity will bring about the implosion of the entire machinery, the mechanism of surveillance and control, the happy (sub)urban family.

Ultimately, this demonstrates that the politicians and planners *and* the users of and participants in the urban public realm all share, to a certain extent, the experience of the possibility and reality of catastrophe. In the near future the debate in the public sphere will play out between the two extremes of a classic and quintessentially modernist fear of catastrophe and a more empathetic and pragmatic attitude, which sees catastrophe as something to be *survived* (as Benjamin suggested). The fact that we can survive catastrophes has already been proved by the history of Rotterdam. It must now be proved again.

Translated by Steve Leinbach

The winter of 1990 saw the publication of *OASE* double issue 26-27, bearing the slightly pretentious title: *his job is to bring about an IMAGINED ORDER, Aldo van Eyck*. As this longish title suggests, the entire issue was devoted to the work of Aldo van Eyck. Its editorial dwelled on the fact that a serious architectural critique of Van Eyck's oeuvre would be possible only by avoiding Van Eyck's person and by steering clear of his digressions on the 'human dimension' and 'poetic design'. That very same editorial indicated that the editorial board had set itself the momentous task of 'incorporating [Van Eyck's work] into the science of architecture', which up until that point had clearly not been possible. The issue addressed a range of topics, among them Van Eyck's approach to living, the journal *Forum*, CIAM, Otterlo 1959, his urban development work, Nagele and finally Joost Meuwissen on Van Eyck's private homes.

The inclusion of Joost Meuwissen was something of a surprise. He had been associated with the journal *Plan* and at the time of this publication he worked for the journal *Wiederhall*. Meuwissen had never shown any affinity with Aldo van Eyck's ideas or finished work in either of these two journals. *Wiederhall* had its heyday in the late 1980s. It had stressed its credentials as a platform for the kind of architecture that infuriated and terrified Van Eyck. Nor does it seem likely that *Wiederhall*'s editorial board, including the likes of Carel Weeber and Umbeto Barbieri, would have inspired much confidence in Van Eyck. In the late 1980s *Wiederhall* was a remarkably polished journal – seemingly the opposite of *OASE* in everything. It had a large, square layout, deliberately designed to prevent photocopying. In the first *Wiederhall* editorial Meuwissen wrote: 'I love architecture because it is old. In its treatises and manuals it has preserved a dead language up until now.'

Judging by his article Joost Meuwissen appears to have little affinity with Aldo van Eyck's work. The title should have read 'Joost in Aldo's Wonderland' rather than evoking an image of Aldo wandering around the catacombs of the giant oak, like some bewildered visitor.

Revelling in his own prose, Meuwissen whirls past Aldo's houses without discovering any real virtuosity. The article's title characterises Aldo van Eyck as a master who, in his homes, conjures with scale and ushers the users into a wondrous world of changing dimensions. At the same time, it also explicitly describes him as a giant stumbling blindly through the china cabinet of architecture.

The homes have a unique logic that is quite different from his public works, because here he does not put together façades. Instead the floor plan gives rise to the finished product. The façades have disappeared and the building derives meaning from its surroundings and the floor plan structure.

Meuwissen's article appears to imply that Van Eyck's homes, which up until that point had gone unnoticed and uncensored, show a weakness and ambiguity that may be more interesting than the meticulous and over-composed clarity of his public buildings. In fact, Meuwissen is carried away by them. The paradox of this article is that whereas Meuwissen wants to provide a dry, analytical description of Van Eyck's work, Van Eyck may ultimately have touched a chord in him. He thus concludes with the poetic image of Aldo van Eyck up in the tree like the invisible cat with the mysterious smile.

Juliette Bekkering
Member of the editorial board
from *OASE* 28 to 40

Translated by Laura Vroomen

Joost Meuwissen

ALDO IN WONDER-LAND

Remarks on the Houses of Aldo van Eyck

FIRST PUBLISHED IN *OASE* 26

Within Aldo van Eyck's body of work, residential buildings form neither a distinct category nor, by any means, a prominent one. Their role is modest. In surveys and other publications about his oeuvre, they are not usuallly presented as a separate group. In his architectural aesthetics, in word and image, Van Eyck does not make a categorical distinction between types of buildings. Each building is called home. His two largest public projects, the Burgerweeshuis and Moederhuis in Amsterdam (a home for orphans and a home for single mothers, respectively), both have a residential function. Van Eyck's aesthetics does include a theory of coming and going, though more of coming than of going – a theory of staying somewhere, of 'dwelling', but not a theory of residing or living somewhere in the strict sense. In the structure of this aesthetics, each work avoids stylistically refining the previous ones; instead, the objective is to 'merge prior experiences' into a rich awareness, and so each work acquires a characteristic tenor that is all its own, offering a truly new and different definition of architecture. Nevertheless, houses seem to have played but a small role in the reception of his oeuvre.[1] Perhaps the concept of architecture that they embodied was less timely, less historically compelling or less urban.

Van Eyck's houses are admired, to be sure, but not often discussed. I do not wish to change this situation radically. Rather, I would like to take their silent builtness and their abstract conceptualisation as a basis, and examine what they

1
The reception history of Aldo van Eyck's works is still too short for us to take any distance from it. For that reason, not much attention is paid here to the secondary literature of prior interpretations, despite the frictions between the hagiographic (Herzberger), empathetic (Strauven) and critical (De Heer, Barbieri) approaches. This article attempts to trace the definition of building, residing and thinking in the houses of Van Eyck, from an angle that is not so much deconstructionist as it is Deleuzian. This is because Gilles Deleuze has formulated more, and more global, descriptive categories, which can serve as keys to the interpretation of an aesthetic system, especially in *Différence et répétition* (Paris, 1968). Or at least, it seems to me that in this approach, the deconstructionist preoccupation with destroying dialectic and constructing equality is coupled with a possibility that has not yet been relinquished, the possibility that an aesthetic system is also thinkable. In this sense, the

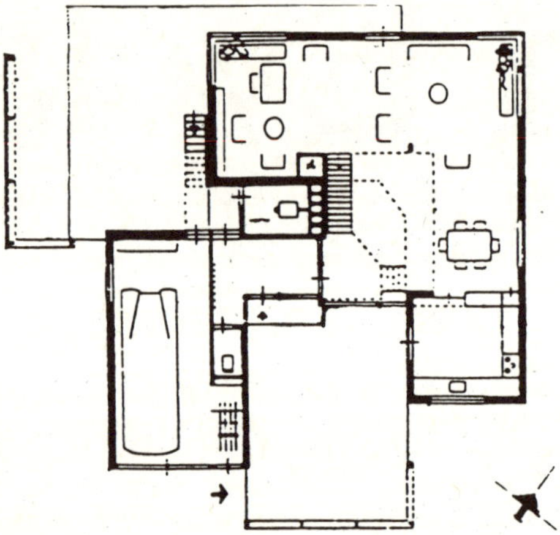

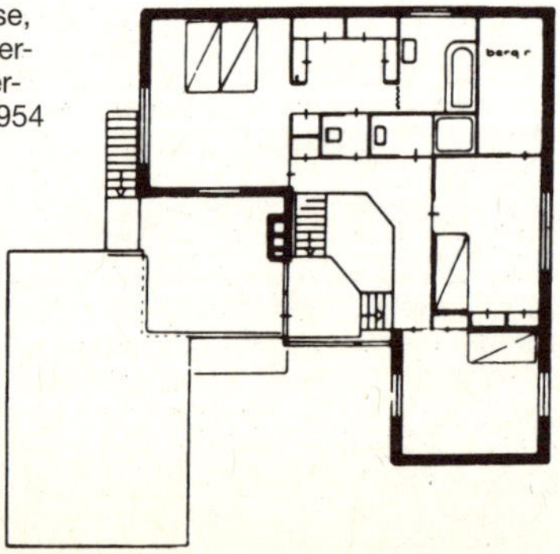

Jan Rietveld and Aldo van Eyck, floor plan of the Damme House, Herman Gorterstraat, Amsterdam, 1951-1954

Jan Rietveld and Aldo van Eyck, Damme House, Herman Gorterstraat, Amsterdam, 1951-1954

present to us from their modern condition, their passive voice – the same voice that speaks to us from the sparse design notes, like the hermetic poet Gerrit Achterberg, singing the praises of something unattainable. The only activity is that of things, the sun entering, the door opening: 'When the door opens, spring has truly arrived!'[2] Truly? Living in the house is waiting for the door to open at last. Deep inside the house, the prime numbers are keeping watch. The play of contrasts, in the larger-scale works, reaches its limit in literary content and ends with a resulting leap towards understanding – the Burgerweeshuis and Moederhuis are run-ups to such a leap. In the smaller-scale works, the monuments and pavilions, that same play of contrasts can – through the restriction of the means of expression – be celebrated directly, as an image: the sign, emblem or logo of an idealised working method. The difficulty is that this play of contrasts in Van Eyck's houses has neither a beginning nor an end. The mode of address is not the 'we' of the architect or the 'them' of the occupants, but reality itself. The game grows more fluid. There are no rules. In his houses, no connection can be made between height, breadth and depth. They threaten to escape not only his oeuvre, but architecture itself. Reality is not rescued there by a concept or image, but because it is indicated as outside. Accordingly, the inside – the interior – is devoid of representation; it is vacated; it creates an almost postmodern emptiness, posing a transcendental question – under what conditions is the play

Deleuzian categories are used here not in an applied manner but in a reconstructive one. If my approach must have a name, therefore, reconstructionism seems most suitable.

2
Jan Rietveld and Aldo van Eyck, 'Huis aan de Herman Gorterstraat te Amsterdam', *Forum*, 1956, 118, 119.

Jan Rietveld and Aldo van Eyck, Damme House, Herman Gorterstraat, Amsterdam, 1951-1954

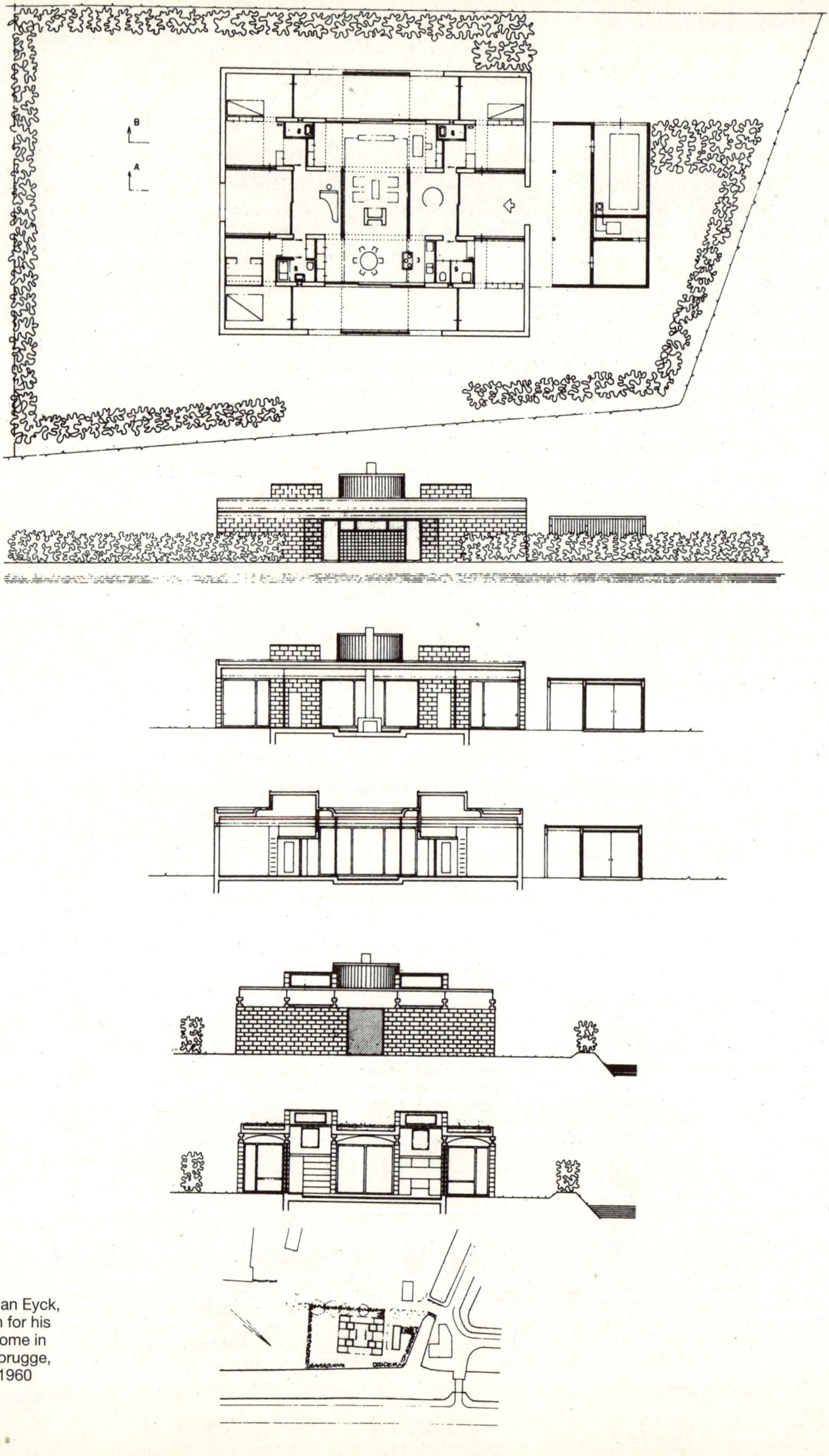

Aldo van Eyck, design for his own home in Baambrugge, 1958-1960

of contrasts possible? – and answering that question by building, by erecting an almost unbridled elevation.

TWISTS

Not that the houses have very different twists than the other works. The entrance recessed deeply into the house, the bayonet reflection in the floor plan, the dominant cornice, the bubbling domes on the roof, or the aggregation of rooms around a larger space, the tectonics of the elevation – these features appear in all his works. But their point differs. For instance, the bayonet reflection in the houses is developed only in one direction, and not in multiple ones. To put it differently, an orthogonal bayonet reflection can prompt a diagonal one on a different scale,[3] but the two are not united in a single system of their own, unlike in the larger-scale projects, such as the Burgerweeshuis, or the design for the cultural centre in Jerusalem, where bayonet reflection seems to be used both lengthwise and breadthwise, occasioning a system of swastikas that aims to unite part and whole within itself and thus achieves its effects through the medium of scale.[4] In the houses, the reflections are more likely to assign a central role to space – or emptiness – than to scale.

Something similar is true of the deeply recessed entrance, which results in the absence of some formal element of the house: the hallway, the courtyard, the separate circulation space, which in the larger works seem to function precisely as an aggregate, as a larger-scale element – at least in the floor plan.[5] In this respect, again, the houses indicate an informal centre to which the smaller rooms will not, in fact, relate in terms of scale. But is this a loss? At first sight, it seems to be experienced as one. The building is too small, as it were, to formalise the complex relations, and so those relations remain informal, like the very experience of living in the house. The hall is absent but, perhaps for that reason, is placed on the upper floor in the houses in Amsterdam and Venlo. But once it is there, is it still because it is missing on the ground floor? In fact, the hall is opened up, by means of one or two voids, opening both outwardly on the upper floor and towards the ground floor. It becomes the central tectonic element, finally indicating that the upper floor is an extension of the ground floor – not merely a second level, but an element in the structure of the house. Here, the hall is not an element of the floor plan and its problem of scale as it attempts to interpret the architecture on the theoretically infinite plane of the earth. It is a tectonic element that indicates the elevation of the house or, rather, suggests that the house is an elevation.

While in the larger projects the twists are necessities, complex and seemingly interlinked and having a function related to scale – a function that is therefore literary and laden with meaning – the serious play of the houses, the elevation erected indoors, requires only one scale. Consequently, the houses

3
Because they indicate different contents, namely inside and outside, I speak of a different scale, although the proportional system does not actually differ.

4
In a recent exchange with Jan de Heer, Johan van de Beek refers to the self-contained compositional quality of these buildings, which have a component structure but whose components never become a model of an infinite structure: 'Een ingezonden brief naar aanleiding van het centrumloze labyrinth: Gerrit Rietveld en de stedebouw', *OASE* 25, 1989, 22, 23: 'In the work of Van Eyck, the point is to use the turbine (swastika) in such a way that it creates a composition corresponding to the size of the particular project. It never becomes a fragment as a model for a theoretically infinite structure. The composition is not acentric, but polycentric. Its dynamics are sometimes kept in balance through a countermovement by a swastika of a different kind . . . Van Eyck creates a specific relationship between the designed composition and the given context, often by leaving one arm of the swastika open to the environment'. But this is not the point at all! The point is how repetition is conceptualised within the composition, how the composition deals with infinity, that of the ground, the materials and the sky. In their elevation, their elevation, these buildings do, in fact, have an infinite structure. Attention is always focused too much, and exclusively, on the floor plan, which is described as if it were the building.

5
Jurgen van Staaden makes a telling observation about this issue in 'Het ontbreken van het plein', *6-nieuws*, 1976-1977, 713-715.

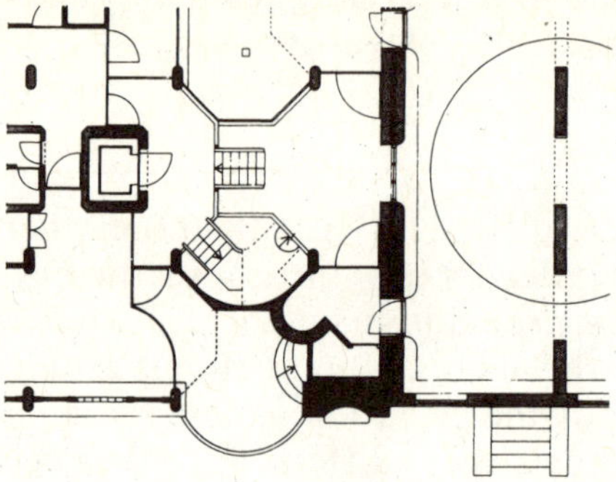

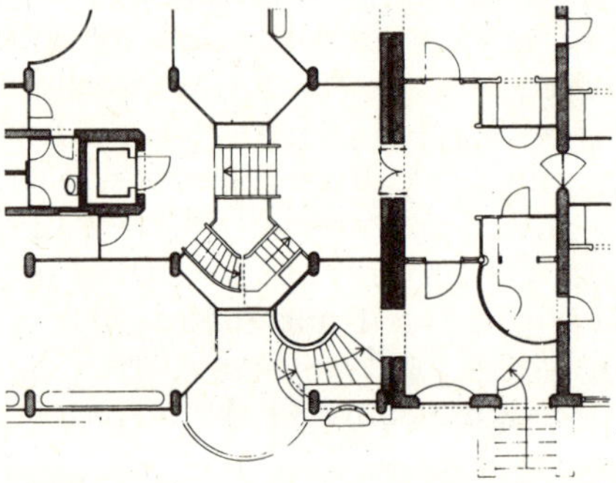

Aldo van Eyck, Hubertushuis, Amsterdam, 1973-1978, entrance hall and stairwell; elevation and floor plans and axonometric projection

Aldo van Eyck, Hubertushuis, Amsterdam, 1973-1978

can celebrate the festival of proportion without much reference to the outside. Or at least, this could form the basis for an analysis seeking not the similarities but the differences within Van Eyck's oeuvre. The houses more strongly resemble the tectonic signs of the monuments and pavilions, which are also pure proportion, but they keep those signs indoors and do not let them shine out over the city – or rather, the woods in which they are found. Perhaps the inside and outside of the private house are not divergent enough in character to enter into a formal merger of scale in the design, or to be significant. Both inside/out and private/public seem barely able to signify a social or cultural value in this work. They can form a psychological content, but that is by grace of their informality, their lack of form. Aldo van Eyck must have been avoiding the educational function that, in the 1950s and '60s in the Netherlands, was associated with living in a small country house in a modern style. For him, in a sense, this work must have been a non-genre and thus have represented a kind of building as such, more so than his schools, playgrounds and other urban creations.

TRANSITIONS

Van Eyck's houses do have transitional spaces between the inside and the outside, but those spaces are almost always incorporated into the volume of the house itself. Within those houses, they manifest more as a vertical absence or void than

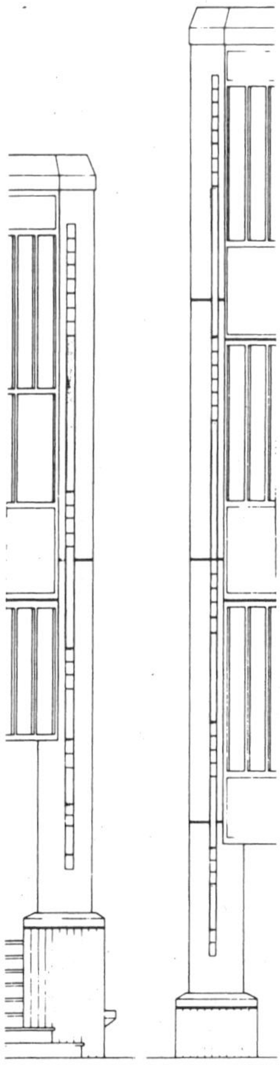

Aldo van Eyck, Hubertushuis, wall columns; at left, coloured tiles in descending spectral order from purple to red; at right, in ascending spectral order from blue to red

Aldo van Eyck, Hubertushuis, coloured tiles in a mirror frame

as a horizontal connection – ultimately, more as a window than as a door. No matter how articulated and linked some houses may seem, their exterior space does little to engage with forms in the vicinity – a square, a circle, a canal, a larger but well-defined space – that could give coherence and meaning to the house as a grouping.[6] Even in the house in Rétie, I would argue, this is in fact the case. The coherence seems to be defined internally, in terms more of composition than of grouping. Although all of Aldo van Eyck's buildings have substantial cornices, the houses seem most deeply embedded in the frames that those cornices provide.

The cornice or the edge of the roof surrounds a surface, the rooftop, where the elements of the composition extrude or intrude, a surface that therefore never manifests as a plane but is always a little more than planar. It is the fractal dimension of the rooftop that forms the compositional reference point for the entire house. As a result, the elements of the composition are in fact all conceived as vertical, reaching upward, towards their fractal levelling in the rooftop, and the house is not erected out of the floor plan but conceived as a complex elevation, a system of towers, from its very inception: the San Gimignano connection that has served as a route in architectural metabolism and structuralism.

'House on the water with four towers' is the phrase used to describe the Baambrugge design.[7] Why four? Why not one, as in the houses in Amsterdam and Venlo, or many, as in Rétie? It is not just that this design is for a house for the architect himself, who could hardly be expected to wall himself up in a single tower, and instead opted for a place of unbridled building in which his many-faceted, 'chameleonic' personality could sojourn. The number four itself must also have been important, because it suggests the four, rather than two, directions in the floor plan – the four points of the compass, the four seasons – in their lack of difference as an elevation, or rather, in the repetition of their elevation. Because the elevation repeats itself, the differences in the floor plan become free, rather than designed, content. The intended message is that in the houses no three-dimensionality will be pursued, or in any case, a different three-dimensionality will be suggested than in the public works, which have more to do with the small and large.

6
Their centre is a horizontal or vertical decentring, a shift, a change, around which the rooms are not grouped but reflected, while in the larger projects the elements of the floor plan are clustered together relative to the centre, which however is too empty to hold them in place. See note 4: More acentric than polycentric. In the Loosduinen church, the actual centre is the drainage channel that ceases to exist somewhere in front of the front door. In fact, this is another decentring and shift, but not a change, except in the material used, namely water, in which the church is reflected naturally but not architecturally. Or at least, the relationship between the church as a grouping and this centre is structural, possibly even symbolic, but not, as I see it, in the nature of a mirroring. Unfortunately, further analysis of this point would take us far beyond the scope and topic of this article.

7
'Four two-storey towers each give access to four independent quarters. Inbetween, covered outdoor living spaces enclosed within the perimeter of the house . . . Recurrent motif in most subsequent projects', Aldo van Eyck, 'In Search of Labyrinthian Clarity', *l'Architecture d'aujourd'hui,* 177, 1975, 15.

ELEVATION

In Van Eyck's public buildings, the vaulted roof and outer wall can be conceived more or less as a single elevation, no matter how complex they may be. In the Burgerweeshuis, the play of open and closed in the flat outer wall is kept in balance by the round, three-dimensional columns that create space around themselves, that make themselves spatial, that envelop themselves in space like the dancers in a George Balanchine ballet. The choreography here, however, with its intense confrontations in the sphere of perception, is not frontal or orthogonal, but solely diagonal, as the path of the building's main circulation routes indicates. But the exterior view of the building reveals no more of this – despite, or precisely because of, the fractal overgrowth of the outside space – than the hint of a perceived diagonal. This fails to add much to the outer wall, however, and the undulations of the roof are weakened by the stacking of the architrave and cornice. The rooftop is flattened, not in its entirety, but in the vicinity of the outer wall. This is unlike the houses.

The result that emerges, in the sectional view, is a reiterable elevation of vaults, a measure, a proportion that can articulate, divide and expand the floor plan. Because the elevation functions as a single material envelopment, the floor plan becomes available. Because proportion predominates, every scale becomes identical, at least conceptually. This is also the case with the foundation and upper floors of the Moederhuis, and certainly at the ESTEC site in Noordwijk. The elevation is vaulting that creates a certain tension between the inside and the outside. Height cannot truly be conceptualised in the outer wall; depth is not truly tolerated. The outer wall, right down to the distribution of glazing bars in the case of the Burgerweeshuis, can in fact only be given form as a stack of horizontal bands, a complex frame, a parergon: that which is found outside the work but, from an outside perspective, is part of that work. Precisely for that reason, the floors of the building cannot also be stacked. The tectonic model of the vaulting militates against it.

The larger buildings are extension, theoretically infinite. They require an elevation that can be horizontally reiterated. This is what leads to the problem of the floors, the levels, that is resolved only with difficulty in the outer walls of the Burgerweeshuis and the Moederhuis. But the houses are elevation. The upper level is part of the elevation, not a true floor. The houses develop vertically, not as domes but as towers. They rise to their peak at the centre. This is one reason that in the outer wall, again, the possibilites are quite the opposite of those present in the larger works. The articulation of the outer walls of the houses serves merely as a transparent or flimsy veiling of the elevation; it is dependent on the arrangement of the towers or the cornice and designed out of a sense of 'weakness'. However much the formal solutions resemble one another, as they undeniably do in the Burgerweeshuis and the house in Rétie, there is a world of difference between the strong, even classical, Palladian, foundation-tectonic physiognomy of the Burgerweeshuis's outer walls – a veritable series of funny faces like those that Aldo van Eyck himself sometimes pulls – and the somewhat textile-like patterns, with no top or bottom to speak of, that are on display in the outer walls of the houses. The house in Venlo does not present the face of the architect but merely wears his inseparable floppy hat. The house front in Rétie is, as it were, no longer designed as a front or outer wall in any sense, but is dissolved into the weak contour of the woods' edge, which borders the clearing that contains the furnished complex. Precisely because this edge is drawn so exactly around the complex, and does not presuppose a different, grander scale, its curve does not appear to be a natural boundary but an unnatural palisade, a dividing line, a front, a defence, a resonance or a response to the ramifications of the development of this clearing for the tectonic evolution of the woods. An outer wall without an outside, a façade without a face.

TEXTURE

The weak outer walls of the house may be the reason that commentators have typically kept silent about them – because their laxness is seen as a deficiency, or because the endlessly eulogised aesthetics of the larger projects rules out any moments of weakness, and where they arise it conceals them from the eye through the simplest of graphic devices. This is what we find at the Burgerweeshuis in the south wing, with an upper level, where the wards for older children are located. The upper level rises too high to be incorporated into the elevation as an architrave or frame. Regular placement of windows would make it an extended architrave or frame with an unacceptably weak, textile-like appearance. The pattern of windows would dominate and somewhat detract from the tectonics of the substructure. Finally, the windows would merge with the dome in an excessively three-dimensional way. The rightmost of the three windows on the upper floor is therefore displaced out of its plane and incorporated between the planes and above the column as a tectonic moment in the elevation of the outer wall over the two floors. Not the plane of the house front for the upper floor as a whole, but only this window is incorporated into the vertical development of the front elevation. This makes the upper floor not only literally but also figuratively asymmetrical. A conceptual difference is also imposed onto the windows: part of the fabric of the upper floor, but also part of the elevation of the entire house front. The upper floor is not seen as a floor, but drawn into the tectonics of the house front by means of the windows. Although the swastika floor plans on both levels offer every reason for such a solution – with Van Eyck's game of bottom corner open, top corner closed – still, you cannot deny that, even from a diagonal perspective, the house front is created through a completely unambiguous shift, a graphic trick which in itself is entirely pointless and has little to do with architecture, but does dominate the view.[8]

The same thing applies to the two left-hand bays – extending onto the upper level – for which the principle of giving every window a face becomes very difficult to maintain on every level. Each bay has a single colour of its own from top to bottom, creating vertical bands of colour that negate the

8
The fractal exuberance of the wall line in the floor plan of the Burgerweeshuis could also be seen as an attempt to make the outer wall visible from within – an attempt that clearly is never entirely successful, not until the house in Rétie. In addition to this minimisation of the outside of the outer wall and the nominal minimisation that results from the inclusion of the outer wall as material in the elevation of which it can then only form the base, there is a third minimisation, which we could describe as open. This minimisation attempts to remove the outer wall from view in order to give direction to the movement. Eye and feet are directed elsewhere, and so the only remaining impression of the outer wall is as a screen. In the Burgerweeshuis it is the horizontal movement, as a result of which the glazing bars around the courtyard enter into a geometrical relationship but are equal in width, because people and their gazes move horizontally rather than vertically. In the Moederhuis it is the vertical movement, 'the distribution of windows on the street side, which distracts you from the houses across the street and leads you (without compelling you) to gaze involuntarily at what is going on in the street below', Herman Herzberger, 'Het twintigste-eeuwse mechanisme en de architectuur van Aldo van Eyck', in *Aldo van Eyck, Hubertushuis, Hubertus house* (Amsterdam, 1982), 23. The architecture does its job without compulsion and involuntarily, but it does get the job done. In *Architectuur als oude wetenschap* (Amsterdam, 1988), 170 (the relevant chapter had been previously published in *Plan* 1982, no. 7-8) I asked whether the distance between the nominal concept of the observed outer wall and the free concept of involuntary observation as experience has not become too great in thise case and in fact comes at the expense of the architecture: 'That the buildings, in other words, are not appreciated in terms of the ideas involved in their design, but experienced in a "different" way . . . An architecture that was about architecture would evoke an experience about ex-

entire concept of stacked floors. The height of the building is involved in the tectonics of the outer wall not as height, but as colour. The simple graphic technique – colour – is not the larger-scale element intended to bring together multiple levels in one colossal order. On the contrary, the bays differ in height. Colour is not a concept relating to scale, but a transcendental category that links the texture of the upper levels to building as an elevation, as an act.

But the difficulty is that just like the displaced window at the Burgerweeshuis, this imaginative trick also dominates the outer wall. The train of thought proceeds in the wrong direction. The non-tectonic element – unambiguous horizontal shifting, colour as surface – is brought into the building process as a last resort available only once, as an element which makes it possible to continue building. It serves as the representation or concept of the possibility of building, instead of building itself serving as the condition of possibility for this concept, this term, for colour, graphics, celebration. As if the party tent was the point of the party. Because the architect cannot give shape to any upper levels, they are covered up and represented by an element that cannot give shape to any upper levels either, but can act as tectonic writing on the wall. The problem is that the textile-like writing is the condition of possibility for the wall on which it is written. That is why in these larger projects the writing also has to play the role of the wall. In the houses, in contrast, the outer wall does not have this function, because it does not have to be seen from outside, unless by a thief or an architecture critic. The textile-like quality we find in the larger projects defines building as a graphic sign, a kind of writing; in the houses, the act of building is instead a condition of possibility for their textility, for the thinking, for the curtains, the house front, for the freedom of difference and the development of ideas. While in the larger projects the idea of building is sought in the identity of the building as 'house', in the houses this idea is stripped of any form or design, to be enjoyed, as it were, as informal, liberated content.

perience'. The result, after all, is that the idea is concealed. Herzberger (see above, page 23) is undoubtedly right to claim that Aldo van Eyck's buildings do not aim to change people's behaviour but rather 'to give people richer opportunities to determine their own attitudes towards one another at all times'. But the problem is that one's attitude towards things disappears from view, not only in involuntary observation but also in the minimal aesthetic system of this architecture. In this respect, of course, the architecture of Aldo van Eyck is a kind of abstract art after all.

WONDERLAND

In the Burgerweeshuis, the window shifts across the wall in a tapestry-like pattern, without a great deal of top and bottom, and then becomes a one-off sign, a single gesture, that rescues the top and bottom of the building's tectonics. Likewise, in the Moederhuis, the spectral colour pattern of the vertical series of tiles that straddles the columns is expressed in two series, one ascending and the other descending. This creates a kind of woven thread pattern, giving the different but uniformly coloured groups of windows in each bay the appearance of a tectonic plane. It is in relation to this building that the architect emphasises unity of scale: 'Between the largest room and the smallest . . . the intensity changes but not the scale . . . because it is only Alice who sometimes

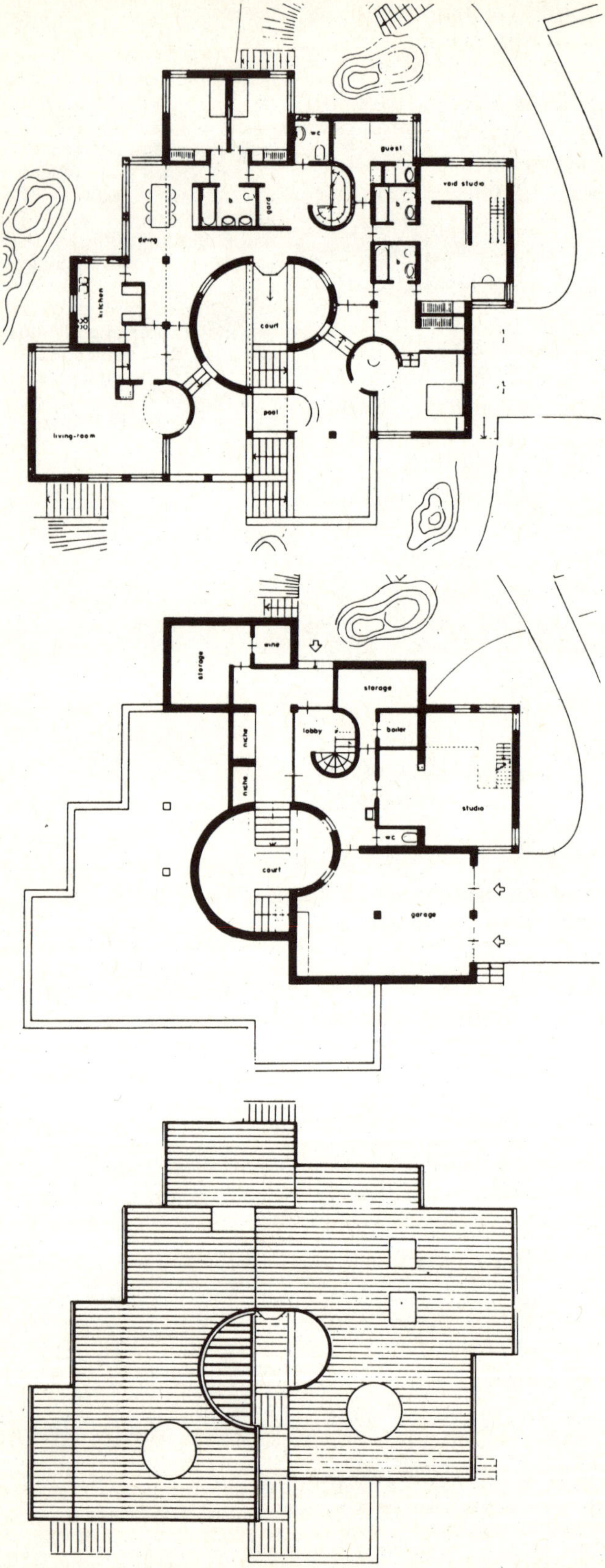

Aldo van Eyck, design for R. van Eyck House in Saint Paul de Vence (France), 1968

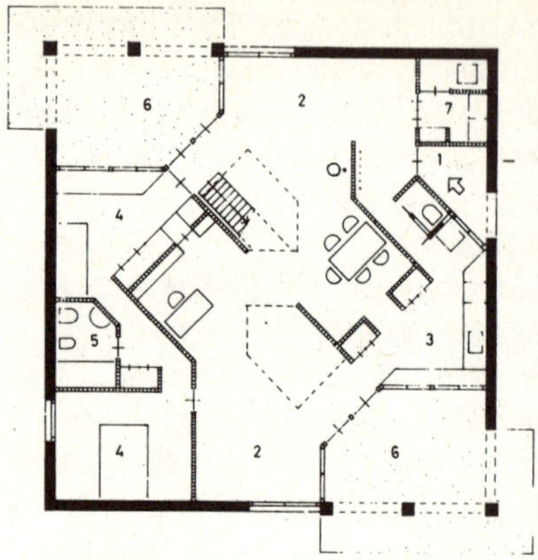

1. entrance
2. living room
3. kitchen
4. bedroom
5. bathroom
6. loggia
7. storage space

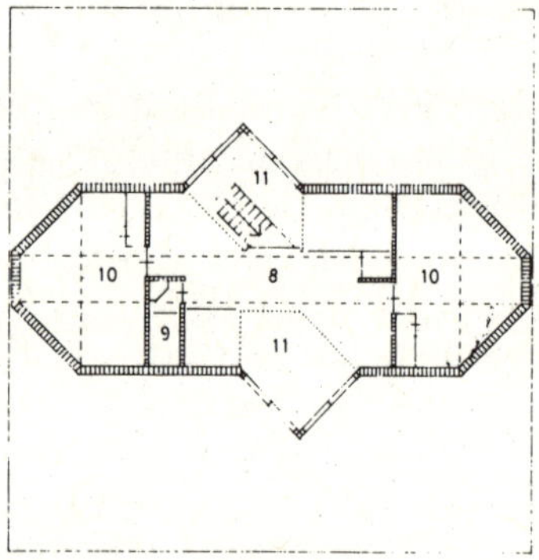

Aldo van Eyck, Verkerk House, Herungerweg, Venlo, 1967-1970

shrinks and sometimes grows.'[9] Here, Wonderland is characterised as the place where things grow and shrink at a gradual pace, and not by fits and starts, as they do in our world. The dream is of a space so continuous that directions mingle with one another and dimensionality becomes entirely weak. The reality is that the elevation and the outer wall cannot be reconciled with one another because they imply different orientations. The elevation can be a single, fluid movement, but the price that must be paid is the minimisation of the outer wall, which must nonetheless be designed. Or the outer wall can be weak, like those of the houses, but the consequence is that the elevation is then internalised and can no longer be observed.

Displacement (in the Burgerweeshuis) and colour (in the Moederhuis) are immaterial but without content. They are intensive quantities and not qualities. Wonderland is the intuition of pure space without extension and without dimensions, without directions, without high or low, without left or right, and so without symmetry, without up or down. Things grow and shrink there without an external scale, become purely dimensional – the power of proportion, of different proportions, is unchained. But the intensity, which in the form of unity of scale (and thus in the form of an egg, essentially) seems to escape observation because it precedes it, is defined as change. Displacement and colour evade observation in the form of change and, for this reason, cannot be assigned any meaning

9 Aldo van Eyck, 'De bouw van een huis', in: *Aldo van Eyck, Hubertushuis, Hubertus house,* op. cit. (note 8), 84.

Aldo van Eyck, Burgerweeshuis, Amsterdam, southern wall of one of the wards for older children

Gerrit Rietveld, Martin Visser House, Eikendreef, Bergeyck, 1956; floor plan

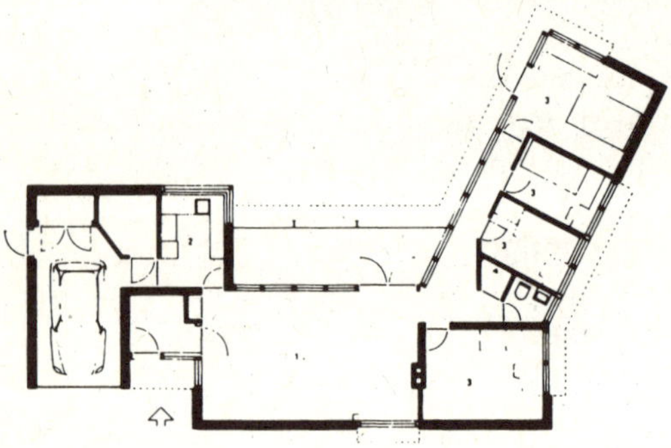

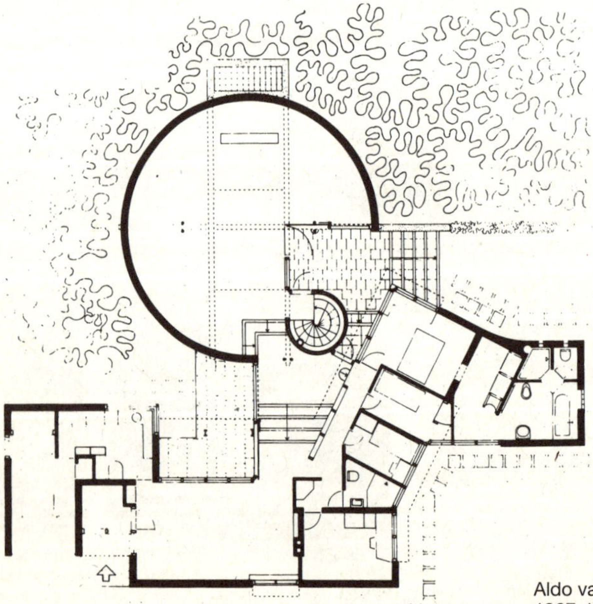

Aldo van Eyck, expansion of Martin Visser House, 1967-1969; floor plan

either. As transcendental categories, they cannot have any content of their own – all they can do is rescue the tectonics.

Displacement and colour are not symbolic but imaginary in nature. They are not an image but a mirror of decline, crisis, architecture. Accordingly, in the Burgerweeshuis it is the window that is displaced, the mirror of inside and outside, and not any other element of the outer wall. And so the colour spectra in the Moederhuis are sometimes interrupted by mirrors or even, at the base of the bays, captured in a frame of mirrors. What a topsy-turvy world, in which instead of the mirror being contained in a frame, the frame becomes a mirror. Intensity is a mirror held up to the observer. 'Space is the undergoing of space',[10] not the experiencing, observing, thinking or discussing of it. The discussing of what? The difficulty for the critic is that he or she, in his or her text, has no choice but to attach meaning to these elements, which throughout the building never wish to be substance, content. They do not wish to mean or to be meant and are not even intended to be observed. As a category of experience, the intensive quantity ('space is the undergoing of space') is passive in this case. The reality of the building can be enjoyed not by seeking but by finding, not by looking but by seeing.[11] But the result is that what emerges from this source, the building itself in its extension, its dimensions, its materials and its completeness as a work of art has no other meaning or purpose than the sheer fact that it was built. Tautology, cycle, identity. It is always this same concept that is brought to the fore and makes the architect's spoken comments sound like a constantly repeated manifesto.

In a sense, it would be impossible to arrive at this concept without the existence of another series in his oeuvre, one which does not found building on thinking in terms of non-tectonic cleverness, but founds thinking on the act of building. Because the cleverness of the architect is then no more than a special case, it makes sense that the latter series – that of building that provides a foundation for thinking – is an earlier, older current in Van Eyck's oeuvre. And perhaps both series could be examined as changes of direction within the chronology of the oeuvre, as the alternation of constructive and deconstructive signs. This is similar to what Theodor Adorno found in the work of Arnold Schönberg, the 'dialectical composer' who changed direction completely in each new work. Building is also repetition and Aldo van Eyck's houses, above all, seem to have been conceived as time machines, *machines à oublier*. It thus seems plausible that thinking, thinking based on living in these houses, will be done in terms of an open or free difference, an unleashing of concepts that are potentially just as unbridled as the elevation hosted in their interior, but without being analogical to it, precisely because that thinking is directed out of the interior and into the world, like a kind of orthogonal. At least, the two staircases in the house in Amsterdam that Van Eyck built with Jan Rietveld can be

10
Aldo van Eyck, 'Inleiding tot de Loos tentoonstelling op de afdeling Bouwkunde, bij de opening woensdag 17 maart 1965 uitgesproken', *Delftse School* 12, 1965, 269-273.

11
Many of Aldo van Eyck's pronouncements and those of his admirers are doctrines and recurring formulations of what Evert van Uitert has called 'faith in modern Art' (in *Het geloof in de moderne Kunst*, Meulenhoff/Landshoff, 1987). They serve to shield the works from misuse by non-believers. It is thus understandable that in the structure of his aesthetic system, uninterested observation is given priority over interested observation, or at least, it is assumed that even the interested variety can be understood and described in terms of lived experience. That is the approach consistently taken by Herman Herzberger: a report of actual visits and actual observations, which are therefore always in the past tense. Despite the suggestion of a Kantian definition of beauty as disinterested pleasure, the only thing this seems to underscore is the importance of this architecture and its aesthetic system. Herman Herzberger's final assessment, however, does not have the character of lived experience at all, but of established causality: 'a question of the correct measurements' (Herzberger, 'Het twintigste-eeuwse mechanisme', op. cit. note 8, 23). But the measurements are always correct if they are measured, and if they are experienced they are equally correct, though only within this aesthetic system. What is more, observation is no longer an adequate response to the metrical feeling, and there is a tension, a quality of intensity, between the observed and the felt measure: 'The intriguing thing . . . is not the shift of accent in itself, but the tension that exists between the accent you expect and feel in your mind and the accent you actually hear' (ibid., 21). A question of metrics and rhythm. The shift of accent is seen not as a complex repetition but as a foundational difference. The observed is observed in a field

interpreted this way, for instance. The inner staircase is part of the unbridled elevation, and seen from ouside, through the openwork glass outer wall of the middle quadrant of the floor plan, it looks like something mobile, some kind of furniture, something abstract – lines – and thus seems to float, while the outer staircase, in contrast, flings itself out casually like an orthogonal around the omitted quadrants of the house (which is actually square), without having much impact on the outer walls, which are so weak as to remind one of Hein Salomonson. In the front view, the landing of the outer staircase seems continuous with that of the inner staircase, which is barely or not at all visible. The result is that where the actual elevation of the inner staircase is apparent in the outer wall, it seems to be part of the outer route.

of expectations. Nevertheless, Herman Herzberger's interpretation is closer than than of any other commentator to the core, the deep obstacle, in Aldo van Eyck's aesthetic system, namely that repetition, the repetition of elevation, materials, large and small spaces, can be observed *hors système* only as an event, as an image in a dream, without any field in which it might take place, and within the system only as measure, as number, as a 'shift of accent in itself'. The concept of identity, having a single scale or at least an unchanging one, is compatible with the repetition but not with the idea of space that is free of concepts. Aldo van Eyck: 'The point is not space, but the interior of that space and the inner horizon (as my wife has called it . . .) of that interior (even if it is outside)' (Van Eyck, 'De bouw van een huis', op. cit. note 9, 80).

SCREEN

It is not always the case that the elements indicating the outside can be drawn so closely around the house, like a virtual outer wall. Or rather, sometimes the surroundings are so patently present that it is impossible to create a conceptual exterior. In such cases, there are two ways in which the house screens itself off. In the design for Saint Paul de Vence, this is achieved by reversing the plan, by turning the house inside-out, and at the house in Bergeyck there is an actual screen, in which the wall entirely coincides with the textile sign. Both approaches arise from the nature of the project. The hilly terrain of Saint Paul de Vence tucks the house so thoroughly into the folds of the landscape that the building cannot, in addition, veil itself in its own drapery. Aldo van Eyck consistently avoids a rhyme that would imply a difference in scale. If the elevation of the outer wall has a stacked structure, the floors of the house cannot be stacked. If the landscape has rolling hills, the outer wall is toothed – though in this case, there is another difficulty, namely that the slopes complicate thinking about building in terms of height and elevation. This is why the house is turned inside-out. The weak spiral in the centre of the house erases the centre of the composition, brackets it and thus makes possible the fragmentary volumetry of the rectangular composition on the outside – which height and elevation, despite their geometry, cannot formulate. This volumetry is somewhat reminiscent of Theo van Doesburg and Cornelis van Eesteren's 1923 *Maison d'artiste*.

While the rectangles are rectangular because they are on the slope, the spiral is spiral-shaped – expansive – because it is at the centre of the house, and not on a slope. But because the centre of the house has more to do with an artificial height, with the elevation of the staircase and the upper level, than with a natural height – or, rather, a height that would serve as a natural sign – the sign of the spiral remains powerless. However, a difference is created that motivates the small, circular motifs in the floor plan between the rectangular volumes and the spiral shape. In terms of their shape, they are halfway between the geometry of the exterior and the uncertain curve in the centre. As an intermediate form, however, they are too inchoate to support the elevation. The result of the idea that the house is toothed where it faces the slope – while the slope folds towards the house and the house folds into its own centre, with the spiral emerging like a tooth from the large fold in the centre – is that everything seems to grow but nothing stands. If the house folds in on itself, the result is that the rooms will have to protrude outward. Outward, not upward. In a sense, the house on the hill requires a horizontal sequence. The sequence of square, circle and oval is too well-tempered and, at the same time, too complicated for the sign of the spiral to mean much. If the house had been built, it would undoubtedly have looked quite different.

Even so, the function of a simple graphic form of this kind will always be the same, whether the wall is a sign or there is writing on the wall. The point is always to make space tectonic by a method that is so minimal, so simple, that where it is unsuccessful the method itself appears to be a potential expansion of the repertoire (and it does not work because the method is so minimal; the application of it is minimalistic precisely because it is not an architectural method). However, it does not make an appearance unless the tectonic possibilities have been exhausted, as a kind of second choice. The working method thus does not involve any investigation of how this means of expanding one's repertoire could actually be used more than once – in multiple projects, for instance.

Graphics defines architecture differently every time as a transcendental category, but always defines it systematically as a field of tectonic dissociations or, more precisely, as a field of dissociations of tectonic modes, as different types of construction, in which the building is always identical. And also because the building is always identical, always the same, always a 'house'. The house in Bergeyck may be the best illustration of this line of thought, precisely because the graphic method is applied as an addition to an existing house designed by a different architect, of which it was necessary to have an opinion.

Bergeyck was in fact one of the most beautiful, if not the most beautiful, of Gerrit Rietveld's houses, the sloppiest zigzag he ever made. The rudimentary butterfly floor gives the central place to a living room that is not really a room at all, but an entrance hall, where home life retains something of its potential festivity, its public character. It may be the finest execution of this somewhat bourgeois aspect of the programme for the Dutch post-war genre of the small country house. This entrance hall had just one wall, the rear wall, along with a fireplace and side entrances. It was a stage on which everything became mobile, a *repoussoir*, part of the scenery, where the depth and shallowness of the room brought into theatrical relief the play of the actors entering and exiting, stage left and

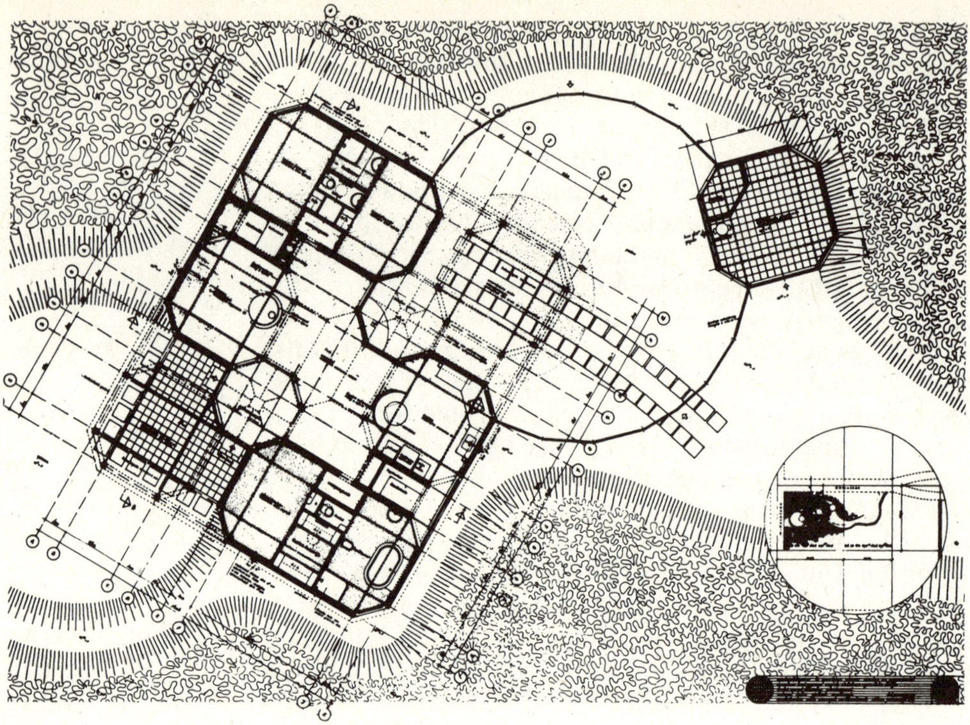

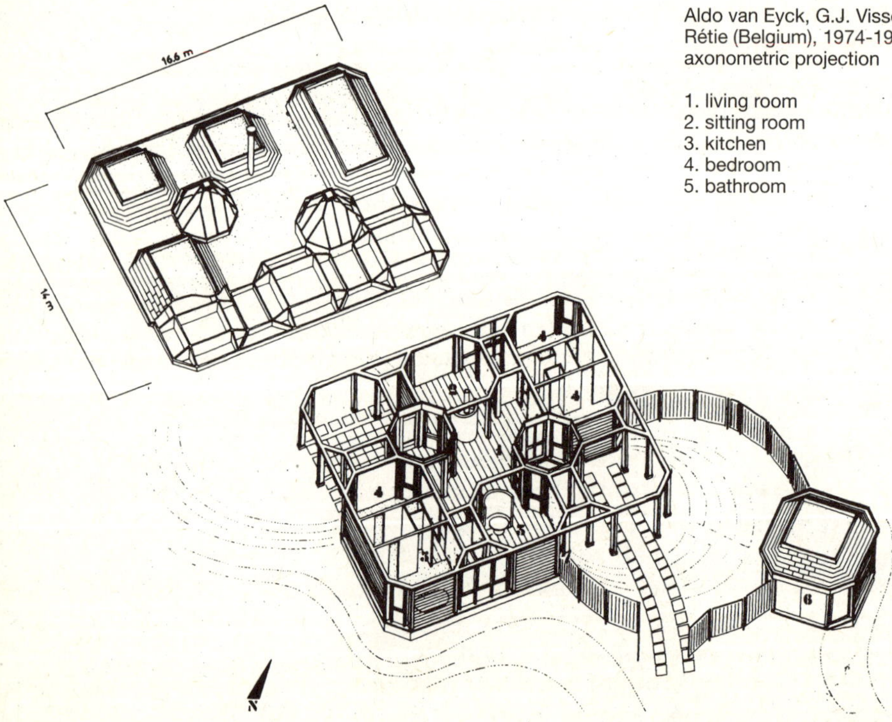

Aldo van Eyck, G.J. Visser House, Rétie (Belgium), 1974-1976; plan and axonometric projection

1. living room
2. sitting room
3. kitchen
4. bedroom
5. bathroom

stage right, whose conversation there could for the last time be considered a form of art, before the dark audience of silent and applauding trees. Was it necessary for this of all houses to be tectonised? Gussied up? Aldo van Eyck's addition looks like a butterfly net. 'Counterpoint', Herman Herzberger calls it.

I would like to quote Herman Herzberger's elegant analysis of this design at greater length here, because it shows so clearly what is going on: 'Although it was not a true Rietveld house, it was still a house by Rietveld, not so very tense, and not really relaxed either, but there was not a great deal of space, especially not for paintings and sculptures. We can only imagine the moral and ethical dimensions of the decision to extend this of all houses, but Van Eyck's masterstroke here dispels all doubt in a single gesture. The circular curve of the wall is placed so that in a single motion it gathers within its rondure the entire, somewhat indistinct openness of the 'garden wall' together with the opposing world. Between the two components, the new and the old, new areas emerge on the outside and new rooms on the inside. The unclear patio takes form, the undefined, blunt corner suddenly has meaning, and the rectangular system of the existing living room is reinforced by a continuation of it. We see that the house was really only a torso, which now has a head. Van Eyck completed Rietveld's house, exposing its weakness and at the same time transforming it into a strength as a component of a new whole, just as a good answer can lend meaning to a trivial

Aldo van Eyck, G.J. Visser House, Rétie (Belgium), 1974-1976

question. . . . Aldo van Eyck's respect for Rietveld would have been clear enough by now, even without this house, but here we find new confirmation of it. To doubt it, you would have to lack all sense of proportion. What architect other than Van Eyck could have come up with such a solution in a place like this? I can only think of one: Rietveld himself!'[12]

12
Herzberger, 'Het twintigste-eeuwse mechanisme', op. cit. (note 8), 16-18.

Nevertheless, there is no getting around the fact that the description of Gerrit Rietveld's house abounds in pejoratives – 'doubt', 'indistinct', 'unclear', 'undefined', 'weakness', 'trivial' – while Aldo van Eyck's addition is referred to as 'a single gesture', a 'masterstroke', 'a single motion', an 'answer', a 'solution', but in fact described solely as the 'opposing world'. I would be more inclined to describe the addition as a problematisation of the existing house than as a solution to a problem. Herman Herzberger chiefly describes what the addition does to the existing house, in terms of 'gathering', giving 'form' and 'meaning', 'reinforcing' and 'completing', 'transforming into strength', 'lending meaning' and 'solving'. Tectonics is reintroduced through a single gesture that is not itself examined in tectonic terms. What is suppressed is the view, the elevation, of the addition itself, which is sketched only as an interior, as a 'world' and as a 'component' – as an egg, in fact – and not as a view, an elevation, something that can be independently examined. Ultimately, the circular form is described as a 'screen' and a 'moderate square' – in other words as a weak, geometrically unsound square without a centre – but only from the inside. Herman Herzberger's description keeps a secret, not on the inside but on the outside, that the architects of this complex are said to share: some reason that no other architect than the two who built it could have thought of this solution.[13]

13
'Obwohl Rietveld dieses Haus selbst kaum schatzte Rietveld-Haus', Aldo van Eyck, in *Dortmunder Architekturaussteüung 1978, Dortmunder Architekturhefte* no. 3, Prof. Josef Paul Kleihues/Abt. Bauwesen der Universitat Dortmund, Dortmund, 1976. The sentence is altered in the errata: 'Obwohl dies nicht das beste Rietveld-Haus ist, ist es dennoch ein Rietveld-Haus' ('Although this is not the best Rietveld house, it is a Rietveld house all the same'). Apparently, Rietveld believed that, after all, this was not the worst of his houses, or he was thought to have believed that.

RÉTIE

This is the secret that is ultimately revealed, as it were, in the house in Rétie, as content without form. The woods, the actual outdoor space, is fractal to the highest possible degree, so that the edge of the woods, the outer wall, is infinite. The screen has become unlimited and infinite, so that the border, the *limes*, has to be repeated in the elevation of the house and its echoes. With an overabundance of types of bayonet reflection that dissect the rooms by decentring and shifting them, the floor plan looks more like a mathematical model, a diagram, a blueprint, than a composition kept in balance by the difference in scale between the inside and outside, or between small and large. In fact, the house understands only proportion, and not scale. This is because the relationship with its surroundings is conceived in terms of materials and fractality, rather than surface or space.

The forest is incorporated into the house in material form – in the form of the wood of which the house is made. It therefore does not have to be incorporated into the house in a spatial sense; it is reflected as an enclosure, a palisade, an outer wall, sometimes vertical, sometimes horizontal, as a dividing line and a screen, but also, in fact, as a movement, a series of material elements. The forest is what is located outside the complex; the wood is a parergon, a frame. From the forest it looks like a wooden house. From the house the wood looks like a forest. The wood, the frame, the dividing line, the elevation – they do not separate the inside from the outside but are both inside and outside, or rather, alternately inside and outside depending on the mindset. The wood, the frame, is ambiguous. The elevation is the domain of difference, not of form. Seen from the frame, the difference between what is inside and outside the frame is arbitrary, but this establishes the difference in content. Or, in the architect's words, the wood makes it possible, within the house, for the difference in form between inner rooms and outer spaces to become so small that only their 'content' still counts as a distinction.[14]

Inside and outside are seen as a thought, a possible concept – or, better said, a condition of possibility for all possible concepts – for a nearly unbridled art of conversation. It would be wrong for us to suppose that the minimisation of the distinction between interior and exterior spaces could, in this case, be based on a lack of difference, a similarity, instead of an intensive quantity. Or in any event, the thesis that becomes the central issue in this house is that when two things resemble each other their content must differ – precisely because they contain a shift, because they are not located in the same place, because they disguise themselves, diverge, decentre. Only by speaking explicitly of content does the artist avoid a situation in which the only difference is natural – for instance, the difference between the indoor climate and the weather – which would emerge from comparison and the experience of which would, after all, not be the primary topic of conversation for the inhabitants of the house. These people do not talk about the weather.

Difference must become open, free – that is one way of summarising the aesthetic programme of this house, of this complex repetition. The aesthetic system finds its sublime moment in the endless fractal boundary, yet in its intensive quality it presents the possibility of informal understanding, of content without form, of smile without cat. Living in Rétie, in Wonderland, is a smile without a cat.

Translated by David McKay

14
Ibid., 'bei . . . Verminderung der formaten Unterschiede . . . inhaltliche Unterschiede hervorheben' (because the size of the difference is reduced, difference in content is emphasised).

Issue 28, 'Snelheid en zwaarte' (Speed and gravity) is the beginning of a new era for *OASE*. The journal finds an ally and a professional publisher in the SUN, the socialist publishing house in Nijmegen that in the 1980s emerged as a major actor in the architectural landscape of the Low Countries, bringing onto the market books whose critical, often Marxist-oriented perspective on society and culture in general – and architecture in particular – had connections with the some of the interests of *OASE* at that time. A smaller, book-like format is chosen and graphic designer Karel Martens and the Werkplaats Typografie in Arnhem take over the graphics of the journal, which will be acclaimed and awarded. From now on not only the message is crucial, the medium is carefully considered as well.

OASE 28	Snelheid en zwaarte (Speed and gravity)
OASE 29	Sprekende architectuur I (Talking architecture I)
OASE 30	Sprekende architectuur II (Talking architecture II)
OASE 31	De tektoniek van de opstand & Het Bonnefantenmuseum (The tectonics of rebellion & the Bonnefanten Museum)
OASE 32	Architectuur en stedebouw in de jaren zestig (Architecture and urbanism in the 1960s)
OASE 33	De transformatie van de metropool (The transformation of the metropolis)
OASE 34	Het interieur (Interiors)
OASE 35	Havenfronten (Waterfronts)
OASE 36	De architectuurtekening (The architecture drawing)
OASE 37/38	Massa en woningbouw (Mass and housing)
OASE 39	Materialiteit en fysieke ervaring (Materiality and physical experience)
OASE 40	Poiésis en architectuur (Poiesis and architecture)
OASE 41	Het wereldontwerp (World-class design)
OASE 42	Over stijl (On style)
OASE 43	Zwischenraumgespenster
OASE 44	Venetiaanse Perspectieven (Venetian perspectives)

Period III

PROFES-SIONALISA-TION

A New Publisher and New Graphics 1990–1996

Gerard van Zeijl

O, OASE, OH

THE NAME EQUALS PRESENTATION

OASE. A more appropriate name for a journal about 'architecture, urban design and landscape' seems inconceivable! The actual intention comes to the fore, undisguised, however these disciplines are represented in its pages. Its name contains its thirst-quenching argumentation and its hunger for more. An oasis is a fertile place, but one concealed in a barren hostile landscape. Is this a case of preaching in the desert?[1] Does it deal with the city as a desert, the limitless metropolis, within which architecture appears as an oasis? Nietzsche has the Devil make Zarathustra[2] choose between the weak-willed return to the city or the brave defiance of the desert. For the desert wanderer, there is no defined destination. To leave the city behind, like the past, means to surrender to adventure, which moves forward without goal or object. Does architecture lie hidden within the defiance of this danger? When it comes to leaving behind certainties and discovering a new potential, yes! The thousand Nietzschian perspectives then coincide with the 'negative horizon', to paraphrase Virilio.[3] An unexpected oasis: he who thinks he sees water and, filled with false hope, bites into the sand of the mirage is still counting on the salvation he expects to be granted. No, this is about an unconditional surrender, love perhaps, passion! Tschumi once remarked, 'If you really appreciate architecture, you may even need to commit a murder.'[4]

A search that goes beyond Adorno's predilection for the goal and 'exclusion of goal-setting'[5] ends the idealising quest of Percival. The oasis in question here offers no salvation, no comfort, and does not represent an answer to catastrophe. A refuge for the desperate, as in 'the gothic novel',[6] perhaps. Tzonis's 'hopeless arcadia'[7] and beyond the 'end of architecture'[8] described by Bekaert. A place beyond.

Nor does the architecture of the oasis contain the origin of architecture, the 'primitive hut' put forward by Rykwert, from Laugier to Viollet le Duc.[9] Aristotle, in the trio of 'cave, hut and tent', saw the last as the moveable habitation of the nomad.

A hut, on the contrary, is static. In terms of origin of the hut, as well as of the oasis, one is dealing with a reconstructed 'beginning', a fiction that 'has never existed', as Derrida observed.[10] This must be an oasis in which false ideals vanish like mirages and the presence of architecture appears nomadically.

The journal *OASE* is actually conducting a nomadic debate, one that constantly shifts the 'parameters' of criticism, as Tafuri advocated.[11] Similarly, Eisenman[12] has clarified the immaterial and Grassi[13] the material presence of architecture. Besides 'the stone and the word', *OASE* also focuses on the image. The critique of normative 'visual quality' and 'fossilised building standards' in government architecture policy was defined by reopening the discourse about self-evident 'speak-

1
See *OASE* 33, C.J. Christiaansen, 'Woestijn, centrum en periferie', 51.

2
Friedrich Nietzsche, *Also sprach Zarathoestra* (1885).

3
Paul Virilio, *L'Horizon négatif. Essai de dromoscopie* (Paris, 1985).

4
Bernard Tschumi, 'Advertisements for Architecture', 1978.

5
Theodor Adorno, *Negative Dialektik* (Frankfurt, 1966).

6
OASE 43, 1995.

7
Alexander Tzonis, *Towards a Non-Oppressive Environment* (Boston, 1972).

8
Geert Bekaert, 'Het einde van de architectuur', 1967.

9
Joseph Rykwert, *On Adam's House in Paradise* (Cambridge, 1993).

10
Manfredo Tafuri, *Theories and History of Architecture* (London, 1980).

11
Eric Bolle, *Afscheid van wat nooit geweest is* (Groningen, 1982).

12
Peter Eisenman et al., *Five architects* (New York, 1975).

13
Giorgio Grassi, *La costruzione logica dell'architettura* (Padua, 1967); see also *OASE* 28.

ing architecture' and pluriform 'style'.[14] *OASE* is conscious of its theoretical independence without becoming elitist. After all, ever since Cacciari thematised commentaries on the metropolis, restraint is appropriate. He considers architecture to be defined by the 'schism' that has arisen between the metropolis that has become 'consumption' and the 'intellectual'.[15] In describing the world as a desert, after all, architecture risks becoming arrogant and unrealistic. Such a description polarises the disciplines of urbanism and architecture. Perhaps we should situate ourselves somewhere between the pronouncements of Rossi, 'the architecture of the city' (as a social work of art), and of Koolhaas, 'where architecture is (in the way), nothing else can happen'.

OASE also expanded the design work along the way. More and more it was nurtured by a secret Benjamin-esque search for the 'sanctuary of art and intellect'. The answer to the contemporary problems of banality, multiculturalism, globalisation – pragmatic matters, in short – was found in an oasis manoeuvre, where 'negative thinking'[16] becomes productive and *realpolitik* is fulfilled by Koolhaas, among others. There where the 'negative confirmation' of compromising conditions turned into its opposite.

In this way, *OASE* contains distance and engagement, a place of critical reflection and thematisation of the building towards architecture. *OASE* also means the stimulus to 'shudder'[17] in the sense of ecstasy, and where possible, poïesis; both form a critical distance, according to Lidy van Marissing.[18] With Adorno, we think of 'illuminating things for a moment'. With Baird we say that because of 'post-utopian pragmatism'[19] and 'image hedonism', critical interventions are imperative.

The 1990-1996 period is also defined by a dark sense of futility and increasing unease.[20] After all, these years of punk and social unease can be considered the extrapolation, but above all the inversion of the oppositions of the 1970s, the dogmatising critique of the 'capitalist conditions' of architecture and 'imagination in power'. Following the resourcing of history in the 1980s, the 1990s dispenses with postmodern aberrations in order to maximise the motto 'everything goes' as Baudrillard's 'simulacrum'.[21] In risky critical fashion, the 'modern' was turned over to the stretched potential of liquid technology and fluid capital. The conflict with architecture, instead of affirming its futility, was detonated.

All of this coincides with the track *OASE* follows during this period. If we think of the complex of editorial tracks, we see a series of conflicting subjects. 'The architecture of reason' (Terlouw) and 'Atlanta' (Koolhaas), architecturalia such as 'the corners' (Bachelard) and 'the sensory nature of architecture' (Meuwissen), poetic themes such as 'the gestures of things' (Wortmann) and 'intimate immeasurability' (Sturkenboom), to end with philosophical theoretical considerations such as

14
See *OASE* 28, 42, 30, 29, 42 and 31, respectively.

15
See *OASE* 42, including Van Nieuwstadt's adaptation of Cacciari's thesis.

16
See *OASE* 30.

17
See *OASE* 29 and 30.

18
Lidy van Marissing, *Het gedroomde leven. Een denkbeeldig onderzoek* (1979).

19
George Baird, '"Criticality" and its Discontents', *Harvard Design Magazine* 21, 2005.

20
Anthony Vidler, *The Architectural Uncanny* (Cambridge, 1992), notably the essay 'Dark Space'.

21
Jean Baudrillard, *Simulacres et simulation* (Paris, 1981).

'The architecture as a fable' (Van Nieuwstadt on Cacciari) and 'The historical project' (Tafuri).[22] With this train of inertia, one anticipates an international course that will dominate during the following period. A course of globalisation in which *OASE*'s intellectual resistance is examined globally in the themes of 'tectonics', 'autonomous architecture', 'ornament' and 'historiography and design practice' and 'literature'.[23]

22
See *OASE* 29, 33, 34, 39, 40 and 44, respectively.

23
See *OASE* 62, 65, 69 and 70, respectively.

FROM *O O O* TO THE INVERSION AND DISRUPTION OF DESIGN

OASE seems, in the course of 25 years, to have returned to its original position. Having started with the three Os of its Dutch subtitle, *Ontwerp, Onderzoek en Onderwijs* – design, research and education – the journal, following its student publication phase, was marked by an instrumental approach. The objective was to clarify the methodology of the architecture programme at Delft University of Technology. In architectural culture, 'plan analysis' was paired with a paradoxical 'cross section'. For even as Colin Rowe's 'transparency'[24] was taught, in reality the by now lifeless power of Modern Building thundered forth. Conversely, the Faculty of Architecture at Delft further disrupted architectural culture by pushing through a democratisation process via the radical pamphlet *de elite*,[25] taking the journal *O*, published by (the same) SUN Publishers, along with it. Once it was realised that the baby had been thrown out with the bathwater in Delft, there emerged, along with the name *OASE*, a journal that began to evolve from an instrumental and politicising approach to a reflective one. In putting its literary and philosophical name to serious use, architectural design was henceforth seen as an expression of an architectural culture. The writing became contemplative, an expansion of the empirical approach. Rational argumentation and research into original materials were linked with criticism. Delft University of Technology was editorially dominant, but Eindhoven University of Technology, through its staff,[26] partly thanks to Kees Vollemans, was not without influence.

24
See *OASE* 31.

25
Stielos, *de elite, een analiese van de afdeling bouwkunde van de techniese hogeschool te delft* (1970).

26
Such as Pieter Jan Gijsberts, Joost Meuwissen and Gijs Wallis de Vries.

In the 1990-1996 period, with the contributions of Nijenhuis, 'The Passion for the Hiatus', and Bekaert, 'Eupalinos ou l'architecte',[27] a restrained visual power was also on the rise along with the philosophical content, in part through the typography of Karel Martens, celebrated as a prize winner with words like 'personal and painstaking'.[28] *OASE* never degenerated into the glossy approach to which many architecture periodicals surrendered due to design practice and the broader audience ever since Postmodernism. Instead, *OASE* reached a pinnacle of integrity without resorting to the dogma of scribes or iconoclasts. On the contrary, visual culture was thematised and problematised by examining its functioning. If we ask which periodicals evolved as architecture tracts

27
See *OASE* 28 and 40.

28
Beginning with *OASE* 28.

during this period, then *Archis*, under Bekaert's editorship, and certainly *OASE* qualify. Among other things, through a convincing historical anchoring by Erik Terlouw, Endry van Velzen, Kees Vollemans and Gijs Wallis de Vries, but also through the theoretical rhetoric of writers like Geert Hovingh, Joost Meuwissen, Wim Nijenhuis and Harm Tilman. In the process, *Oase* established an independent and expert position within the disciplines of architecture, urbanism and landscape design by establishing the sovereignty of a 'sanctuary of art and intellect' in the interaction of architecture theory, architecture history and architecture criticism. When *OASE* stretches this sanctuary for a trivialising contribution by Gijsberts (the inundation of the gaze) and a humorous article by Sierksma (anecdotal architecture), it is clear that the journal is both 'subscribing to' (*inschrijven*) and 'deregistering from' (*uitschrijven*) its time.[29] To ensure that *OASE* continue to escape contemporary development mechanisms based on the three Os mentioned above, Tafuri's adage, to examine current events from a historical distance in order to take the discourse beyond even the *Fragwürdige* (dubious), remains. During the last period, from 1997 to 2007, *OASE* has established an even more international profile, but the demand for historical reflection continues to set the agenda.[30]

29
See *OASE* 34 and 39.

30
Op cit. (note 26).

In short, *OASE*'s progress runs from student publication, through a period of growth, to maturity, to finally explore the world. It is comparable to Vasari's *Le Vite*.[31] The mature state has been reached through a process, starting out as the house organ of Delft University of Technology, then orienting itself via translations towards a discourse broader than design, and finally to participate, via the call for papers in the debate that evolved via graduate research, international publications and symposia. Incidentally, the articles selected by *OASE* from the 1990-1996 period do open up the possibility of escaping from a discourse that is merely tributary to design practice and the *Zeitgeist* connected with it. The authors reject all compromises in order to create a critical distance through their sovereign position. They are a testament to the shift from the instrumental and utopian notion of design to a position of independent criticism aimed at revealing the intrinsic functioning of architectural culture. The term 'intensive coherence'[32] opens up a new perspective on the metropolis, in order to describe this reality generically and flexibly.

31
Giorgio Vasari, *Le vite de 'piùeccellenti pittori, scultori e architettori* (Florence, 1568).

32
The term, notably explained by Deleuze in 'Folding' (in *Architectural Design Profile* 102), is part of an architectural debate among Jeffrey Kipnis and Greg Lynn, Peter Eisenman and Rem Koolhaas, Zaha Hadid, etc.

A PAINFUL ANTHOLOGY

The contributions by Erik Terlouw, Geert Bekaert and Wim Nijenhuis are painful to the reader. A farewell to the peaceful oasis. They address the idea of 'beyond', a period that no longer tolerates division into periods.[33] Selecting a few anniversary contributions out of 25 years of production seems to make time evaporate in order to find *OASE*'s critical odour

33
See *OASE* 44.

through distillation. *OASE*'s anniversary thus becomes a celebration of edited source material, reasoned manifestoes, in short a shopping list of intellectual pleasures. These are not messages from the world of arguments, in which the familiar categories of past and future are relevant; rather it is about bringing a transhistorical thinking up to date. For instance, through the 'Architecture of Reason',[34] beyond the 'positive and arbitrary rules' of Perrault, Terlouw points out above the decline of the Platonic idea of architecture, and subsequently 'taste', which jettisons its rational explanation through Ledoux. He argues that 'an architectural language that is not judged as to a predetermined content, but as to what it makes possible . . . as a formal, complete in itself and already meaningless, yet ordering and designing instrument.' Bekaert's adaptation of Valéry's text, 'Eupalinos ou l'architecte'[35] leads to the following pronouncement: 'Yet all the delicate care for the durability (*la durée*) of the building expressed in the care for detail is nothing compared to the attention Eupalinos displayed when he worked out the emotions and the vibrations of the soul of the future viewer of his work.' Nijenhuis[36] uses Virilio's perception of time to provoke 'transhistoricity', besides the conventional notions of syn- and diachronous time, the vanishing of the perspectivist and finite view of time and space. This is about the filmic 'hiatus' in which we become conscious of a world that is 'separate from memory' in order to 'challenge our expectations'. 'Time, stripped of dimensions . . . has no end.' Such a 'sudden' time 'interrupts the habituation to continuous time in a normal progression in reality and thereby generates mental processes and the passions related to them'.

34 See *OASE* 29.

35 See *OASE* 28.

36 See *OASE* 44.

Has this architecture debate lost its object as an artefact? No, the building appears as an architectural statement and retains its validity as a mouthpiece for rhetoric. Thanks to reflection, the debate has been intensified, but also expanded. Bekaert, for instance, has Valéry observe that 'it is the architect who transforms seeing into the visible'. The result is 'a completed building that presents us, at a glance, with a sum of intentions, inventions, insights and powers'. Quoting Germain Boffrand, Terlouw makes the connection between architecture and building: 'The detailing of the mouldings and the other elements that comprise a building are to architecture what words are to an oration.' Nijenhuis, finally, shows us the Fiat factory in Turin so admired by Le Corbusier, but beyond what Jencks terms his 'tragic perspective', the building and its test track is situated in Virilio's perspective, that of speed and vanishing. A posteriori we see the building differently, yes, 'every observation leads to optical illusion'.

OASE AS HOST

As a journal, *OASE* has also provided a podium for a number of favourite writers, including Michel van Nieuwstadt and many designing, teaching and researching writers such as

Jurjen Zeinstra. Van Nieuwstadt invites, as it were, Cacciari, who had not only floridly summarised his articles himself, but more importantly, edited them himself.[37] Should we say that his 'aesthetic and philosophical questions' largely coincide with *OASE*'s agenda, specifically 'to become an exile in one's homeland', an exile in search of the nearly exhausted sources of the intellect? Should we also note, however, that the article 'Houses of the Future' (Zeinstra)[38] risks resorting to the utopian rhetoric of design? Fine, it is an 'exploration of the limits of the discipline' through 'extremely fascinating experiments' such as those of the Smithsons and Archigram. Yet would it not have been interesting, with Cacciari in mind, to adapt the text in order to update it with current experiments, via Kiesler's Endless House, Van Berkel's Möbius House and Lebbeus Woods's New City, for example?

37
Op cit. (note 35).

38
See *OASE* 32.

OASE consisted of a fairly constant and sometimes alternating series of hosts who, in addition to consulting and balloting their guests, also seasoned their texts in the kitchen themselves. Their expertise is that of haute cuisine. They merit praise for a balanced series of articles, translations and editorials. They measure up without question to leading architecture journals. A comparison with journals that set out to document and describe design practice falls short a priori, because *OASE* is about a definitive disengagement from the codes of the practice of the profession. This necessary detachment allows an unbiased yet critical discourse about architecture based on a dynamic complex of perspective in cultural science and aesthetic philosophy. In the process, *OASE* has gradually carved out a position and incorporated the capacities of such journals (some of them no longer extant) as *Lotus*, *Daidalos* and *Oppositions*, such as their capacity for theoretical thematisation, historical situation and substantive polemic, respectively. *OASE*'s relevance is increasingly grounded in the capacity to formulate productive rather than operational criticism. A criticism that is sufficient in itself by relying on its sovereign position to examine architectural culture from the inside as well as the outside, based on history and theory as well as on a perspective beyond the familiar, the unpredictable.

THE EDITORIAL LANDSCAPE

Let us sketch the landscape. 'Splendour is tragic', 'The green grass . . .', 'Fence, labyrinth and cave', 'Periphery of the heart' and 'Architecture on the rocks', 'An excess of sensations', 'Cornfield and poppy', 'Shadows in the green . . .'.[39] A series of narrative introductions and articles with a literary bent. Let us compare the landscape of all the texts in *OASE* to those of the anthologies of, among others, Michael Hays,[40] Hilde Heynen et al.[41] and Kate Nesbitt.[42] The first two limit themselves to identification and reading advice, the third might inspire *OASE* if we set the *OASE* editorials alongside her introduction.

39
See, respectively: *OASE* 40, Gijs Wallis de Vries; 33, Philippe Panerai cs; 34, Michiel Riedijk; 35, Juliette Bekkering; 34, Willemijn Wilms Flot; 39, Johan Meyer; 42, Joost Meuwissen; and 43, Dirk van den Heuvel.

40
K. Michael Hays (ed.), *Architecture Theory since 1968* (Cambridge, 1998).

41
Hilde Heynen et al., *Dat is architectuur. Sleutelteksten uit de 20e eeuw* (Rotterdam, 2001).

42
Kate Nesbitt, *Theorizing a New Agenda for Architecture: An Anthology of Architectural Theory 1965-1995* (Princeton, 1996).

If we situate the 'small editorial narratives' within her larger narrative, they should 'light up' like pearls. Her work covers the period from 1965 to 1995 but represents a possible agenda for *OASE* on its way to issue number 100. Her thematisation is admittedly somewhat categorical, but *OASE* can use it to outline its rhetorical landscape, as Hays does carve in Deleuzian style on the cover of his book but fails to elaborate in terms of content.

The 'compilation of editorials and articles'[43] from the 1990-1996 period can be seen as an emergency landing in the desert. Saint-Exupéry's little prince would hear various fragments of a strange civilisation: 'the collective longing of architects for an individual course-setting in architecture' answers the 'storm of irresistibility' as a result of trendy 'images' by opposing it with 'gravity and self-evidence'. Back to a 'speaking architecture'![44] Moreover, the question of 'form' must be faced, as well as the 'tectonics of resistance'. Does the 'intelligent membrane' (of Kas Oosterhuis) offer a solution?[45] The 'cryptic demand for a collective identity' in government policy documents on architecture and space must provide an answer to the 'pluriformity' observed by Jencks and the NAi.[46] What's more, the 'shudder' may be an instrument to 'appeal to the individual without the mediation of a convention'. Nor does the 'end of the avant-garde' mean that architecture should dress up as Pop Art in order to appeal to the 'masses' through 'medium and technology' – perhaps via 'hardware' in relation to 'freedom' and 'software' in relation to 'identity'? In any event, a 'master plan' (by Richard Meier), which led to 'a shocking mediocrity' in Antwerp, should be avoided. 'Architecture should contribute to a broadening of the mind.'[47]

Isn't all of this a 'prison' that, according to Bachelard, is 'as familiar as it is hostile'?[48] And doesn't the unbridled excess of Koolhaas's 'Atlanta', together with the evocation of the 'underground cave, Rome' not point to a necessary 'internal quality of urban design' as a consequence of the negation of the 'external'? If, along with the pilots of *OASE*, we surrender to these metropolises, these designed deserts, yes, then we see the architecture of oases, a complex network entailing the challenge of intensifying architectural rhetoric. These countless Bergson-esque 'moments' even take us beyond the *Fragwürdige* to keep rediscovering, via the 'mental builder par excellence', the power of 'poïesis'.[49] O, *OASE*, Oh, let the plea, in its simply constructed theoretical force, not be swept away to the four winds, but instead go bravely forth to explore, in a 'clairvoyant' way, Virilio's[50] view of today's 'desert of chaos'! Perhaps Vattimo's nomadic ability could lead the way: the 'weak thought'[51] that, devoid of a 'solid foundation' continues to interpret the flowing character of reality.

43
Compiled by Filip Geerts and Marc Schoonderbeek, among others.

44
See editorials in *OASE* 28, 29 and 30.

45
See editorial in *OASE* 29.

46
See editorial in *OASE* 42.

47
See editorials in OASE 32, 35 and 39.

48
See editorial in *OASE* 33.

49
See editorials in *OASE* 33, 34, 40 and 44.

50
Paul Virilio, *A Landscape of Events* (Cambridge, 2002), with an introduction by Bernard Tschumi.

51
Gianni Vattimo, 'Il pensiero debole' (Milan, 1983).

OASE 28 (*Speed and Gravity*) was published in December 1990. At the time, architecture and architecture criticism were experiencing the after-effects of the deliberate confrontation with other intellectual disciplines including cinema, literature and, above all, philosophy. Tschumi, Eisenman and Derrida, the pioneers of this debate, were keen to see architecture 'put itself on the line' by opening up to other practices. This would help architecture, put forward as a metaphor for slowness and stasis, meet the major challenges posed by mobility and the new media. During this process, two different approaches are in constant conflict. The first ascribes to the politics of the *Gesamtkunstwerk*, positing architecture as a kind of slate for these other arguments. The second, more or less classic approach accepts slowness as a sobriquet: Giorgio Grassi's article on education as the basis for an architectural community, which appeared in this issue, can be read as such, as well as De Nijl's design study with its emphasis on typology as the theory of architecture.

The article by Wim Nijenhuis formed the theoretical core of *OASE* 28. Drawing on philosophical terminology, it outlines the development of an 'aesthetics of disappearance' prompted by the general acceleration caused by the revolution of means of transport and the media. The order of transport and mass communication is characterised by the destruction of place, distance and 'presence'. After all: amid general mobilisation everything is always moving (on). Nijenhuis claims that this puts great pressure on architecture and urbanism as disciplines of 'appearance' and 'presence'. What's more, he argues, the set of instruments deployed by architecture has become obsolete. After all, since the Renaissance it has been used for the production of a transparent, objective and stable spatial order, a order that is material, solid, slow and sustainable and formed by physical elements such as thresholds, walls and floors and dependent on land surveying and perspectival insight. Any architect will recognise in Nijenhuis's argument the deliberate and provocative – because somewhat caricaturing – (lack of) insight of his discipline that appears to be inherent to philosophy. The philosopher Hegel once described architecture as the 'lowest', because heaviest, most physical form of art, the kind of art that sees the mind struggle to overcome matter (a vision masterfully parodied in Peter Greenaway's *The Belly of an Architect*).

The hyperbolic finds its paradoxical expression in Nijenhuis's 'calm reasoning': his argument is entirely plausible. The more the architect is prepared to pursue Nijenhuis's train of thought, the more he will be provoked. But it is precisely this provocation that leads to reflection on the architect's part, to the need to formulate his own answer to the question posed, or to phrase it as an architectural question. The fact that architecture has succeeded in doing so is evidenced by the extent to which it has itself become immaterial and 'de-realising', targeting the in-between and the hiatus, and prepared to carve its own way amid the new media . . .

Frans Sturkenboom
Member of the editorial board
from *OASE* 14 to 22 and
from *OASE* 28 to 34

Translated by Laura Vroomen

Wim Nijenhuis

THE PASSION FOR THE HIATUS

FIRST PUBLISHED IN *OASE* 28

Artefacts: artificial structures or phenomena encountering and dealing with natural phenomena, all feeling reduced here to an optical illusion.
Paul Virilio, *Aesthetics of Disappearance*

Architecture and film are vision machines. Before the invention of rapid modes of transport such as the train and before the invention of the dynamic prostheses of memory such as film, the most important instrument with which a society could express its cosmology was architecture. This was true for cities such as Babylon, Niniveh and Thebes in ancient times, as well as for the Renaissance and baroque eras. The value, meaning and splendour of the *locus* were expressed in the age-old phenomenon of the fortified city, which derived its form and its restriction from the embodiment of the boundary in a system of walls, towers and gateways. Ranked above the interminable journey of nomadism, it celebrated an order in which the sojourn and the delay prevailed, an order wherein the intramural was also equated with safety, certainty and rationality.

In its restrictive form the city offered its inhabitants a system for spatial and mental orientation that established the meaning of the here and the there, the inner and the outer, the near and the far, and the familiar and the foreign. Because the city was geographically fixed and had fixed dimensions, its boundaries produced the *mundus imaginalis* of infinity, a world that was unfamiliar with nomadism. Fixedness and permanence also implied a special relationship with time, contained in the theme of duration and continuity. These qualities of the space-time vector made it possible to establish a society on the basis of solid forms, and thus instituted a perception of the world that was static. From the nineteenth century, under the influence of the train and cinematography, this static world traversed by moving bodies was starting to be replaced at an alarming rate by a dynamic world that spins around a static body. Looking out from the train or watching a film, our field of vision is filled with a fast-moving, flowing world.

Although our tradition attributes more reality to the fixed than to the fluid, and even equates the fixed with the evident, the static forms of the city, just like the flowing forms of dynamic perception, are 'arte-facts', artificial structures or manifestations perceived through the man-made structures of architecture and the artificial manifestations of film. In both cases the world appears as a phenomenon mediated by these arte-facts, which is made manifest through the order of perceptibility, but which also disappears into or behind this order. The world is a relative phenomenon, relative to the order of our perception. However, the world that appears and disappears through architecture is different to that of film and that which is held up to us from our rapid forms of transport. Architecture and (communication) media enter into a discordant relationship at the moment the (mental) worlds that emanate from the respective modes of perception start to interfere with one another.

SPEED AND DISAPPEARANCE

'No more delay!' was not only the adage of the founders of the nation-state in the nineteenth century, bringing us the standardization of weights and measures, the abolition of tolls and dissolution of guilds, and the introduction of national time; we find a similar idolatry of flow among the engineers who introduced the train. 'No more delay!' expresses an attitude that equates the rapid flow with survival. The territory is put into perspective and the physical environs are marginalized in favour of a unidirectional movement that is fixated on its goal or terminus. In its form and direction the train re-enacts the offensive column of the penetration strategy known from the art of warfare that, under Carnot and Napoleon around 1800, definitively replaced the besiegement and encircling of the fortified city.

'No more delay!' means above all: the emptying of the route and its immediate surroundings. Anything that does not sustain the goal-oriented movement is a potential hindrance and a source of danger. The railway is cleared and declared off-limits to man and beast; the dissidents are intercepted with cowcatchers and kept at bay by means of barriers and gates. Delay has acquired all the characteristics of a contentious and combated adversary force. The battle against delay turns into a battle against the earth's surface, which disappears beneath the levelling projects of civil engineering, such as bridges, railway embankments and tunnels. The levelling of the route, of which the Gotthard Tunnel and the Moerdijk Bridge are a case in point, shifts the manifestations of the earth's surface with its obstacles and objects to the *fond* of perception. This fosters the desertification of space, which finds its psychological counterpart in the 'panoramic gaze',[1] the dreamy and mentally retreated orientation towards the distant horizon. The material and mental-visual desert-form of space is the necessary complement to speed. That the train, as it put the territory into perspective, would come to represent an assault on and liquidation of the city and the urban community, was astutely presaged in 1873, by Victor de Stuers, the founder of the Dutch Historic Building Council,[2] when he protested against the demolition of Maastricht's city ramparts and gateways for the sake of the railway line.

Once the violence of penetration has superseded the traditional encircling of the fortress, the speed of transport demands further excavations and tunnelling. The breakthrough, levelling and clearance will soon be followed by penetrations into the subterranean, because it not only necessitates the absence of obstacles, but also the guarantee of the inaccessibility of the track. Because speed requires emptiness *it shifts underground*, as foretold by Jules Verne in his story, 'An Express of the Future':[3]

> 'No doubt you are asking yourself who I am?' said my guide: 'Colonel Pierce, at your service. Where are you? In America, at Boston – in a station.'
> 'A station?'
> 'Yes, the starting-point of the "Boston to Liverpool Pneumatic Tubes Company".'
> And, with an explanatory gesture, the Colonel pointed out to me two long iron cylinders, about a metre and a half in diameter, lying upon the ground a few paces off.

Colonel Pierce had linked up Europe and America by means of a 'peashooter of interminable length' for passengers. The 'inventor' has laid two long, steel cylinders with a length of more than 3,000 miles and a total weight of over 13,000,000 tons. An extremely powerful current of air propels Pierce's carriages through the cylinders at a speed of 1,800 km an hour 'in the same way that despatches are conveyed pneumatically round Paris'. In 1989 this idea was revived with the 'High-Speed Tunnel Route',

1 Wolfgang Schivelbusch, *Geschichte der Eisenbahnreise. Zur Industrialisierung von Raum und Zeit im neunzehnten Jahrhundert* (Munich/Vienna, 1977), translated by Anselm Hollo as *The Railway Journey: The Industrialization and Perception of Time and Space in the 19th Century* (Berkeley, 1987).

2 Victor de Stuers, 'Holland op z'n smalst', *De Gids* 1873, 320-403.

3 Jules Verne, 'An express of the future', *The Strand Magazine* 1895.

which envisions a system of tunnels under Europe that will interconnect its population centres by means of vacuum transport. Here, speed will be coupled with radical emptiness.

The subway gives us a glimpse of what the empirical world will become under the regime of speed. In the tunnels of the underground tram, the world of urban objects had already become a desert, dotted with a few oasis-like stations. In the subway tunnel we experience the eclipse of urban forms, which reappear in memory like a *fata morgana*. Thanks to the evocative power of the names of stations, the old world once again becomes a *mundus imaginalis*; however, no longer a world of the imagination, but of memory.[4]

4 Henri-Pierre Jeudy, 'Metrobeelden', *OASE* 23 1989, 44-48.

THE AESTHETICS OF DISAPPEARANCE AND THE PASSION FOR THE VOID

The Greek word *aisthesis* does not so much signify the rule or theory of beauty, as: perceptible with the senses. In this sense the metro and the train provide us with an experience of the aesthetics of disappearance.[5] This aesthetics, which is closely connected to the performance of the rapid vehicle, carries a logic of abduction. Deep down, it suggests something of the forced separation and melancholy of such an abduction. The moment one frees oneself from the geographical and territorial body to board a form of transport is also the start of a process of de-socialization, which has evolved steadily from the warrior-horseman of ancient times to the present. Whereas in the past, when people still lived in neighbourhood communities, the other was both identified and familiar in the everyday recurrence of the encounter, now, in step with the revolution of the means of transport, this neighbour will swiftly fade into a 'shadow' that is only re-encountered by chance. Eventually, the stranger will reside among us in secret . . . The liquidation of the delay by the power of transport will not only facilitate better communication between groups and improve trade, but it will also bring about this fleeting presence of the other. Many a passer-by will then disappear for good. The kinetic habituation to the sudden disappearance of fellow humans will assume the tragic character of a social divorce; the physical presence of fellow man will become less real. Both as passer-by and as passenger, the Other will soon be identified with its cinematic image. Hence the supremacy of fashion and looks. The same retinal retention that enables us to watch a film must grasp the transience of fellow humans. Yet in the improbability of the cinema, the physical probability of the corporeal will be banished in favour of a terrifying persistence of the signs.

5 Aesthetics: from *aisthesis*: perceptible by the senses.

Just like a camera, rapid vehicles are machines for taking 'shots'. Their relationship with film lies in the 'linearization' of the observed surroundings. The mental image they produce is the 'strip'. Rapid vehicles allow us to see the geographic planes and reliefs of the areas traversed as they pass by, as we might at a parade. Unfortunately, this speed-induced optical illusion produces a double-edged phenomenon: in the frenzy of accelerated movement the passenger sees things as if they were moving, whereas in reality they are standing still and it is the passenger who is passing them. Conversely, in modern-day urban life those who surround us create the impression they will stay, whereas they will actually disappear forever.

We have, strangely and tragically, become accustomed to these phenomena that belong to the meta-stability of the cities we inhabit. This meta-stability is not so much a product of the journey as a romantic voyage of discovery, but of the disintegrating and destabilizing forces of a wind: the wind generated by the speed of a transport system that accompanies the pneumatic breaths of the commuter city. This wind deports the inhabitants and turns them into 'displaced persons'. It is remarkable that nobody notices this wind and that nobody is concerned about the fact he is always interacting with spectres. Paradoxically, the eradication of delay does not result in an 'arrival' or 'home-coming', but drags us down into an interminable 'departure' or 'leave-taking', while at the same time all sense evaporates. The experience of this in the desert-form of space and the desert-form of the social moulds our passion for the aesthetics of disappearance.[6]

6 Jean Baudrillard, 'Transparenz, Probleme des Nihilismus', *Berliner Hefte* 17, 1981, 35.

However, something of the temporal desert-form already resides in the eclipse of the subway, and this would eventually be made explicit in the *special effect* in film. The wonder of the special effect is a supplementary phenomenon, extracted from reality by the speed of the film camera. Around 1900 the French film maker Méliès claimed that the cleverly deployed trick would make it possible to show the supernatural, the imaginary, indeed even the impossible. Méliès thus freed film from realism, which had ceased to captivate the audience, and saved the medium. This is what he had to say about the film-trick:

> One day, when I was prosaically filming the Place de l'Opéra, an obstruction of the apparatus that I was using produced an unexpected effect. I had to stop a minute to free the film and started up the machine again. During this time passersby, omnibuses, cars, had all changed places, of course. When I later projected the reattached film, I suddenly saw the Madeleine-Bastille Bus changed into a hearse, and men changed into women. The trick-by-substitution, soon called the stop trick, had been invented, and two days later I performed the first metamorphosis of men into women.
>
> Paul Virilio, *The aesthetics of disappearance* (translated by Philip Beitchman), 15-16, quoted from: Georges Sadoul, *Georges Méliès/presentation et bio-filmographie. Choix de textes, correspondence et propos de Méliès* (Paris: Éditions Seghers, 1961)

The miracle stems from a technical coincidence, which causes the de-synchronisation of film-time and real-time. Although the film appears to represent an identifiable unity of life, the trick interruption evokes a sense of the hallucinatory. The film thus creates an improbable world of special effects, analogous to the traffic illusions of the meta-stable commuter town and the subway eclipse.

We can explore the passions stirred by the de-synchronisation of real time and film time using psychological phenomena. At breakfast, the cup is suddenly dropped and its contents spilled across the table. The absence lasts several seconds and its beginning and end are abrupt. Although the senses remain alert, they are not susceptible to external impressions. But as immediate as the absence, so immediate is the subject's return from the accident of the absence. Speech and gesture are resumed where they were left off. The two ends of conscious time are automatically joined together to form continuous time without obvious gaps. These absences can be quite numerous, several hundred a day, and generally go unnoticed by those around us. For people who go through this, nothing has happened. The absent time never existed. Children who have many of these episodes have a tendency, when asked, to add what they did not see. They draw on other memories to fill in the gaps. If such a child is placed in front of a bunch of flowers and asked to draw them, it will draw not just the flowers but also the person who put them in the vase and even the meadow where they were picked. Having grown secretly apprehensive and insecure about the truth of the world that surrounds him, the child must time and again penetrate the frontiers of his memory in search of the missing information. The described over-totalization is an indication of our habit to join together the sequences, harmonise their contours and match what we see and what we failed to see, what we remember and fail to remember. The fusion-confusion of reality and imagination, the real and the imaginary, must be invented and constructed by the interrogated consciousness in order to lend its 'discourse', [from discursus: to run to and fro/haste and division], a 'verisimilitude' [from *veri similis* = like the truth] vis-à-vis social intercourse. If perception means accepting as true that which has the appearance of truth, then this 'acceptance of truth' is impossible without an artificial addition. It makes probable that which is *conceivable*.

The technical coincidences of Méliès' camera reproduced the same desynchronised conditions as the child that joins flower girl and meadow. Méliès, who lets the machine interrupt the systematic sequence of film takes, is doing the same as the child that joins together the two experiential sequences from before and after the crisis, thus undoing any conspicuous temporal disruption. Both play a game with the hiatus, or the time-gap. They work with a disappearance of time. The child, however, deploys its imagination to achieve probability, whereas Méliès' 'gap' has become so substantial that the 'reality effect' is utterly transformed into a 'supernatu-

Deserted FIAT factory Lingotto in Turin

ral phenomenon', an improbability that challenges the 'conceivable' aspect of perception.

Through the constant recurrence of the time hiatus, the film reveals a world that has never been seen before. In other words, it reveals a world that is independent of the memory as the subconscious storeroom of traces of experience. By creating a world without memory and with unfixed dimensions of space and time, the film shows configurations that ordinarily appear to us in dreams and memories: fleeting and phantasmagorical. The trick interruption reveals that part of our true nature that never ceases to respond to events that are, in fact, in the past and absent. It is the omitted 'in-between', the *hiatus* that challenges our memory and our expectations, as a result of which we see the configurations as marvellous and improbable. The jolt of the hiatus is nothing but a ploy. A ploy directed at the 'conceivable' aspect of perception by suddenly interrupting our habituation to the continuous time typical of a routine reality, thus generating certain mental processes and their associated passions.

According to Dostoevsky, a powerful eclipse of consciousness, such as it occurs during an epileptic seizure, is presaged by an aesthetic perception or an aesthetic awareness. The crisis reveals itself, like a bolt from the blue, by the beauty of this shade. The epileptic, such as Dostoevsky, does not welcome the seizure as a moment of lust, rather he dreads it. Yet he is informed of its arrival by a state of bliss, by a youthful exhilaration.[7] The epileptic is imbued with the divine muse, in the true sense of the word, and at the same time enraptured, transported . . . until he regains consciousness. In his book *Annäherungen*[8] Ernst Jünger writes that this exhilaration should be seen as the effect of a *mortgage on time*, which must be paid on the due date. It is a claim that is cruelly confirmed by the epileptic seizure itself. Nevertheless, the accident of consciousness, the hiatus of time, is preceded by an inexplicable exhilaration.

An exceptional and intense phenomenon, which turns out to be the infra-normal, manifests itself through the hiatus. An interval in time leads us to the difference. In the difference we experience a transience, a liquidated reality. This is what poets such as Hölderlin and authors such as Nietzsche, Rilke and Robert Musil took as the subject of a heroic, anticipatory battle against the metaphysical 'fixedness' of reality, in an effort to liberate the oppressed exhilarating forces. Perhaps it is this *power of the difference* that we encounter on a daily basis in traffic and through the media. At any rate, the difference offers a way of to eradicate the fixedness of reality and to put the metaphysical proof of perception into stark perspective.

'I can no longer think my own thoughts, the moving pictures have replaced my thoughts,' a writer remarked in 1930 regarding the introduction of big cinema buildings. His words are a conscious or subconscious allusion to the warlike onslaught of images outlined in Paul Virilio's *Guerre et Cinéma*.[9] The military power lies less in brute force than it does in the psychological deterrence that is exercised through an impressive display. Just as the warrior of old used to deter by the sudden appearance of his person and by sabre rattling – think, for instance, of the terrifying appearance of the samurai in Kurosawa's films, causing mortal fear that cancels out all thought and sense of reality – any strategy of the appearances is nothing more than sabre rattling. The ubiquitous information is reminiscent of the sudden appearance of the warrior, but having grown accustomed to the accompanying shock we have become desensitized.

7 Plato: So the Muse herself inspires men (*enthéous*), and the inspiration passes from them to others, till we have a whole chain of men possessed (*entheousiadzontoon*).

8 Ernst Jünger, *Annäherungen, Drogen und Rausch* (Frankfurt am Main, 1980).

9 Paul Virilio, *Guerre et Cinéma I. Logistique de la Perception* (Paris, 1984), translated by Patrick Camiller as *War and Cinema: The Logistics of Perception*, (London, 1989).

As a result the primary perceptions are not converted into individual perceptions, because the 'conceivable' is constantly interrupted by the obtrusive presence of the media, which have created a mass consciousness. They provide the masses with a store of information and programme their memories. Walter Benjamin, in his account of the demise of the story, deeply regretted this state of affairs.[10] An a priori occupation and hyperactive defence mechanism of our consciousness prevent the penetration of daily stimuli and impoverish our experiences. Thus storytelling is deprived of its basis and source of inspiration.

The informative address and the striking image, which the artistic avant-gardes intended to be educational tools, now achieve the exact opposite. A dense network of stimuli and signs forms a continuous interruption of the potential aesthetic surprise and the budding insight. The stab at independent observation is overwhelmed by the speed of information. Nowadays this no longer applies solely to memory and experience which, as inner illuminations of reality, are expelled by the glare of the shock, but applies mainly to the gaze. The gaze is captured by the dynamic play of light of the vehicles and the media, which takes us by surprise by means of rapid changes. We have grown accustomed to this surprise, so much so that we now only experience these stimuli from the *nothingness* of the transition, from the hiatus. It explains why Alexander Kluge can present us with a blind film director in his film *Der Angriff der Gegenwart auf die übrige Zeit* (The Assault of the Present on the Rest of Time, 1985). The director focuses exclusively on what, in the near future, will become film's essence: the eclipse of the image. The blind film director limits himself to the black of the interruption, which accompanies the exposed image 24 times per

10 Walter Benjamin, *Charles Baudelaire: A Lyric Poet In The Era Of High Capitalism,* translated by H. Zohn (London, 1983).

Deserted FIAT factory Lingotto in Turin

second. The fact that for most of the time he aims his camera at something other than the dramatic film action is of marginal importance here. The blind director is a master of the art of 'overlooking' and 'looking askance'. The strategy of the appearances, which is based on the hiatus and change, uses de-synchronisation to generate the desert-form of time. By making the consciousness hasty it creates insensitivity and insecurity as correlatives of an image of the world that now exists only in the mind. The strategy of the appearances liquidates the material realm of activities and experience in order to create a world in which seeing precedes being.

THE LIQUIDATION OF ARCHITECTURE

The great(er) vehicle through time and space – the vehicle of traffic and the visual media – fosters the disinterest in the perceived world. Architect Jean Nouvel estimates that 85 per cent of people perceive architecture subconsciously. The crisis of the object, and hence that of the city and architecture, is well-nigh inevitable. The power of the obstacle as an intersection of sightlines, a multiplicity of detail and a combination of textures, whose form and materiality are highlighted by the light of the sun, is steadily being displaced by the machines of dynamic perception. The static carriers of memory, such as architecture and the city, pay their daily toll to the active prostheses of memory, such as film and television.

In *The World as Will and Representation*, Schopenhauer celebrates the static nature of architecture for its ability to embody gravity, cohesion, rigidity and solidity. In his view, architecture is countered by the tragedy, which affords us a glimpse of chaos and transience. For George Bataille[11] architecture is the embodiment of an ideal state of society, because it blocks the moving elements that remain out of sight behind the façades. Both viewed architecture as an aesthetics of appearance that was, generally speaking, an aesthetics of the material carriers of objects and works. The aesthetics of appearance revolved around materiality, the interaction of form and *fond*, the emergence of a painting on the canvas, the materialization of a sculpture from stone, and around an architecture that took pride in its brotherhood with the stone, that was tied to its foundation and yet sought to defy gravity, an architecture that set itself the task of creating the city as an entity against the backdrop of the sky, the fields, the forests and the roads. Ultimately, society as a whole was based on the fact that these material carriers arose as something solid, as something valuable and meaningful, as expressed in the principle and form of the fortified city.

11 George Bataille, *Inner Experience,* translated by Leslie A. Boldt (New York, 1988).

The advent of film, or more precisely cinematography, the take and the technique of sequencing did not herald the era of the tragedy or the inner experience, but that of the aesthetics of disappearance. Things no longer touch our hearts through their presence and solidity, but through the fact that they are closer and more solid the more they fade. The aesthetics of disappearance intensifies (mental) presence through the relative removal of the world of objects from perception in space and time. Things exist because they disappear. The fact that they owe their impact on memory to retreat, blur and transience actually signifies the revolution of the monument, or rather, the monumental. The monument presents what is absent with the help of a solid carrier. Conversely, the monumentality of the aesthetics of disappearance rests on the fleetingness and flight of the sign. It monumentalises the moment.

With the dynamic camera position, the combination of the camera with vehicles, the cinematographic technique of the disappearance joins the set of train, subway, car and airplane, which has launched its assault on mental distance in name of the remote. It reduces the time-distance to a moment and shrinks space into a kind of ubiquitous proximity. Film, television and forms of transport bring everything closer, so we appear to acquire an overview of the world. Whereas in the past ubiquity, or omnipresence, was the reserve of God, now it lies at the feet of man. However, what is awaiting us is no panoptic ubiquity, no omnipresent omni-vision. Foucault's panopticism[12] is betrayed by synopticism, which arises out of the technique of the 'hiatus' in space and time. As a result we develop, within our individual field of perception, a fragmentary, broken and contracted, constantly changing, fluid, liquid worldview, complemented by uncontrolled reminiscences that infect the image of the true world with the imaginary.

12 Michel Foucault, *Surveiller et punir. Naissance de la prison* (Paris, 1975), 251-295, translated by Alan Sheridan as *Discipline and Punish: the Birth of Prison* (New York, 1995).

But how does the world's liquidation impact on the experience of and approach to space and time? The media's inherent destruction of time-distance creates effects of iconological distortion, causing the rapid disappearance of the most elementary landmarks. Our traditional topology and morphology, which were dominated by the size of an area, our traditional conception of geographical expanse as mapped in cadastral plots of land, are fading in favour of a view of the world in which the notion of physical dimension loses its significance and analytical value. We are witnessing the co-production of an empirical reality in which *direct* and media-driven observations merge to produce an instantaneous and momentary representation of space. The difference in scale between the actual distance in time and space and the size of the representations that used to guarantee the readability of the map, the design drawing, the model, etcetera, ceases to exist. Direct observation of empirical facts makes way for a tele-observation, which leaves the observer without any direct contact with empirical reality. The absence of any mediation of *scale*, and the chance to see planes that in reality cannot be seen with the naked eye, renders the images *accidental*. They no longer have a referent, which produces a serious imbalance between what is perceptible by the senses and what is intelligible. This forms the first disruption of our familiar topology and morphology.

A second disruption derives from the fact that the visual angle is displaced by the projection time. The time depth of the media projections replaces the field depth of the Renaissance perspective. The vantage point, the omni-present axis of a perspectivist point of reference, makes way for the fleeting, remote view (tele-vision) of an observation aiming at transparency and penetration. In other words, an observation that penetrates the biggest and most remote appearances, establishing a gaze without horizon. An event that will lead us to God, if we are to believe the portrayal of this theme in the film *The Man with the X-Ray Eyes*. Radical transparency and penetration will enlighten us and bring us closer to the light, which will be the last thing we see. Initially, the man with the X-ray eyes is thrilled with his newly-acquired faculty, bestowed on him by a chemical solution. He sees through people's clothes, displaying a special interest in women. Yearning for his faculty to be improved, their skeletons are revealed to him. Ultimately, even the mass of the earth and planets no longer obstruct his view. What remains is pure visibility, light, which extends from his retina to the remotest vistas.

The eye of the camera, our technical prosthesis of transparency and penetration and remote vision that operates just like the X-ray eye, therefore heralds less of a reversal of matter or the revelation of a kind of extra-reality that until then had been buried within the things and is now projected in the 'distance'. This was Walter Benjamin's view.[13] Rather, this 'eye' opens up an *open field* of perception, whose objective frontiers will never be known, an integral dispersal and fragmentation, a broken morphology/topology of immeasurable magnitude. Such a tele-capture of the world by the eye of the camera and the simultaneous aesthetics of disappearance corrode the old geometric and architectural configurations and thus overthrow the way of seeing of the Renaissance, which was based on the monumental arts.

13 Walter Benjamin, *The Work of Art in the Age of Mechanical Reproduction* (1936), 34.

The dissolution of scale, distortion and perversion of forms and sites, elimination of intervals in space and time, compression of images and data – the mediatized précis of the world brings us face to face with a *trompe-l'oeil* effect, with a representative order that is reminiscent of anamorphosis and which has been emptied of its points of reference. Whereas the baroque had relied on architecture and plaster for the distortion of forms, these have now been superseded by the immateriality of light and electronics, the true baroque architecture of our time.

Although a foot remains a foot and the east the east, today's model of the city is no longer determined solely by squares, rivers, high-rise blocks, a succession of streets and a patchwork of plots of land. This gaze on the city's architecture is harassed by a lucid doppelganger. A technological time-space, a tele-time-space of the hiatus, is interfering with the city's materiality. As a material foundation of our collective perception and as a set of volumes under the sun, made visible by the light and caught up in the cycle of day and night, the city is besieged by the technical temporality of the length of the transmission, the false day of the screen without depth and the exposure time of rapid vehicles. A construction consisting of a set of temporal-spatial mutations now positions itself opposite the solid stasis of structural engineering. It creates an invisible and improbable order, an order of change and renewal, fragmentation of the whole and dispersal of the constituent parts *ad infinitum*. This is an order that disturbs the senses and grips us in a vertiginous fascination for the unreal and the unstable. If we take the cadastral mapping of the land and the creation of monuments and landmarks as the foundations of urban monumentalisation, its intended effects are continuously dissolved and reconstituted by the systems of transfer and their aesthetics of disappearance. The construction of 'an image of the city', as fantasized by Kevin Lynch in the previous century,[14] has become a troublesome assignment in as far as it aimed to produce psychic stability and territorial identity. As both essence and recollection, the geographical site no longer functions as the basis of human experience. Our modern monumental city, our *metropolis*, is rapidly morphing into an invisible and vertiginous *omnipolis*.

14 Kevin Lynch, *The Image of the City* (Cambridge, MA/London, 1960).

Architectonic counter-movements of postmodernism and those who want to compete with the fascination of the media constructions often forget that architecture was originally a discipline of measures and stasis. It consisted of a body of knowledge and a practice, which enabled us to harmonise a society with a natural environment and thus manage its time and space. Well, this ability based on geodesy to establish a unit of time and place for social activities has now come into open conflict with the (de)constructive forces of the mass media and means of mass communication.

We now have two opposing orders:

- A material one, which is formed by physical elements such as walls, thresholds, floors and exact dimensions and settings. It is an architectonic and urbanistic order, which relies on land surveying and perspectival insight into a situation. It organises and constructs geographical space in a relatively sustainable way. Thanks to its solidity of time and space, this order is slow and exploratory.
- An immaterial one, whose representations, images and messages allow no localisation. As the result of a momentary expression, they are not familiar with solidity, stasis and fixedness. This order sets up an incoherent space-time, which is subsequently disrupted again. Analogous with the tools of our memory, it establishes a de-realised world, a world with a receding reality.

TRANSFINITY

Would it be fair to say that the efforts of architecture and urbanism, which are aimed at the output of and control over the urban dweller's mental pictures and thus try to bring about a stable order in the domain of the imaginary, are based on an obsolete theory of space, perception and orientation? Is our relationship with the city in fact the relationship with a relic, which we view through nineteenth-century eyes? Most probably, since the liquidation of architecture suggests that our society gravitates towards a de-territorialized state, in which the city will lose its obvious functional and cultural centrality. So far, the challenge of the 'greater vehicle' facing the complacency of the urban form has remained concealed behind the masque of history and hidden from view by a naïve trust in the certainty of the geographical place.

Today's impossibility to arrive at a consistent and persistent city concept and urban design has its roots in a rationality which has itself become accidental. The changing theoretical perspectives and 'conceivable' references, that derive from the fact that theories too are subject to fashion, bring us face to face with the disappearance of duration and continuity. The development of thought about the city thus assumes the character of an accident, that is, an incident that escapes the clutches of reason and human initiative through the infinitesimal small time span in which it initiates its disruptive development. The city reclaims in a parodic way the actuality it possessed before the era of planning. Actuality here means: at the mercy of the vicissitudes of fate. From this we learn how the accident of time finally impacts on the condition of space and how the fragmentation of space correlates with the fragmentation of time.

The state of affairs in architecture theory shows how our time implies an endless *commutation* or change. Commutation lacks an objective dimension and therefore rules out reflection. Permanent innovation is steeped in a potent illusion of progress, but in reality it boils down to an accelerated cycle of principles and configurations. So time, too, has become a kind of salt desert, whose surface allows all great speeds, both deceleration and acceleration. The decline of *duration* within *commutation* does *not* mean a transition to eternity, but a transition to the eternity of speed.

Thanks to the absence of frontiers and obstacles within the networks, space and the social can be traversed like a desert. *Transfinity* means we have reached the frontiers of time and space and that no further transgression, or transcendence, is possible.[15] We are no longer faced with a natural limitation, such as the finite nature of space or time, which envelops and encloses us and which afforded metaphysicians of earlier generations a glimpse of infinity. We are instead facing an artificial finiteness, the outcome of the depletion of the time-space horizon that once inspired history and progress. Familiar with all frontiers, we have transgressed them, without this affording us a glimpse of infinity. The upshot of transfinity is that we dispose of all time, of all kinds of time, and therefore have suddenly no more time ahead of us or behind us. It dissolves in its contemporary effect. Accelerating, we have used up our reserves of time and space. In and through acceleration, time and space become mass, or a kind of fluidity, similar to the kind that builds in front of the nose of a projectile. Compressed and condensed, they ultimately form an obstacle to development or progress. They become an unassailable wall: the horizon-negative. The process is similar for the artificial build-up of communication and data, as they ultimately form a mass that thwarts and destroys the development of the social itself. Our present time is an assault on all other times: past, future and eternity.

15 Jean Baudrillard, 'Die Abschreckung der Zeit', *Tumult* 9, 1987, 109-118.

FRAGMENTATION AND BROKEN MORPHOLOGY

This condition of time has an unmistakable effect on the condition of space. We might say that the fragmentation of space is a direct result of the fragmentation of time. In architectural discourse, the whole problematic of fragmented space and the fragmented city is governed by the memory of the image of the complete. However, the problem of fragmentation is not so much the loss of totality, as it is the loss of a restrictive totality that was still governed by the boundary. What emerges in the desert of time-space is not so much the fragment, but the unlimited, sprawling, extensive totality of a *broken morphology*.

The broken morphology is above all a mental configuration that can be identified through memory. It is triggered by the momentary and instantaneous character of the images and concepts generated by the rapid means of transport and the media. The key feature of the broken morphology is the crisis of the concept of dimension. This crisis manifests itself to us as the crisis of a whole, or a totality, as the crisis of a substantive, continuous and homogenous space. Through a process of rupture and dispersion, the continuous and homogenous time-space of archaic geometry appears to turn into the relativity of an accidental time-space. A discontinuous space in which elements and particles, scattered points and fragments become essential again in the context of the instantaneous.

Nevertheless, the media, the view from the car, train, subway, and so forth, as well as the perspectives afforded by the constantly changing frameworks provided by theory (the commutations), never cease to project an image of a city forming or representing a totality. Be it a totality that is now composed of fragments scattered in time and space and of heterogeneous speeds, that is, accelerations and decelerations. The totality they present us with is truly a totality without dimension. The problem of space is therefore not so much its fragmentation as the loss of its dimension generated in the mental picture. As a universe of fragmented spaces, a broken morphology is a totality that lacks dimension because . . . it lacks duration.

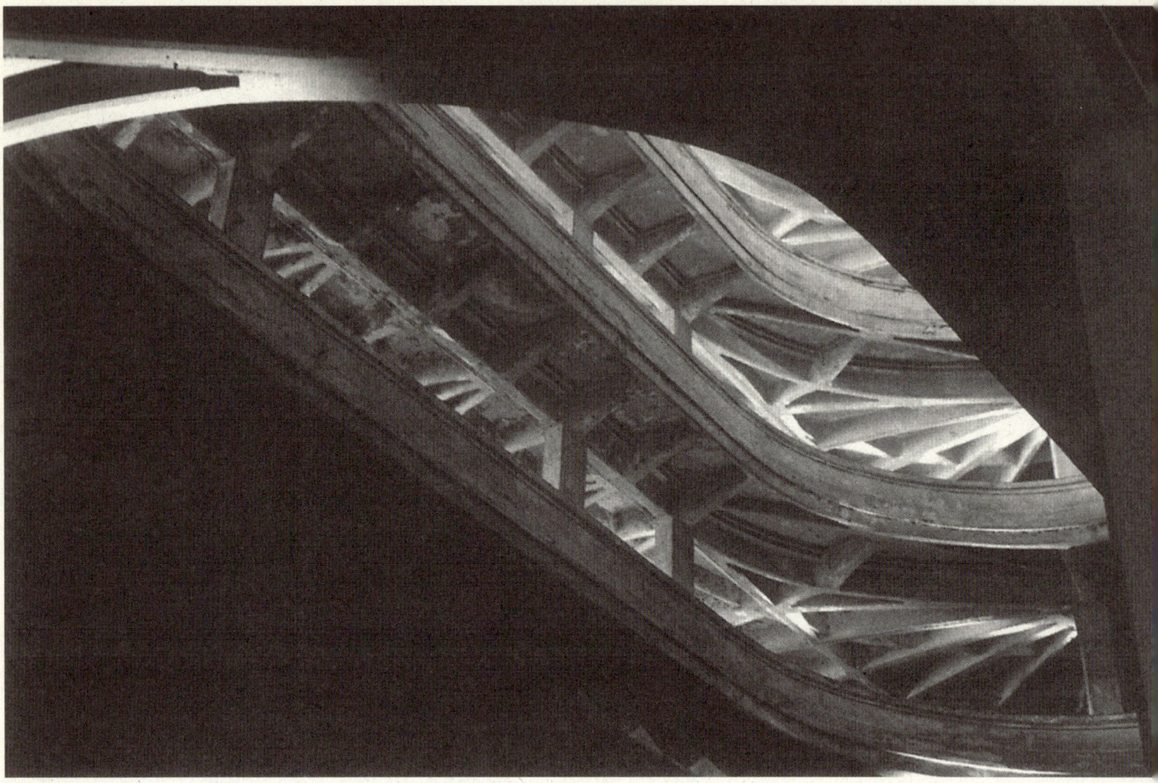

Deserted FIAT factory Lingotto in Turin

For this kind of space I would like to propose the concept of *tele-topology*: a topology that is distinct from the classic notion of time-space, which was measured in terms of expanse and duration.

Topology is essentially the geometry of the form, whereby distance and size are eliminated from mathematical formulae. Although in a topological prescription distance and size may vary from zero to infinity, the formulae nevertheless describe a specific set of manifestations. The topological formulae know how to capture the distanceless mathematically in a series of systematic variations. But, topology cannot deal with absence or lack. This is where tele-topology enters the game, because it considers phenomena such as the elimination of the interval in time and that of the gap in space – everyday phenomena in transport and the media. Although tele-topology cannot measure what is lacking, it does helpfully suggest we conceive of the *hiatus*. What happens in this 'nothingness', in this 'absence', in this 'omission', in this 'something' that no longer matters?

Perhaps the eliminated interval or the vanished gap is a desert-form, a kind of absolute and empty sign, which has no presence of its own and is determined by its context, and thus resists recognition and unambiguous decoding. In his essay on Carlo Scarpa's fragments, Manfredo Tafuri defines the desert-form as the *topos* of the imagination.[16] In doing so, he follows Maurice Blanchot's theory of the *incomplete*.[17] The fragment need not only be seen as the residual part of a whole, which has been lost, but could also be considered as something demanding completion in the viewer's imagination. The fragment thus serves as a stimulus for 'thought'.

In addition, or in contrast, it is clear that the desert of time is caused by change and acceleration. Deserts emerge out of the comprehensive explo-

16 Manfredo Tafuri, 'Carlo Scarpa and Italian Architecture', in: Dalco et al. (eds.), *Carlo Scarpa: The Complete Works* (New York, 1985), 77.

17 Maurice Blanchot, *L'espace littéraire* (Paris, 1955), translated by A. Smock as *The Space of Literature* (Lincoln, NE, 1990); *L'entrétien infini* (Paris, 1969), translated by Susan Hanson as *The Infinite Conversation* (Minneapolis, 1993). See also: Emmanuel Levinas,

ration of earthly phenomena and the subsequent process of contraction, as has been explained by David Harvey.[18] His word has become canonical in postmodern discourse in the 1980s and '90s. This contraction consigns to desolation all non-privileged zones that are outside the scope of a general economy of attention. Following Baudrillard, we might call this desolation, which also includes the forgotten things and devaluated people, the *fourth world*. The fourth world is not robbed and plundered by a kind of European expansionism, as experienced by the third world. Rather, the fourth world is simply abandoned to nothingness. It is abandoned to nothingness by the motion of contraction. The over-concentration of the exchange of images, goods and information abandons the fourth world to its non-existence, to its disappearance. Excluded from the circuits of this world, it is condemned to an erasure, akin to the erasure of the Atlantic Ocean by the Concorde. The fourth world is the real desert. It is created by the desertification of time, bodies and territory. This fourth world is now the *repoussoir* of the social as network.

The deconstruction of space is not carried out by the Deconstructivists, but is instead provoked by the development of transport and the media. Or, to put it in broader terms, by speed and acceleration, including those of the commutation of architectural fashions and theories. Although the fragment and the broken morphology exert a powerful allure, one cannot avoid the impression that we are dealing with a kind of act of war, a 'traumatising' strategy of appearances playing a disappointing game with us – a game that is not too dissimilar to the primitive and shamanistic strategies that draw on the 'wound' and the 'cut' to breed 'a nation of thinkers'.[19]

Sur Maurice Blanchot (Montpellier, 1975), translated by Garth Gillan as 'About Blanchot: An Interview', *Sub-Stance* 14, 1976, 54-57.

18 David Harvey, 'The Experience of Space and Time', in: *The Condition of Postmodernity, An Inquiry into the Origins of Cultural Change* (Oxford, 1980).

19 Friedrich Nietzsche, *On the Genealogy of Morals* (Oxford, 1996), 59.

MACHINES OF GRAVITY

Today all output, architectural and otherwise, takes place on the basis of de-realisation and disappearance. The predicament of architecture is that it is forced to operate on a foundation that is being deconstructed. What is being deconstructed is the homogenous, perspectivist time-space of the Renaissance. Architecture and the city are facing forces that initiate a propensity for pure circulation and pure dissipation. This propensity for formlessness and emptiness is born of speed, while speed in turn springs from the accelerated output and circulation of signs. We, the agitated producers in the field of culture, art and science, produce the acceleration ourselves. What if we decided not to plunge into the wake of the disappearance, but instead attempted to defer the desertification and disappearance or even have our own way with it?

This brings us to the machines of delay.[20] Both within and out of disappearance and transparency, these machines generate a minimum degree of gravity, that is, some degree of gravity, and thus enable us to recover ourselves, at least for a time. The key issue is the paradoxical will to not be an accident, to postpone the accident that in the end will, inevitably, be provoked by the context. Perhaps this gravity may be seen as the stake that lends the game its intensity and hence its passion.

The machines of gravity seek to affirm gravity against the propensity for pure circulation, against the propensity for pure commutation, against the brutality of the confrontation, against transience. Without a doubt, many are in operation already, while many more may be invented. I would like to highlight one possibility here. Gravity is displayed by post-modern

20 Jean Baudrillard, 'Jean Nouvel en het franse denken', *OASE* 25, 1989, 48.

melancholy and perhaps also by Paul Virilio's *humility in thought*. In the case of melancholy and humility the central place is occupied by the body that has become heavy as a result of the circulation speed of the signs. Enough strength is drawn from this heavy body to withstand the pressure to accelerate of the social networking deserts. Its gravity delays the thought process and the thought process is capable of slowing down even more by focusing on a single point: the empty space of the possible future event. Thinking the unthought can be one of them. The thought process has to be slow, because if it accelerates, the tools of knowledge it produces turn into weapons once more and once more they enter into an alliance with the panic that is the basis of the circulation speed of the signs, and thus insist on their deployment in society. To counteract the repetition of the thought patterns in the accelerated circulation, the machine of gravity tries to mould the circulating material in both thinking the accident and developing thoughts by accident. These will bring us into contact with an exterior that could erase the too significant tracks of the life path cleared through speed.

To avoid speed (which is not the speed of writing or drawing), these machines of gravity advocate a special thought pattern. When one focuses on a single point on the artificial frontier of transfinity, at the perimeter of the end without confirming the end as End, imperceptible distortions and minor semantic changes will come into effect. The machine of gravity, of which Paul Virilio's *The Negative Horizon* is a striking example, steers clear of the depression for which our modernity is heading. It does so with the help of a thought process that harks back to its predecessors: melancholy and *acedia* (weariness of the heart), which may be sources of a *poiesis*, providing they remain incomplete and disorganised. These forms resist the departure of the body and the territory and stand by the notion that imagination and territory go together just like fantasy and body do. The thought processes of the machines of gravity constitute a game with secret rules; it takes place against a backdrop of uncertainty. Certainty perverts the game and transforms the stake into a power struggle revolving around the rules. The introduction of gravity in a manner that is not perverse has to echo symbolically what happens in reality. The difference with reality must be kept alive via linguistic symbols.

The end that this machine of gravity inhabits with its melancholic effects is the transfinite. This end has two manifestations: the eschatological acceleration, which projects us onto the wall of time, and the post-historic era with its tedium and listlessness. However, the *apocalypse without transcendence* and the *expansiveness of the post-historic* are only superficially at odds with one another. Ultimately, both contribute to speed. To counter this we must take advantage of the chance to talk about the Apocalypse, yet without being prophets of doom. We must contemplate the post-historic, without contributing to its expansion.

Fundamental perception, producing gravity in the sense outlined above, is alert to negativity and is always open to the recurrence of the primordial fear (in a Kantian sense) that can break the compulsion to produce concepts and understanding quickly. This respite and perhaps the complete loss of conceptual certainty is not immediately compensated for with a ready image, while individuation is not cancelled out by a sense of the universal or the whole. The relativity of the moment of perception leaves matters undecided.

Dyed-in-the-wool melancholy means: being convinced of the end. A fixation on the end cannot be accompanied by the opposite of melancholy. Even the stimulation machines of utopian urbanism or the gigantic effort of space exploration, and also the heroic self-affirmation of Nietzsche ultimately failed to provide a solution. In other words, although a machine of gravity cannot escape the end and the 'weighty' mechanisms it produces, it can lend them a new destiny, by using stylistic expressions which are not averse to irony and bear witness to and show some distrust of themselves.

A protest against the desert-forms, against the fourth world of bodies and territories is appropriate, although perhaps one thing is even more important: the game that revolves around thinking, which itself wants to be the end. The game that revolves around thinking, which itself wants to be finality and which locks itself into definition and terminology. Thinking directed at itself will render itself superfluous. It ultimately boils down to the fact that thinking is itself time, received into a grammar that creates future, past and present. Time, stripped of direction and dimensions, like Virilio's trans-historic time, has no end.

Translated by Laura Vroomen

In the late 1980s, architecture in the Netherlands found itself in an ambiguous, yet interesting position. In the knowledge that an outline based on a series of 'isms' could hardly do justice to the extraordinary character of those years, I would like to describe them as follows. With the storms of postmodernism and deconstruction seemingly confined to the international scene, in the Netherlands the worn-out 'structuralism' of the Forum generation is quietly replaced by a light-hearted neomodernism, which fuses effortlessly with the emerging visual culture of those years. With the arrival in Rotterdam of 'superhero' Rem Koolhaas the storms, or their aftermath, finally reach our shores, to the delight of a new generation of architects.

The youthful *OASE* editors with their varied, burgeoning ideas about architecture are part of this generation and, from their deliberate position on the sidelines, use a series of special issues to try and find some depth amid all the hype.

Erik Terlouw played an important role in all this. He has, without doubt, been one of the most prolific editors in the magazine's history. With few exceptions, his texts and translations are lengthy and erudite. Through a meticulous analysis of historical precedents, they focus on the essence of architecture and architectural thought. They use history as a source: it would be a mistake therefore to read his texts purely as historical tracts. His articles explore several closely linked themes. These themes tie in with the contemporary architectural development outlined in his article 'Image building' (*OASE* 28), in which the old architectural categories 'presence' and 'place' make way for 'representation' and 'time'.

For Erik Terlouw the dissatisfaction with this development triggered his search for the roots of architecture's visual culture. His study of the source material and the connections he establishes were impressive and yielded a series of three lengthy articles published in three issues of *OASE*: 29, 30 and 42. To some extent they rewrite the history of Western architecture as a history of the concept of style. (The text included here is the first in the series.) It is a fascinating history, precisely because of Erik's meticulous and nuanced account of his search and the understated style of his fierce criticism. Perhaps this is why these texts have lost none of their value.

Jurjen Zeinstra
Member of the editorial board
from *OASE* 18 to 41

Translated by Laura Vroomen

Erik Terlouw

THE ARCHI-TECTURE OF REASON

FIRST PUBLISHED IN *OASE* 29

The detailing of the mouldings and the other elements that comprise a building are to architecture what words are to an oration.

Germain Boffrand, *Livre d'Architecture,* 1745

The wealth of materials used, the grandeur of the building, the precision and neatness with which it was built and its symmetry: these were the fundamental beauties that Claude Perrault ascribed to architecture in a 1683 text that can be seen as the beginning of rationalism in architecture, the *Ordonnance des cinq espèces de colonnes selon la méthode des anciens.*[1] This collection seems very much removed from a view of architecture that seeks to find in it something akin to a language, that is to say a structure that in its capacity to visualize, represents something. Even the term 'symmetry', which in the sixteenth and the first half of the seventeenth century meant a harmonious, proportional relationship between the elements and the whole of the building, and which thus linked architecture to the world of (neo-Platonic) ideas, did not signify anything more to Perrault than it does to us.[2]

ARBITRARY BEAUTY

Yet, as the rest of his text makes clear, these 'positive beauties', precisely because of their unquestionable nature, are actually of little import for architecture as a science. In their

1
'In order to judge this correctly we must suppose that there are two kinds of beauties in Architecture, that is those grounded in persuasive reasons and those that depend solely on prejudice. I consider the beauties grounded in persuasive reasons those through which works must be pleasing to all . . . such as the wealth of the material, the grandeur and the magnificence of the edifice, the precision and the neatness of the construction and its symmetry,' *Ordonnance des cinq espèces de colonnes selon la méthode des anciens* (Paris, 1683), iv ff. The wealth and grandeur were not perceived as such by everyone. Simplicity also had a beauty of its own. François Blondel assailed Perrault on this point; see Wolfgang Herrmann, *The Theory of Claude Perrault* (London, 1973), 133. But of course Perrault did not mean that every building should be as grandiose and as big as possible. In his *Abregé des dix livres d'architecture de Vitruve* (Paris, 1674), he had already spoken of a 'reasoned use of the posi-

Claude Perrault, *Mémoires pour servir à l'histoire naturelle des animaux*, frontispiece by S. Le Clerc, 1671. Louis XIV and Colbert visit the Académie des Sciences. In the background the new observatorium, still under construction, can be seen

stead, Perrault posits beauties he calls 'arbitrary', 'for they depend on the will to give a certain proportion, a form and a certain shape to things that could be different in all of these things without being misshapen.' Architecture is about knowing this latter form of beauty: 'It is a fact that knowledge of the arbitrary beauties is most essential in forming what is called taste, and that only in this do true Architects stand out from those who are not.'[3]

The distinction that Perrault draws is in the same vein as that drawn by Malebranche a few years earlier in his *De la Recherche de la Vérité* between two kinds of judgements *(Jugements)*. The first, which coincides with Perrault's positive beauties, is 'a judgement of the senses . . . which exists within us, without us and even in spite of us'. The second is 'a free judgement of the will, which one can also discard if one wishes to avoid errors'.[4] Claude Perrault, even though he had designed the Paris Observatory and the new east wing of the Louvre, was not primarily an architect, but a man of science. He had been a member of the *Académie des sciences* since its founding in 1666, where he concentrated mostly on comparative anatomy and the invention of all manner of machines and measuring instruments.[5] Colbert, the driving force behind the founding of this academy, likely commissioned Perrault to write a new translation of Vitruvius's *Ten Books on Architecture*, the *Libri Decern,* in 1667.[6] In the annotated translation of this book, which had functioned as a sort of law book for architecture during the Renaissance, and in his own architecture treatise, the *Ordonnance des cinq espèces,* Perrault endeavours to subject architecture to the same kind of analysis that others, particularly Descartes and Malebranche, had previously applied to the other sciences.

The writings of Descartes, Malebranche and Perrault cover different domains, of course, but they converge in their method of analysis. In general terms we can say that this is an analysis of the imagination, of an explication of the representation present in thought. During the classical period defined by Michel Foucault, this also entailed, and without any clear distinction, an analysis of the language, of the sentences, the sequence of words, regulated by grammar, through which this thought was expressed.[7] The imagination that earlier, in the sixteenth and the beginning of the seventeenth century, had been the quintessential faculty by which to acquire knowledge, through the transformations that it could engender in representation, was now, in the latter half of the seventeenth century, the domain of prejudices and errors, because it linked things and their characteristics in a vague, never actually extant similarity. Wherever Jean Martin, in his 1547 translation of Vitruvius, uses the word 'imagination', Perrault resorts to the Cartesian 'meditation'. Even the image evoked by architecture now emerges, in Perrault's texts, as a bias *(prévention),* which places atop one another or groups things that do not do this in reality. A bias that blurs judgement and begs for dissection.

tive beauties' – Antoine Picon, *Claude Perrault ou la Curiosité d'un Classique* (Paris, 1988), 137.

2
Perrault himself went into detail about this difference in meaning. He argues that the term symmetry as it was used by Vitruvius is synonymous with proportion, and uses the latter in his translation. For the use of the term symmetry in French architecture treatises, see Werner Szambien, *Symmétrie, Goût, Caractère, Théorie et Terminologie de l'Architecture à l'Age Classique 1550-1880* (Paris, 1986), 61-78. For the link between harmonious proportions and neo-Platonic ideas, see Erwin Panofsky, *Idea: A Concept in Art Theory* (New York, 1968), 53 ff. For the precise development of these ideas in architecture, see Rudolf Wittkower, *Architectural Principles in the Age of Humanism* (London, 1952).

3
Perrault, *Ordonnance,* op. cit. (note 1), vii.

4
Malebranche, *Oeuvres, I* (Paris, 1979, 1st ed. 1674), 117. William Chambers, after studying Perrault's treatise, drew a distinction between 'particular qualities in Visible Objects that Act immediately upon the organs of Vision' and qualities that owe their power to 'the Ideas we connect with them', see Herrmann, *The Theory of Claude Perrault*, op. cit. (note 1), 159-160. This division coincides exactly with that of Malebranche, but has the disadvantage that in architecture, virtually everything has to be relegated to the second category, making it unsuitable for the critique Perrault envisioned. In Perrault's categorization, it is not the 'immediate effect' of a particular beauty that is the decisive factor, but its unquestionable nature.

5
For Perrault's scientific activities, see Antoine Picon, *Claude Perrault*, op. cit. (note 1), 29-101, and for the relationship between his ideas and those of Descartes, see Alberto Pérez-Gómez, *Architecture and the Crisis of Modern Science* (Cambridge, MA, 1983), 23-27.

Already in his annotations to his translation of Vitruvius, Perrault puts the knife into what had been one of the key concepts of architecture theory up to that point: proportion, that is to say the dimensional relations of the elements of a building and of the orders in relation to one another. This application of proportion, in the Renaissance, was one of the crucial means to bind, in the design, the elements of a building into a whole, into a harmonious affinity. These proportions were conceived in a direct analogy with the differences in length of, for example, the strings of a harp or the pipes of an organ, necessary to enable these instruments to produce musical harmonies. As late as 1677, this doctrine was set out in rigid form by the music master of the Sainte-Chapelle, René Ouvrard, in a pamphlet entitled *Architecture Harmonique ou Application de la Doctrine de la Musique à l'Architecture.* Yet, Perrault asserts based on his physiological studies, 'the proportions of the elements of Architecture have no beauty with the same positive foundation as the state of natural things, such as the beauty of musical chords, which is pleasing as a result of a correct and immutable proportion and is in no way dependent on fantasy.'[8] The eye does not possess anything like an eardrum that immediately registers proportions as an effect, as a vibration, whether pleasing or not. In the domain of the image, therefore, there are, according to Perrault, no proportions that are beautiful in and of themselves, through the pure operation of nature. In representation, the positive and the arbitrary beauties are mixed together. This unreflected, unanalysed mixture and the force of habit are the cause of the incorrect judgement that these proportions contain an inherent truth: 'because these proportions were found in buildings that also possessed other positive and persuasive beauties, such as the materials used and the precision of the construction, they have come to be approved of and cherished, even though they held nothing positive.'[9]

In architecture, proportions, unlike in music, neither belong to the positive beauties, nor, in Malebranche's categorization, to the *jugements des sens*, but to the *jugements libres*, that is to say the uncertain, slippery domain of knowledge: 'the ear is not capable of communicating the knowledge of this proportion; but the eye, which is capable of making the proportion it loves knowable, can make none of the effect of this proportion palpable to the mind except through the knowledge of the proportion that it communicates'.[10] Architecture, for the most part, must be considered in relation to the world of ideas – to the more or less correct ideas that are expressed in architecture in the representation it communicates. It is in this, within classical epistemology, that a specifically architectural formal canon was comparable to a language. In the *Ordonnance des cinq espèces,* but also in the theoretical treatises that would follow, architecture is seen, in its formal methods of arrangement, as an instrument that, in its categories and distinctions, should produce a clearly legible representation of itself and of the use for which it is intended. Whenever, in the last quar-

6
Les dix livres d'architecture de Vitruve, corrigés et traduits nouvellement en français avec des Notes et des Figures . . . par M. Perrault (Paris, 1673). A second, extended edition was published in 1684, and would remain the sole authoritative Vitruvius publication until the nineteenth century. That same year, 1667, Colbert established a committee, consisting of Louis Le Veau, Le Brun and Claude Perrault, which was commissioned to produce the definitive design for the new east wing of the Louvre. This situation is comparable to that around 1545, when Jean Goujon collaborated on the first French translation of Vitruvius, and at the same time, by commission of François I, was working on the design of a new wing for the Louvre, a design that can be seen as an architectural manifesto, in which the rediscovered science of architecture is proclaimed.

7
Michel Foucault, *De woorden en de dingen, een archeologie van de menswetenschappen* (Baarn, s.a.), 110, published in English as: *The Order of Things: An Archeology of Human Sciences* (New York, 1973). Perrault's distinction between positive and arbitrary beauties coincides with the distinction drawn by Cordemoy in his *Discours physique de la Parole* and in *La Logique* by Port Royal between *signes naturels* and *signes d'institution*. Picon, *Claude Perrault*, op. cit. (note 1), 154, had already pointed out this analogy, but subsequently sets aside the analogy with language. It would take us too far afield to attempt to refute his interpretation of Perrault's ideas here. Picon poses the question as follows: is architecture, in Perrault's view, a language, or isn't it? In this respect, as the rest of this article will show, architecture, ultimately, is not a language. The point, however, is that Perrault considers architecture in a way that is structurally similar to the way in which his contemporaries looked at language, and in so doing sets out the first outlines of rationalism in architecture.

ter of the seventeenth century and the first seven decades of the eighteenth century, a link between these formally defined building forms and the use made of them is discussed, we must see in this link, first and foremost, a form of representation. The point is never that these forms follow from their function through some sort of natural process, but as insightful and appropriate an articulation of that use as possible. This part, that is to say the precise form and the formal structure of a building, is the arbitrary part of architecture. It consists, we might concur with Perrault in saying, of 'opinions'. With this term Perrault designates all forms of knowledge. These forms are not simply arbitrary because, as he says in the preface to his *Essais de Physique,* it is impossible in science to arrive at a perfect knowledge of things, but also because the 'language' in which they are represented (like any other language) has come about through coincidence and habit and thus is essentially characterized by a certain randomness.

8 Perrault, *Les dix livres,* op. cit. (note 6), 1684 edition, 106, n. 12.

9 Ibid., 105, n. 7.

10 Perrault, *Ordonnance,* op. cit. (note 1), iv.

RULES

Perrault himself draws a clear comparison between architecture and language only once, when he wants to emphasize the necessity of regulating the forms of architecture: 'Given that beauty has no foundation except in imagination, which causes things to be pleasing insofar as they correspond to the idea that everyone has of their perfection, there need to be rules that form and rectify this idea, and it is clear that such rules are particularly necessary for all the things from which Nature withholds them, such as language, the characters of writing, clothes and all those things that depend on chance, will and habit; it is necessary that human institutions provide for this, and therefore people submit to a certain authority that replaces positive reason.'[11]

Language, in general conceived as an instrument for acquiring knowledge and in its complete sentences considered a representation of this knowledge, must be defined in its structure and in its elements in order to arrive at an unequivocal order that displays this knowledge, capable of being communicated and discussed. Only this sort of taxonomy can make possible specific experiments that contribute to the structure of science. The principles of publicness and the exchangeability of knowledge, and of the comparison and rational reduction of all 'opinions' to as limited a set of principles as possible, are among the pillars upon which the scientific revolution of the mid-seventeenth century was able to take place. Rules, orders and classifications were necessary in order to achieve more positive results.

The state, with its authority, should contribute to the establishment of such rules, and would, in return, derive its stature from the beautiful and profitable results of these rules. This, at least, was the ideal, as outlined in the early seventeenth century in the utopias of Francis Bacon and Tomasso Campanella.[12] The same century witnessed the birth of sci-

11 See Herrmann, *The Theory of Claude Perrault*, op. cit. (note 1), 127.

12 Francis Bacon, *Nova Atlantis* (1624); Tomasso Campanella, *Citta del Sole* (Frankfurt am Main, 1628). In 1634 Campanella travelled to Paris, where he was generously received by *les grands* at court. In 1637 an edition of the *Citta del Sole* was also published here. The same year, his *De sensu rerum et magia* was also printed here, a work in which Campanella, in his dedication to Richelieu, urges the cardinal to build the sun city he has sketched. Campanella prophesized a new golden age for the French monarchy; it would become the new, shining centre of a reformed world. See Frances Yates, *Giordano Bruno and the Hermetic Tradition* (London, 1964), 360-379.

entific academies directly linked to the regulatory authority of the state. In 1635, Richelieu transformed the *Académie des beaux esprits* – a meeting place for a few patricians, founded in the 1620s – into the *Académie française*. Its primary mission was to establish a standard dictionary and a standard grammar for the French language.[13] In 1648, Mazarin founded the *Académie royale de peinture et de sculpture*. The model of enlightened absolutism found its definitive form under Colbert. At his instigation, the latter academy, from 1660 onward, was to apply itself to a deduction of an aesthetic doctrine, by means of study and consultation. In 1666, as previously mentioned, the *Académie des sciences* was founded. Following the death of the elderly Louis Le Veau, who had hitherto served as the *premier architecte du Roi* , the *Académie royale d'architecture* was founded in 1671, with François Blondel as its director.

Perrault's own architecture treatise, the *Ordonnance des cinq espèces,* was intended as a rational proposal for the regulation of the proportions of the five architectural orders (Tuscan, Doric, Ionic, Corinthian, Composite) and their 'characters', that is to say the identifying signs that differentiate them, like the letters of an alphabet, such as the *mutules* under the Doric cornice, the *serrated moulding* under the Ionic, and the *modillons* he ascribed to the Corinthian and Composite orders.[14] In intention, the document can be seen as a sort of rational standard dictionary, or a standard signature of architecture.[15] Perrault called his arbitrary proportions 'probables' or *vraisemblables*: 'yet even if in Architecture, in an essential sense, no proportions exist that are true in themselves, it remains to be inquired whether one can deduce probable or reasonable proportions that are based on positive reasons.'[16] In essence, his methodology was simple. He compared the proportions identified in the works of Vitruvius, Palladio, Scamozzi and other architecture treatises and laid them alongside the proportions of the surviving structures of antiquity as pictured and meticulously measured in Antoine Desgodets' *Les Édifices antiques de Rome* (Paris, 1682). From this he simply determined a median, except when rational considerations told him otherwise. In this he was acting according to the doctrine proposed by Descartes in his *Discours de la Méthode*: 'Among divergent, equally received opinions, I choose only the most moderate . . . not only because they are the most convenient in practice but because they are probably the best.'[17]

The conceptual basis of the *Ordonnance* only becomes truly clear in Chapter IV, which deals with the problem of the ratio between the height of the entablature and the diameter of the column. Up to this passage, the text can easily give the impression that Perrault is relegating the whole idea of a system of proportions to the trash heap of an absolute and pointless randomness.[18] The beginning of this chapter, however, tells us otherwise: 'There is nothing on which architects agree less than on the proportion of the entablature in relation to

13
Louis Hautecoeur, *Histoire de l'architecture classique en France* (Paris, 1943-1957), Part III, 462. The official investiture was delayed by the parliament, and did not take place until 1637.

14
Claude Perrault, *Ordonnance,* op. cit. (note 1), 66.

15
Joseph Rykwert compares the *Ordonnance* to the establishment of a standard typeface, the *Romain du Roy,* accompanied by a voluminous report, by a committee of the *Académie des sciences*: *The First Moderns, The Architects of the Eighteenth Century* (Cambridge, MA, 1980), 40-42.

16
Claude Perrault, *Ordonnance,* op. cit. (note 1), xvii. For Perrault's *probabilisme*, see Herrmann, *The Theory of Claude Perrault*, op. cit. (note 1), 127-129.

17
René Descartes, *Discours de la Méthode* (Paris, 1946), 73.

18
François Blondel, presumably after reading several excerpts from the unpublished manuscript, also seems to have interpreted the text in this way (François Blondel, *Cours d'architecture enseigné dans l'Académie royale d'Architecture,* 1675-1683, Bk. V, 1683, 761, 762; see Herrmann, *The Theory of Claude Perrault*, op. cit. (note 1), 131 ff). Yet in fact Perrault's and Blondel's concepts coincide in their broad outlines. Ultimately, Blondel felt architecture, and its ordering in particular, should be an expression of 'a stable, constant and indubitable principle', which, as in the other sciences, should be found 'through induction and as a result of multiple experiments'. Their main difference of opinion lay not in this, but in the question of what status should be accorded to the proportions found in the buildings of antiquity, and the related question of whether optical corrections are desirable (see the following text). Modern interpretations have found an early example of relativism in Perrault's 'arbitrary beauties', in which the conventions of building are entirely tied to history, that is to say

the thickness of the columns . . . This proportion, nevertheless, should be the most regulated of all: none is more important, or shocks more when it is not rational. It is certain that of the rules of Architecture, the most important are those that are intrinsic to solidity, and that nothing destroys the beauty of a building with greater power that when one notices, in the elements that constitute it, proportions that are contrary to that which should create this solidity, such as when it seems as though the elements are not capable of supporting that which they must support, or do not seem capable of being supported by that which supports them.'

One of the most crucial proportions for the composition of the orders is here linked to the question of solidity. Perrault, as the text makes clear, is not concerned with actual solidity, but with the apparent, or to put it more accurately, manifest solidity, that is to say a rational proportion between load and support that can be clearly read from the representation that the building presents, a kind of tableau of the mechanics of architecture. In addition, the text implicitly makes clear that architecture, in essence, might also be capable of representing other kinds of rational connections.

Hitherto the height of the entablature had not been linked to the thickness, but to the height of the supporting columns, and in such a way that the height of the main structure increased as the length of each order increased. In Perrault's view, this went entirely against reason. The solidity of a col-

to a specific place and time. Alexander Tzonis reprises this interpretation in *Het architektonisch denken. Ontwerp, rationalisering van de architektuur en maatschappelijke macht* (Nijmegen, 1982), 98. Herrmann, *The Theory of Claude Perrault,* op. cit. (note 1), 61, has previously clearly asserted that there is no question of any such relativism here. But he does not arrive at a complete and clear interpretation either. The text only becomes clear when we place the emphasis on the 'in themselves' (*en elles mesmes*), when Perrault argues, 'properly speaking, in Architecture, there are no proportions genuine in themselves', and we keep in mind that Perrault viewed his arbitrary beauties in the same way that his contemporaries viewed a scientific *language*.

Claude Perrault, *L'ordonnance des cinq espèces*, 1683

Claude Perrault, Le Louvre, colonnade, 1670-1680

Emmanuel Héré, l'Hotel de Ville, Nancy, 1752-1755

Jacques-Ange Gabriel, La Place de la Concorde, 1755-1763

umn depends primarily on its diameter and, Perrault points out, decreases as its length increases. In this situation, 'in which things are so confused that even the most enlightened judges (*Juges)* cannot know them', Perrault opts for a solution that remains as close as possible to existing 'opinions' yet removes the greatest, unquestionable irrationality. He proposes making the entablatures of all the orders equal to twice the diameter of the column.

He opts here, as elsewhere in his treatise, for a simple, easily memorized proportion. In calculating these proportions he ensures that the other principal proportions of the orders can be set out in the same simple, linearly increasing sequence. Given that there are no 'intrinsically true proportions', and that this ordering, like a language, must be seen as a means to represent certain rational connections with some probability, making this as convenient as possible seems an obvious criterion.[19] Perrault's concepts might be summarized as stating that the elements of architecture and their proportions must be regulated so that these rules, as a covenant, can clearly reproduce a certain idea as an agreed-upon sign. Deviations are defensible only when rationales can be given for them, rationales of which they are the depiction, which can therefore be clearly read from the building as a difference. This is why the main structures of all the orders must have the same proportion to the diameter of the columns that support them. This is also why, for instance, the *astragal,* the moulding profile that forms the culmination of the column and can be clearly defined, in the Ionic order, in its proportion to the volute, must have the same dimensions, in Perrault's opinion, in all the orders: 'Given that this proportion is defined in this Order, I see no reason to deviate from it in the others.'[20]

In the fourth chapter of the *Ordonnance* Perrault provided, for the first time, a clear, demonstrable, positive reason for a given proportion, and his reasoning, moreover, was so rational that the *Académie* could find no way around it. In the last weeks of 1688, the *Académie* had reluctantly and with great reservations set out to study Claude Perrault's treatise. In January 1689 it reached the fourth chapter. Its contents must have struck the members of the *Académie* hard. The reading of the *Ordonnance* was suspended, and in subsequent meetings they attempted to regulate 'those proportions that they feel can best be followed'.[21] The *Académie royale d'architecture* now applied itself to the mission for which it had essentially been founded: establishing a rational architectural doctrine.[22]

CLEAR ARTICULATION

Within Perrault's thinking, other uses that had found their way into architecture could now be denounced as abuses, such as the custom, adopted by Palladio and Scamozzi, of allowing the frieze and the architrave to merge, as it were, by the use of

19
Compare Foucault, *De woorden en de dingen*, op. cit. (note 7), 84: 'If, on the contrary, one designates an agreed-upon sign, one can always (and one should!) select one that is simple, easily recalled, applicable to a large number of elements, capable of being distributed and connect to something else.'

20
Claude Perrault, *Ordonnance,* op. cit. (note 1), 33.

21
Herrmann, *The Theory of Claude Perrault*, op. cit. (note 1), 142-144.

22
On the progress of this regulation, see Wolfgang Herrmann, 'Antoine Desgodets and the Académie royale d'architecture', *Art Bulletin* (New York), 1958, XL, 35. In 1701, with no mention of Perrault, the *Proces Verbaux* listed as a decision of the members of the Académie that 'the height of the entablature . . . can be determined by the diameter of the column, by always assigning two diameters to the entablature'; Herrmann, *The Theory of Claude Perrault,* op. cit. (note 1), 124.

Juste-Aurèle Meissonier, project for the façade of the St Sulpice, 1726

a concave profile, or the baroque custom of allowing pilasters and columns to 'mix with and contaminate one another'.[23] Just as in the other sciences, the point was to arrive at a clear definition and classification of the different elements.

It is no wonder that it was neither Bernini nor Le Veau, but Perrault who drew the eventual design for the new colonnade of the Louvre.[24] This work, as Emil Kaufmann argued in his *Architecture in the Age of Reason,* became *the* example for subsequent generations of architects, because it presented a persuasive image of 'clarity and elegant circumspection'.[25] For a historian who prefers to direct his gaze to the great differences and profound controversies that can be deciphered from the changing face of edifices, the 'classical' period that began here, one of the few periods in later history to have found a style, in the sense of a stable form shared by large groups, is of little interest. In Kaufmann's words: 'A period of peace and quiet then dawned. From a historical point of view this period is of lesser interest than the struggles that preceded and followed it . . . It is up to the historian to find out whether life, in this interim period, went on under the surface.'

Perrault's analysis can be seen as a somewhat late application of the new scientific concepts to architecture. Once established, it would, in its broad structural outlines, form the basis of architectural thinking. The *Ordonnance*, in spite of its lukewarm reception by the *Académie royale d'architecture,* was recommended in Rome in 1696 by the director of the *Académie de France* as 'the best book of its kind'.[26] In the domain of formal classifications, which in this case is to say the way of classifying the elements of the orders and the use made of them in the design of floor plans and elevations, the break with the past was definitive. The baroque or Mannerist play of reflections that, presented in its contaminations and tricks or in a crowded formality, characterized the architectural designs of the early seventeenth century, was broken up into a clearly articulated classification and transformed into an orderly and elegant representation.

As late as 1683, François Blondel, just before the publication of Perrault's treatise, described the broad outlines of the old theory of proportions as set out by Alberti, as well as the analogy between these proportions and the musical harmonies, in the penultimate part of his *Cours d'Architecture*. He was the last to do so. Only Charles-Étienne Briseux, in his *Traité du Beau Essentiel* in 1752, would make a not very successful attempt to provide a basis for the harmonic, musical proportions as a design rule, now using the authority still held by Palladio's designs as well as the harmonic distribution of the colours of the rainbow postulated by Newton.[27] Briseux, 92 years old and looking back on 70 years of architecture theory, saw only loss: the loss of generally accepted rules that had lent architecture a positive, non-arbitrary foundation. The professors who had succeeded Blondel at the *Académie*

23
Claude Perrault, *Ordonnance,* op. cit. (note 1), chapter VIM, 'De la hauteur des entablements'.

24
The design of this colonnade was and continues to be generally attributed to Perrault. This attribution was immediately controversial from the end of the seventeenth century, as a consequence of the commission Colbert had given to the trio of Perrault, Le Brun and Le Veau, which included a stipulation that no one was permitted to claim authorship of a particular design at the expense of the others. In any event, Perrault had a significant influence. The final design was virtually certainly achieved in 1669 and 1670 in a constant consultation between Perrault, the draughtsmen's offices of the *Agence des Bâtiments du Roi* (which was officially led by Louis Le Veau) and Colbert. See Picon, *Claude Perrault*, op. cit. (note 1), 157-184.

25
Emil Kaufmann, *Architecture in the Age of Reason, Baroque and Post Baroque in England – Italy – France* (New York/Dover, 1955), 127-128. Kaufmann rightly argues, 'There is not much difference between the Louvre Colonnade by Perrault and the buildings on the Place de la Concorde by Gabriel.'

26
Herrmann, *The Theory of Claude Perrault,* op. cit. (note 1), 142.

27
On this rainbow, Briseux wrote, 'everything is made distinct, and yet everything is reduced to a single entity. This marvellous effect, according to the experiment of the famed Newton, comes from the fact that the seven colours we distinguish in it occupy spaces that relate in the same proportions as those of the intervals of the seven Tones in Music: a natural Tableau the Creator presents to our eyes, in order to initiate us into the System of the Arts.' Briseux's treatise enjoyed little success; Jean-Francois Blondel dubbed it 'of little esteem' (Herrmann, *The Theory of Claude Perrault,* op. cit. (note 1), 173). Marc Antoine Laugier likely reflects the opinion of his

Jules Hardouin-Mansart, Versailles, Royal chapel, 1699-1710

'have put an end to the teaching of the fundamental principles of architecture', the old architect wrote.[28]

This is not to say that the proportions set out by Perrault for the different orders were simply accepted. On the contrary, aside from the previously discussed simple rule for the main structure, they virtually seem never to have been applied.[29] Other classifications of the principal proportions of the order were laid out, in particular by Amédée Frézier and Charles Dupuis, characterized, however, in imitation of Perrault, by a simple linear progression expressed in simple numbers and set out in a single clear tableau.[30] In 1745, the *Académie* adopted the proposition set out in the report Gamier d'Isle had drawn up at its request, in which the proportions between the diameter and the length of the different columns were stipulated in the series 1:7, 1:8, 1:9, 1:10 for the Tuscan, Doric, Ionic and Corinthian order, respectively.[31]

THE STATUS OF THE PAST

These proportions, however, were no longer termed 'probable', but 'median', a designation that implied that the design could deviate from this rule. In this difference of opinion between Perrault and the *Académie*, the authority of the examples of antiquity as well as a certain design freedom were at stake. The surviving Roman edifices, as the meticulous measurements of Desgodets, unhindered by preconceptions, clearly showed, displayed great variation, which could not be simplified into a single, unequivocal rule. To Desgodets this did not mean that randomness had played a major role in all of these designs. He assumed that there had been rationales underpinning all of these variations, which for him and his contemporaries, however, had reverted into the darkness of shadowy reflection: 'The proportions of Architecture contain mysteries that only the learned can penetrate.'[32]

The fact that positive reasons cannot be given for every element of the examples of antiquity does not mean that these reasons do not exist. When François Blondel, in his *Cours d'Architecture,* is compelled to admit that for several elements of classical architecture, in particular the Corinthian capital, 'one might with sufficient probability say that the pleasure it gives the eyes is merely derived from custom and the authority of those who first applied it to the work', he immediately adds, 'at least, if there is not a more hidden reason, no less natural, and that causes the pleasure we experience when we see them.'[33]

Is the age of Louis XIV deficient in knowledge in relation to the ever-shining example of antiquity, or may we think, no, *must* we think that our science and arts are superior to the 'great age of Augustus'? This was the crux of the polemic between the *anciens* and the *modernes* that formed the politically charged backdrop against which the controversy between Perrault and Blondel unfolded. This struggle had been

contemporaries when he says of Briseux's proportions doctrine: 'He should have told us what they consist of; he merely repeated to us the arbitrary opinions of a few ancients and gave us, more arbitrarily still, as a directing principle, musical chords'; *Essai sur l'architecture,* xxvi; Antonio Hernandez, *Grundzüge einer Ideengeschlchte der Franzosischen Architekturtheorie von 1560 – 1800* (Basel, 1972, dissertation from 1965), 102.

28
Charles-Étienne Briseux, *Traité du Beau Essentiel* (Paris, 1752), 2; 'The disparity of opinions and the controversy between Blondel and Perrault are like the era of the decadence of Architecture in France. Ever since, truth has been concealed beneath the veil of the false and the arbitrary.' His thesis, Briseux writes in this introduction, is born of discussions he had with a great number of his colleagues at the *Académie*, of whom 'most march confidently under Perrault's banner and refuse to make the beautiful contingent on proportions'.

29
Herrmann, *The Theory of Claude Perrault,* op. cit. (note 1), 172.

30
Amédée Frézier, 'Dissertation sur les ordres d'architecture', 1738, in *Théorie de la coupe des pierres* (Strasbourg, 1737-1739), T. 3, 18; Charles Dupuis, *Nouveau Traité d'architecture comprenant les cinq ordres des Anciens* (1768). On these propositions, see Szambien, *Symmétrie, Goût, Caractère*, op. cit. (note 2), 42-45.

31
Szambien, *Symmétrie, Goût, Caractère*, op. cit. (note 2), 44. These principal proportions are equal to the proportions set out in Vignola's treatise. This treatise, because of the regularity and relative simplicity of the proportions set out in it, had become highly popular in France; see Herrmann, 'Antoine Desgodets', op. cit (note 22), 37, 38.

32
Antoine B. Desgodets, *Les Edifices antiques de Rome dessinés et mesurés très exactement* (1682), preface; Herrmann, *The Theory of Claude Perrault,* op. cit. (note 1), 43.

ignited in earnest with the founding of the *Académie française* and would continue to smoulder into the eighteenth century. It mostly flared in the world of letters and poetry, but the other arts and sciences were also drawn into the rhetorical tumult.[34]

Claude Perrault, himself a declared *moderne,* summed up the position of the *anciens*, clearly and succinctly, in the foreword to the *Ordonnance:* 'There has been a desire to reason on the basis of authority, derived from the assumption that the authors of the admirable works of antiquity did nothing without reasons, even if we do not know them.' He accused the *anciens* of seeking to elevate the status of their discipline by means of a deliberate mystification: 'Aside from a few honest people who, perhaps because they have not given the matter sufficient thought, sincerely believe that classical antiquity deserves the honour of being infallible, inimitable and incomparable, there are many who know full well what they are doing when they cover up this blind respect for the buildings of antiquity, and who are well aware of the desire they have to represent the elements of their profession as mysteries they alone can interpret.'[35]

It would not be accurate, however, to portray the *anciens* as a bunch of reactionaries who attempted to block all scientific enlightenment. Isaac Newton, to name the most obvious example, can clearly be considered an *ancien*. He arrived at his concept of gravity after a detailed study of ancient, often occult scientific literature and after performing numerous experiments in alchemy, which gave him the conviction that there were 'active forces' at work in nature.[36] More precisely formulated, the controversy that divided the two parties came down to the value that the products of the past hold for thinking, for the forming of hypotheses.

The great variation in proportions displayed by ancient edifices was explained, in general terms, by the assumption that the architects of antiquity had carried out optical corrections in the final design. This explanation had some authority, because Vitruvius himself had pointed out this necessity for correction. Perrault had attempted to refute the legitimacy of optical corrections, but had not entirely succeeded.[37] In the wake of his arguments, the simple, purely perspectivist correction method developed by Sebastiano Serlio in the early sixteenth century and illustrated in his 1545 treatise could be jettisoned, but they were not persuasive enough to exclude every modification a priori. Contrary to what Perrault would have wanted, deviation remained part of the arbitrariness of the rule. More than 70 years after the publication of the *Ordonnance*, Pierre Patte would conclude: 'No one has yet had sufficient authority to establish laws that can be inviolably enforced – the reason for this being either the difficulty of finding rules that contain an intrinsic truth . . . or the impossibility of subjecting the human mind to decisions that are not based on principles derived from nature.'[38]

33
Blondel, *Cours,* op. cit. (note 18), 767.

34
On this struggle, see Rykwert, *The First Moderns,* op. cit (note 15), 25-27; Picon, *Claude Perrault,* op. cit. (note 1), 104-111.

35
Perrault, *Ordonnance,* op. cit. (note 1), xx.

36
See Betty Jo Teeter Dobbs, *The Foundation of Newton's Alchemy or 'The haunting of the Greene Lyon'* (Cambridge, 1975).

37
See W.D. Brönner, *Blondel – Perrault. Zur Architekturtheorie des 17. Jahrhunderts in Frankreich* (Bonn, 1972), which is primarily devoted to this difference of opinion about the necessity of optical corrections.

38
Pierre Patte, *Etudes d'Architecture* (Paris, 1755), 2; Herrmann, *The Theory of Claude Perrault,* op. cit. (note 1), 143.

The analysis carried out by Perrault, the analysis of imagination, had produced an awkward arbitrariness. An arbitrariness that continued to haunt architecture, in written theory and built practice, without really creating problems: in its structure, the analysis allowed for arbitrariness in the realm of unverifiable hypothesis. Architects, in particular the members of the *Académie*, tended towards the position of the *anciens*. Antiquated, Roman architecture remained the shining, ultimate promise and the simultaneously visible yet unknown rule. It gave architecture a hallmark and above all an instrument for internal consistency: a formal order, something like a language. At the same time it established a relative freedom: in the wealth of its forms it provided considerable room to adapt the rules that the academy was constantly deducing to the judgement of the eye and above all, as well, to the specific conditions presented by the design.[39]

39
François Blondel, for instance, spoke of 'the beauty that the difference in places, of use and of order might have altered', *Cours,* op. cit. (note 18), 703.

Translated by Pierre Bouvier

The appalling beauty of the razorblade and the slit eye from Luis Bunuel's *Un chien andalou* has a counterpart in a photograph by Lucio Fontana that produces a very similar sense of shock. It shows an arm with an awl punching holes in a canvas. The canvas has been partially perforated already but it is clear that the hairy forearm, with its neatly rolled-up shirt sleeve and paint-splattered thumb, could strike again any moment. The photograph evokes an air of spontaneity, yet casually depicts the horror of a brutal assault. Its beauty lies in the violence with which the white, tautly mounted canvas appears to be desecrated.

In his last known interview, Fontana explained that for him the process of perforating the canvas and its outcome said something both about the art of painting and about abandoning painting or breaking down the boundaries of the profession. These holes and his later knife cuts in canvases show us space in the broadest sense of the word. To paraphrase Fontana's own words: the imagination stretches from the Argentine pampas to the infinite Universe.

The spring 1992 issue of *OASE* looked as if the binder forgot to cover the spine. On the folded sections, visible on the spine, was written the word 'zero'. Both the journal's title and issue number were gouged out of the paper like a work of art by Fontana. The title was visible only when the front cover was turned. The cuts were revealed by the movement of the cardboard. The back cover showed a silver-coloured photograph of a helmeted astronaut.

A great many *OASE* issues explored the margins of Architecture, investigating its interfaces with areas such as cinematography, philosophy, literature or urban sociology. The zero issue was like a return to the source, a return to the heart of the profession. The issue dealt with the essence of architecture, independent from debates on its manifestation or the aesthetic desires and formal preoccupations of a single, random architect. It dealt with the meaning of architecture and its practice at a time of great prosperity and any sense of discomfort this might engender. It focused on the opposition to modernism as a style while at the same time embracing the modern condition. It explored modernity's impact on architectural principles and practice independent from any prevailing fashions. And drawing on the work of Archigram, Superstudio and the Russian NER group it explored and highlighted mass production concepts and the fight against mental erosion caused by increased prosperity and consumption.

Jurjen Zeinstra's article in the zero issue, 'Houses of the Future', looked at the concept of 'living' in the work of Alison and Peter Smithson. He paints a picture of the increasing 'mechanisation' of living via the dichotomy between the work of the Smithsons and the Archigram group. Will the house of the future be pulled from a rucksack, such as Mike Webb's Suitaloon, or does it look like a hovel from the favelas as in the Smithsons' design for the 'This Is Tomorrow' exhibition? Both designs seek meaningful interpretations of place, reclaiming some private space from the infinite void. Superstudio provides us with the most compelling image of this. A little girl is sweeping up in the post-apocalyptic remains of what may have been a home. She is surrounded by endless fencing. Having cut a rectangular base from the mirrored grid her space has been reclaimed from infinity. What we see here is the epitome of architecture in its most naked essence: it is the void that determines form.

Michiel Riedijk
Member of the editorial board
from *OASE* 19 to 43

Translated by Laura Vroomen

Jurjen Zeinstra

HOUSES OF THE FUTURE

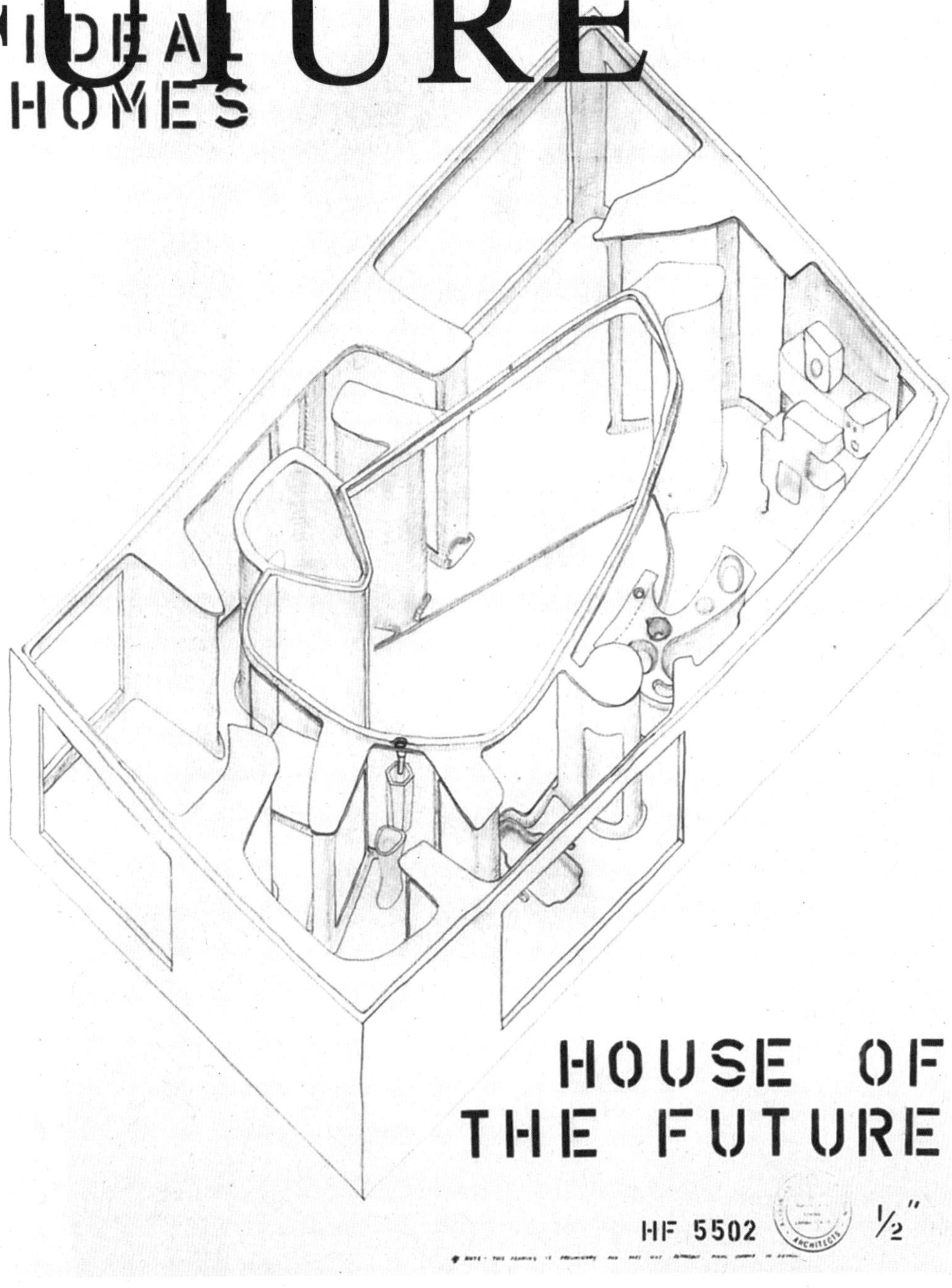

Alison and Peter Smithson, House of the Future, axonometric projection

FIRST PUBLISHED IN *OASE* 32

In the world of architecture there is a long tradition of experiments that test the boundaries of the discipline. The 1960s witnessed a flurry of such experiments, many of them quite intriguing, though it is fair to question whether their significance goes beyond that of the well-timed joke we often take them to be. Do they undermine the foundations of architecture? Or do we, as critics, tend to inflate their importance? To answer these questions it is necessary to gauge the architectural content of the experiments. Only then can we speak in any meaningful way about their ultimate significance to the field. It should come as no surprise that the most fascinating experiments are the ones undertaken on the very fringes of the discipline (or even just beyond), the investigations that attempt to establish the contours of a new architecture.

In this article we will be taking a look at a number of experiments related to the fundamental architectural concept of 'living'. We'll begin with an early experiment: the House of the Future by Alison and Peter Smithson. It is a seminal design, both within the Smithson's own oeuvre and in the field as a whole. The *Archigram* group, for example, would go on to create an interesting series of follow-up experiments. By contrasting these *Archigram* projects with a number of works by the Smithsons, we gain a sense of what creative minds in the 1950s and 1960s thought about the architectural (im)possibilities of the house of the future.

HOUSE OF THE FUTURE, 1956

In 1956 Alison and Peter Smithson designed their House of the Future, which was displayed at the *Daily Mail*'s 'Ideal Home Exhibition' later that

Living room

same year.[1] The house is a somewhat disguised variation on the modernist patio home, adapted to an urban context. Peter Smithson sketched out the principles behind the house and its relationship to its surroundings in one of his 'private air' diagrams from 1955-1956. Here we see how the patio forms the central and most intimate part of the dwelling, thus giving each house a 'vertical tube of unbreathed private air'. It is a design that makes it possible for the buildings to be joined together in a highly dense grid structure.

The House of the Future is built on a rectangular base, 9 x 15 m in area. On this base, various rooms are arranged around an irregularly shaped patio. While each room has its own characteristic shape and dimensions, it also forms an inextricable part of a continuous space. This continuity is the result of the omnipresent plastic panelling: a honey-coloured skin, stretched over all the walls, floors and ceilings. Between the rooms and the patio is a fully transparent façade that exerts a unifying force over the rooms, both in relation to one another and with respect to the patio.

Two different elements are used to establish spatial boundaries: hollow walls and hollow objects. The hollow wall consists of a double shell that is deep enough to accommodate appliances, sanitary amenities and storage space. This element is used three times in the House of the Future. We first encounter it at the entryway, where the visitor quite literally 'breaks through' both shells, experiencing the depth of the wall before coming into the house. There is another one by the kitchen; here, the shape of the wall is determined by the standard appliances, which are contained inside and thus hidden from view. This particular wall is also notable in that it is one of the few large rectangular elements in the house. Household appliances figure prominently in the design; of particular interest is the

1 The description of this work draws from the following articles: Jeremy Baker (ed.), 'A Smithsons File', *Arena* (February, 1966), 177-218; Alison and Peter Smithson, 'The Shift', *Architectural Monographs* 7 (1982).

trance

Kitchen

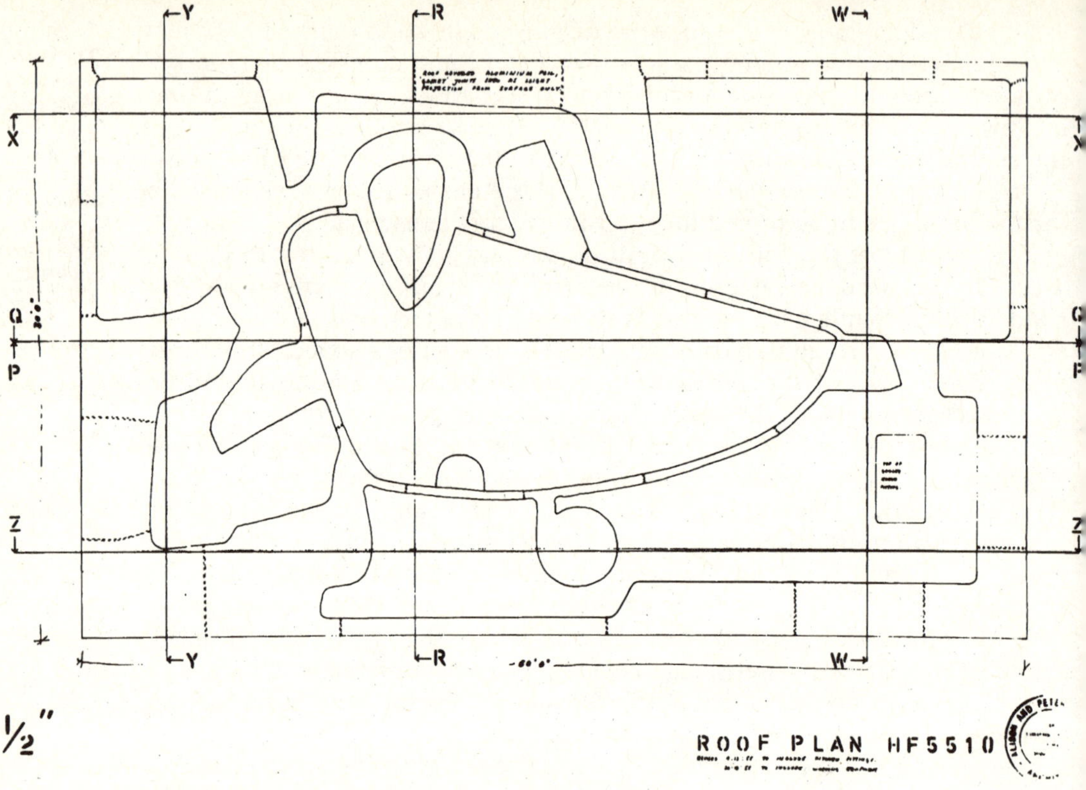

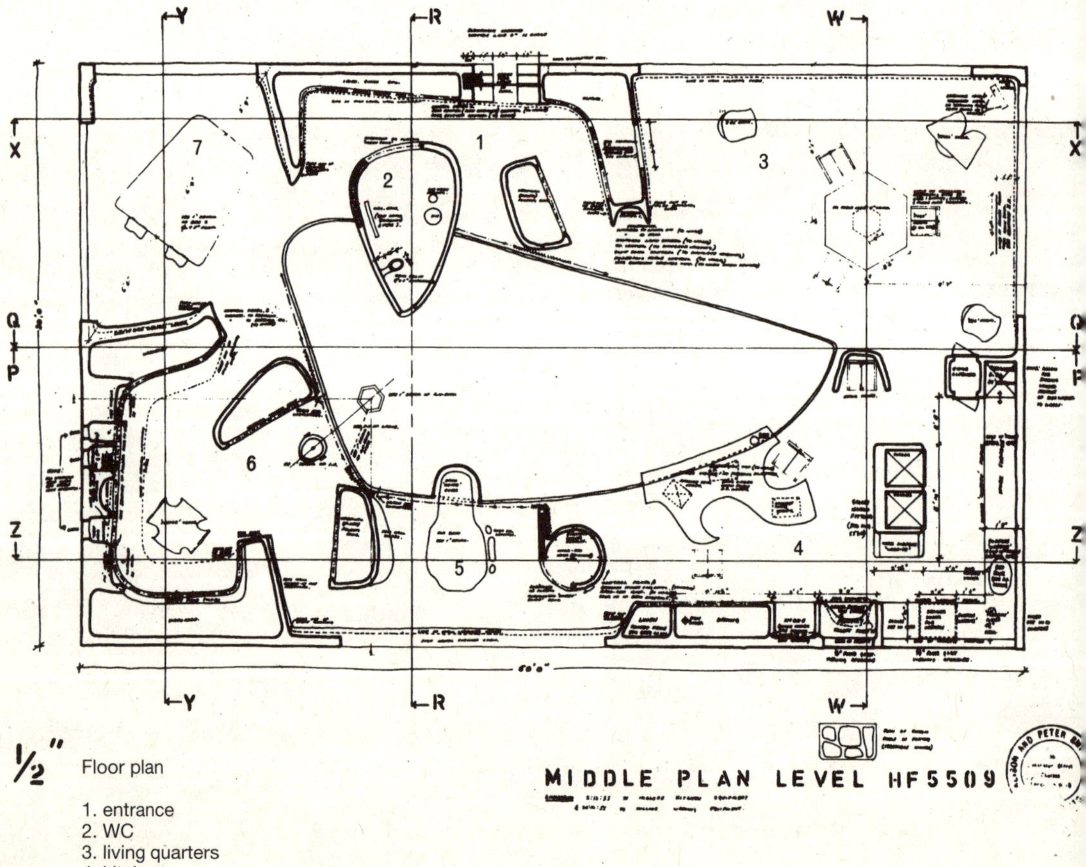

Floor plan

1. entrance
2. WC
3. living quarters
4. kitchen
5. bathroom
6. boudoir
7. bedroom

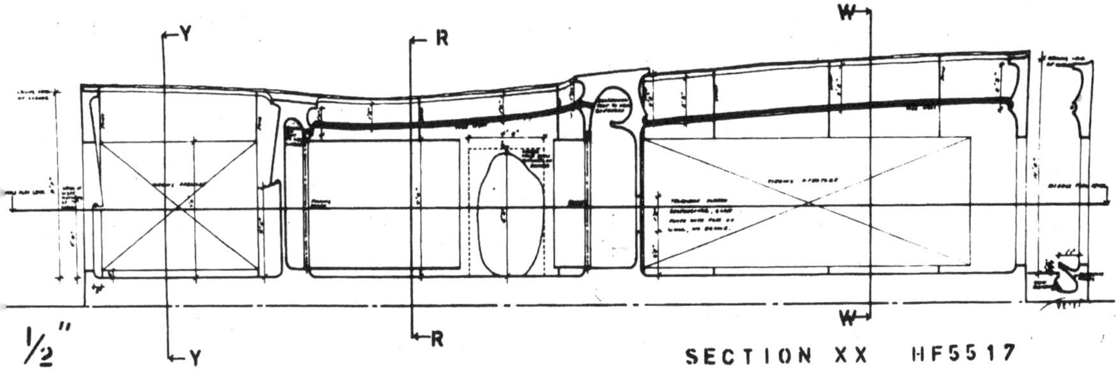

Cross section XX

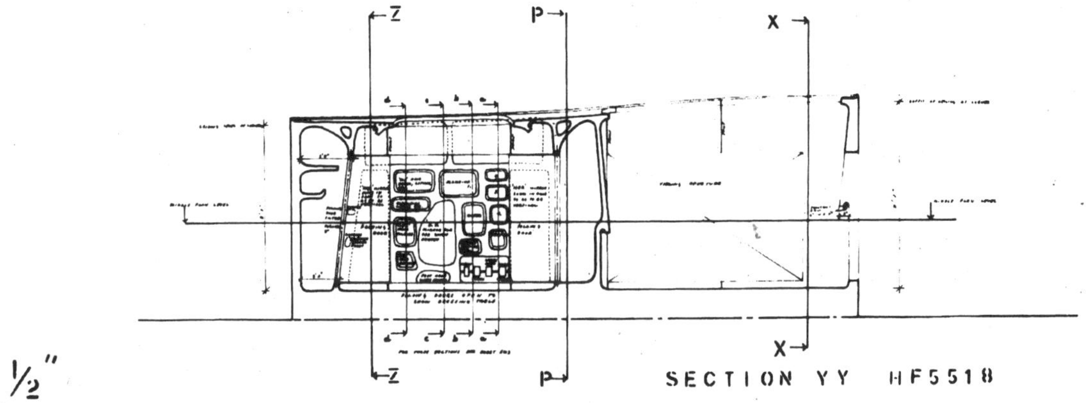

Cross section YY

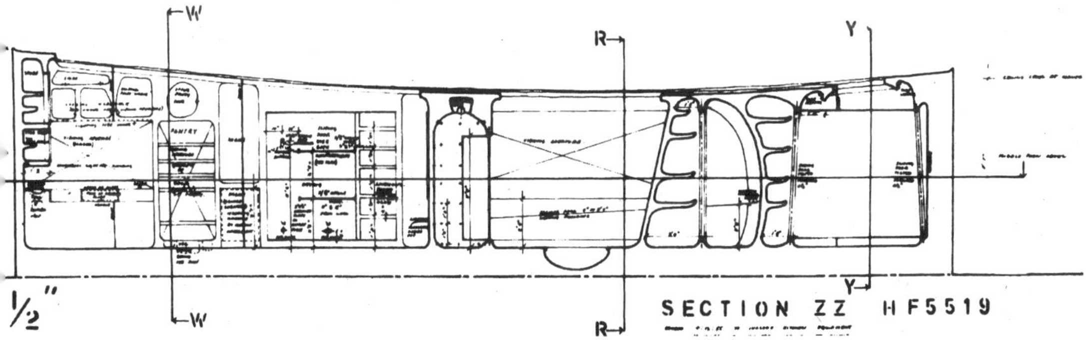

Cross section ZZ

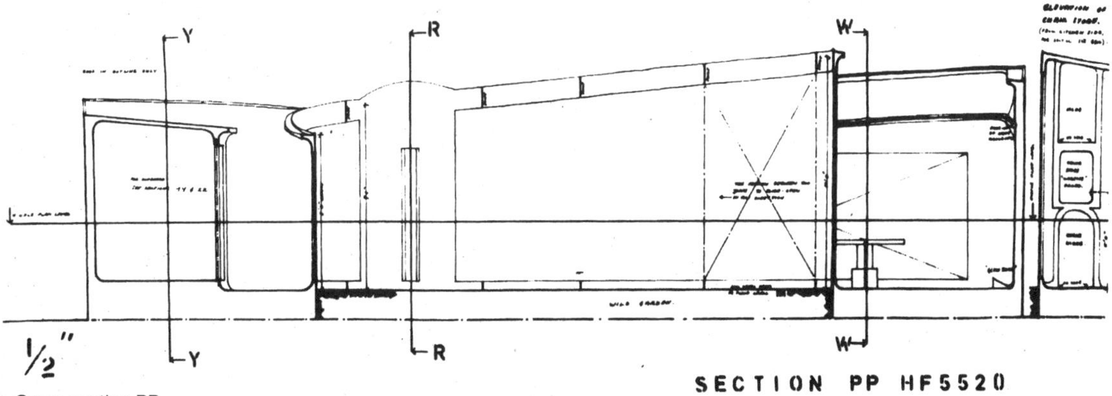

Cross section PP

choice to encase the appliances in the walls. By the 'boudoir' we encounter the final hollow wall, which holds everything relating to the occupant's personal care and attire. Each of these walls not only acts as a highly elaborate container of appliances and storage space, but also serves to define the spatial structure of the house. Certain facilities, such as a wardrobe or the shower stall, are positioned around the house as free-standing objects.

The House of the Future can be seen as an attempt to achieve a perfect fusion between such facilities, which exist in the form of a wide range of appliances, and architecture itself. These facilities (including the storage space and sanitary amenities) are assigned a specific form and location within the house. In the case of the free-standing objects, this location is explicitly linked to the patio. The solid wardrobe by the entrance, for example, is situated partly on the patio; the bath, which is nestled in a recess in the floor, pokes its way into the green of the interior garden; a section of the kitchen island protrudes through the transparent façade, and finally, the elevated sink by the boudoir is echoed in the rainwater basin. All the actions performed by the occupant with respect to these facilities take on a quasi-theatrical significance in relation to the patio. This is intensified by the curtains and the radical openness of the rooms vis-à-vis this central space. Although the objects do have an autonomous shape, which is closely bound up with their specific function, the ubiquitous panelling serves to reimpose a large measure of unity.

Material plays an essential role in this house: the dwelling is made entirely out of fibreglass panels, into which the lighting and heating systems are fully integrated. The panels consist of shells, connected by dark strips, producing a strong graphic effect. The association with the body-

Overview patio

work of a car is almost unavoidable. A conscious decision was made not to include such connecting strips in the transparent patio wall; this house is devoid of any styles or rules. The wall is made of Perspex panels which are glued on at the top and bottom.

Plastic, the quintessential material of the 1960s, has always evoked strong associations with the notion of progress. The odd thing about the material is its intrinsic blankness and shapelessness: plastic can be made to assume or suggest any form. When the material began making its appearance in the fields of architecture and industrial design in the 1950s and '60s, a new visual and formal language was created to accommodate it: clear-cut shapes, rounded corners, a shiny surface and bright primary colours. Thanks to the artificial origins of the material, the variety of applications is potentially boundless, a fact which is often vividly expressed in the designs incorporating it. A textbook example of this is the domed cities proposed by Buckminster Fuller in the 1960s.

But this boundlessness is also a feature of the House of the Future. Here, plastic is taken to absurd extremes, creating the impression that the material is ever-present and overpowering: the occupant is ensconced in the material. The rooms appear to be recesses in an enormous plastic mass, holes in a gargantuan Swiss cheese. Yet the paradox is that the material itself has been reduced to a shell, the bare minimum.

In the 1950s plastic took over the role that concrete had played in the 1920s: a material whose characteristic shapelessness endowed it with unprecedented potential. But whereas concrete bore the burden of its own substantial weight, plastic combined the adaptability of concrete with an unparalleled lightness, holding out the possibility that buildings would at

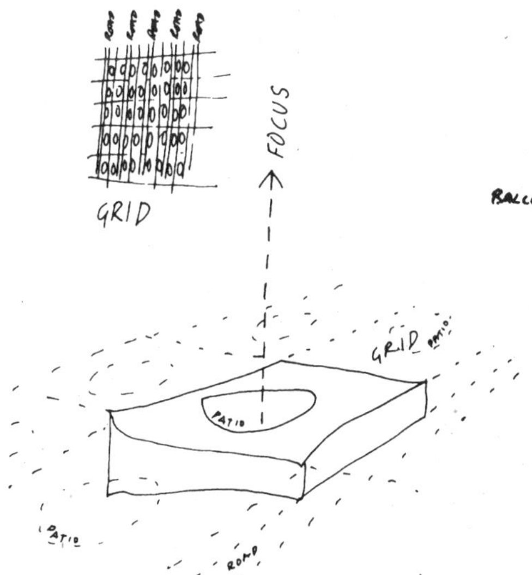

Private Air Diagram, 1955-1956

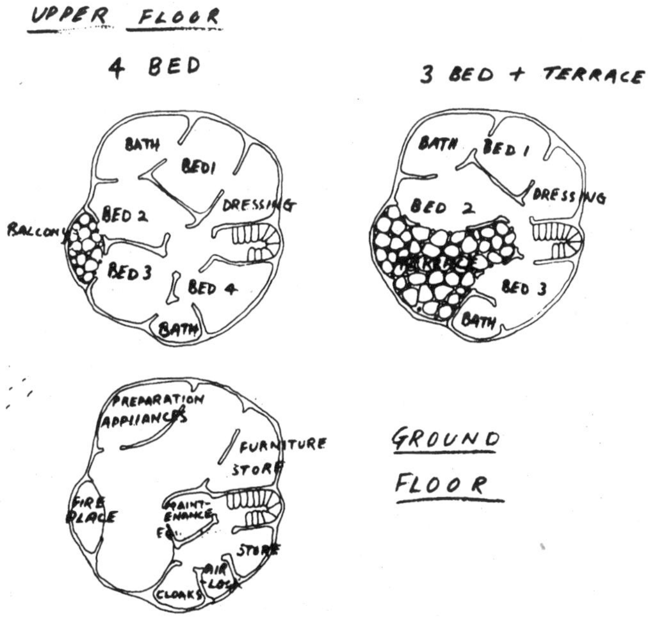

Bread House, 1975, floor plans

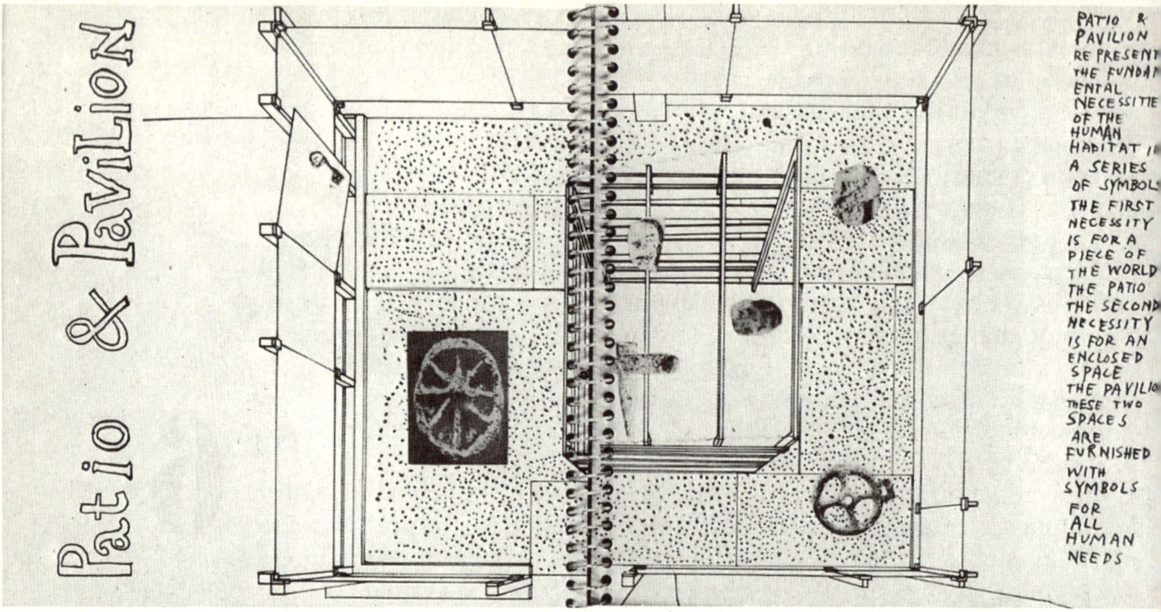

Patio & Pavilion, ‘This Is Tomorrow’ exhibition, 1956

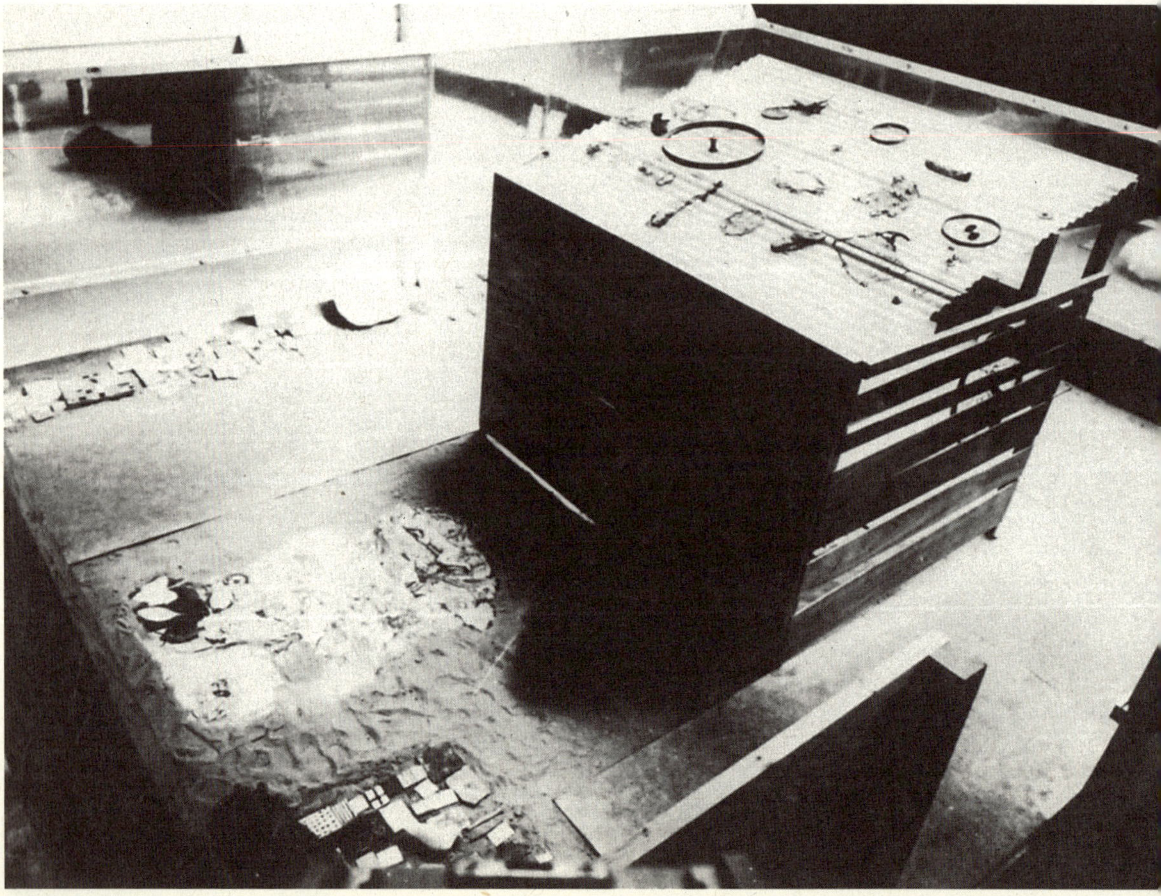

last succeed in wresting themselves free of the pull of gravity. The advent of plastics severed the traditional and obvious relationship between weight and volume, giving rise to the wild, expressionist fantasies of the 1920s.

Yet there is a striking difference between those fantasies and the House of the Future. In the House of the Future, the walls, floor, ceiling and furniture merge into a spatial continuum in which the tension between matter and gravity, so often depicted in constructivist experiments, has disappeared completely – everything flows. The apparently random shapes and the whimsical, door-less doorways that connect the rooms strengthen the illusion of viscosity and literal flexibility.

The Smithsons strongly emphasised the material and its tactile qualities, making reference to Le Corbusier's Maison aux Mathes from 1935.[2] At first glance this allusion seems rather far-fetched. The Maison aux Mathes is a simple house, with a wooden beam construction and massive natural stone walls. It is one of Le Corbusier's lesser known villas, in which the material is visible and speaks a language of its own. The Smithsons take their cue from the natural stone walls, which ensure that the materiality is literally palpable throughout the entire house, thereby establishing a tactile continuity. In the House of the Future the Smithsons sought to attain the same continuity. At the same time they were in search of a different style, a different language,[3] attuned to the world beyond architecture: mass culture.

In the 1950s the Smithsons were part of the Independent Group, a collective that had emerged from the Institute of Contemporary Art. The Group was interested in the effects of technology and mass media on the arts. Other members were the artists Richard Hamilton, Nigel Henderson and Eduardo Paolozzi, all of them pioneers of pop art. The Group also included the theoreticians/critics Alan Colquhoun, Reyner Banham, Lawrence Alloway and John McHale. Alloway described the Independent Group as follows: 'We discovered that we had in common a vernacular culture that persisted beyond any special interest or skills in art, architecture, design or art criticism that any of us might possess. The area of contact was mass-produced urban culture: movies, advertisements, science fiction, pop music. We felt none of the dislike of commercial culture standard among most intellectuals.'[4]

The Smithsons, for their part, were primarily interested in advertising. In the essay 'But Today We Collect Ads'[5] they speak of the increasing influence of advertising on the norms and aspirations of the consumers of architecture, an influence it appropriated from the social reformers and politicians. As evidence they point to the ways that large areas of the house (kitchen, bathroom, garage) are dominated by the products of industry, over which the architect has no control. The Smithsons make much of the growing role of mass culture and its significance to architecture, and the House of the Future can certainly be seen in that light. But unlike Reyner Banham and the *Archigram* group, the Smithsons never wanted to see architecture merge with or disappear into this mass culture. They always had an ambivalent attitude towards the Pop Art movement, chiefly because they remained preoccupied by traditional architectural concepts, like materials, urban design and the pursuit of a style.

Like the House of the Future, 'But Today We Collect Ads' first appeared in 1956. In that same year, the husband and wife team made a pavilion that would seem to be the complete antithesis of the House of the Future. It was displayed at the 'This is Tomorrow' show at the Whitechapel

2 Alison and Peter Smithson, 'The Shift', op. cit. (note 1), 44.

3 'We put photographs of the House of the Future – as evidence of another language – on the walls of a spare room,' Alison Smithson remarked, referring to the CIAM congress in Dubrovnik in 1956. See Alison Smithson (ed.), *Team 10 Meetings 1953*-1984 (Delft, 1991).

4 Quoted in Charles Jencks, *Modern Movements in Architecture* (Oxford, 1973).

5 Baker, 'A Smithsons File', op. cit. (note 1), 194.

1. bedrooms
2. shower cabin
3. kitchen cabin
4. furniture storage cabin
5. maintenance cabin
6. boudoir for her
7. boudoir for him

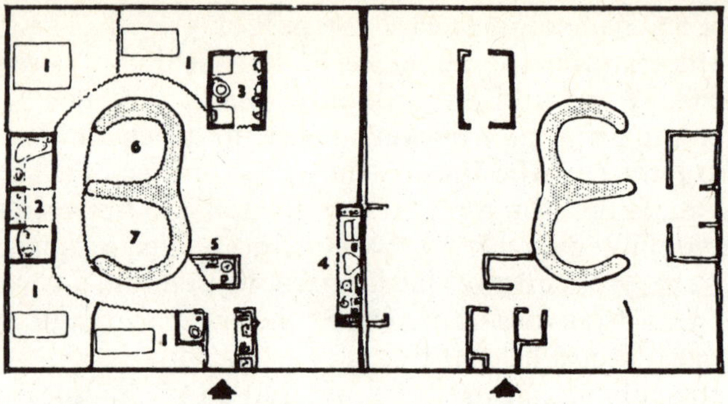

Strip Appliance House, 1958, floor plan

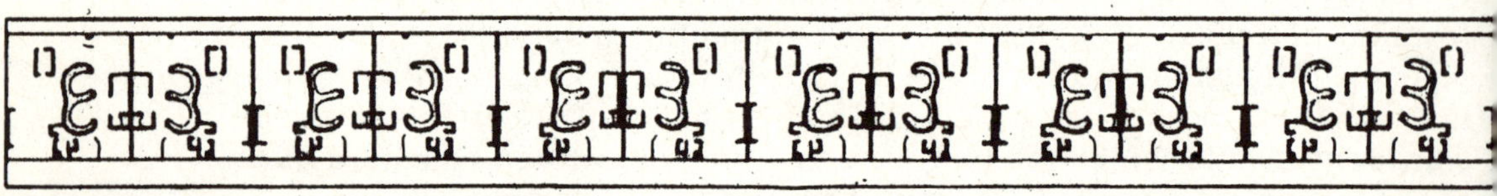

Strip Appliance House as part of terraced housing

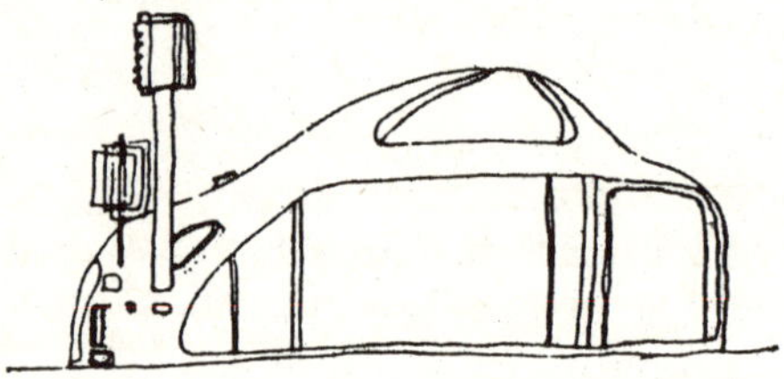

Elevation to main space

Entrance elevation

1. bedrooms
2. bathroom
3. kitchen cabin
4. storage cabin
5. maintenance cabin
6. boudoir

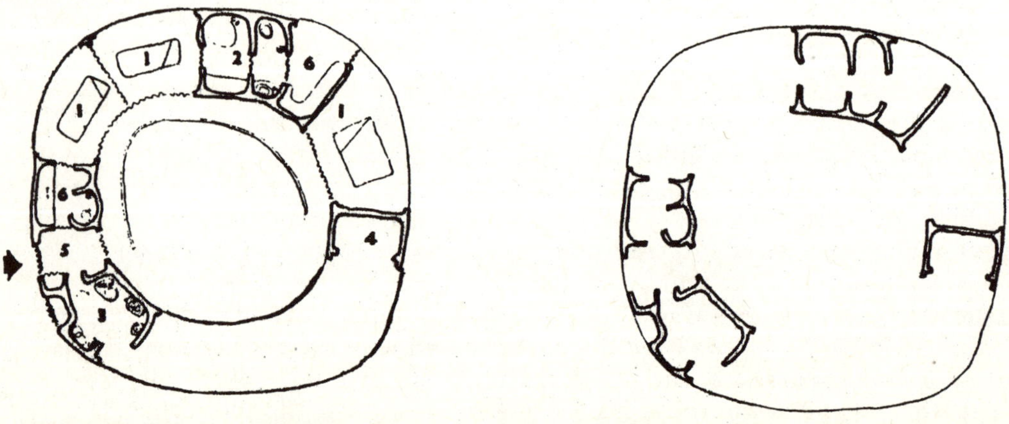

Snowball Appliance House, 1958, floor plan

Gallery in London. The exhibit showcased a number of pieces that could be regarded as the earliest examples of Pop Art, in terms of both their content and presentation. Amid the onslaught of Pop Art images, the Smithsons set down a fenced-in patio on which sat a primitive hut. In, on and around this structure, Paolozzi and Henderson placed a number of *objets trouvés*, giving the Smithsons' project the air of a fragmentary slum, surrounded by garish billboards. Here, the Smithsons depict 'the fundamental necessities of the human habitat', as they put it in the accompanying catalogue. They go on to explain this statement as follows: 'The first necessity is for a piece of the world, the patio; the second necessity is for an enclosed space, the pavilion.'[6]

Despite the deliberately provocative differences, the House of the Future bears an unmistakable resemblance to the Whitechapel pavilion with regard to these necessities. The House of the Future, too, comprises a 'piece of the world' (an enclosed patio) and a space 'furnished with symbols for all human needs'. These symbols are not *objets trouvés* though, but appliances.

6 Alison and Peter Smithson, 'The Shift', op. cit. (note 1), 32.

APPLIANCE HOUSES, 1957-1958

The House of the Future should not be seen as a stage in a straightforward progression within the Smithson's oeuvre, but rather as both an experiment with a particular material and an investigation of the influence of furniture and household appliances on the architecture of the house. That investigation was taken a step further in the Appliance Houses.

The Bread House (November 1957), which was presented as Appliance House I, is a fairly crude application of the 'language' of the House of the Future to a traditional dwelling with a living room on the ground floor and bedrooms on the two upper levels. The Snowball Appliance House plays with not only the language but also the architectonic nature of the House of the Future: the patio totally dominates the ring-shaped house.[7] The rooms, which were initially partitioned off by the hollow walls and objects, have now been sacrificed to a continuous living space with only screens to preserve their individuality. The interior is defined by the cubicles, and it is there that the household appliances are concentrated: the cooking, washing, changing and storage cubicle. The cubicles hide the appliances from view, deliberately segregating them from the interior, as they are highly dependent on trends and thus more subject to obsolescence. The shell walls of these cubicles are the fixed structural elements in the house, rudimentary signposts that suggest the main architectural structure. This is the Smithsons' response (or hypothesis, to use their term) to the breakdown of the home, a phenomenon they draw attention to in the House of the Future as well: 'The House of the Future demonstrated the architectural consequences of, amongst other things, the disintegration of the kitchen by means of mobile appliances and pre-packaged food etc.'[8]

7 The Snowball Appliance House and the Strip Appliance House are discussed in Alison Smithson, 'The Appliance House', *Architectural Design* (April, 1958), 177.

8 Baker, 'A Smithsons File', op. cit. (note 1), 197.

With its ring shape, the Snowball Appliance House does not lend itself to being grouped together in large numbers with others of its kind, a consideration that always played a central role in the Smithsons' work. An attempt was made to remedy this shortcoming in the Strip Appliance House, a prefab, rectangular component of a larger residential system. Again we find cubicles as strictly rectangular elements. Together with the highly pronounced male and female 'boudoirs' they dictate the layout of the house.

In 1959, the Smithsons applied the Appliance House concept to their

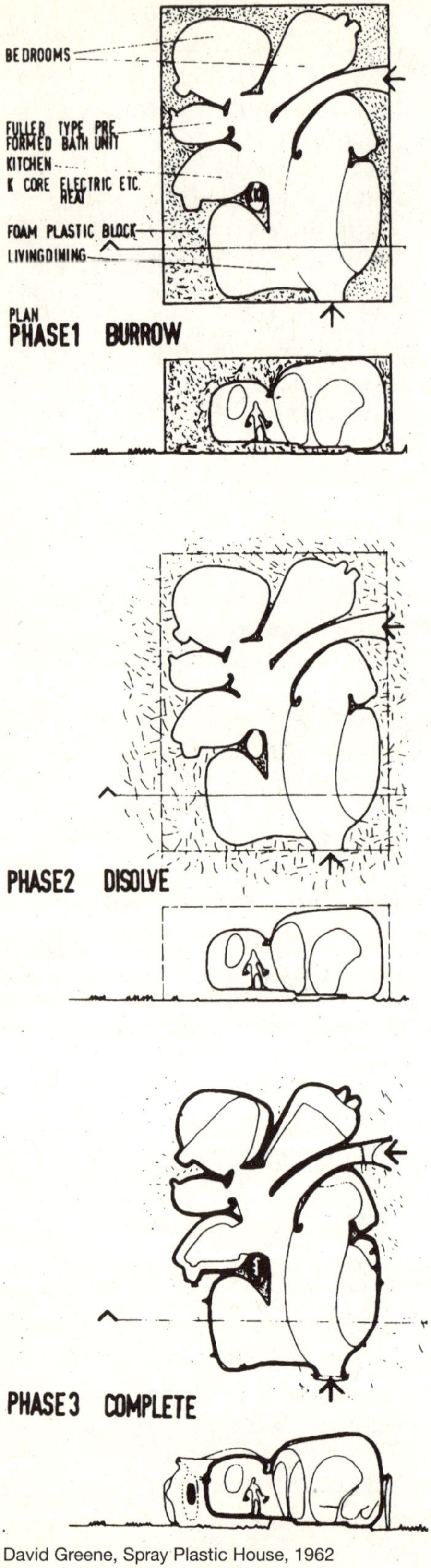

David Greene, Spray Plastic House, 1962

Warren Chalk, Tower with Capsule Homes

Warren Chalk, Plug-in Capsule Home, 1964

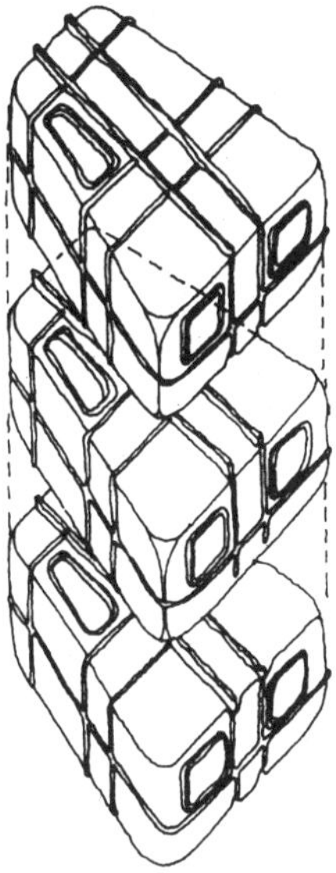

Stacking method

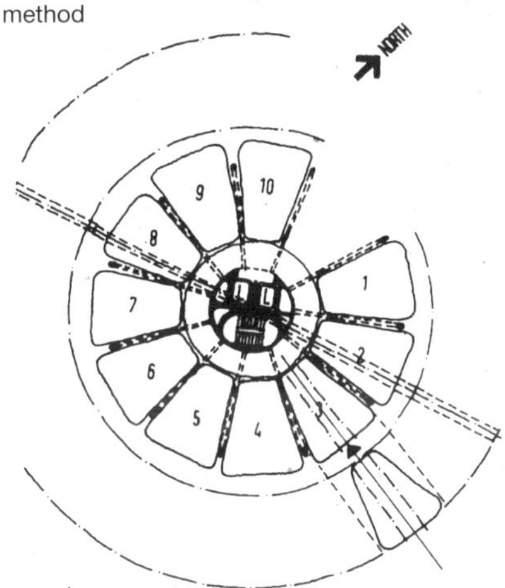

Chain of capsules

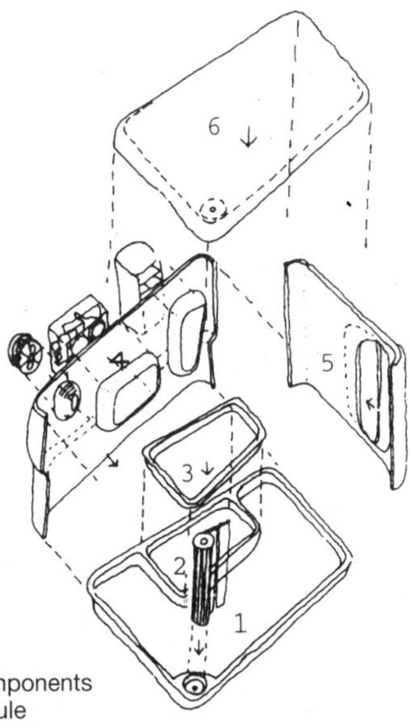

Capsule components
1. floor module
2. sliding screen
3. bed module
4. audiovisual component
5. inner wall
6. ceiling module

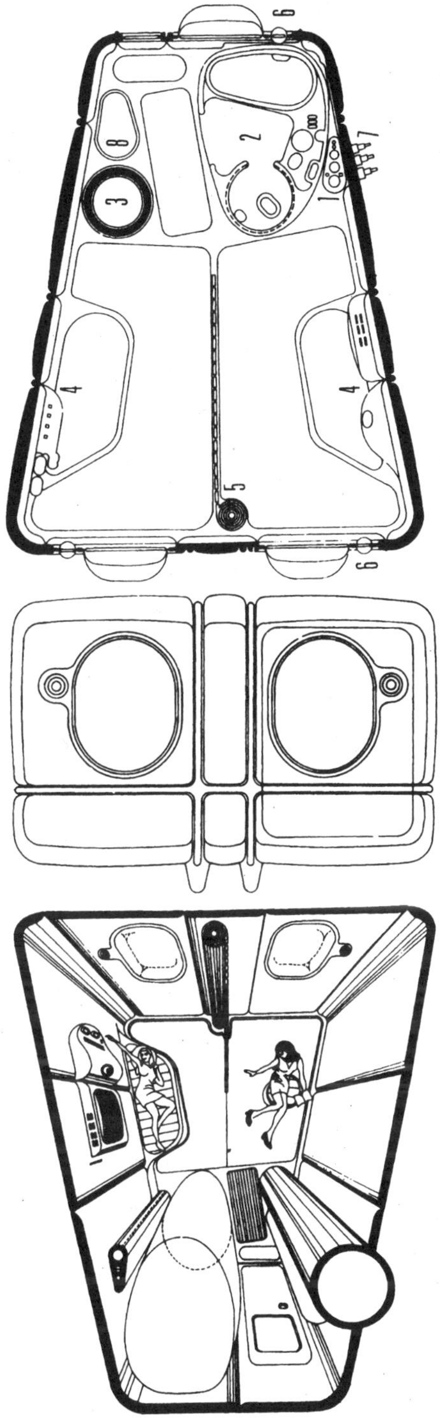

1. service duct
2. bathroom
3. pneumatic lift
4. variable electric wall system
5. sliding wall
6. window
7. connection points for ducts
8. storage space

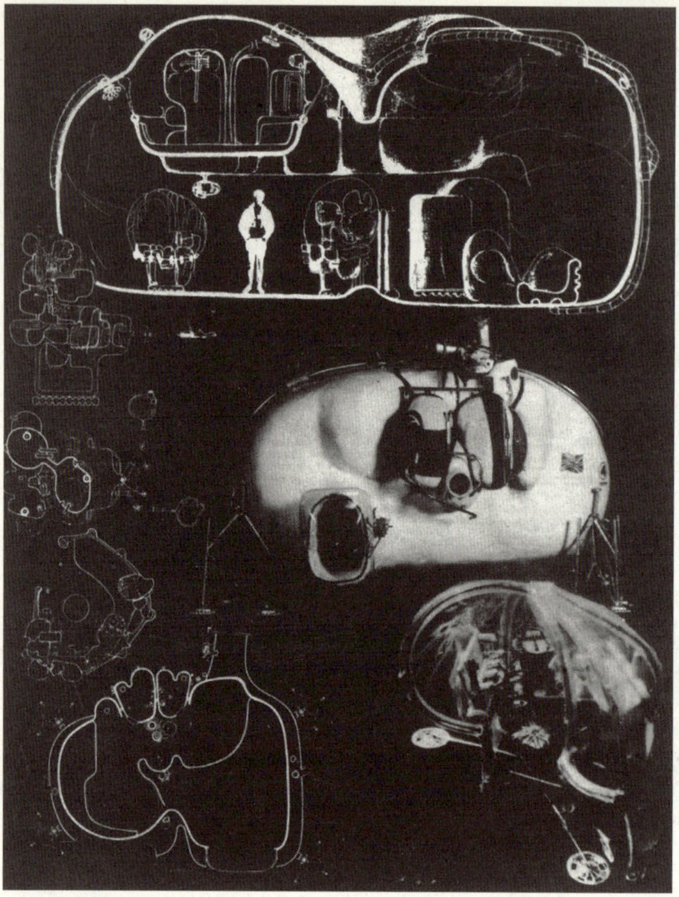

Collage featuring (from top to bottom): cross section, cooking station, model, workstation, floor plan

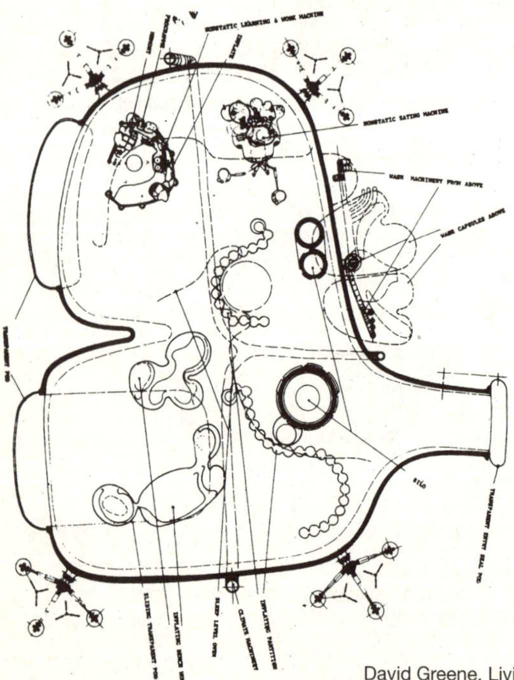

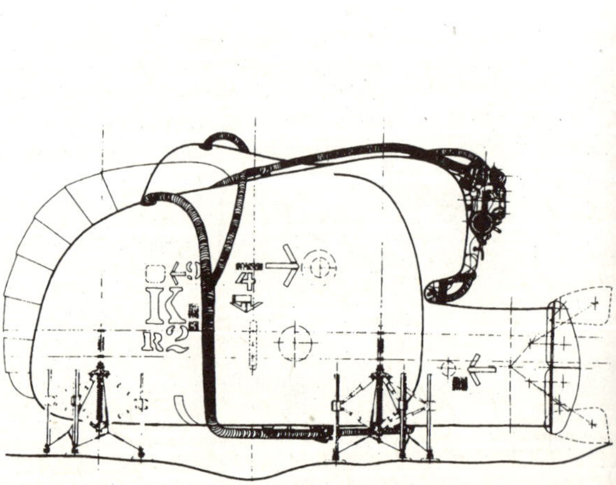

David Greene, Living Pod, 1965, floor plan, façade

blueprints for a country house in Kent. Here, we again encounter the design of the Strip Appliance House, devoid of the last remnants of the organic formal language of the House of the Future. The cubicles are arranged so as to partition off the rooms – literally as well as figuratively – thanks to the sliding walls inside the cubicles. Overhead lighting accentuates the cubicles in the exterior while simultaneously ensuring, in the interior as well, that these elements are more than cupboards stuffed with appliances.

The Appliance Houses concentrate on the architectural significance of the proliferation of domestic appliances. In 'The Future of Furniture'[9] Alison Smithson argues for a new approach to these appliances, whereby the living area would no longer be a workroom for machines. By reducing their size and weight, the designer can scatter them about the house. This decision opened up the possibility of a new spatial concept: separate rooms are replaced by a continuous space. Alison Smithson contrasts traditional Japanese homes, where the closets are oriented away from the room, thus creating continuity, with Western homes, where the furniture and appliances always face towards the room. In the latter set-up the architect is robbed of any control over the interior and left to the mercy of the fashion-driven whims of the interior designer. Alison Smithson sees the cubicles of the Appliance Houses as an architectural solution to this problem: 'Inside the cubicle, under control, the changing world of high-pressure advertising, styling, etc., plugs in.'[10] This is a clear illustration of the Smithsons' architectural approach: even though they are well aware of the growing role of disposable products and the variable elements in a house, they attempt to develop an architectural approach in which these things must be kept in check to maintain and reinforce space as an essential element of the dwelling.

9 *Architectural Design* (April, 1958), 174-178.

10 Baker, 'A Smithsons File', op. cit. (note 1), 178.

SPRAY PLASTIC HOUSE, DAVID GREENE, 1962

In the work of the *Archigram* group, the house of the future is treated as an ongoing experiment.[11] The Smithsons' House of the Future acts a source of inspiration for this experiment, several stages of which are described below.

The preoccupation with plastic as a material and the fervent attempts to forge an appropriate form of expression (a formal language, if you like) are two elements of David Greene's Spray Plastic House from 1962. The three small drawings that illustrate the genesis of the building can be seen as a preview of what will happen to the house in a series of *Archigram* plans. In the first phase the house is 'dug out' of a rectangular block of polystyrene, like a burrow in the earth. In this massive body, the rooms are connected like organs, complete with two 'orifices' and a heart which feeds the installations and heating. In the second phase the surrounding body disintegrates so that by the third phase only the materialised outline of the various rooms (or organs) remains. The material that enveloped the rooms has literally shed its mass and become a skin. Here we are treated to a concise demonstration of a recurring theme in the *Archigram* plans. As David Greene puts it in the first issue of *Archigram*, 'You can blow up a balloon – any size / You can mould plastic – any shape.'

11 The descriptions of the *Archigram* pieces draw on Peter Cook (ed.), *Archigram* (Basel, 1991, originally published in 1972).

PLUG-IN CAPSULE HOME, WARREN CHALK, 1964

The third issue of *Archigram* showcases another important (and related) theme for the first time: 'Expendability: towards a throwaway architecture'.

The issue features collages in which domes, Buckminster Fuller's prefab bathroom and Dymaxion car, and various container houses are depicted alongside packaging material and disposable items as serious and successful attempts to design objects or buildings with a limited lifespan. The periodical criticises a large number of these prefab objects, such as caravans, bungalows and garden houses, for concealing their industrial origins behind a traditional facade. *Archigram*, by contrast, propagates a look that mimics that of popular disposable products.

The Plug-in Capsule Home can be regarded as an elaboration of these ideas. The design is one of the results of an experimental project carried out by members of *Archigram* on a commission from the Taylor Woodrow Design Group. The assignment was to make a prefab dwelling that could be integrated into a tower-shaped support structure. The Capsule Home is an adaptable unit, assembled from a number of industrially manufactured interchangeable parts, like wall, floor and ceiling elements. The Capsule Home strips away the house to the bare minimum: a cell connected to other cells, embedded in a larger structure. The Capsule's form derives from this defining characteristic (that is, its ability to 'plug in'). In the interior we recognise the 'organs' of the Spray Plastic House, but they have now been transformed into appliances and objects that are tightly packed together and often hidden from view by control panels. The Plug-in Capsule project exhibits a number of striking similarities with Georgi Krutikov's degree project from 1928.[12] In the latter work the capsules are minimised even further, resulting in elegant, teardrop-shaped space capsules which are only large enough to accommodate a reclining chair. Here too, the capsules are designed to be connected, like the petals of a flower. Even Krutikov's visual points of reference, which he included with the presentation of his project as a collage, correspond to the aesthetics of *Archigram*: Krutikov's collage, like that of the periodical, is populated by caravans, zeppelins and teardrop-shaped vehicles.

12
S.O. Chan-Magomedow, *Pioniere der Sowjetischen Architektur* (Dresden, 1983), 284, 307-308, 333. Model of the interior. Collage showing (from top to bottom): section, cooking station, model, working station, floor plan.

LIVING POD, DAVID GREENE, 1965

After the Plug-in Capsules and the related Gasket Homes from 1965, the Living Pods represent a further development of the third phase of the Spray Plastic House. Many plans from this period feature a two-part structure: on the one hand, there is the open living space, without the traditional division into rooms that had previously been necessitated by the separateness of various facilities; on the other hand, there is the 'service section', which houses all the high-tech machinery.

We see this same pattern in the Living Pod: the occupant lives in the pod (or cocoon) while all the necessary appliances and power cords are attached to the structure as autonomous components. The look of the Living Pod is derived from the popular visual language of space travel and deep-sea exploration.[13] The interior makes use of the same division described above: organically shaped inflatable couches and an inflatable partition plus a number of highly advanced robots that can move through the pod as cooking and work stations. In this respect the robots are the next step in the evolution of the 'kitchen on wheels' in the House of the Future. Those rooms where machines and facilities play an important role, such as the kitchen or bathroom, are thus rendered superfluous.

Whereas the Plug-in Capsule was still clearly subordinate to a mega-structure, the Plug-in City, the Living Pod is plainly an anti-urban, nomadic

13
In 1967 *AD* put out a special issue devoted entirely to trends in this area, under the editorship of a former member of the Independent Group: John McHale, *2000 + (Architectural Design)* (February 1967).

object with its roots in that other urban *Archigram* fantasy, Ron Herron's Walking City from 1964, which conceives of the city as a giant object.

LIVING 1990, *ARCHIGRAM*, 1967

In 1967 the *Archigram* group was given a chance to repeat the Smithsons' experiment of a decade earlier, under very similar conditions. This time it wasn't the *Daily Mail* but the *Weekly Telegraph* that issued the challenge of designing a house for the year 1990. The traditional architectonic elements, like floors, walls and ceilings, which the House of the Future had treated as a continuous skin that bound the whole structure together, are given an entirely new significance here: they have become conditions or temporary stages, due to the fact that they are in constant flux. They move up and down, in and out; they can become hard or soft. Inside, there is a control panel connected to a large-scale infrastructure, and two mobile robots from which partitions can emerge, to screen off certain areas. The occupants move through the house on their hoverchairs in the same way they move through the city, which is presented as an enormous megastructure. According to its creators, the *Archigram* design is a first attempt to create a house that is capable of immediately responding to the occupant's every whim, thanks to the presence of the latest cutting-edge technology. The last traces of any architectonic organisation have been rigorously eliminated thanks to the treatment of the appliances, just a short ten years after Alison Smithson's warnings in 'The Future of Furniture'. With a rigid consistency the *Archigram* group follows the trail it has blazed for itself, moving further and further away from architecture. They even go so far as to

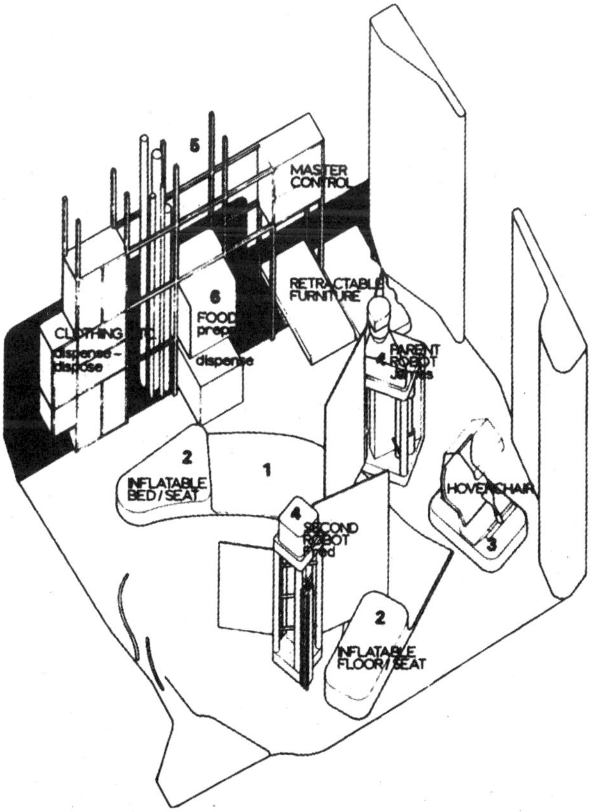

Archigram Group, Living 1990, 1967, axonometric projection

Layout for the exhibition

Robots

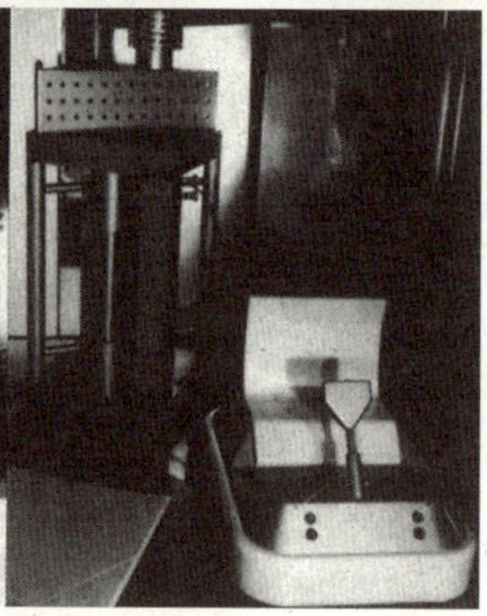

Hoverchair

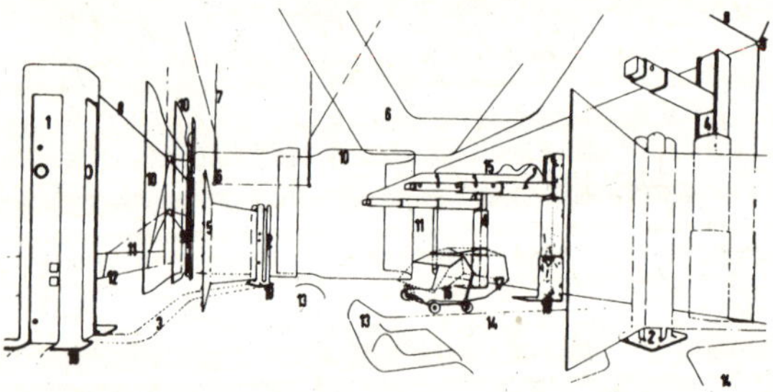

Perspective of an earlier version

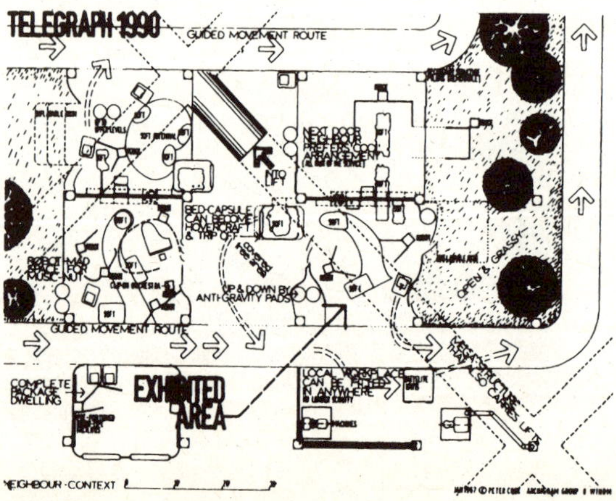

Site plan

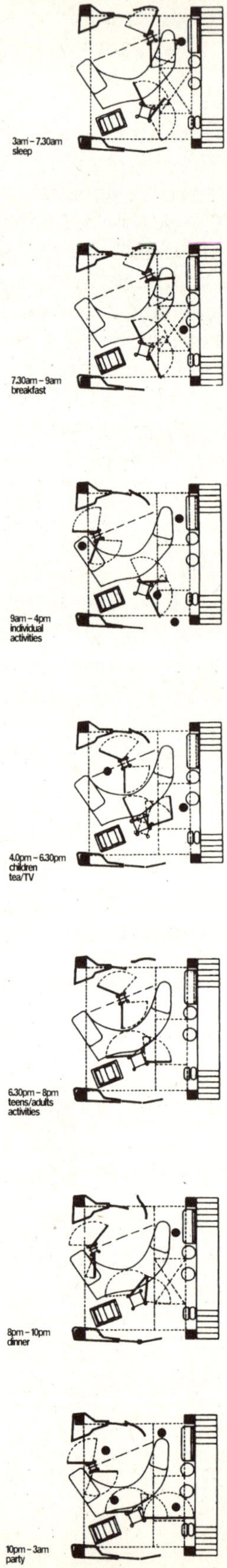

Changes to the house over the course of a single day

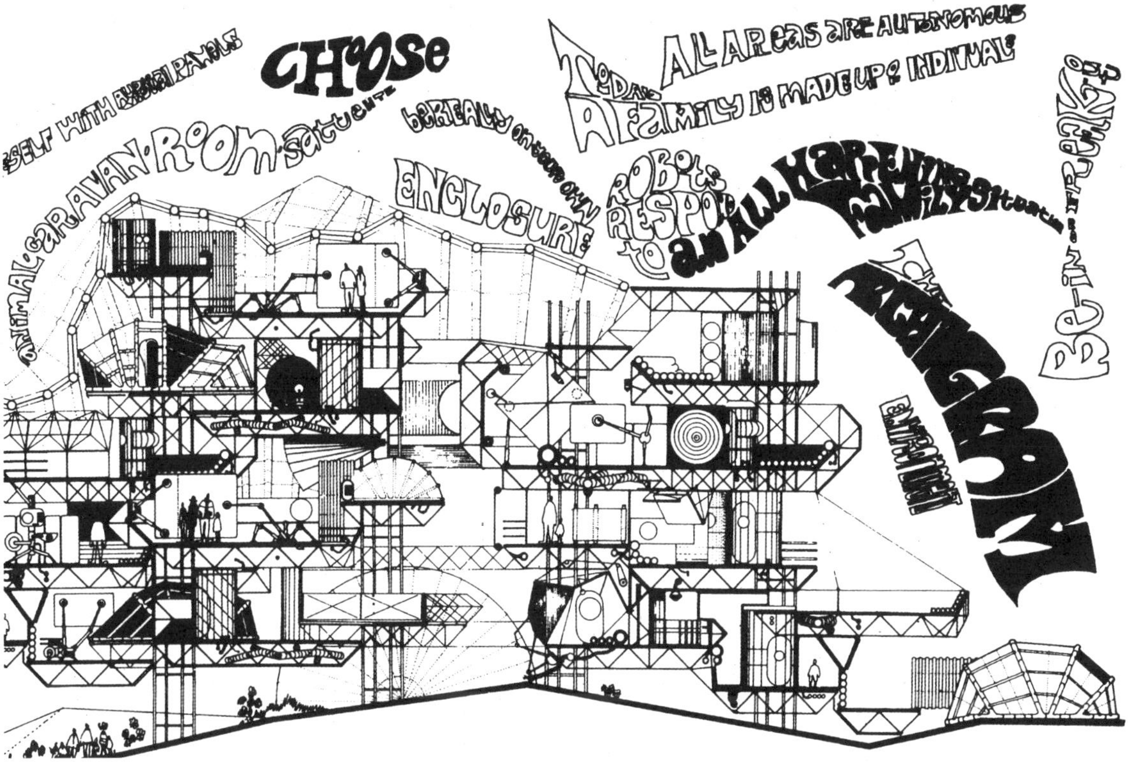

Archigram Group, Control and Choice project, 1967

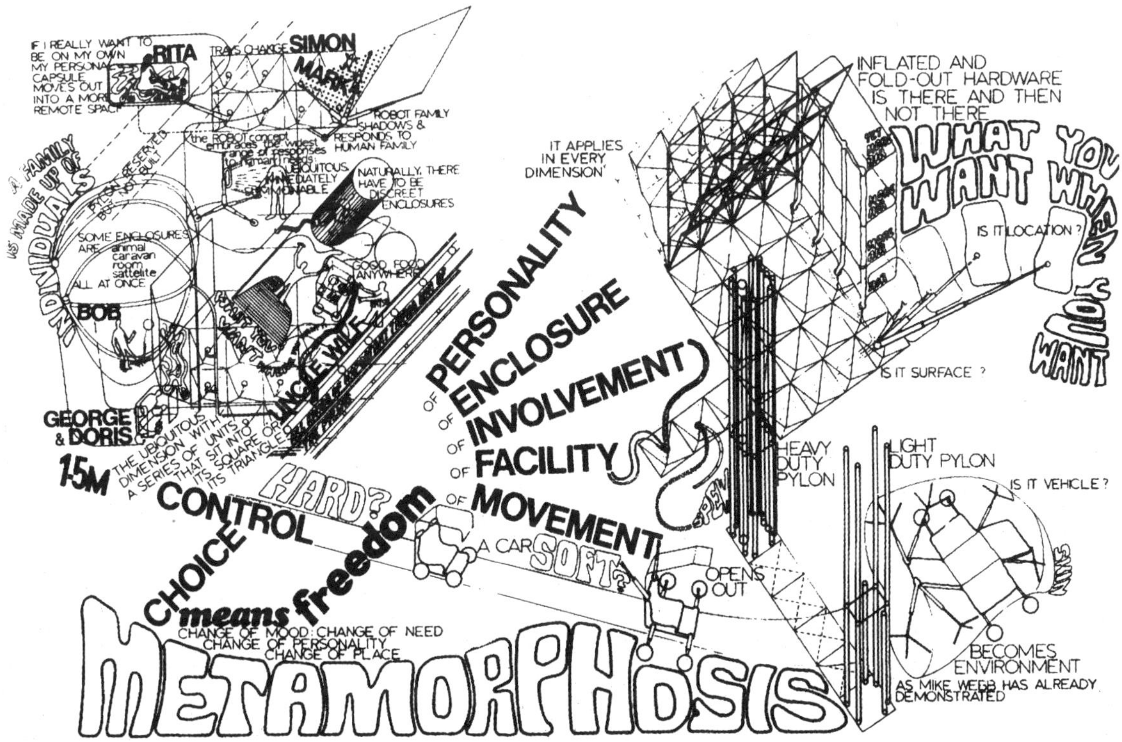

Archigram Group, Control and Choice project, 1967

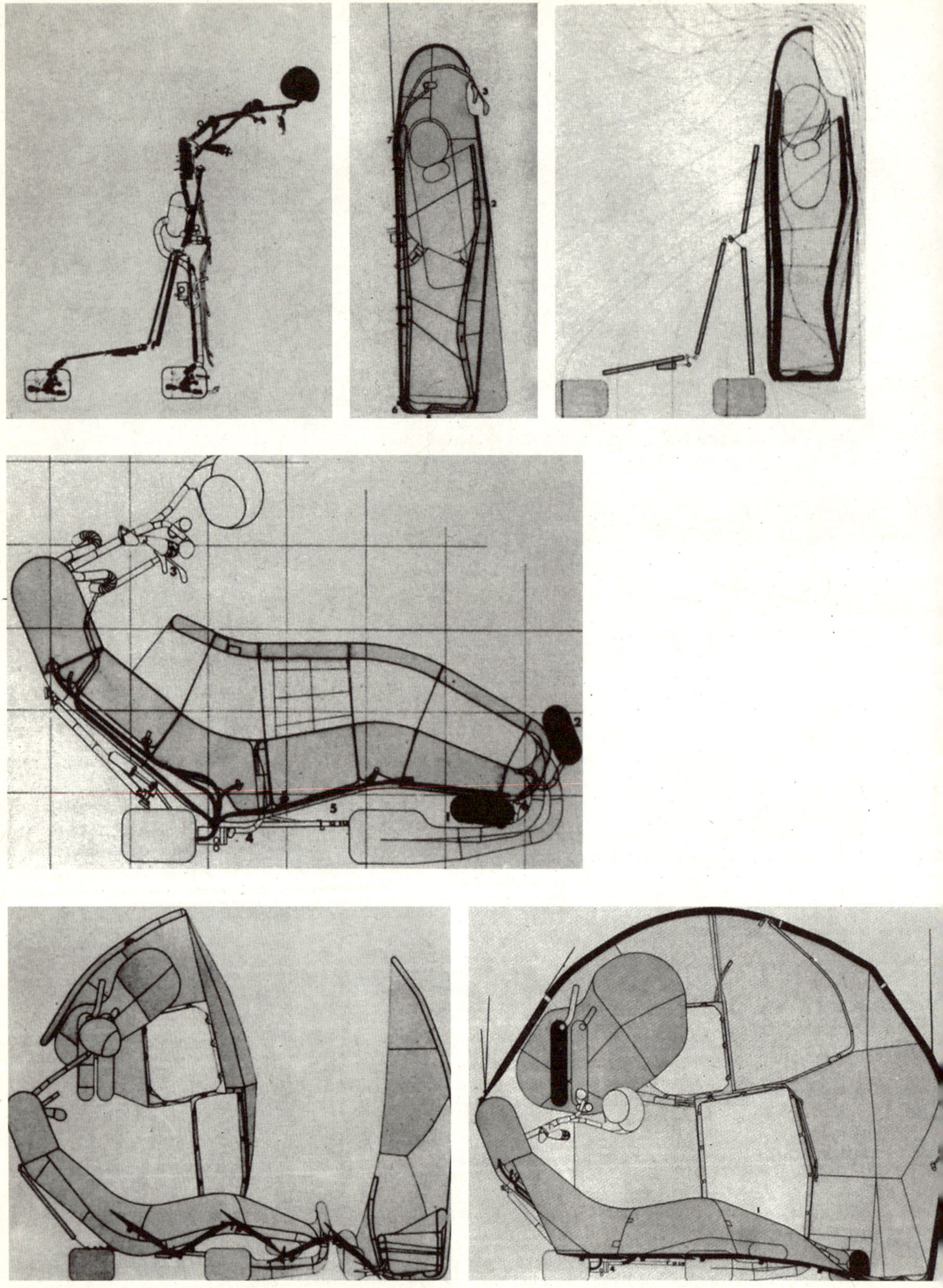

Mike Webb, various stages of the Cushicle, 1966-1967

refuse to provide a design for the numerous appliances that are meant to populate the house. The Control and Choice project, which was also conceived in 1967 (for the Paris Biennale des Jeunesses), is even more radical, blurring the distinction between hardware and software: the robots have lost their defined shape and can no longer be identified as a recognisable appliance or item of furniture. The entire living environment consists of nothing but continually shifting systems. The pursuit of absolute freedom has led to absolute formlessness. The photos of the model bear witness to the tragedy of this project: a bleak carcass, from which any hint of domesticity or architecture has been assiduously erased. And what is more, the occupant has no motivation to stay in such cheerless surroundings, now that he or she can simply glide right out the door on a hoverchair.

CUSHICLE AND SUITALOON, MIKE WEBB, 1966-1968

When walls, floors and ceiling are perceived as merely obstacles to the occupant's total freedom, a house need not be anything more than an apparatus that shelters the person inside while meeting his or her needs. 'With apologies to the master,' wrote David Greene, 'the house is an appliance for carrying with you, the city is a machine for plugging into.'[14]

The Cushicle is an inflatable house that can be carried around by the nomadic 'occupant' like a backpack. A backpack with a frame: the Cushicle consists of both a 'spine', which acts as a support structure, and a tent, which can unfold itself around the occupant. The Cushicle consists of all the basic facilities: food, water, heat and even radio and television. The house has become an appliance itself, a sort of intravenous drip that gives the occupant immediate access to all the necessary facilities. The living area, which in the case of the Living Pod still constituted the dominant spatial element (in the form of an organically shaped 'shell'), has been reduced to a tent of minimal dimensions.

In a later version of this project Mike Webb took things a step further with the introduction of the Suitaloon, a spacesuit that could be seen as the most stripped-down 'house' imaginable. The suit, which provides all the necessary facilities, can be connected to means of transport, to larger 'balloons' where the occupant can shed his or her suit, or to other spacesuits, in order to make direct physical contact with fellow nomads.

The house is in danger of becoming nothing more than an envelope, an article of clothing, a blank spot in which we can perceive the prototypical dwelling, according to Reyner Banham: 'Architecture, indeed, began with the first furs worn by our earlier ancestors, or with the discovery of fire – it shows a narrowly professional frame of mind to refer its beginnings solely to the cave or the primitive hut.'[15]

It doesn't take much imagination to see the House of the Future as this primitive cave. Banham, however, regards the House of the Future chiefly as a Pop Art phenomenon: a conscious attempt to design a stylised, stylish home in the manner of other mass produced articles, like cars. He bases this view on a number of physical characteristics of the house, like the chrome strips and the use of paneling.[16] Yet it is the Smithson's 'narrowly professional frame of mind' that allows this house to show more than what Banham sees in it. The House of the Future gives the house a future.

Translated by Steve Leinbach

14 From the explanatory notes accompanying the plans for the Living Pod; see Cook, *Archigram*, op. cit. (note 11), 52.

15 From Reyner Banham, 'Stocktaking', *Architectural Review* (February, 1960), reprinted in Reyner Banham, *Design by Choice* (London, 1981), 51.

16 From Reyner Banham, 'The Atavism of the Short Distance Mini-Cyclist', *Living Arts* 3 (1964), reprinted in Banham, ibid., 88.

1

2

3

7

8

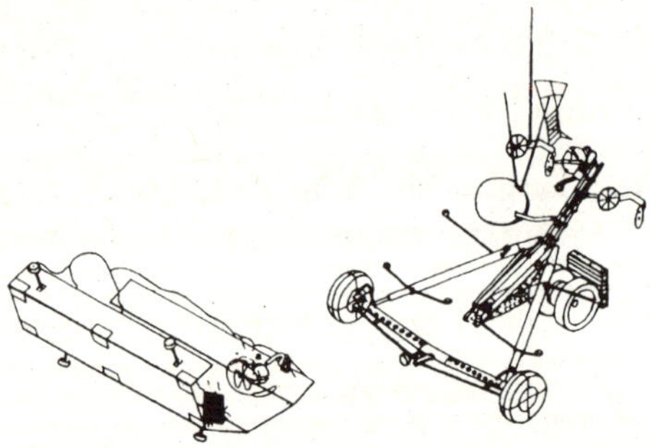

12

13

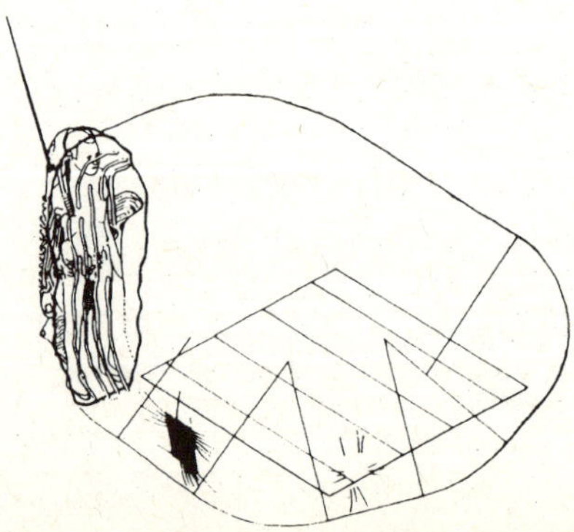

16

17

Mike Webb, Suitaloon, 1968

4

5

6

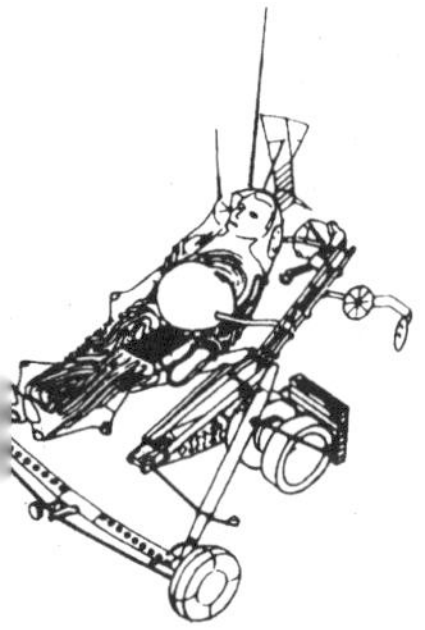

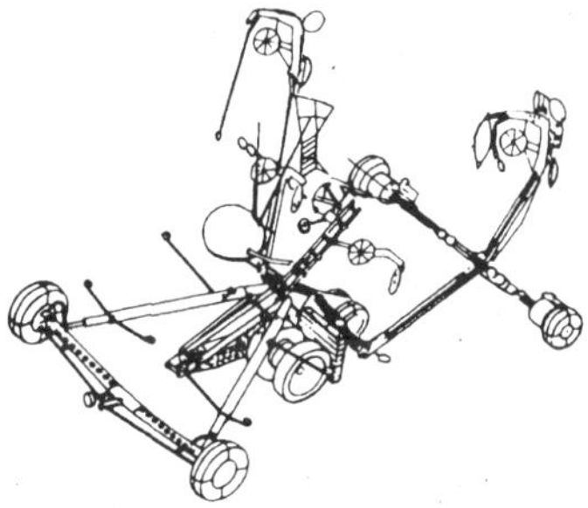

10

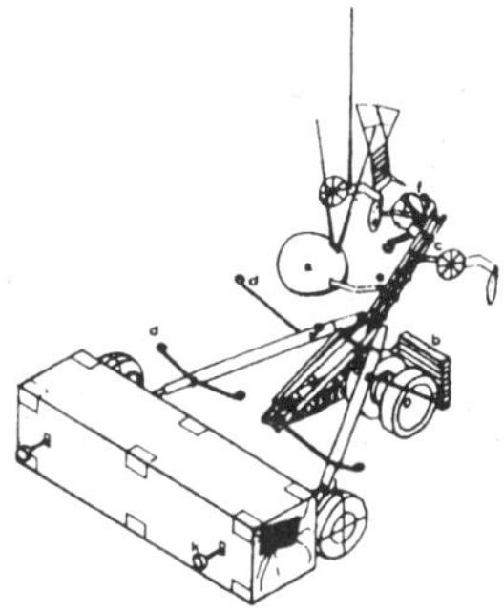

11

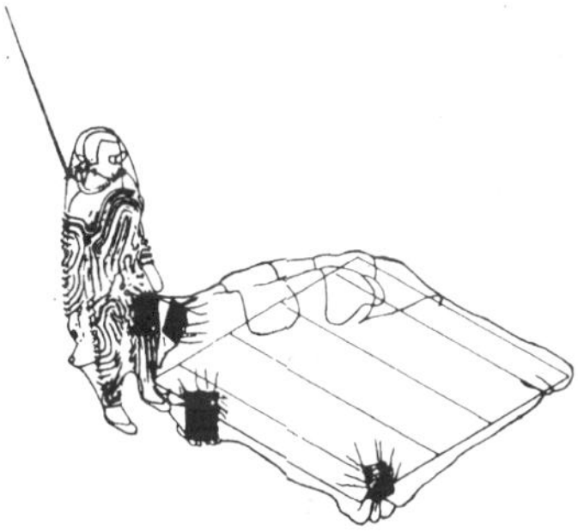

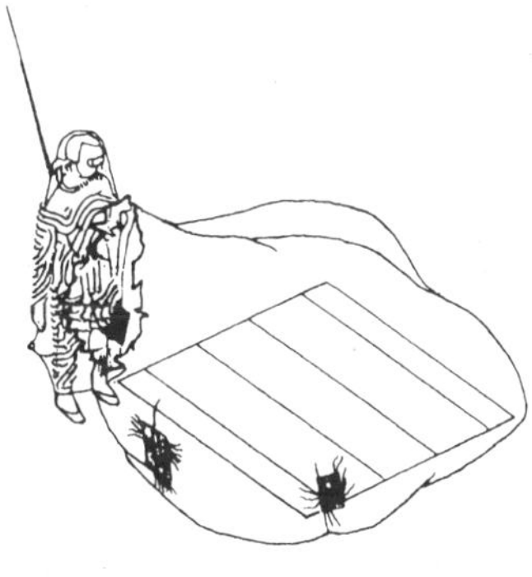

14

15

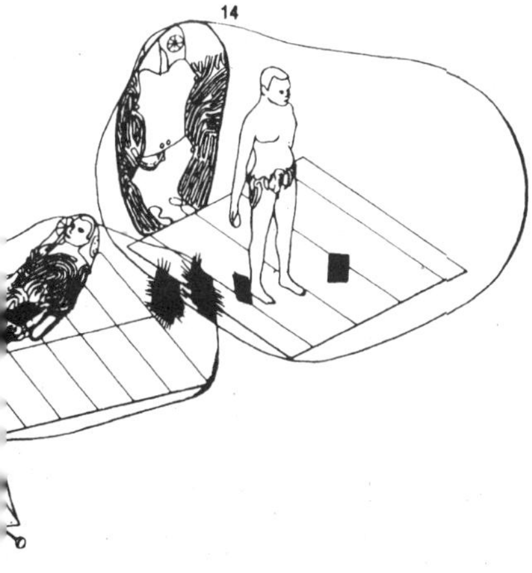

To fully appreciate the Dutch interest in poiesis and architecture, one should keep in mind that the two main schools of architecture in the Netherlands are embedded within universities of technology. One with a standing tradition, namely Delft, which was established in the nineteenth century, and the other with the freshness of relative youth, namely Eindhoven, established in the post-war years as part of the large-scale project of the welfare state. The context of educating engineers for Shell, Philips and the civil works that keep the Netherlands dry and running, is not always favourable to educating architects, who need to be trained in understanding culture beyond the sheer pragmatics of the applied sciences.

'Poiesis and architecture' was a symposium organised by the Eindhoven chair of history and theory in 1987, and the *OASE* editors, at the time based in Delft, gladly offered the journal as a platform to publish the lectures, which ranged from reflections on the writings of Martin Heidegger, Paul Valéry, Julio Cortázar and Paul Celan to the work of Mies van der Rohe, Aldo Rossi, Cesare Cattaneo and Gianbattista Piranesi. The focus on *poiesis* and its manifold relations with architecture should be understood as part of the discursive politics at stake, and as such the symposium was one of the various attempts to reclaim the territory proper to architecture.

At the time Geert Bekaert held the Eindhoven chair of Architecture History and Theory. The title of his contribution, 'Le réel du discours', immediately illustrates his intention to firmly defend the hermeneutic tradition as another discourse parallel to the one of scientific knowledge. 'Le réel du discours' represents to Bekaert a discourse that is equally real and without which we can't grasp the construction of the human universe. Clearly, among others, Heidegger and Valéry belong to this tradition, yet in this text, Bekaert reframes Valéry's dialogue 'Eupalinos ou l'architecte', a Socratic dialogue, in order to demonstrate how poetry and thinking is primarily construction when marking the transition from chaos to order.

From thereon – after establishing 'thinking' as 'building' – Bekaert starts to weave his argument. He proposes various paradoxes, including the one of a 'thinking' that is absolutely free yet cannot go beyond the limits of construction. Eventually, Bekaert's profound humanism also becomes clear from this text, when he situates the paradox of human existence within the act of construction. According to Bekaert, construction itself already implies the possibility of change, and the imagination of another world. Construction and thinking, then, are also acts of distortion.

Dirk van den Heuvel
Member of the editorial board
from *OASE* 35 to 53

Geert Bekaert

LE RÉEL DU DISCOURS

Eupalinos ou l'architecte*

* A slightly different version of this text was previously published in the *festschrift* for Geert Bekaert, *Wonen tussen gemeenplaats en poëzie* (Rotterdam: 010, 1993).

FIRST PUBLISHED IN *OASE* 40

Parthenon, 440 BC

If there is one text that takes the theme of the symposium, 'Poesis and architecture', as its element, then it is Paul Valéry's dialogue *Eupalinos ou l'architecte*. I became familiar with this text in the elegant Gallimard edition published in 1944[1] – the year before Valéry's death – which also contains the dialogues *L'âme et la danse* and *Dialogue de l'arbre*. I mention these titles in passing because dance and trees are two subjects of Valéry's that are closely connected to our theme. While reading Valéry's text, I was sent a review copy of the proceedings of the 1951 Darmstädter Gesprach, *Mensch und Raum*, including the Sunday lecture 'Bauen, Wohnen, Denken' by Prof. Martin Heidegger of Freiburg. By sheer coincidence, those texts, written 30 years apart, were brought together for me in an almost organic association. Recently, Massimo Cacciari made this association the theme of an article with the altered title 'Eupalinos ou l'architect*ure*' (rather than *l'architecte*), which appeared in *Critique*, no. 476-477, January-February 1987. This alteration, whether conscious or not, is not unimportant in our context.

It is tempting to take Cacciari's thesis, or the comparison between Heidegger and Valéry in general, as a point of departure, but I fear that Valéry's text will then remain underexamined. Cacciari offers a Heideggerian reading of Valéry, in such a skilful and thought-provoking way that you are almost convinced it was meant to be. I too believe that it can be useful to juxtapose those two authors (Heidegger was 19 years younger than Valéry), just as it can be useful to juxtapose Valéry with authors such as Barthes, Deleuze, Derrida, Cioran and Bataille. I cannot escape the impression, however, that Cacciari's all too direct interpretation of Valéry's writings with the aid of certain Heideggerian concepts does violence to Valéry's text. I will stay with Valéry's text itself.

Valéry's text is of a different order than Heidegger's. It is above all text, form, construction, publication. Valéry plays with thoughts as if with bricks/building stones. He does not develop them. He provides no explanation. The spoken language, the writing in statements and counterstatements, the cessation, the continuation of spoken language and writing, carefully, cogently, but also playfully, parodically, speaking and writing is important. His thoughts about poiesis are the text itself. Outside the text they do not exist. His approach to architecture is the architecture of his text.

Le réel d'un discours, Socrates says in *Eupalinos*: '*c'est après tout cette chanson, et cette couleur d'une voix, que nous traitons a tort comme détails et accidents*': 'The reality of a discourse is, after all, that song, and that colouring of the voice, which we unjustly view as details and accidents.' Elsewhere Valéry says: 'The highest goal of art is charm, enchantment.'

The most obvious thing to do would be to read the text itself aloud, to listen to it. It is rhetorical or poetic enough for that. But our symposium leaves no scope for this approach. Reading or 'reciting' the 127 pages in the above-mentioned elegant edition would take too much time. But what is the alternative?

Narrating a condensed version of Valéry is impossible, summarising him even more impossible. Explaining his system of thought is likewise impossible, because it does not exist, or if it does (as a kind of wish), it contains its own destruction. Just as Loos' buildings cannot be photographed, Valéry's texts cannot be translated. They are attached to their language. Their reality lies in their appearance, their form, their sound, their body.

1 A Dutch translation by Piet Meeuse was published in 1991 by De Bezige Bij in Amsterdam, under the title *Leonardo en Socrates*. Translator's note: The English translations of quotes from *Eupalinos* are based on the Dutch translations in the original article, but with reference to both the original French version and a published English translation of the complete dialogue: 'Eupalinos', in Paul Valéry, *Dialogues*, trans. William McCausland Stewart (New York, 1956), 65-152. These translations thus reflect both the original dialogue and, in many cases, Geert Bekaert's interpretation of it. Moreover, they reflect his decisions on issues such as whether to provide the French, a translation or both, what words and phrases to omit from the quotes, and whether to indicate those omissions. The English version of the excerpt from *La Pythie* is largely based on a translation by Elizabeth Sewell, as

All we can do here is take a few shots – following Valéry's own method, *à la mode des artilleurs* – in the direction of the target, the target unknown to us, which remains eternally mysterious, and for all we know may not even exist. The text, as a text, remains out of reach. No construction or deconstruction whatsoever is capable of neutralising it.

Eupalinos ou l'architecte is an occasional piece – like the vast majority of Valéry's works, one might add. This occasional character is in fact essential to its viewpoint on the functionality of a text. It was commissioned by the architects Louis Suë and André Mare as an introduction to the monumental edition of their work *Architectures . . . la présentation d'ouvrages d'architecture, décoration intérieure, peinture, sculpture et gravure, contribuant depuis mil neuf cent quatorze à former le style français*, an attempt to naturalize the Wiener Werkstätte in France. The book was published by Editions de la Nouvelle Revue Française in 1921. (That same year, Loos's *Ins Leere gesprochen* was published. Le Corbusier's *Vers une architecture* followed in 1923.)

Valéry was allotted precisely 115,800 characters, not one more or less. In a letter to Paul Souday, he remarks: 'It's true that they are sumptuous characters.' And the fonts used were luxurious! The oversized proofs gave the author the impression that he was holding a sixteenth-century book and had been dead 400 years himself.

The same letter includes other remarks of potential relevance to our theme: 'They are works made to order,' Valéry says, 'in which I could not place an authentic thought in the most favourable light. I have tried to show that pure thought and the search for truth itself cannot aspire to anything but the discovery and construction of a *form*.' Here is all poiesis in a nutshell: *découverte*, *construction*, *forme*.

Valéry explicitly draws in philosophy: 'The contrast is not between a philosopher and an artist, but between an artist and a philosopher who does not arrive at a *perfect* form, who does not realise that *only this* can be the object of a rational and conscious investigation.' Sculptors have never complained about also having to carve sculptures for the scalene triangle of a temple pediment. In a letter dating from 1934, 11 years after the previous one, Valéry returns to the subject of *Eupalinos*. He still recalls the precise number of characters. At first, he writes, this restriction put him off. But as a poet, used to fixed forms, he discovered that all the difficulties could be resolved through a flexible form of dialogue, in which a reply without meaning could be added or left out.

The name Eupalinos he finds in an encyclopaedia. It is no more than a name. But he needs a name, Poiesis is not anyonymous. It is the work of a 'master', 'whose art gives beings and things a duration longer than many centuries and a contemplative and interpretative value comparable to that of a sacred text'.

The name is tied to the work, not to the person. 'One can never infer from the work to the person, but from the work to the mask and from the mask to the machine.' The author is a machine for writing; the writer is a typewriter. Valéry says, about himself, *Je ne suis pas celui que je suis* – 'I am not who I am . . . I exist in order to find something', to make something. '*That* which makes a work is not the person who lends his name to it. *That* which makes a work has no name.' A name is no more than 'a useful notation for a virtual collection of partial connective systems'.

cited by Denis Donoghue in *Partisan Review*, LXVII (1), 2000, but has been altered to more closely reflect the Dutch translation in the original article. One noteworthy difference is the second line (in this version; Sewell presents her translation as prose), in which Bekaert interprets *paré* as meaning 'prepared' or 'forearmed' (*paraat* in Dutch), while Sewell renders it as 'adorned'. The English translations of quotes from other works in French are based entirely on the Dutch versions.

(In reality, Eupalinos was apparently more of a bridge-builder than a builder of temples. Valéry never went to Greece, and with his grammar-school Greek he could not read Plato's dialogues in the original language – in translation they struck him as terribly long and tedious.)

These comments by Valéry are more than anecdotal. They reveal his relationship to the text. What matters to him is not the reality of the Greek landscape or of Plato's text, but the form that his text assumes. In *Triomphe de Manet*, Valéry makes the following remark about the poetic art of Mallarmé, his great predecessor and friend: 'Far from wishing to reconstruct beings and things through literary adaptation and painstaking description, he [Mallarmé] understood that poetry exhausted them; he dreamed that they had no other purpose, that they could be intended for no other use than to be consumed by it. He thought the world had been made to end up in a beautiful book.' And Valéry would not have had any objection if we replaced the beautiful book with the beautiful building.

Reality provides only the occasion and the materials for *le réel du discours*. For Valéry, every text is an occasional text, or vice versa – every occasion is worth a text, can generate a text, just as a stone (in Valéry's view) carries an image within it, or even awaits an image.

In one of Valéry's earliest works, which not coincidentally is about architecture or, in fact, about the architect, *Paradoxe de l'architecte* (1891), this conviction comes to the fore. There Valéry says of Flaubert that *il taillait les mots longuement comme des pierres dures*: 'he carved words for a long time, like hard stones.' And he added, in italics, *le héros . . . conçoit en dehors du monde*: 'the hero conceptualises independently of the world.'

For Valéry, the real world is language. *Honneur des hommes, Saint LANGAGE*, he says in his long 1919 poem *La Pythie*. I quote the final stanza, which sums up Valéry's entire poetics:

> Honour of humanity, Sainted LANGUAGE,
> Discourse prophetic and adorned,
> Fair chains in which the god
> Lost in the flesh binds himself,
> Illumination, generosity!
> Here speaks a Wisdom,
> Here sounds that august voice
> Which when it sounds
> Knows itself to be no longer anyone's voice
> So much as that of the waves and the woods!

Accordingly, there can be no poiesis outside of language. Poiesis is where language, through bodily participation, obtains its immediate and universal significance. In *Dialogue de l'arbre*, Valéry speaks of an *étrange voeu de trame universelle*, a strange wish for a universal framework, in which the individual is dissolved – in the words of his well-known poem *Le cimetière marin: ouvrages purs d'une éternelle cause*. In *Paradoxe de l'architecte*, quoted above, he describes the soul of the future architect as 'a musical one, long sheltered in the pure loneliness of its dream'.

The deliberate, pure loneliness of the poet, the maker, the *constructeur* sets his work apart from the history around him. There is another reality besides the historical. Valéry did publish a collection of writings entitled *Regards sur le monde actuel*, which contains some surprisingly incisive analyses of current events, but his *monde actuel*, his present-day world, is above all a world of the spirit, a universal world in which references to the anecdotal world around him – in which, it should be said, he made his way with great ease, though also with detachment – are signally lacking.

The surrealists Paul Eluard and André Breton once entertained themselves by altering Valéry's texts, replacing a given word by its opposite and thereby making a mockery of the utterly equivocal nature of Valéry's statements. In fact, they were very nearly applying Valéry's own method.

In *L'idée fixe ou deux hommes à la mer*, written in 1932 for the Medical Society – another *enfant de la hâte*, 'child of haste' – Valéry writes: 'Among people who know each other well enough not to misjudge the proportion of seriousness and unseriousness that makes up their dialogue, everything amounts to a match without consequences. Just like the kings painted on playing cards, the most serious subjects are thrown onto the carpet, taken up again, mixed with all the nothings of the world and the moment.' A dialogue does not offer the reader any ideas. The ideas are no more than incidental to the game, in which the essential thing is the rapidity of the exchange. Then comes the marvellous sentence: *Ces messieurs perdent vivement leur temps.* Those gentlemen are wasting their time in a lively (and rapid) manner, just as we are now. *Nos propos font des ronds à la surface de nos ennuis* – 'Our words make circles on the surface of our boredom.' Or put more prosaically (for Valéry can do that, too): *La façon de parler en dit plus que ce que l'on dit . . . Le fond n'a aucune importance . . . essentielle* – 'The manner of speaking says more than what one says. The content is of no essential importance whatsoever.' Like the ambiguous object that Socrates picks up on the beach in *Eupalinos*, any sentence forms an occasion for contemplation, for wordplay. When one has had enough, he throws it back into the sea. But his spirit remains in the grip of its riddle. Socrates hastily runs inland 'like someone whose thoughts, after having long been tossed in all directions, seem at last to find their bearings and gather into a single idea, engendering in his body at the same moment the decision for very definite movement, along with a resolute bearing'.

This clears the way for *Eupalinos*. *Eupalinos* is not an architectural treatise, much less a philosophy of architecture. The best way to describe our text is as a poetics, not the poetics of a particular discipline, but a poetics of spiritual activity, laying bare 'the inevitable ways in which the spirit functions'.

It is in Hades, the underworld, the realm of ghosts, the domain of philosophy, that this poetics of the spirit is formulated and thus put into perspective too, because there thought is utterly 'free', unfettered. It can no longer 'think in materials' and so, Valéry believes, it can no longer truly think. *Nous ne savons que ce que nous savons faire* – 'We know nothing but what we know how to make.' In the underworld, knowledge has become no more than allusion, memory. It is utterly dependent on itself. It no longer has a body, as the living do; it can no longer enter and exit, distance itself. After all, the living are made *d'une maison et d'une abeille*, 'of a house and a bee'.

The house which the living wish to make eternal, and which thus leads them to erect desperate monuments of stone or thoughts, is nothing but transience and madness. But the unquenchable, foolish longing to protect it from time is what makes a person a person, belongs to him and no one else and sets poetry into motion. *Il n'y aurait pas d'hommes sans l'amour* – 'There would be no men without love,' Socrates says, and lets his thoughts drift onward: 'And from where do you think we have drawn the primal idea and the energy for those immense efforts which have raised so many illustrious cities and useless monuments that reason admires but would have never been capable of conceiving?' Elsewhere, Valéry speaks of *cet éclair qui illumine instantanément des années*.

Man's fate is his poiesis, his love (the discovery and acknowledgement of the other), the creation of the other, the awareness of the nonexistent, the unknown, the hidden, the *possible*. This brings us close to the concept of *Technik* (technique, technology) in Heidegger. In a commentary accompanying his *Introduction à la méthode de Léonard de Vinci*, which was first published in 1894 and remained his credo for the rest of his life, Valéry says: 'It is not living, but making, that is of interest.' Living is *se transformer dans l'incomplet* – 'transforming oneself within the incomplete'. *La construction . . . implique les conditions a priori d'une existence qui pourraït être TOUT AUTRE* – 'Construction . . . presupposes the *a priori* conditions of an existence that could be ENTIRELY DIFFERENT.'

From this perspective, architecture – along with music – is the ultimate paradigm for the 'work of the spirit', the 'potential of the spirit' in matter. This point is emphasised in his *Paradoxe de l'architecte*, but also in many other texts in his daily *Cahiers* or his introduction to melodrama, *Amphion* (for which Honegger wrote the music). *Amphion* is an ode to the constructive arts, music and architecture. In Valéry's version, the tragic Amphion, the son of Zeus and Antiope, receives the lyre from Apollo, an act by which the god wishes to benefit the human race. When building the Temple of Apollo in Thebes, Amphion plays his lyre and the stones move into place of their own accord.

La marche des pierres

O miracle, o merveille!
Le roc marche! La terre est soumise a ce dieu,
Quelle vie effrayable envahit la nature?
Tout s'ébranle, tout cherche l'ordre
Tout se cherche un destin!

O miracle, O marvel!
The rock is walking! The earth is subjected to this god,
What fearsome life has overrun nature?
All things start moving, all seek order
All seek a destiny!

'Like prey, work and beauty are pursued.' But Amphion, too, is seized like prey. When the work has been completed, the Muses, one of whom is none other than Hope, seek a new master. And after a veiled form has taken Amphion's lyre away, he hides his face in the lap of someone who could be love or death.

In his introduction to *Amphion*, Valéry confesses: 'Architecture has assumed an important place among my spirit's first loves. My young self passionately imagined the act of construction . . . and even the idea of *construction*, which is the transition from chaos to order, the use of the changeable to arrive at necessity, took hold of me as the most beautiful and complete type of activity that a person can imagine. A finished building gives us, at a single glance, the sum of intentions, inventions, insights and forces that imply its existence; it brings to light humanity's combined work of desire, knowledge and ability. Uniquely among the arts, and in an indivisible moment of vision, architecture charges our souls with the sense of human capacities as a whole.'

The building in *Eupalinos* is at first a Greek temple, but it is also a ship. Both Eupalinos of Megara and Tridon the Phoenician are artists of surprising spirit, who possess the power of Orpheus and work *à la manière de Dieu*. It is said that Eupalinos *s'élévait à la suprème connaissance de son art*.

We approach architecture through the architect. It is he who 'changes the seen into the visible'. Phaedrus reports on his conversations with the architect. He speaks, as Adorno says, about Valéry from the perspective of the design studio, not from that of the work of art.

The temple is not described as a result in a formal, archaeological or art-historical sense. The form itself is not dissected. Form is formation, poiesis. And this encompasses everything. Eupalinos controls not only the physical materials, but also the living workers. For him, they are pliable material in the creation of his work of art, because he can fill them with such inspiration that they become a kind of romantic brotherhood, carrying out his orders (which are no longer orders) with enthusiasm. In his speeches to the workers, no trace remains of his own nocturnal struggles for the idea. 'He gave them nothing but orders and figures.'

Phaedrus sums up his story: *Je ne sépare plus l'idée d'un temple de celle de son édification* – 'I no longer distinguish between the idea of a temple and that of its construction. When I see one, I see an admirable act, even more glorious than a victory and more in opposition to wretched nature.' *Le détruire et le construire sont égaux en importance* – 'Destruction and construction are of equal importance, souls are required for the one and for the other, but construction is dearer to my spirit.'

The remainder of the dialogue elaborates on this poiesis of architecture – a tautology – on this architecture. It takes a number of turns that at first seem surprising, but on further scrutiny, they all refer back to the fundamental themes of Valéry's poetics.

The first principle of this poetics is, *Il n'y a point de détails dans l'exécution* – 'In execution, there are no details.' Or, in Mies van der Rohe's terms, God is in the details. A professional's working principle must give a philosopher like Socrates valuable food for thought. It is a *lingot d'or brut*, an ingot of raw gold, at least 'if it is truly clear, and the direct product of work, in a brief act of the mind that sums up its experience, without allowing itself the time to fantasise'.

Socrates takes up this point in his remarks on *le réel d'un discours*. The reality of any speech lies in its form, the way it is phrased. This rule, it should be added, applies to every domain, except to the philosophers, 'whose great misfortune is that they never see the worlds they have imagined collapse, because they simply do not exist'.

Still, the very meticulous care devoted to the durability (*la durée*) of the building, which is manifest in this attention to detail, is nothing compared to Eupalinos' attentiveness *quand il élaborait les émotions et les vibra-*

tions de l'âme du futur contemplateur de son oeuvre – 'when he worked out the emotions and vibrations in the soul of the future viewer of his work.' And Phaedrus continues, in a marvellous passage: *Il préparait à la lumière* – 'He prepared a matchless instrument for light, which spread it, entirely saturated with intelligible forms and almost musical qualities, into the space where mortals move.'

Accordingly, the second rule of Eupalinos' poetics is, *Il faut que mon temple meuve les hommes comme les meut l'objet aimé* – 'My temple must move people as a cherished object moves them.' Valéry uses *mouvoir* here, rather than *émouvoir*.

Socrates responds by telling a surprising and enlightening story about a friend who, confronted with the well-made body (*le corps si bien fait*) of Alcibades, cried out, *En le voyant, on se sent devenir architecte!* – 'Seeing it, you feel yourself becoming an architect!'

This story prompts the further exploration of ideas about the corporality (materiality, sensory nature) of poiesis, of the poetic and the poet, and thus about their inherent transience. *Ce qu'il y a de plus beau ne figure pas dans l'éternel* – 'What is most beautiful has no place in the eternal. Nothing beautiful is separable from life, and life is that which dies.'

Beauty is not, however, a kind of intoxication or stupor. Socrates has known ecstasy. Experience has taught him 'that our souls, in the very bosom of time, can make sanctuaries for themselves impenetrable by duration, internally eternal, transient with regard to nature; where they at last are what they know, where they long for what they are, where they feel themselves to have been created by what they love, and give back to it light for light, silence for silence, giving and receiving themselves without borrowing anything from the material of the world or from the Hours.' These abysses 'presuppose the life that they suspend'.

'But these marvels, these meditations and these ecstasies do not clarify for me,' Socrates says, 'our strange problem of beauty. I cannot connect these supreme states of the soul to the presence of a body, or any object that brings them into being.'

These claims provoke the accusation from Phaedrus that Socrates, the philosopher, has always disapproved of beauty, of poiesis. By the end of the dialogue, this leads to a sort of conversion of Socrates, who becomes an anti-Socrates, a *constructeur* rather than a philosopher.

Again, the example of the architect is used to show that inner thoughts cannot be detached from external actions. *A force de construire*, Eupalinos confesses with a grin, *je crois bien que je me suis construit moi-même* – 'By building, I do believe I have built myself.'

And Eupalinos clarifies by making another confession: 'Listen, Phaedrus, that little temple I built for Hermes, just a few steps away – if you only knew how much it means to me! Where passers-by see nothing but an elegant chapel – it's nothing much, four columns, a very simple style – I placed the memory of a bright day in my life. O sweet metamorphosis! This delicate temple, nobody realises, is the mathematical image of a Corinthian girl whom I loved happily.'

Because Phaedrus shows that he understands Eupalinos, the architect is ready to tell him all his secrets. But they are inexpressible; they slip away from language. What can be said about them tends to be tedious, since it relates to the purely technical side of the profession.

But here again, the analogy between architecture and music sheds some light on the issue. There are buildings that are mute, Phaedrus says, buildings that speak and, very rarely, buildings that sing.

Buildings that do not speak deserve only contempt. They are inferior even to a heap of stones 'that amuse the sharp eye because of the accidental order they borrow from their fall'.

Buildings that speak clearly deserve our respect, like a prison that expresses the rigour and fairness of the law. Socrates replies, in a twist characteristic of Valéry's work, that he does not even know how his prison looked.

But Phaedrus continues with the story of Eupalinos, who waxes lyrical about the beauty of the miraculous, half-natural theatres at the ports and on the coast. Maritime construction had fascinated Valéry since his youth in Sète. But as impressive as they are, Eupalinos says, they cannot compare to a work of art made entirely by a single man, as the temple was made by Eupalinos. 'Even if, we have to make a fairly serious effort in defiance of ourselves, we must keep at a certain remove from the glamorous things in life and from immediate gratification.' *Ce qu'il y a de plus beau est nécessairement tyrannique* – 'That which is most beautiful is of necessity tyrannical . . . True beauty is as rare as is, among men, the man who is capable of defying himself, that is to say, choosing a certain self and imposing it on himself' – *de choisir un certain soi-même et de se l'imposer*.

Eupalinos then gives a rapturous description of an architecture that could partake in the purity of musical sound, thanks to the architect whose meditations (with Minerva's help) have penetrated to the outer limits of his being and thus the outer limits of reality. Eupalinos can imagine this only as a dream, and not as a science. *Je ne suis pas en possession d'enchainer, comme il le faudrait, une analyse à une extase* – 'I am not capable of joining analysis with ecstasy, as one should be.'

Ecstasy overtakes the artist. But it is not the ecstasy that is creative. 'O most important of moments and supreme heartbreak! . . . Far from accepting these excessive and mysterious favours as they are, inferred solely from a great desire, formed naively from the extreme anticipation of my soul, I must hold them back, O Phaedrus, and they must await my signal. After I have obtained them through a kind of interruption of my life (an adorable suspension of ordinary duration), I still wish to divide the indivisible and to temper and interrupt the very birth of the Ideas . . . to be free. Above all, the important thing to me is *d'obtenir de ce qui va être* – 'to obtain some part of *what is to be* which, with all the force of its newness, satisfies the reasonable demands of *what has been*.'

The spirit is a bodily, sensory spirit. It thinks in material terms. It lives by seeing, as Valéry says in his *Discours en l'honneur de Goethe*. *Il vit de voir.* And elsewhere: *Laisse l'oeil vivre de sa vie.* He quotes Goethe: 'I have never thought about a thought.'

'When I design a dwelling,' Eupalinos says, '(whether for the gods or for a man), and when I search for that form with love, setting myself the task of creating an object that delights the gaze, fuels the spirit, accords with reason and the many proprieties, I will tell you something strange: *it seems that my body is playing a part*.' *Corps* is of course a term with architectural associations, perhaps more so than 'body'.

Eupalinos goes on, in a moralistic tone, saying that people do not know how to put the miraculous instrument of the body to full use. 'Beasts one moment and spirits the next, they do not realise what universal connections they contain. 'Through their bodies, they are part of the world, they are stones, they are trees.'

Each morning, Eupalinos calls on the muse of the body in a long prayer: 'Living instrument of life, for each of us you are the only object comparable to the universe.' And he ends with the words, 'But this body and this soul, this invincibly real presence and this creative absence which fight for being and must ultimately be brought together, this finite and infinite that we carry with us, each according to his nature, must now unite in a well-ordered construction . . . of which the profit is the imperishable wealth that I call Perfection.'

After his long silence, Socrates speaks, using the relationship between architecture and music to further explore the 'perfection' of the body and soul in the creative work. Music and architecture are unlike the other arts, because they carry us away with them. 'We are, we move, we live in the work of man.' We can leave it and return to it. (Here too, there are promising points of departure for a Heideggerian approach.) These two arts enclose man in man, or rather, they incorporate man into his work, and the soul into its acts and the products of those acts.

Through two arts, man surrounds himself in two different ways with laws and acts of inner will (*volontés intérieures*). 'And each one fills our knowledge and our space with artificial truths and quintessentially human objects. By means of numbers and numerical relationships, they bring forth in us not a fable, but the hidden force that creates every fable.'

'Music and Architecture make us think of things entirely different from themselves. They exist in this world as monuments from another world, or as examples, spread [disseminated] here and there, of a structure and a duration that are not those of beings, but of forms and laws.' The architect imposes intelligible forms on stone. He gives shape to laws or deduces their forms from the laws themselves.

But he cannot do that without words. *Pas de géométrie sans la parole*. 'No geometry without words. Without words, forms are mere accidents and neither manifest nor serve the power of the spirit.' Language itself is a *constructeur*. The altar of language, like that of architecture, has three sides: that of the ordinary word, 'which vanishes into the bread one asks for, the road one points out', that of the exalted word, 'from which a crystalline torrent of eternal water flows', and finally, that of severe, subtle, inhuman clarity and simplicity, that of 'numbers, which are the simplest of words'.

And then comes Socrates/Valéry's confession: 'There was an architect in me, which the circumstances did not form completely.' A meditation on the beach, a personal memory of Valéry's own, leads him to the distinction between a work of nature and a work of man.

The structure of every human creation is disorder. It is the result of a thought, and to think is to disrupt something (*déranger quelque chose*). Man creates by abstraction, by underappreciating or forgetting many of the properties he uses. Wine and milk and water are drunk from the same vessel, made of glass, onyx or clay and in a diverse array of shapes. 'Even the maker of that cup could only ever roughly harmonise its material, form and function with one another. For the intimate subordination of these three things and the profound connection between them can only be the work of creative nature (*nature naturante*) itself. The artisan cannot do his work without violating or disrupting some form of order through the forces that he applies to matter to adapt it to the idea he wishes to imitate and the use he anticipates. He is thus inevitably led to make things which, as a whole, are less complex than their parts', just as in an army in formation, each soldier is infinitely more complex than the formation as a whole.

Only philosophers try to grasp everything. Man, who wishes to live, is capable of action only because he can forget, and content himself with part of the knowledge that is his special quirk (*bizarrerie particulière*), knowledge which is a little bit more extensive than it need be. And this little bit shows that living beings are not precisely adapted to pure utility. Like dogs barking at the moon, people (*les humains*) try to fill or break the eternal silence of these infinite expanses that frighten them.

The things that people make stem from 'acts of a thought'. The principles are distinct from the construction (this does not contradict the higher statement that the idea of the temple cannot be separated from its construction); they are imposed on the material by a foreign tyrant who communicates them through his actions. 'The human condition (*le fait de l'homme*) is to create in two kinds of time, one of which passes in the domain of pure possibility, in the bosom of the subtle material that can imitate all things and combine them unto infinity.'

This brings Valéry to the Vitruvian categories: utility, beauty and durability. Utility is focused on the body, beauty on the soul and durability on the outside world, in which the object must resist its destiny, which is to perish. Only architecture requires these three properties of the complete 'work' and carries them to their highest point.

Those who succeed in that have no reason for modesty. They have discovered the means to mix necessity and artifice inextricably, and to bring forth ultimate freedom from ultimate severity. Their secret is well known. They replace nature, against which other artists struggle, with a nature more or less derived from the first, but in which all the forms and beings are nothing other than acts of the spirit, well-defined acts preserved by their names. In this essential manner, they construct worlds that are perfect in themselves, which sometimes grow so distant from our own as to become unimaginable, and sometimes approach ours so closely that they partly coincide with reality.

The example of the Phoenician, which Phaedrus presents at this point, introduces a new aspect of poiesis: the perfect work cannot imitate what already exists, but continually delves into the unknown regions of art, recapturing things at their source, in sensory experience. Most people reason with the aid of concepts that are not simply 'readymade' (*toutes faites*) but made by no one. No one is responsible for them, and so they are of no use to anyone. Only *les clartés personnelles* can be universal. Only they enable the artist to choose his form, 'for it is the task of the form to take from the resistance of nature what it needs in order to go on, but to take from it only what will impede its motive force as little as possible.'

'Man's deepest gazes are for empty space. They converge beyond the All.' Man never learns to overcome his hubris. 'What soul would hesitate to turn the universe upside down to be a little more itself?' We grant everything else only the right to be of use to us. We believe that all things, and all the richness of Time, are merely morsels for our mouths, and we cannot conceive of the contrary. We ghosts defend ourselves from non-existence with illusions, just as the living defend themselves from existence with illusions.

The God that Socrates sought is nothing other that a word born of words that returns to words. Only action can break the circle. It is in action, and in the combination of actions, that we must find the most direct sensation of the presence of the divine, and that is the best possible use of the portion of our capacities that is unsuited to life and seems to have been reserved for the pursuit of an indefinable object that infinitely surpasses us. It is through action that one is most naturally able to take God's place. And of all actions, building is the most complete.

Towards the end of the dialogue, Socrates summarises what poiesis is to him, and he at once shows to what a great extent the digressions in the dialogue fit into a coherent structure, are a construction in their own right.

'A work demands love, contemplation, obedience to your most beautiful thought, the discovery of laws by your soul and so many other things in yourself that you never suspected you possessed. This work arises from the most intimate part of your life, and yet it cannot be confused with you.'

The creation story of the great *formateur*, who defeated chaos, is a story about the organisation of inequality, the introduction of diversity. The *constructeur*, as Socrates imagines him, departs from this established order, disrupting it or building on it. *Il ne faut pas que les dieux demeurent sans toit, et les âmes sans spectacles* – 'Gods should not remain without a roof, nor souls without spectacle. Marble should not remain interred in the earth's solid night. Cedars and cypresses should not be content to rot; they can become fragrant beams. Rich people's money should not sleep idly in their urns.'

In the face of all prior expectations, the *constructeur* says, *Je suis l'acte* – 'I am the act.' I am the one who designs what you desire, a little more precisely than you do yourself. The whole world benefits. Even if I am mistaken, my failed work will be a step towards greater beauty. (Phaedrus: 'It's fortunate that you're a dead architect, Socrates!') And after Socrates has recited an authentic bit of architectural treatise, he concludes, ironically or cynically, 'But here [in the netherworld] there is no "now", and everything we have said is both a natural game of these netherworlds, and the fantasy of a certain rhetorician in the other world who has taken us for marionettes!'

'That [that game, that eternal metamorphosis] is precisely the nature of immortality,' Phaedrus answers. And that is the final word: immortality, poiesis.

Translated by David McKay

OASE 44 is entitled *Venetian Perspectives*. This issue was put together – by Dirk van den Heuvel and myself – in response to the passing of Manfredo Tafuri in 1994. Alongside Dal Co and Cacciari, Tafuri was the main proponent of the so-called 'Venetian School', a group of architecture historians associated with the IUAV. The historical scrutiny of these Venetians derived its impetus from the intellectual sources of neo-Marxist and post-Marxist thought, such as the Frankfurt School, Benjamin, Nietzsche, Heidegger and Foucault. In other words, predominantly philosophical sources, imbuing the historical work with a critical dimension that yielded an extraordinarily rich and profound output of architecture historiography.

For many years, intellectually voracious architecture students at Delft University of Technology found inspiration in the work of Tafuri in particular (translations of *Teorie e storia* and *Progetto e utopia* circulated during the 1970s and 1980s). The Venetian philosophy thus constituted standard baggage for many members of the *OASE* editorial team (the bulk of whom had links with this degree programme).

OASE 44 features articles by Tafuri and Cacciari (including his beautiful oration given at Tafuri's funeral), and commentaries by the Dutch/ Flemish authors Hilde Heyen and Michel J. van Nieuwstadt. The latter's contribution is reprinted here. Writer and translator Van Nieuwstadt is extremely well-versed in the Venetian School's intellectual sources, especially Nietzsche's oeuvre. Van Nieuwstadt reviews the English edition of Cacciari's 1993 book 'Architecture and Nihilism'. This book revolves around the Nietzschean concept of 'complete nihilism', which Cacciari sums up quite pithily as a critique of the greatest dogma of our time, namely that everything is relative and interchangeable (goods, products, fashions). In short, it is a critique of the eulogy on the 'death of the ideology'. This dogma symbolises the world of the modern metropolis, the city without qualities. As such, the metropolis serves as the central allegory in Cacciari's book.

Tafuri's death seems to have heralded the demise of critical thought in architecture. After all, the closing decade of the twentieth century was characterised by the pragmatism of supermodernism. Likewise, the field of architecture theory seems to have turned into an autonomous, hermetic cultural-philosophical 'discourse' that has lost sight of its true object – architecture. Perhaps Nietzsche was too naïve and optimistic in thinking that man may ultimately conquer nihilism.

François Claessens
Member of the editorial board
rom *OASE* 39 to 52

Translated by Laura Vroomen

Michel J. van Nieuwstadt

ARCHITEC-TURE AS FABLE; OR CACCIARI IN AMERICA

FIRST PUBLISHED IN *OASE* 44

But let us not forget this either: it is enough to create new names and estimations and probabilities in order to create in the long run new 'things'.

Nietzsche, translated by Walter Kaufmann

With some authors, especially the most prolific – those whose productivity makes a comprehensive view of their work nearly impossible – it can reasonably be called a happy chance when their work is suddenly summarized. It gives us an aerial view, as it were. This type of happy chance may come about when the work is presented to a 'new' public, in a translation that – to promote a basic understanding of what the author has to say – brings together his insights in the most concise possible form. That is what has now taken place with Massimo Cacciari's theoretical insights in English: they are available in a representative reader, which at the same time is a new book.[1]

What we see at once when we attentively leaf through this collection are the interventions that the author has allowed himself in his original texts. In two of three essays that otherwise appear unabridged in this translation, Cacciari interrupts himself and adds lengthy interpolations from a different context. One would like to echo the author in his brief preface and say that 'this edition brings together [his] most significant essays on aspects of modern architecture viewed in the light of aesthetic-philosophical problematics' (page vii). But the inquisitive reader will also want to seek out the assemblage techniques at work in this newly formed mosaic.

The interventions are quite revealing, and may help to uncover a secret principle behind this body of thought. Along with the surprising title – which serves to introduce 'nihilism' as an umbrella term for the modern and postmodern – and the new epilogue 'On the architecture of nihilism', written especially for this edition, which clarifies this term, the interventions are the real surprises in this book. Even beyond that, the fact that this is the first true presentation of Cacciari's architectural philosophy in the English-speaking world makes its publication a major event; it facilitates a basic understanding of Cacciari's thinking about the architectural. Before now, only 'Eupalinos or architecture', which appeared in *Oppositions* no. 21 in 1980, was available to English speakers.

Furthermore, all these surprises are festively wrapped and skilfully tied up with a bow in the form of a highly edifying introduction by Patrizia Lombardo: 'The philosophy of the city'. The only misleading thing about it is its title, with its implicit promise of a 'synthesis', because it is precisely a philosophy of the city that is no longer conceivable for Cacciari. Beyond that, this exemplary edition, complemented by Lombardo's introduction, is sure to make its readers wish that all border traffic between cultural zones could flow so smoothly. The only thing it may be lacking is a bibliographic survey and timeline of Cacciari's theoretical development, which could have brought his selected writings into sharper relief.

1
Massimo Cacciari, *Architecture and Nihilism: On the philosophy of modern architecture* (New Haven, 1993). Throughout the article, the page numbers in parentheses refer to this work. Translator's note: Passages quoted from Cacciari's work have been taken from this 1993 English edition. Likewise, the quote from *Modern Architecture* is from the English edition cited in note 4. The quotes from Benjamin and other German-language authors have been translated into English from Michel Nieuwstadt's Dutch renderings.

I

Aside from Lombardo's introduction and Cacciari's epilogue, the essays presented here are divided into three major parts. Even typographically, they are distinctly separated from one another, and they represent stages in the uninterrupted progress of Cacciari's thought, which seems to possess its own continuously reformulated law of motion in the explication of what the metropolis 'is'. Part I of this collection, entitled 'The dialectics of the negative and the Metropolis', roughly corresponds to the lengthy piece with which Cacciari opened his 1973 book *Metropolis. Saggi sulla grande città di Sombart, Endell, Scheffler e Simmel*, except for one major intervention, the final paragraph, which is drawn from a different context and put to work here.[2] The main point of reference for this 'Metropolis text', as it is usually called, is Simmel's 1903 article 'Die Grossstadte und das Geistesleben', which from the very start has figured as a boundary in Cacciari's work, because what Simmel calls the *Nervenleben* of the big city no longer leads the inhabitant back to the deeper regions of the personality. This *Nervenleben* dissects individuality into a stream of impressions, a process which has the effect of integration into something new. Between the publication of this work in 1903 'and the appearance thirty years later of Walter Benjamin's fragments on Baudelaire and Paris' – as Cacciari writes, juxtaposing the two milestones that had the greatest initial impact on his orientation in architecture theory[3] – 'falls the entire avant-garde and its crisis.' And he immediately follows this up with the question: 'Why is it that the limits of this historical period can be determined by two comprehensive historico-philosophical discussions of the Metropolis? What is meant by Metropolis?' (pages 3-4)

The Metropolis – as one might sum up the still somewhat astonishing insight of Cacciari's approach after 20 years – is the crystallisation point of a generalised process of rationalisation that nevertheless resists generalisation into any 'synthesis'. Cacciari's diagnosis commences with the anatomy of this non-'synthesisable' metropolis. But this diagnosis is also the self-diagnosis of the intellectual, arising from the awareness that his role has been compromised through the normalisation of mass production and mass consumption. From the first appearance, in the mid-nineteenth century, of the contours of the modern city, a place inimical to psychological introspection and experience regulated by individual consciousness, there has been a growing divide between intellectuals and the Metropolis. This divide can only be expressed effectively in the paradoxical form of a disagreement, a rejection – also referred to by Cacciari with a term he defines much more generally, *Entsagung* (roughly, 'renunciation' or 'self-denial') – and it can never be bridged. The fact that the crisis in the relationship between the 'intellectual' and the 'Metropolis' can no longer be patched over lends a new, unique cipher text to many intellectual positions. The philosophers, poets and rare

2
See Massimo Cacciari, *Metropolis. Saggi sulla grande città di Sombart, Endell, Scheffler e Simmel* (Rome, 1973). The first part (7-97) consists of the essay 'Dialettica dei negativo e metropoli'. The second part, entitled 'Città e metropoli', consists of selected writings of Werner Sombart, August Endell, Karl Schemer and Georg Simmel. Cacciari's opening essay is a revised, much longer version of an earlier essay on Simmel, which appeared in *Angelus Novus* 21, 1971, 1-54: 'Note sulla dialettica del negativo nell'epoca della metropoli'.

3
Cacciari's references to Simmel's renowned essay are usually to the following edition: Georg Simmel, *Brücke und Tür. Essays des Philosophen zur Geschichte, Religion, Kunst, und Gesellschaft* (Stuttgart, 1957), 227-242. The phrase 'Walter Benjamin's fragments on Baudelaire and Paris' refers primarily to the texts collected in Dutch translation in: Walter Benjamin, *Baudelaire. Een dichter in het tijdperk van het hoogkapitalisme* (Amsterdam, 1979), translated and with an afterword by Wim Notenboom.

architects who have proclaimed the uninhabitability of the world and city are awarded the rank of commissioning authority. How do architecture theory and the Metropolis look under the patronage of Schopenhauer, Nietzsche, Baudelaire and perhaps even Rilke? Those who are now without a home will never build themselves one.

In their 1976 tome *Modern Architecture*, Manfredo Tafuri and Francesco Dal Co (whose work and Cacciari's were often produced in close collaboration) described this condition of disunity: 'The intellectual, in substance, discovered that his own singularity no longer had its place in the massified metropolis dominated by a technical capacity for infinite duplication which, as Nietzsche saw with utter lucidity, had killed off once and forever all sacredness and divinity. But at the same time the metropolis became the very sickness to which the intellectual felt himself condemned; exile in his homeland, he could make one last attempt at dominating the evil that assailed him by deciding to abandon himself of his own free will to a holy prostitution of his soul.'[4] It is no mere coincidence that at this point Tafuri and Dal Co refer to Baudelaire, whose 'poet' literally loses his aureole in the streets and is overjoyed to be able to go about incognito and behave just as crudely as any other mortal. But that is already the Baudelaire of the fragmented intellectual gaze, of the *Trauerspiel* that Walter Benjamin identifies in the French poet's *Fleurs du mal* as a modern counterpart of the baroque German tragedy. Baudelaire describes himself as *coudoyé par les foules*, and Walter Benjamin identifies this experience of being jostled by crowds as a decisive one for the poet.

4
Manfredo Tafuri and Francesco Dal Co, *Architettura contemporanea* (1976). English translation: *Modern architecture*, 2 vols. (London, 1980), 98-99.

II

According to Benjamin's interpretation, Baudelaire made it a point of honour to confront this experience of shock and integrate it into his literary work. He turns this capacity to absorb – in mental and physical terms – this jostling and these experiences of shock into the most basic element of the atmosphere in which his poetry takes place. The jostling, jabbing masses were the moving, stirring veil through which Baudelaire saw Paris. Benjamin arrives at his image of these masses as concealed by a veil primarily because the poems in *Fleurs du mal* do not depict or portray them directly. Likewise, he adds, in the description of their character traits, they cannot be pictured as a 'class', or as a collective that is structured in any way. This is why Benjamin sees the amorphous urban crowd – whose existence Baudelaire never forgets for one moment, but which never serves as a model for his work – as active in that work by means of a 'hidden pattern' and a 'secret constellation'. In 'On Some Motifs in Baudelaire', he calls it the 'hidden constellation . . . [of the] phantom crowd: the words, the fragments, the beginnings of lines, from which the poet, in the deserted streets, wrests poetic booty.'[5] And it may be

5
The Dutch translation, 'Over enige motieven bij Baudelaire', is found in: Benjamin, *Baudelaire. Een dichter in het tijdperk van het hoogkapitalisme*, op. cit. (note 3), 109. Translator's note: For an English translation, 'On Some Motifs in Baudelaire', see: Walter Benjamin, *Selected Works, Volume 4: 1938-1940*, translated by Edmund Jephcott et al., edited by Howard Eiland and Michael W. Jennings (Cambridge, MA/London, 2003), 313-355.

important to point out at this juncture to what extent thought itself, in Benjamin's work, feels compelled to make itself equal to this hidden constellation, like writing that is only readable in the light of its banished 'meaning', in the light of a darkened firmament of ideas that no longer casts an a priori, salvatory gleam on the written characters. Those characters do not refer to any possibility of synthesis, any intact mode of experiencing subjectivity, any continuity or any community.

At the end of the above-mentioned 1939 Baudelaire essay, Benjamin says that the poet's heroic accomplishment was that 'he named the price for which the sensation of modernity could be had'. Then Benjamin, too, names that price: 'The disintegration of the aura in the immediate shock experience.' He adds – tellingly drawing on Nietzsche – that Baudelaire's consent to this shattering is what lends his poetry the peculiar quality of being a 'constellation without atmosphere'.[6] It is part of the peculiar quality of Cacciari's thinking, in turn, that it takes this atmospherelessness both as its starting point and as its final objective. That is another way of saying that the Archimedean point in Cacciari's thinking is anchored in the other universe of Walter Benjamin's thinking, which it constantly presupposes and in which no consolation is offered for the disintegrated aura. At this point, a brief digression is required, on the 'how' of this anchoring and the question of how to theorize the relationship between Benjamin and Georg Simmel.

6
See the conclusion of 'On Some Motifs in Baudelaire', 145 in the Dutch edition (343 in the English edition). Just as I prefer not to omit the first word in the translation of Benjamin's title 'Über einige Motive bei Baudelaire', it seems preferable to me to translate 'Gestirn ohne Atmosphare' as 'constellation without atmosphere', rather than 'star without atmosphere'.

III

After finishing his 1928 work *Ursprung des Deutschen Trauerspiels*, at latest, Benjamin must have had various writings of Simmel's within arm's reach. In a number of *Nachträge* (appendices) to the *Trauerspiel* book, Benjamin develops the transition from the terminological framework of that work to his image of an 'ur-history' of the nineteenth century that was of groundbreaking importance for the store of ideas behind his voluminous and unfinished *Passagen-Werk* (Arcades Project).

These *Nachträge* include notes on Simmel's 1913 Goethe monograph. In those notes, Benjamin says that Goethe's conception of the *Urphämonen*, as explained by Simmel, has once again made it undeniably clear to him 'that my idea of "origin" in the *Trauerspiel* book is a strict and compelling translation [*Übertragung*] of this fundamental concept of Goethe's from the sphere of nature into that of history. . . . "Origin" – this is an ur-phenomenon in the theological sense.'[7]

When Benjamin later incorporates this *Nachträg* almost word for word into what is known as the epistemological convolute of the *Passagen-Werk*, with additional text that includes *Nun habe ich es in der Passagenarbeit auch mit einer Ursprungsergründung zu tun* (Now, I am also dealing with a fathoming of origins in the *Passagen-Werk*),[8] then one is not only on the trail of the fundamental shift in Benjamin's thinking in the sec-

7
See 'Nachtrage zum Trauerspielbuch', in: Walter Benjamin, *Gesammelte Schriften*, Band I, 3 (Frankfurt am Main, 1974), 953-954.

8
See Walter Benjamin, 'Das Passagen-Werk', in: *Gesammelte Schriften*, Band V, 1 (Frankfurt am Main, 1982), 577.

ond half of the 1920s. In addition, one has an impression of Simmel's emphatic influence on this radical process of transforming theological concepts relating to the comprehension of language and nature into a materialist view of history and modernity.

This influence on Benjamin's own arsenal may have been indirect, but Simmel's interest (often dismissed as 'impressionistic') in objectifications of culture, down to the very smallest details and the most fleeting peripheries – he argues that fashion, for instance, belongs to this domain – compellingly combined with an updated interpretation of Goethe's *Urphänomen*, is in itself almost paradigmatically related to an essential vein of Benjamin's thinking. He did not keep that relationship secret.

IV

Among the 850 books that Benjamin consulted while writing the *Passagen-Werk* is Simmel's *Philosophie des Geldes*, along with a French-language edition of a number of essays, *Mélanges de philosophie rélativiste*, and a first edition of the 1991 collection of essays entitled *Philosophische Kultur*.[9] But at the same time, the similarities between Benjamin's thinking and Simmel's theoretical approach were a bone of contention from an early stage. When those similarities became too great, they even led to a minor parting of the ways. Because the very status of Benjamin's theoretical structure was at issue, this was more than a tempest in a teapot.

In a letter (now lost) to Ernst Bloch in the autumn of 1934, Adorno said that he did not believe he had gone too far when he described it as a 'terrible affront' that Bloch had drawn a link between the anti-systematic impulse in Benjamin's thinking and Simmel's 'impressionism'. Bloch had done so in a review of Benjamin's 1928 book *Einbahnstrasse* and included the essay, in an adapted form, in his masterful 1934 collection of essays *Erbschift dieser Zeit*, under the telling title 'Revueform in der Philosophie'.[10] That same year, in early December, Bloch sent Adorno a long, angry letter. The following passage illustrates the general tenor: 'Your objection regarding Simmel is entirely off-target, in fact, and wildly far-fetched [lit. 'dragged in by the hair he did not have']. Benjamin, as I know, is deeply impressed by Simmel, as an impressionist. Simmel is present at the scene of the crime only as an example, to show that the coherence of the system has been disrupted. If that is a "terrible affront", then you do not know what an "affront" is, and I hope you never receive a more severe one.'[11]

The controversy is much more general than this type of carping might lead one to believe. In 1938, when Benjamin sent review copies of his detailed Baudelaire studies to individuals who served as patrons and prominent early readers – Max Horkheimer and particularly Theodor W. Adorno – the latter raised far-reaching methodological objections to the text.

9 The editions in question are: Georg Simmel, *Mélanges de philosophie relativiste. Contribution à la culture philosophique* (Paris, 1912); Georg Simmel, *Philosophie des Geldes* (Leipzig, 1900, this is the large, hardcover edition published by Verlag von Duncker & Humblot); Georg Simmel, *Philosophische Kultur. Gesammelte Essays* (Leipzig, 1911, published as Band XXVII in the series 'Philosophisch-soziologische Bücherei' by Verlag von Dr. Werner Klinkhardt).

10 Cf. Ernst Bloch, *Erbschaft dieser Zeit*, Gesamtausgabe, Band 4 (Frankfurt am Main, 1962), 368-372. See also: Michel van Nieuwstadt, 'Doortocht', afterword to: Walter Benjamin, *Eenrichtingstraat* (Groningen, 1994), 85-113, esp. 93.

11 See the letter in question and the annotations in: Ernst Bloch, *Briefe 1903-1975*, edited by Karola Bloch et. al. (Frankfurt am Main, 1985), 423-437.

Adorno lamented the drastic forms of expressive specificity that Benjamin had managed to achieve in tracing mid-nineteenth century cultural phenomena back to their social substrate, calling them an impending farewell to a theory that had to maintain its connection to the *Gesamtprozess*. In a now-famous letter dated 10 November 1938, in which he advised Benjamin not to publish this first Baudelaire manuscript – in the *Zeitschrift für Sozialforschung* – Adorno again suggested that Benjamin's essay showed too much affinity for Simmel's thinking. According to Adorno, that specificity showed nothing more than short-sighted behaviourist tendencies; in other words, he believed Benjamin was much too quick to label cultural phenomena as consequences of material phenomena. In the second letter, again, Adorno objected to a prominently placed Simmel quote in Benjamin's work: 'I can't help thinking that in the treasure chamber of the *Passagen-Werk*, there must be more sharply honed daggers on this subject than the Simmel quote.'[12]

Much later still, in an essay on the occasion of Ernst Block's eightieth birthday, Adorno characterised Simmel's thinking as 'woodland and heath metaphysics' and dismissed his aesthetics as timidity in aestheticising or – at its worst – as simple, dainty 'teatime witticisms'.[13] But there are other, lesser-known replies by Benjamin to Adorno's original criticisms of Benjamin's essay about Baudelaire. These letters have an immediate claim to classicism, with their measured quality mixed with courteous concealment of the chagrin that Benjamin felt about the rejection. This is not the place to examine the import of Benjamin's two replies for cultural theory, but in the latter, written on 23 February 1939, Benjamin says of Simmel, 'Might it not be time to recognise and respect in him one of the forefathers of cultural bolshevism?' And about the *Philosophie des Geldes*, which he had begun to read, he says, 'I was struck by the criticism of Marx's theory of value.[14] If one is searching for the conditions under which both Simmel and Marx were reread in Italy in the late sixties and after, the keys are hidden here.' In the anti-systematic and anti-philosophical rereading of Marx in Italy lies one of the impulses behind the formation of Cacciari's theory. The resurgence of interest in Simmel is of more than secondary importance in this context.

12
Theodor W. Adorno and Walter Benjamin, *Briefwechsel 1928-1940*, edited by Henri Lonitz (Frankfurt am Main, 1994), 392. For the two letters with Adorno's remarks about Benjamin's first major essay on Baudelaire, written for the *Zeitschrift für Sozialforschung*, see that same work, 364-376 (letter of 10 November 1938) and 388-402 (letter of 1 February 1939).

13
See Theodor W. Adorno, 'Henkei, Krug und frühe Erfahrung', in: Siegfried Unseld (ed.), *Ernst Bloch zu Ehren. Beiträge zu seinem Werk* (Frankfurt am Main, 1965), 9-20.

14
See the letter from Benjamin to Adorno dated 23 February 1939 in: Adorno and Benjamin, *Briefwechsel*, op. cit. (note 12), 402-407, esp. 405-406.

V

Although in Germany, Simmel's writings have been republished in recent years, it must be said that his re-evaluation is mainly an Italian phenomenon. In Simmel's rediscovered relevance, his essay 'Die Grossstadte und das Geistesleben' is the glorious touchstone for an early concept of modernity. On the other hand, precisely the neo-Kantian, *verstehende*, general background to Simmel's philosophical work must be banished from the idea of modernity to which the text can lay claim. Theodor W. Adorno's oversensitivity to the overly harmonic ('aestheticising') aspects of Simmel's *esprit* resurfaces in Italian theorising about the metropolitan as a boundary and a critical dividing line drawn straight through Simmel's philosophical work. This separates the analytical acuity that Simmel achieved in his studies of the depersonalising tendencies at work in culture as objectification from the comforting reservoir of a subjective counterweight, and thus from the particular conditions of *Kultur* in the traditional sense.

Two quotes from Cacciari's perceptivc and detailed arguments regarding the Simmel of 'Die Grossstadte' (1903) and the earlier *Philosophie des Geldes* (1900) should clarify this point, illustrating the domains between which this dividing line is drawn.

First of all, there is the blasé personality that Simmel developed as the new ideal psychogram for the metropolis-dweller: *keine seelische Erscheinung, die so unbedingt der Grossstadt vorbehalten wäre* (no mental phenomenon belongs more unconditionally to the big city). Here is Cacciari's summary of this idea and his commentary: 'The blasé attitude exposes the illusoriness of differences. For Simmel, its constant nervous stimulation and quest for pleasure are in the end experiences totally abstracted from the specific individuality of their object . . . The object reveals its historic essence as exchange value, and it is treated as such. The simple act of consumption is in constant relation to the equivalence of all commodities. . . . The blasé type uses money according to its essence, as the universal equivalent of the commodity; he uses it to acquire commodities, perfectly aware that he cannot get close to these goods, he cannot *name* them, he cannot *love* them. He has learned, with a sense of despair, that things and *people* have acquired the status of commodity, and his attitude internalizes this fact. Universal equivalence expresses itself in *spleen* – but this spleen is only the product of the Verstand's omnipotence. The concentration of the life of the nerves, which seems to preside over the blasé experience, thus manifests itself "in the devaluation of the entire objective world", in the futility of the search for the *unicum*, in the desecration of the transcendent aura that once enveloped inter-subjective relations.' (page 8)

Simmel's analysis, in which appropriate conduct in the metropolis hinges on the negative, blasé attitude, is fundamental for Cacciari. This analysis later forms the backbone of the brilliant essay 'Die Grossstadte und das Geistesleben', which, it should be added, is no longer than 15 pages.

But in Simmel's 'geometry' of light and dark sides, objectifying and subjectifying tendencies that partly neutralise or counterbalance each other, the construction of the blasé personality remains an extreme. A Dutch doctoral thesis on 'philosophy and sociology in the work of Georg Simmel', published in 1982, was called *Geometrie van de samenleving* (Geometry of Society).[15] The geometry of synthesis is the whole Simmel. Cacciari engages only with the extreme, isolating and salvaging it from the geometry as a negative axiom.

15 See A.M. Bevers, *Geometrie van de samenleving. Filosofie en sociologie in het werk van Georg Simmel* (Deventer, 1982).

That brings us to the second point. Simmel's extreme view of modes of conduct within the metropolis is literally rectified by Simmel himself in the final pages of 'Die Grossstadte', and Cacciari makes the following remark about this correction: 'Just when negative thought begins to point to the isolation or the perception of a historically specific form of capitalist domination, by presupposing this form as such – and thereby to break away from any nostalgia as well as from any utopia – Simmel immediately reduces this form to a simple expression of individuality in the Metropolis: an individuality that asserts itself, asks for the fulfillment of its rights, and demands freedom. The essay's final synthesis . . . answers this demand. But this synthesis is completely unrelated to the actual discussion of the blasé type and negative thought, and is not at all required by Simmel's concrete development of the material discussed. It is a synthesis that recuperates the value of community, of the *Gemeinschaft*, in order to reaffirm it in society, in the *Gesellschaft*.' (page 12)

It is that dream of 'community' that Cacciari wishes to eliminate as an element antithetical to the essence of Simmel's analysis. He wants to abandon geometry, which in the further development of the disorderly transgressions of Cacciari's 'negative thinking' sees its circles thrown into confusion. In the Metropolis, every regressive or utopian divergence from the news of the hour runs the risk – according to the unwavering chronology of 'negative thinking' – of *falling out* of the present.

What is initially misleading about this is the Marxist register in which this body of thought armours, as it were, its philosophical categories and conditions. Yet the nihilistic élan of these categories derives precisely from the fact that beneath this philosophical armour, as with Dadaist costumes, a wristwatch is tracking the restlessness of a categorical unattainability. The Marxist categories, including their content, are detonated, detuned and deactivated. At the end of the book, in the epilogue 'On the architecture of nihilism', the history of the past century, of the Modern Movement and Rationalism, is summed up as a unique tragedy. This tragedy, Cacciari writes, is the rise . . . of an architecture of effectuated nihilism that perfuses the image of the Metropolis: 'it is the very figure of pro-ducing, of leading-beyond, of continuous and undefinable *overcoming*. The obsession with overcoming is embodied in the work of "radical uprooting" carried out by this architecture: an uprooting from the limits of the *urbs*, from the social circles dominant in it, from its *form* – an uprooting from the place . . . It is as though the city were transformed into a chance of the road, a context of routes, a labyrinth without center, an absurd labyrinth. The great urban sociologists of the early century perfectly understood the uprooting significance of this explosive radiating of the city. In these sociologies, the Metropolis appears as the great metaphor of the calculating intellect devoid of all ends, whose *Nervenleben* (life of the nerves) is immersed in the succession of equi-valent cases. The architecture "without qualities" of the Metropolis – a conscious image of fulfilled nihilism – excludes the characteristic of the place; in its project, every place is equi-valent in universal circulation, in exchange. Space and time are arithmetically measurable, detachable, and reconstructible.' (pages 199-200)

The writings in this collection do not take us through the entire meltdown that these categories must undergo in order to go on describing this tragedy. In other words, *Architecture and Nihilism* does not offer an unobstructed view into the actual engine rooms of Cacciari's thinking, where the most important process taking place – as expounded in Cacciari's 1976 book *Krisis*, subtitled *Saggio sulla crisi del pensiero negativo da Nietzsche a Wittgenstein* (Essay on the crisis in negative thinking from Nietzsche to Wittgenstein)[16] – is the conversion of Nietzsche's concept of the *Wille zur Macht* into the descriptive category of factual rationalisation. This turns the *Wille zur Macht* into the opposite of subjectivism, the opposite of exaltation and late Romantic glorification of creative genius. In the readings in *Architecture and Nihilism*, we no more than catch glimpses of this meltdown. Is it possible that the purpose of the interventions mentioned in section I was greatly to magnify a couple of these glimpses?

16 Massimo Cacciari, *Krisis. Saggio sulla crisi del pensiero negativo da Nietzsche a Wittgenstein* (Milan, 1976).

VI

The basic postulate is that the Metropolis leaves behind any synthesis into the 'city', including elements of the latter such as 'community' and 'individuality'. The desire to bridge the manifest contradiction between the two quantities of the 'city' and the 'Metropolis' is – in Cacciari's analysis – the inherent limit of the activity of the Deutsche Werkbund and the contemporary sociological work of Grossstadt. This is where the impossibility of synthesis, demonstrated in relation to Simmel, begins to bear fruit. The Werkbund was founded in 1907. The writings by Sombart, Endell, Scheffler and Simmel that are included in *Metropolis* are responses to an 1898 piece about Rome by Simmel, and they all date from the brief period 1906 to 1913. At the 1914 Werkbund conference, the conflict between the absence of any concept whatsoever of capitalist development and the utopia of an all-inclusive 'new style' came to a head. The artistic nature of design is an impossible, unworldly thing. Better to be left with nothing than to elevate the utopia of this impossibility to an a priori artistic truth. That is why Cacciari says the following about the episode in the Werkbund immediately prior to the conflict: 'To give an order to the absence of synthesis – to posit this absence and explore its implications to the end – was the real "mandate" and the real question. . . . This is precisely where the Werkbund failed: it was incapable of planning the Metropolis *of negative thought*, the social relations of alienated labor.

That is, it failed to construe the Metropolis as conflict and as the functionality of conflict . . . The Metropolis as synthesis is not Metropolis, it is city, family, organism and individuality.' (page 37)

One might have identified the weakness of Cacciari's original introduction to Metropolis as the very limited extent to which his concept of 'negative thought', which is not specifically tied to architecture theory, leads to more than . . . negativity, the unachievable. But on the contrary – and in contrast to Adorno's *Negative Dialektik*, to which it is related only through coincidences of terminology – this line of thought is full of functionality within the system that it rejects, because it also rejects all the comforting alternatives to it. It is thought that in its trembling is condemned to signify, an inevitable *tremblé du sens*, as Patrizia Lombardo describes it, drawing on Roland Barthes' understanding of language. One step further and this line of thought, which like Nietzsche's *Wille zur Macht* is situated at the end of philosophy, must anchor itself in existence without illusions in order to conquer that existence in any way other than dialectically. I believe this is the unspecified motivation for the decision – in Part I, the part about the dialectics of the negative and the metropolis – to follow the section on the mystifications and utopias of the Werkbund with a much more political section dealing mainly with Walther Rathenau as a theoretical opponent of the Werkbund and the head of the AEG (*Allgemeine Elektricitäts Gesellschaft*). Given the new monopolist organizational form towards which all the forces of mechanization and rationalization were tending, only a politician, we are told, could head the AEG from then on (page 53). But in this context, Rathenau also stands for everything that is actualized in the designs and buildings of 'his' master architect Peter Behrens.

VII

For Cacciari, the significance of the designs made by Behrens for the AEG culminates in the exemplary tension between interior and exterior, between labour and the Metropolis, that we find at the Kleinmotorenfabrik in Berlin's Voltastrasse: 'Clearly the facade, given rhythm by the monumental pilasters, encloses a space that is set up as separate from the urban context. The activity that goes on behind these walls must appear to be *exceptional* and hence set apart from the anonymous labor of the large city. What takes place within such buildings is labor par excellence, whose very repetitiveness (this is precisely the signification behind the sequentiality of the façade) assumes a ritual, sacred value. Here repetition is much more than a mere symbol of the Metropolis. It actually expresses the stability (*Festigkeit*) and permanence (*Dauer*) of the power that is founded on labor and emanates from labor. Like all monuments, the factory stands out from its urban context, but at the same time it maintains a singular relation with it: and this relation is one of *dominion*. Behrens's form is supposed to emphasize that the factory governs the hustle and bustle, the kaleidoscopic multiformity of life in the Metropolis.' (pages 54-55)

This is typical of the concretization achieved in Cacciari's analyses. Where 'negative thinking' can express itself in the act of building, the organization of space, it is a moment torn out of the chain that forms the Metropolis, because it coincides with the present of the Metropolis in a unique way. If it is therefore true, as Patrizia Lombardo suggests to us in her introduction, that the name of Metropolis should be interpreted allegorically (and it is written with a capital letter for good reason), then this concretization is comparable to the moments at which, as Benjamin allegorically expressed it, an empty and homogeneous history is frozen mid-flow. Perhaps at some point, the movements of stasis as figures in Benjamin's thinking and in thinking that is opposed to Cacciari's synthesis will become more than comparable.[17] In the limited space available here, however, the most important point is that this section about Rathenau and Behrens has been integrated into Part 1 of *Architecture and Nihilism* from a different original context. In this new context, under the title 'Merchants and heroes', it remains more or less identical to two successive chapters of Cacciari's 1979 study *Walther Rathenau e il suo ambiente* ('Mechanisierung & Seele' and 'Mercanti e eroi'), which served in part as an explanatory introduction to a collection of the later writings and speeches of Rathenau, the businessman/politician/minister.[18]

Here, although they postdate Loos's position, they serve to anticipate and clarify it – specifically, his relationship to the Metropolis on the one hand and the Werkbund and Vienna Secession and their desire for 'style' on the other. Compare the following passage from Part II of *Architecture and Nihilism* with the excerpt quoted above about the Kleinmotorenfabrik. Cacciari makes grateful use of the nickname that the journalist Ludwig Hevesi gave Loos's Café Museum in 1899: Café Nihilismus. It had stark, untattooed outer walls and an almost bare interior. Polemically enough, it was located near Joseph Olbrich's Haus der Sezession, built in 1897-1898. But Cacciari's analysis emphasizes above all the sign value of the famous 1911 Looshaus on Michaelerplatz. The 'Nihilismus House' and the terms of that analysis are analogous to those of his analysis of Behrens' factory. 'The Cafe Nihilismus and the Nihilismus house . . . are necessarily situated in the Nihilismus city, the Metropolis where all the social circles of the Gemeinschaft have been shattered. City and style, as community organism or the nostalgia for such, are synonymous. . . . Loos, on the other hand, isolates with great precision the regressive implications of the communal ideologies that serve as a foundation for the concept of style. Style is not Metropolis, but *hangs over* its structure.' (pages 112-113)

Cacciari then tries to probe further and further into the dynamics of this negation, which begins by positing differences, but above all into the riddle that lies beneath it, where

17 That would necessitate an analysis of the epilogue entitled 'On the architecture of nihilism' with which *Architecture and Nihilism* closes. One of the final allusions in this epilogue is to Benjamin's angel of history, before whose eyes a series of separate catastrophes unfolds. Among Cacciari's many essays that bear comparison to the level and intellectual tendencies of Benjamin's philosophy to an extent unequalled in the reception of Benjamin's work, let me name just two: 'Di alcuni motivi in Walter Benjamin (Da "Ursprung des deutschen Trauerspiels" a "Der Autor als Produzent")' in: Franco Rella, *Critica e Storia. Materiali su Benjamin di: M. Cacciari, F. Desideri, G. Franck, R. Infelise-Fronza, G. Mensching, F. Rella, J. Derrida & W. Benjamin* (Venice, 1980), 41-71; and 'Necessità dell'Angelo', *Aut Aut* no. 189-190 (May-August, 1982), 203-214.

18 See Massimo Cacciari, *Walther Rathenau e il suo ambiente. Con un antologia di scritti e discorsi politici 1919-1921* (Bari, 1979).

the difference in value – in Loos's interior – makes its presence known once again. And there, in the middle of the problematic of 'nihilism', negative thinking must, as it were, depart from itself and posit itself in a new and different form, not without an analogy to Nietzsche: 'The *negatives Denken* posited as a condition of the analysis of the multiplicity of languages is overturned and transformed into a stylistic condition aimed at the affirmation of its value – no longer a synthesis, of course, but in any case a "superiority" of interior over exterior, of the space of art over that of functions . . .' (page 118)

All the analytical categories in Cacciari's study *Loos-Wien* pave the way for this about-face, this interpretive displacement. Part II of *Architecture and Nihilism* consists entirely of a translation of this study, here entitled 'Loos and his contemporaries'. The original work was published as Cacciari's contribution to *Oikos da Loos a Wittgenstein*, which he co-authored with Francesco Amendolagine in 1975. The pages of Part II are the only ones in which Dutch readers can catch their breath and feel they are on familiar terrain; a translation of *Loos-Wien* by Ineke van der Burg and Marga van Mechelen was included in the Dutch-language edition of *Oikos* published by SUN.[19] But the remainder of *Architecture and Nihilism*, including the epilogue, exposes precisely the ground covered here to the many-sidedness of an interpretation that fans out in the most radical way, which I will not attempt to summarise here. To encapsulate the dynamics of this interpretation in the rather smarmy motto 'Not a home but an adventure', as Lombardo does at the close of her introduction, suggests to me a half-misapprehension, if the phrase is indeed anything more than a slogan – for in Part III, which everyone must read for him or herself, these dynamics lead not only to the swirling void referred to here as *Entortung* and total *Mobilmachung*, but also to something fundamentally different.

19
See Francesco Amendolagine and Massimo Cacciari, *Oikos. Da Loos a Wittgenstein* (Rome: Officina, 1975). The Dutch translation is entitled *Oikos. Van Loos tot Wittgenstein* (Nijmegen, 1982).

VIII

Part III, 'Loos and his angel', is the unabridged translation of Cacciari's introduction to the new edition and complete Italian translation of Loos's curious one-man periodical *Das Andere*, two issues of which appeared in 1903. This new edition, which in itself was nothing less than a typographical and editorial miracle, was published in 1981 by Gruppo Editoriale Electa.[20] Again, in the English edition of Cacciari's text, material from another context was inserted: one section on Lou Salomé's box of buttons and another on Bruno Taut's *Glaserne Kette*. They come from Cacciari's 1980 work *Dallo Steinhof* and are included here to dispel any naive, childish notions about an intact interior and the glorious rebirth of urban architecture.[21]

Of the box of buttons, in other words, because the saved button 'is the opposite of money: it opposes division, circulation, and exchange with the principle of the secret and the hidden. Money exists in a dimension exclusively external

20
Adolf Loos, *Das Andere/L'altro. Festschrift/Per i sessant'anni di Adolf Loos* (Milan, 1981).

21
Massimo Cacciari, Dallo Steinhof. *Prospettive viennesi del primo Novecento* (Milan, 1980).

and public; the button, on the other hand, is the unattainable maternal relic, preserved in the most interior part of a virgin mountain . . . But how does one collect buttons? and where does one collect them? Is there still the possibility of a space of the "collected," a space opposed to the market of things visible? This space is an interior, but not every interior can be the place of the collection of that which resists in unproductivity. The difficulty of defining such a space derives from the fact that it must correspond to the unhappiness of the productive and the sacrifice that this implies. . . . But if the button does not become the margin and remains of the Metropolis, it is transformed into a fetishistically guarded treasure, and ceases to exist as true childhood. It becomes again a possession, though an unproductive one. Unproductivity is not enough to "surpass" the language of the Metropolis – childhood must find its own interior within the relations of the Metropolis.' (pages 179-180) The rest is usually just *Heimatkunst*.

The opposite of the button-box interior is *Glasarchitektur*, which Benjamin also emphatically greeted in his essay 'Experience and poverty' as the appropriate setting for the modern impoverishment of experience. Specifically, it reveals the progressive, barbaric destitution that consists in the little, the little with which one must make do. But 'Glaskultur's critique of possession is conducted exclusively from the perspective of circulation and exchange. In the uninterrupted flow of stimuli-perceptions made possible by the city of steel and glass, in the continual enrichment of the life of the spirit, what is desecrated is not so much the ancient auras, but the very possibility of experience – what is pro-duced is the poverty of experience. In universal transparence every thing is assumed to be of equal value, equivalent. . . . Glaskultur decrees that experience is already dead, and declares itself its only heir. Its glass reflects the present poverty. In spite of its avant-garde pose, which rejects the paternal language and opposes its presumed organicity with the arbitrary and freely constructive, Glaskultur belongs to a perfectly logocentric civilization. Its will to render transparent, to lay bare, to demystify, expresses a utopia that fully and progressively identifies the human with the linguistic: every secret must be spoken aloud, every interior made manifest, every childhood pro-duced. Language, and its power, are here absolute. . . . The very fact of its being a cause of the present poverty is precisely what Glaskultur tends to obscure.' (pages 188-189)

Glasarchitektur or Lou Andreas-Salomé's box of buttons? The past and present cannot stand in a synthesising relationship, any more than the interior and exterior. No salvatory look back at the past is permitted. There is no project that will produce a guarantee for the future, just as there is no language that says everything. The only ones here, in what must be described as an intellectual no-man's land, are the Viennese *Sprachlehrer* Karl Kraus and the Viennese *Baumeister* Adolf Loos, planted firmly between the past and the future, and perhaps most inclined to swear by silence.

Thanks to Cacciari's interpretation, thanks to his reading of their language and their silence, we know that they learned and borrowed their attitude from Benjamin's *Angelus Novus*: 'But though their [Loos's and Kraus's] eyes be turned to the past, never do they seek therein an "eternal image," or a model with which to oppose the ephemeral present. There is no respite in the past that they see, just as there is no flight toward the future: their backs are turned to it. The past is transformed into the vision and hearing of a living, incessant questioning – into a problem par excellence. It is in this relation . . . that we are pulled away towards the future. Indeed, what we call the future occurs in this dialogue. The very language of Kraus and Loos is this dialogue: it is the relation – which is all the more indestructible as it is less nostalgic – not with tradition *tout court*, but with tradition that has preserved in language the "search for a lost image of the primordial" . . .' (page 147)

The final reference here is to Karl Kraus's book of aphorisms *Nachts*, and specifically to an aphorism that deserves to be quoted in full here, at the close of this article: *Die Sprache tastet wie die Liebe im Dunkel der Welt einem verlorenen Urbild nach. Man macht nicht, man ahnt ein Gedicht.*

What we call 'future' carries with it a forgotten prototype of happiness. The ultimate message of these analyses must be summed up as follows: architecture theory is not capable of establishing the possibilities of architecture by proclamation. Instead, the simultaneity of Cacciari's theory with the continuity of the modern lies in the fact that he is silent about this point as well. That silence displays an intensely ambivalent eloquence, in that Cacciari – without doing any violence to his past – is now mayor of the city of Venice. On this topic, it is precisely Simmel whom Patrizia Lombardo – who may not yet have known that Cacciari would soon hold public office – quotes at the end of her introduction. The passage comes from a text which once, in that early collection of texts at the end of *Metropolis*, accompanied Cacciari's entrance into the contemporary architectural debate: 'In Venice one can see realized the duplicity of life: here it becomes flesh and blood. Double is the sense of these squares, which, because of the lack of vehicles and the narrowness of streets, look like rooms. Double is the sense of meeting, pushing, and touching of people in the *calli*, which gives this life an appearance of familiarity, of Gemütlichkeit, precisely where every trace of Gemüt is absent. . . . That Venice has been and will be the classic *city of adventure* is just the most perceptible expression of the fact that it cannot be a home for our soul, cannot be anything but adventure.'

This may be a superior version of the motto *Not a home but an adventure . . .*

Translated by David McKay

The first English text appeared in *OASE* in issue 45/46 (*Essentiële Architectuur/Essential Architecture*). The first entirely bilingual issue (Dutch/English) is number 48 (*Diagram*), published in 1998. From then on, there are more and more international contributions to the journal. In 2003, *OASE* establishes stronger relationships with academic institutions in both the Netherlands and Flanders, thus becoming a potential forum for publishing the work of often upcoming scholars and researchers from a broader scientific milieu. This initiative serves as leverage for the status of the journal, by introducing a peer-review procedure and installing an academic board. *OASE*, however, deliberately chooses not to develop along the common standards of an academic journal, but to preserve its role as a space in which more speculative and/or personal reflections might also be given a voice. The membership of the editorial board is more stable, yet its diversity ensures that the tradition of addressing a broad spectrum of themes is maintained.

OASE 45/46	Essentiële architectuur / Essential Architecture
OASE 47	Bekleding / Dressing
OASE 48	Diagrammen / Diagrams
OASE 49/50	Conventie / Convention
OASE 51	Rearrangements, A Smithsons Celebration
OASE 52	Consumptie en territorium / Consumption and Territory
OASE 53	Netwerk stedebouw / Network Urbanism
OASE 54	Re: Generieke stad / Re: Generic City
OASE 55	Huis en tuin / Home and Garden
OASE 56	Huiselijke natuur / Domestic Nature
OASE 57	1970s Revisited
OASE 58	Het zichtbare en het onzichtbare / The Visible and the Invisible
OASE 59	Nagel op de huid / Scratching the Surface
OASE 60	Het land in de stad / Urbanism Out-of-Town
OASE 61	Neoliberalisme in de buitenwijk / Suburbia and Social Democracy
OASE 62	Autonome architectuur en het stedelijk project / Autonomous Architecture and the Project of the City
OASE 63	Platteland / Countryside
OASE 64	Landschap en massatoerisme / Landscape and Mass Tourism
OASE 65	Ornament
OASE 66	Virtually Here: Ruimte in cyberfictie / Virtually Here: Space in Cyberfiction
OASE 67	After the Party: Nederlandse architectuur 2005 / After the Party: Dutch Architecture 2005
OASE 68	Thuis-Land / Home-Land
OASE 69	Posities / Positions
OASE 70	Architectuur & Literatuur / Architecture & Literature
OASE 71	Stedelijke formatie & collectieve ruimten / Urban Formation & Collective Spaces
OASE 72	Terug naar school / Back to School
OASE 73	Gentrification
OASE 74	Inventie / Invention

Period IV

INTERNA-TIONALISA-TION *OASE* Goes Bilingual 1997–2007

Maarten Delbeke

RECENT HISTORY

If articles, books, artefacts, buildings or even single issues of a journal necessarily – but sometimes reluctantly – impose themselves as an entity in their own right, several years of a journal rarely do. At issue is not the sheer volume of the material, the complexities of a journal's institutional position or the vastness of its horizon, but the very nature of the object itself. Over the course of their existence, journals very rarely coalesce into a coherent (if necessarily multifaceted) argument that could be attributed to the intentionality of an 'author', whether that author is a person, a board or an institution. In the particular case of the last ten years of *OASE*, moreover, there are no declarations of intent or position papers that reach beyond the single issue. The 'oeuvre' of *OASE* is shaped by the succession of the selected themes and their treatment by the editorial teams and the contributors. Since the choice of themes and authors largely depends upon the composition of its editorial board, and therefore at least indirectly on the institutional context of the publication, it would certainly make sense to examine this context to gauge what the journal attempts to say and why. Here, however, it will be attempted to take these themes and what they signify in *OASE* at face value in order to treat the last ten years of the journal as a body of work, and to ask what that body could be about.

One way to arrange the themes of the 30 most recent issues of *OASE* is to relate them to architectural design. In fact, it doesn't require excessive license with regard to the actual content of the journal to class every issue under at least one of five aspects of architectural design: the design process and its tools, important (yet hitherto partly neglected) architects and bodies of work, the qualities or properties of architecture and/or buildings, the tasks of the designer (generally an architect), and the conditions of their practise. Interest in the design process is apparent in discussions of dressing (*OASE* no. 47), the diagram (48), convention (49/50), ornament (65), invention (74), and – through the case of schools – typology (72). Important figures in the history of architectural design were commemorated with the celebration of the Smithsons (51), and the issue on the 1970s (57) introduced a neglected body of work and the concomitant preoccupations of the discipline. The qualities or properties of designs and buildings that have been identified are essence (45-46), (in)visibility (58), surface (59), autonomy (62), monumentality (71), or the relation of architecture to literature (70). As different tasks of the designer one thinks of the house (52), the garden (55, 56), the (semi-)public building (again schools), and the suburb and the city (53, 60). These task are shaped in a permanent negotiation with the conditions of architectural and urban design practise, building and use, and these conditions are examined under the headings of post-capitalist society (52, 54, 61), again the 1970s, the countryside (63), tourism (64), virtual reality (66), immigration (68), gentrification (73) or architectural culture itself, both in the issues *After the Party* (67) and *Positions* (69).

To propose design as the centre of attention of an architectural journal might seem too self-evident. But in *OASE*, design figures under particular conditions. *OASE* is not associated with a professional organisation, nor does it explicitly address the profession of architects, like for instance *de Architect* in the Netherlands or *A+* in Belgium. In other words, in *OASE* the topic of architectural design does not serve to define a profession or a professional practice, and if the journal certainly seeks to address themes that might be of interest to professionals, its content is certainly not confined to that task. Nor does *OASE* see it as its prime mission to inform a wider public about what is going on in the profession, both in terms of recent production or the preoccupations of its practitioners. That is left to the aforementioned journals, or to *A10* or *MARK*. At the same time, however, *OASE* is definitely not centred on the discursive environment in which architecture is said to exist. *Forum* (in its final incarnation) and *Archis*, now *Volume* and associated with among others AMO, have embodied the notion that architecture dissolves in a wide field of discourses, activities, practises and research programmes, and that it is therefore as much the task of the architectural journal to register this field as to reflect what architecture, understood rather as a form of 'intelligence', can contribute to it. Certain issues or essays of especially the last couple of years certainly veer into this direction, such as no. 68, on immigration. Immigration is an essentially political, economical and geographical phenomenon, and proposing this phenomenon as the theme of an architectural journal suggests its relevance for architecture even if its direct implications for architectural practise are not immediately clear. But generally *OASE* rarely loses sight of design or the designer. Even if it is not defined by the needs and questions of a professional practise, *OASE* believes in architecture as a design discipline with a specific, if not always clearly delineated field of action that has buildings and their context writ large at its centre.

As such, *OASE* is probably not unique; *AAFiles*, for instance, is sometimes a close counterpart. This parentage stems probably from both journals' close association with architecture schools and universities. Would it be too far fetched, then, to read *OASE* as a forum where different strains of a predominantly academic input coalesce into an undeclared (and certainly not homogeneous) theory of design? Does *OASE* produce architectural theory, not in the sense that it examines the discursive practises involving architecture, but in the more classic meaning of the word, that it defines what architecture is by describing how it is made and should be understood? And, if this were the case, is it possible to characterize this theory?

When the last 30 issues are arranged around architectural design, slight shifts in focus become visible. The design process and the 'properties' of architecture reoccur more or less regularly, while the tasks of the designer and the conditions of their practise received more attention around 2000-2003. The distribution of the different themes over time suggests that the theoretical aspects of architectural design are the backbone of *OASE*, and that this backbone vertebrates into reflections upon the conditions of architecture in sync with the sometimes short-lived preoccupations of academics and designers (many of whom are affiliated with architecture departments as well). Probably the clearest example of actuality catching up with design is the issue 'After the Party', which attempted to examine what was left of Dutch architecture once the phenomenon of *Superdutch* had blown over, a question that seemed acute to a surprisingly large portion of the field. This issue also announced a move away from an examination of 'conditions' towards 'design' and 'architecture' proper, which chimes well with a more general trend in architectural culture that seeks to combine an investigation of the proper tools of architecture with an acute 'ideological awareness', to borrow Pier Vittorio Aureli's phrase from the same issue.

If architecture and its design are a permanent preoccupation, *OASE* contains remarkably few papers on the exact status of architectural theory and by extension, criticism, with regard to design. It has been noted above that position papers are confined to single issues; very few essays reflect on the kind of work that is being done in the journal itself. The mainly North-American involvement with 'theory', 'criticality' and its aftermath, the post-critical and projective, have left remarkably little traces in *OASE* (and it is hard not to feel a sense of gratitude about that). When John Macarthur and Naomi Stead invoke the North-American debate in *OASE* no. 69, the only issue entirely dedicated to the relative positions of design, design theory, criticism and history, it is to reassert the rights of criticism as 'the place where a concrete, disciplinary conception of architecture, such as that held by most practicing architects, meets the historical-aesthetic conception of the specialist critic'. This view very well describes the practice of *OASE* as a journal, yet now under the heading of criticism, not design theory as I proposed above. It is the slippage between criticism and design theory, I believe, that characterizes the 'historical-aesthetic conception' of the journal.

Following Macarthur and Stead, criticism positions buildings and projects in history, not only because the critic decides to address and thus to canonize them (an effect that is as unavoidable as it inspires resistance), but also because of the historicity of the critic's knowledge, judgement and even individuality. Design theory operates on an altogether different level. To borrow Andrew Leach's reading of Manfredo Tafuri in the same issue no. 69, architectural theory is a necessary corollary of architecture. Theory defines architecture's disciplinarity, delimiting its proper goals, tools, field of action by means of a discourse that, while employing examples, models and tropes from the past, essentially stands outside of history.

In other words, if criticism constructs the pastness of the present, architectural theory – here still understood as design theory – implies the permanent and unchanging presentness of the past (to invoke Robert Venturi quoting T.S. Eliot).

In *OASE*, the past and its translation into history assume both roles, as a context for criticism and as a point of reference acting in the present, but not in equal parts. Discussions of the conditions of architectural design necessarily treat history in a critical mode, since these conditions are investigated when they are the subject of change or acquire new importance. Yet the other four 'themes' I distinguished at the outset, the design process and its tools, the properties of architecture, the tasks of the designer and important oeuvres and bodies of work, are often treated in terms that presuppose a disciplinary core that remains largely 'present' throughout time: historical precedents, (more or less) forgotten authors, and concepts with sometimes very long histories, such as invention, are 'remembered' as building stones of present architectural practice. In *OASE*, the past and its history serve as abstractions, not because history is made operative by describing models for contemporary practise or buildings are isolated from their historical and intellectual context (quite to the contrary), but in the sense that a quite homogeneous set of present preoccupations steers the interest in the past.

These preoccupations are the issues relevant to a community of architects, critics and academics whose basic frame of reference is modernism and its post-war mutations. As such, *OASE* closely mirrors the intellectual framework of many if not all architecture schools in and around the Netherlands, which are almost without exception tributary to modernism in their attitude towards history, theory and design. In fact, *OASE* has shown a predilection for the different challenges that modernism has faced, ranging for instance from the issue of decoration and ornament, addressed repeatedly and successfully, to the infiltration of the notion of the 'everyday' in architectural discourse (echoing a trend in the architectural discourse of the 1990s that picked up the threads of, among others, the *Forum*-group and Situationism) and the substitution of large-scale urban planning and publicly funded social housing by market mechanisms or 'wild' interventions. One effect of this predilection is the recanonisation of the 1950s and 1960s, and figures or movements like Team 10, the Smithsons, and James Stirling.

OASE's interest in these architects, buildings and issues is only historical in form, and less 'critical' than 'theoretical' (still in the classic sense). It has the aim to examine the internal dynamics and complexities of modernist design theory and the architectural discipline as it was construed by modernism. Symptomatic of this fact is that over the last ten years in *OASE* history starts with modernism, in 1890. If issues of *OASE* before the mid-1990s displayed a more extensive historical interest (if still very much predicated upon the so-called 'long history' of modernism from the eighteenth century onwards), in more recent times only a few essays have reached back before that date. This has lead to some missed opportunities and surprising choices. For instance, readers with a working knowledge of the history of architectural theory will be startled, yet also stimulated, to see a concept like convention (no. 49/50) treated through the prism of the everyday rather than classicism (the notion does surface in the contributions by Irenée Scalbert and François Claessens, however each time with regard to modernism).

Whether or not this focus on the twentieth century has impinged on the quality of the journal is not the issue. After all, *OASE* is nearly consistently worth reading. Rather, it is justified to ask to what extent *OASE*'s stance towards history is deliberate and premeditated. For, if my reading of the journal has any validity, it is this stance that has produced a body of ten years worth of *OASE* that can be read as 30 building blocks of a design theory imbued with the heritage of modernism. This is probably the most visible effect of *OASE*'s connection with the agendas of the writers, researchers and institutions constituting its editorial board and core team of authors, but it is unlikely that these agendas are the only rationale underlying these ten years of work. This is why a proper assessment of the place of history in *OASE* would, I believe, benefit the journal. Such a reconsideration would and should not transform the methods and approaches proposed in the journal as it exists today. Rather, it could induce a better awareness of *OASE*'s own historicity, the position it chooses to occupy with regard to twentieth and early twenty-first century architecture, and the very nature of its own theoretical endeavour.

During the late 1980s, the debate in architecture was dominated by the emergence of deconstructivism. A version of postmodern architecture, deconstructivism presented itself as an alternative to architectural postmodernism. Both formulated a criticism of modernist architecture and its dogmas such as *purity of form*, *truth to materials*, and *form follows function.* Postmodernist architecture did this through the conscious and sometimes ironic reorientation towards earlier historic periods and a renewed interest in decoration, while deconstructivism exercised the distortion and fragmentation of form, space and surfaces and therefore developed complex, if not complicated geometries.

In the lee of this debate, an architectural approach developed that is often associated with the notions *purity of form* and *truth to materials*, but nonetheless is not a rectilinear continuation of modernist ideologies.

Instead of the truth of materials, this position explores the richness of materials. It does not attempt to reveal a single truthful essence of construction, but it rather considers construction to be an essential means of architecture that can narrate the rise of an edifice in various ways and in multiple layers. It is not interested in having the form of structures follow the lines of their load-bearing function alone, instead it considers the form of load-bearing structures to be just as important in relation to the articulation of space and how it is experienced.

Architectural practices that are sympathetic to this approach came to be labelled as 'minimal' in the mid 1990s, because of their formal similarities to the well-known art movement of the same name. This is perhaps the reason why the equally, if not more, important orientation towards architectural examples that diverged from the dogmas of the International Style in the period before and directly after the Second World War, remained much less discussed. The work of architects Sigurd Lewerentz, Rudolf Schwarz and Max Bill belong to these precedents, to which *OASE* 45/46 draws attention.

The affinity for the use of essential architectural means and the realization that this design attitude often 'seemed reserved for assignments that reminded people of essential matters of life and death – churches, cemeteries and crematoria' brought the editors of *OASE* 45/46 to entitle the issue *Essential Architecture.*

Although the questions that the editorial raised – 'What happens when the often religiously motivated rejection of architectural rhetoric mutates into a design strategy in the non-committal context we live in today? What meaning does architecture have that aims at creating authentic experiences when this is used as one of the many possibilities to distinguish architecture on the vanity fair? And is architecture in a position to fulfil this need – an experience that really has the power to move – or will the inevitable result be one style among many, a lifestyle variant?' – remain largely unanswered, it is the merit of this issue that both the close reading of the works of Lewerentz, Schwarz and Bill, and the reflections on this work by a younger generation of architects nonetheless give an understanding of an attitude and modus operandi, which achieve magnificent architectural qualities that range outside the reach of labels such as minimal architecture.

Christopher Woodward is well-disposed towards the work of Max Bill, who of the three discussed predecessors still operated most of all within the ideological legacy of modern architecture. Woodward sees in the *Hochschule für Gestaltung* at Ulm Bill's theories of artistic, industrial and architectural design aligned in a building that proved to be influential for a generation of architects that reoriented itself through the serious consideration of robust building techniques, processes of production, and the thoughtful assembly of material and components.

Udo Garritzman
Member of the editorial board
from *OASE* 42 to 53

Christopher Woodward

BAU, BAUKUNST, ARCHI-TEKTUR

The Work of Max Bill

FIRST PUBLISHED IN *OASE* 45/46

In the early 1960s I was a student at the Architectural Association School in London and in one of the winter vacations worked as assistant for Colquhoun and Miller preparing a door schedule for a secondary school in East London. The office (now that of Cedric Price) was in a cold attic near the AA and was heated only by two extraordinary objects: new turbo fan heaters made by Braun. These were sleek and rectangular, pale grey and about the size of a brick. Their form challenged both the then accepted willed plasticity of British architecture with its emphasis on craggy forms and 'real' textures and finishes, and the fag end of the rococo impulses of the 1951 'Festival of Britain' which still infected British industrial design. Their origins and authors had to be investigated. Rather like the characters in Truffaut's Jules et Jim *(1961), I and three fellow students set off to Germany to find out. In Düsseldorf we found an exhibition of* Gute Form *displaying the full range of Braun appliances, by various designers but all of a family and all eminently desirable, although we could not afford the luxurious record players with their wood veneer-clad side elevations. We traveled via Stuttgart to Ulm and visited the Hochschule where we found Herbert Ohl conducting research into 'ideal' prefabricated building components whose clever universal junctions ignored the direction of gravity or the possibility of the rain which was falling outside. We were entertained to tea in his small designing cutlery. The building by Max Bill, then unheard of in the English-speaking world, although not exactly the equivalent in architecture of Braun's appliances, was forthright, its detailed language tough, the distribution*

of its parts around the summit of its hill wildly romantic. England knew nothing like it. Later we ordered a wholesale consignment of the stacking TC100 catering crockery designed at Ulm by Nick Roericht and now displayed in design museums all over the world. I still eat my meals off it.

1908 was a fecund year for the birth of architects. Max Bill, son of Winterthur's stationmaster, shared the year of his birth with the British knights Frederick Gibberd and Leslie Martin, as did Enrico Peressutti and Gordon Bunshaft. Albert Speer had been born three years earlier, and Konrad Wachsman seven. Aged 16, in 1924 Bill enrolled in the silversmith course at the Kunstgewerbeschule in Zurich, the nearest large town to his birthplace of Winterthur and the one of the centers of German Switzerland's artistic activities. A lecture by Le Corbusier at the school in 1925 persuaded the young Bill to transfer from silversmithing to architecture and in 1927 he left Switzerland for the Bauhaus, Dessau. In the period during which Bill studied there, architecture was taught by Walter Gropius, Mies van der Rohe, Ludwig Hilberseimer, Hannes Meyer and Marcel Breuer. Marcel Breuer and Josef Albers were in charge of the metal workshop, Oskar Schlemmer of stage design, and Georg Muche of painting. Even with hindsight, what we know of the later careers of these teachers, their effect on a very young Swiss must then have been overwhelming, and their powerful ideas in both the theory and practice of architecture, and of Gropius' organization of the school may have determined much of his later development.

In 1930 Bill set up in practice in Zurich, not just as architect but offering services in product design and advertising. He already saw himself as a painter as well as a sculptor. His marketing must have been excellent, for in 1936 he was chosen from Switzerland's architects to design the country's exhibit at the Milan Triennale (as he was again later, in 1951). The contemporary black-and-white photographs of this work suggest that the design closely followed the examples of his Bauhaus teachers, particularly of Marcel Breuer.

In 1944, Bill was invited to organize an exhibition at the Kunstmuseum, Basel. It's title, *Konkrete Kunst*, and the lecture he gave at its opening suggest the first stirrings of Bill the theorist. The term *konkret* presents difficulties. Untranslatable – *abstract* and *concrete* can be antonyms – but most simply rendered in English as abstract it was so propagated by Herbert Read in his *Art and Industry* from 1934. The word had first been used polemically in 1930 in the manifesto of the Paris *Art Concret* group which included Van Doesburg, Hélion and Carlsund. This group's aim was to rid art of its representational duty so that it could promote and serve spiritual ends.

Bill also used the word to describe a new plastic art uncontaminated by the requirements of representation; an art which is *essential*. This art, systematic and objective and using mathematical methods, would not aspire to the transcendental but, cleansed of among other things associations with earlier ideologies, would serve particularly the democracy of Switzerland and, Bill must have hoped more generally, the new Europe which might emerge from the World War then in its final stages. The lecture proposed an analogy between such a plastic art and the formal structures of music without, however, considering that the composing of and listening to music might be culturally circumscribed. He implies that the music of Bach, for example, is in some way absolute and affects our sensory and perceptual apparatus in the same way that, say, a painted red square might. One needs to listen to a classical Japanese composition alongside a work by Bach to conclude that, apart from the most rudimentary rhythms, the analogy was false.

The case for the *konkrete* art or design was supported by an appeal to the design of utilitarian objects (quite often spoons) which at its most successful could be imagined to be free of ideological associations. The idea that utilitarian objects should be designed at all had been proposed and to a certain extent practiced by William Morris and his associates. It was taken up at the end of the nineteenth century by the English Arts and Crafts movement. The Deutsche Werkbund had been established under its influence, which also pervaded the early years of the Bauhaus. Morris intended to bring that beauty already available to connoisseurs to mass consumers, or at least the British middle classes.

Max Bill in 1949

Stackable tableware TC 100, design by Nick Roericht

The extreme puritan and iconoclastic position, to which Bill as practitioner of the fine arts could have subscribed, had been adopted by Hannes Meyer in a Bauhaus lecture published in 1928 as *Bauen* (Building). This text was saturated with anti-art rhetoric: 'all art is composition and therefore unsuited to achieve goals. . . . architecture as *emotional act of the artist* has no justification.' It concluded: 'building is nothing but organization: social, technical, economic, psychological organisation.'

Bill himself seems clearly to have understood the difference between designing a spoon, a building or a painting. Nevertheless, he never made the case for the similarity between utensils and buildings as *types*. In his production of the plastic fine arts he allowed for the 'flash of inspiration' or for using the work of earlier artists as a jumping off point, and he accepted that his mathematical and geometrical *methods* could only be used once a type or kernel existed.

In the same year that Bill gave this lecture he started teaching design ('Form') at the Kunstgewerbeschule in Zurich, and four years later, aged 40, he lectured for the first time outside Switzerland, at the Technische Hochschule at Darmstadt. On Bill's initiative, the Musterausstellung at Basel in 1949 included an exhibit about design, 'Gute Form', sponsored by the Swiss Werkbund.

In 1949 Bill was asked to participate in setting up a *Volkshochschule*, a centre for adult education, in the South-

Philip Webb's 'Sussex Chairs' in the Morris and Co. catalogue, ca. 1860. When designing their chairs, William Morris and his friend Webb would often hark back to older designs from the English countryside

Example of a painting cited by Herbert Read in *Art and Industry* (1934)

ern German town of Ulm. This invitation to Bill, a neutral German speaker, to help rehabilitate German culture in the post-war years is one of the most remarkable episodes of patronage in European twentieth-century architecture, and it produced one of its outstanding buildings. The story of Ulm's early years is fully documented in the highly recommended dissertation on Max Bill *Konkrete Architektur?* By Hans Frei, a Swiss architecture historian.[1] The initiative to found the *Hochschule* was taken by Inge Scholl and Otl Aicher, two young Ulm residents. Scholl's brother and sister had been student members of the *Weisse Rose*, an anti-Nazi resistance group based in Munich. They were both killed in 1943. After the war Inge Scholl conceived as their memorial, under the influence of the ideas of among others the Catholic theologian Romano Guardini, an institute, 'an active school for science art and politics', devoted to re-establishing a German culture purified of Nazi ideology.[2]

In 1948 a delegation from the Ulm Volkshochschule, including Scholl and Aicher, visited Switzerland to study the arrangements for adult education. Aicher had read and been impressed by Bill's article *Erfahrungen bei der Formgestaltung von Industrieprodukten* in the Swiss magazine *Werk*. In Zurich, Scholl and Aicher met Max Bill for the first time. They tried to persuade him to go to Ulm as a teacher in their new institute.

In 1949 the administration of the American occupied zone of Germany passed from its military commander to a civilian

1
Hans Frei, *Konkrete Architektur? Über Max Bill als Architekt* (Baden, 1991).

2
Otl Aicher was born in Ulm and from 1947 ran his own graphic studio there. He and Scholl married in 1952 and his subsequent career included the graphic design for the Munich Olympics in 1972. In later life he became typographer to Sir Norman Foster and Partners and designed the typeface now used for the practice's buildings and publications. He was killed in a traffic accident in 1991.

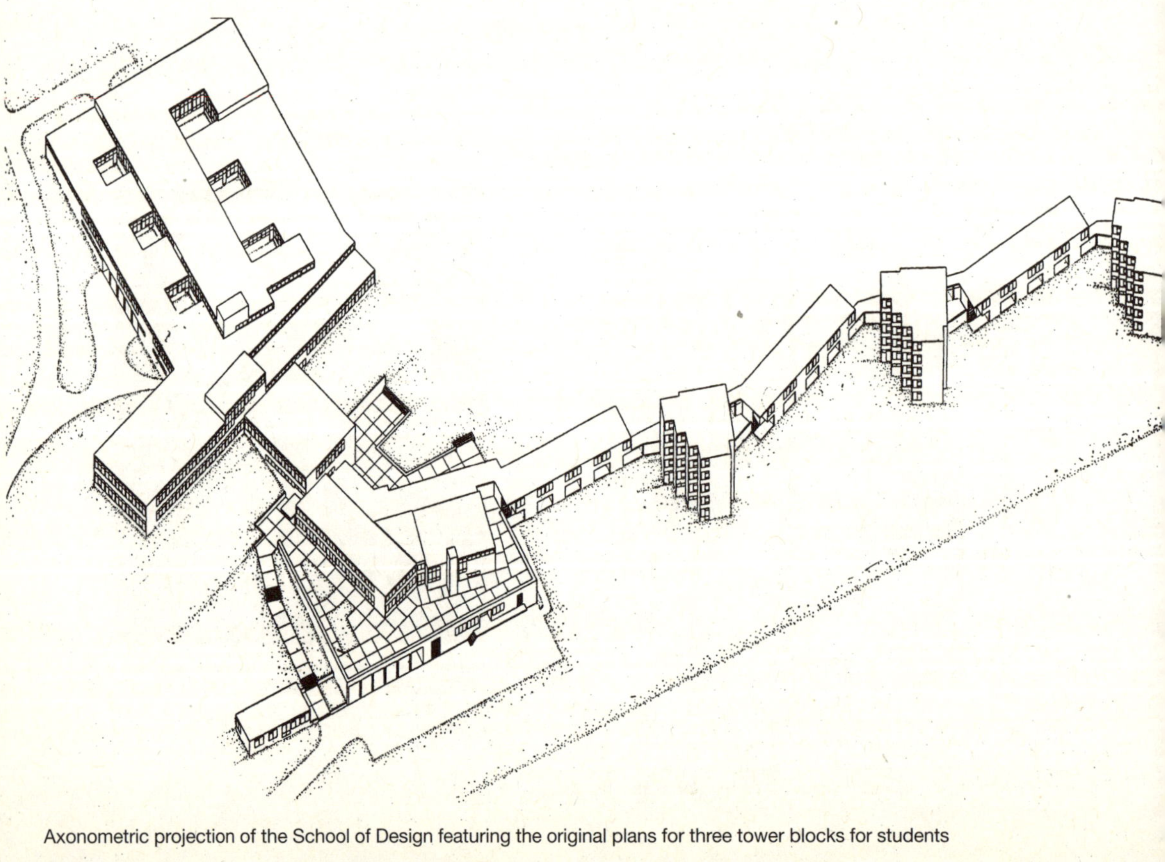

Axonometric projection of the School of Design featuring the original plans for three tower blocks for students

High Commissioner, John J. McCloy, who governed it until the international recognition of the Bundesrepublik in 1952. McCloy administered a US-sponsored fund for a 're-education' programme for high schools and universities. Scholl met McCloy, who was touched by her enthusiastic petitioning for her institute, and involved himself in propagating the idea of the school and in arranging its finance. At this time the designated Rector for the institute was the author Hans Werner Richter, appointed to run a political and scientific programme, but McCloy found Richer uncongenial. In a dramatic move during one of the meetings with the Americans, Inge Scholl proposed Bill as an alternative and more acceptable candidate. Bill agreed to join Ulm on the spot. At the same time he also got the commission to design the buildings.

A site was found on the south-facing side of the summit of a formerly fortified hill looking away from the city of Ulm and the valley of the Danube.[3] By July 1950 Bill had prepared the first layout for the site and by August 1952 the design in its present form was confirmed. The early schemes demonstrate a 'functionalist' composition: each function is identified and then housed in its separate appropriate form and clearly separated from its neighbours, but reconnected to them by neutral elements of circulation. This is one of the canonical modern compositional methods, much liked because it easily gave rise to the asymmetrical arrangements which CIAM promoted over the symmetrical. Gropius had employed the method in his 'pinwheel' design for the Dessau Bauhaus. That this method arose from the early picturesque stages of neoclassicism, most notably in the work of Schinkel, was unknown to or ignored by most modern architects except Frank Lloyd Wright and Mies van der Rohe.

Placed on the highest part of the site, and to its 'back', a two-storey rectangular block of workshops was lit and ventilated by small internal courtyards and a continuous glazed attic. To the south of this the social facilities standing on a platform extended from the side of the hill and looked out over the valley. To the east was strung a necklace of alternating terraces of studio flats and stumpy residential 'towers' of five storeys (of which only one of the proposed three was built), their rooms stepped on plan to provide views. Finally, separate flats and houses for staff were isolated to the west. While the individual parts employ conventional orthogonal geometry, from the very first designs the parts are skewed in relation to each other.

The usual explanation for this departure from Schinkelesque practice is that the buildings 'follow the contours'. This description is inadequate: while parts of the site undeniably slope, much of the remainder on which the residential buildings are placed was flattened when the hill was terraced into fortifications. Something less utilitarian and more poetic was being considered: Bill was a declared admirer of Klee, and was perhaps influenced by the painter's working method.

3
The isolation of the site from the contaminated ruined city may have been deliberately significant, but its distance from the city could have been no help when friction between city and school later developed.

View of the south façade of the School of Design, featuring the three tower blocks and the communal facilities and the school and workshop buildings at the back

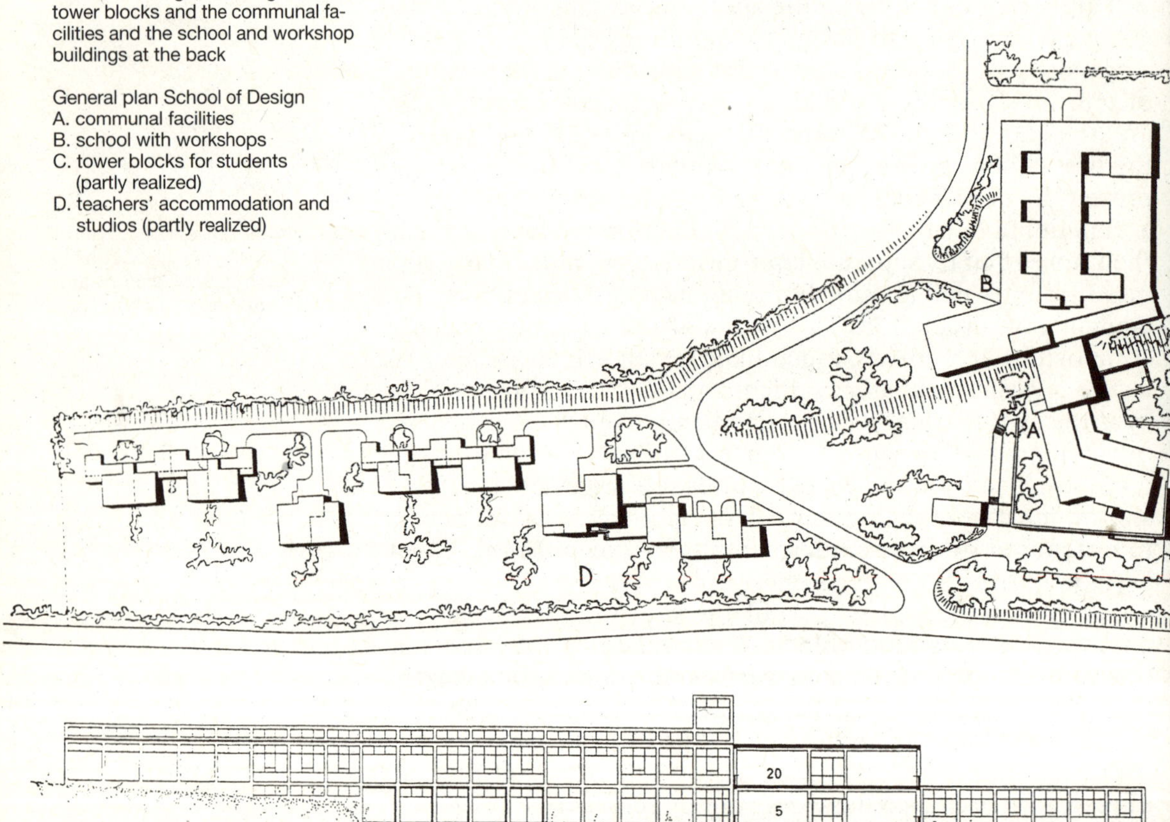

General plan School of Design
A. communal facilities
B. school with workshops
C. tower blocks for students (partly realized)
D. teachers' accommodation and studios (partly realized)

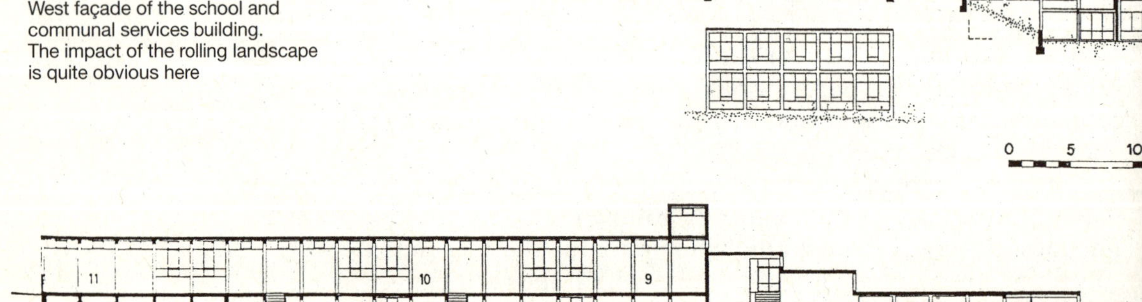

West façade of the school and communal services building. The impact of the rolling landscape is quite obvious here

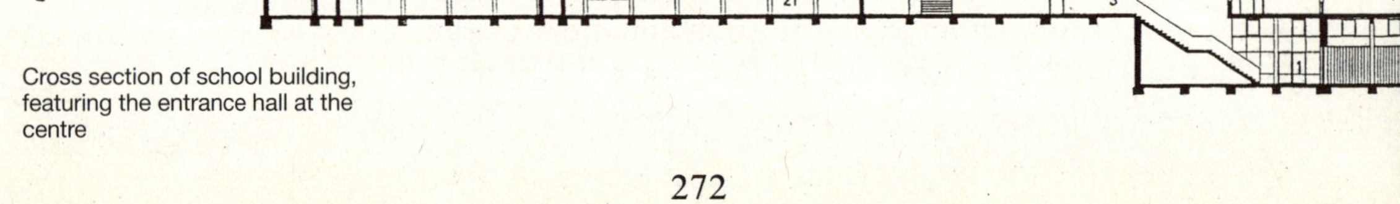

Cross section of school building, featuring the entrance hall at the centre

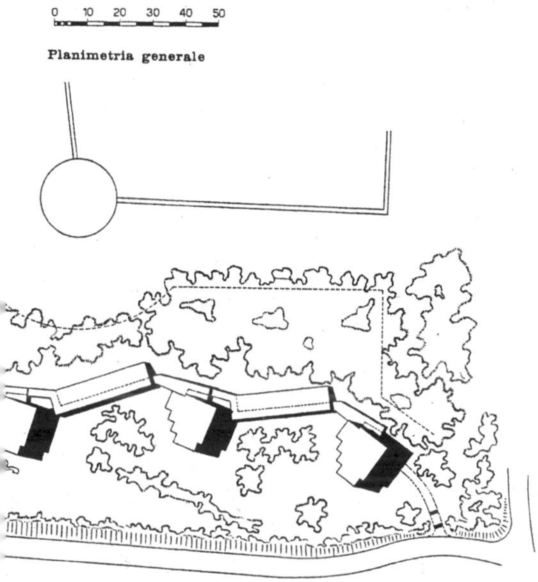

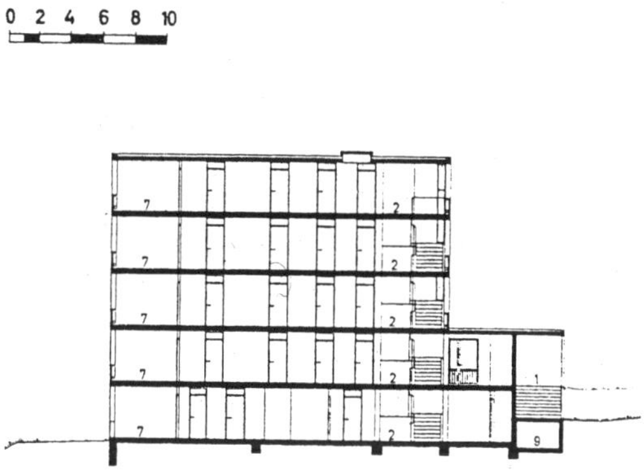

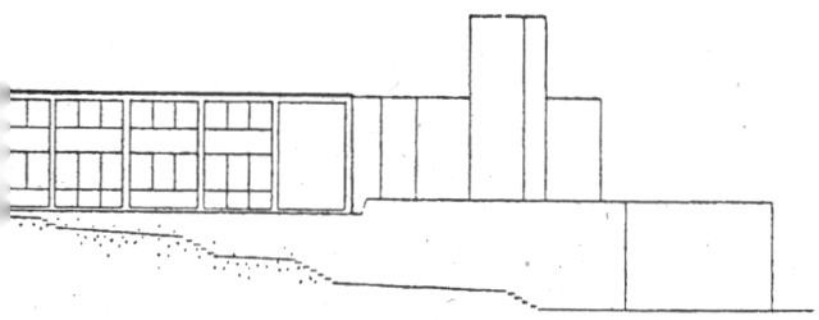

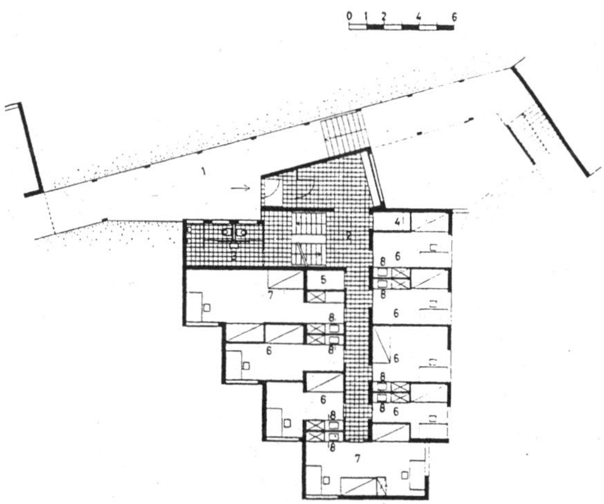

Floor plan tower block

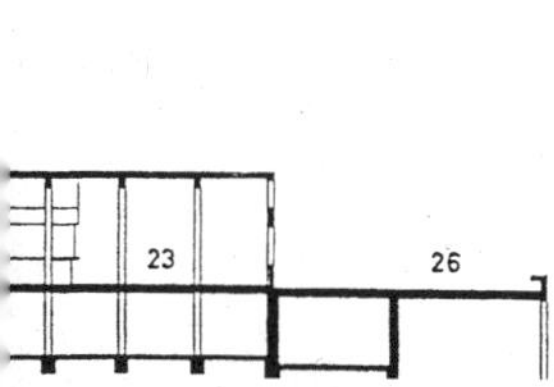

To the extent that it has one, the main and continuous circulation of the building promenades its way through the various parts to provide a rich variety of architectural events, mostly indoors, but some, like the beautiful stoas under the overhanging studio apartments, open to the air.

The paradoxical consequences of the skewing are that a reading of the plan emphasizes the different parts, while the building appears as an amorphous continuum from a distance. An alternative reading might suggest that, since axial planning and irresistible right angles had been used in the buildings of the previous regime to demonstrate its power, the angles may be a conscious or unconscious evocation of the expressionist and organic architecture suppressed as 'entartet' (degenerate) by the Third Reich. If those buildings had rather obvious entrances, their reforming successor could demonstrably ignore these: the Hochschule is remarkably open, its 'front door' is unobtrusive, and many of its parts could be entered without passing through the others.

The most radical and final shift in the development of the design was the 'train-crash' resulting from the compression between the previously separate workshops which set up the main orthogonal on the site, and two differently-angled sub-elements of the social facilities. This produced between them the extraordinary and masterly circulation spaces including the doubled-height lobby with its angled walls. Rudimentarily detailed stairs connect two levels of the social facilities.[4]

4
At about the same time, Hans Scharoun was starting to develop such angled organic plans, but his junctions are more elegantly resolved, less deliberately clumsy.

Stairs connecting the school and workshops

Detail stairs

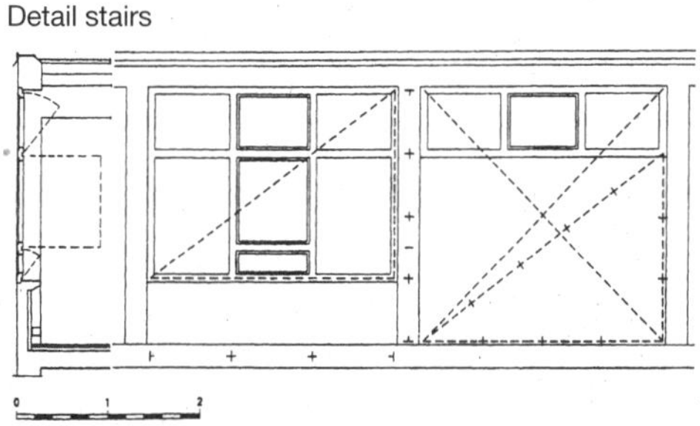

Fragment of the façade

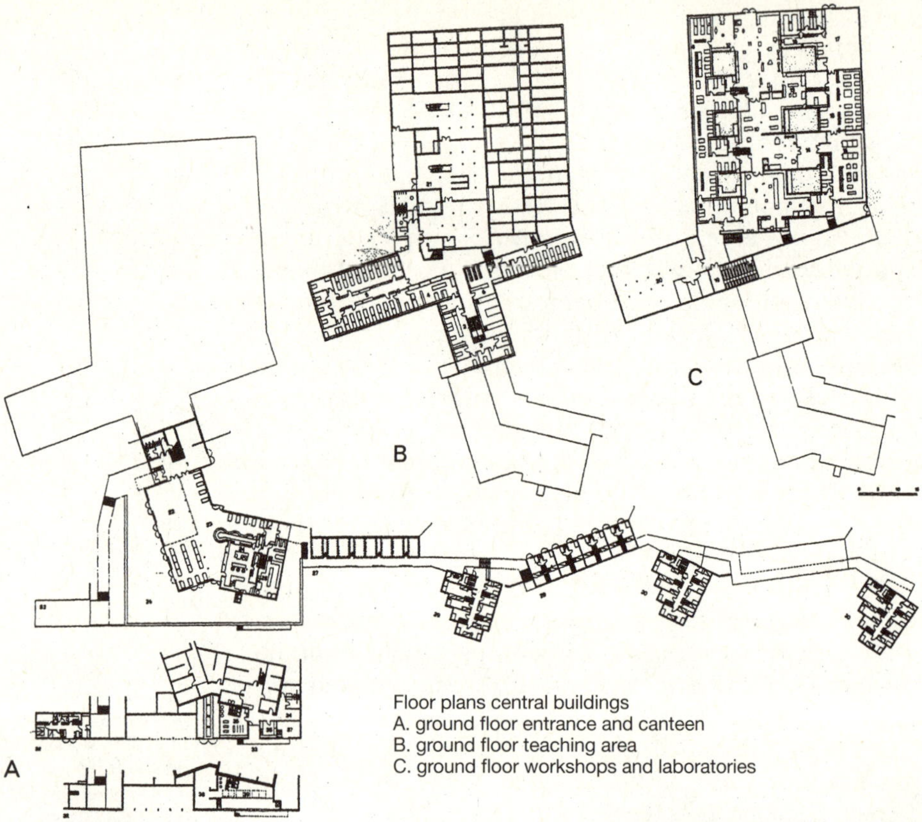

Floor plans central buildings
A. ground floor entrance and canteen
B. ground floor teaching area
C. ground floor workshops and laboratories

Promenade through the building (1955)

The whole complex is constructed, by what must for the time have been a heroic effort of the re-emerging south German building industry, of reinforced concrete, a frame of slim columns or piers and beams supporting profiled precast flooring units for the regular parts, and the irregular parts of smooth *in-situ* concrete. Bill deliberately used an extremely restricted repertoire. Much of the exterior is clad in storey-height glazing units of square format placed between the exposed frame and subdivided on a simple scheme of four vertical divisions and three horizontal. Where not glazed, the exterior is filled with panels of concrete or rendered masonry clearly separated from the frame by narrow recesses. Glazed and masonry elements are set flush with the outside surface of the frame where possible, conferring on the exteriors a taut and constrained quality. In the interiors, by contrast, the full tectonic plasticity of the frame is evident. The brightly lit interiors were and still are strikingly Spartan, with few decorative surfaces. Many of the fittings and much of the furniture was designed by Bill.

The unwillingness to be involved in 'representation', was of course part of Bill's general theoretical position, but here the reticence was particularly appropriate to the circumstances. The bourgeoisie, fed for twenty years on a diet of architectural bombast of fine materials or fake regional decorated folk architecture were being re-educated into accepting what Bill and others had defined as the new style of democracy.

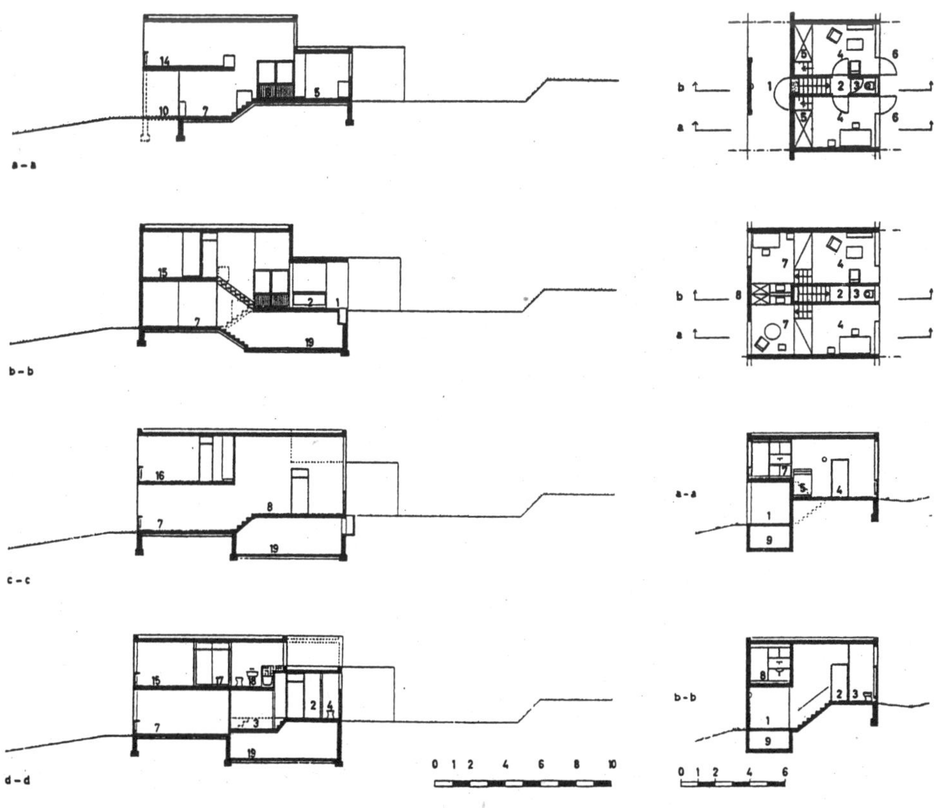

Cross sections and floor plans assistants' studios

Ulm School of Design, lecture hall

Ulm School of Design – stool, design by Max Bill, Hans Gugelot, Paul Hildinger

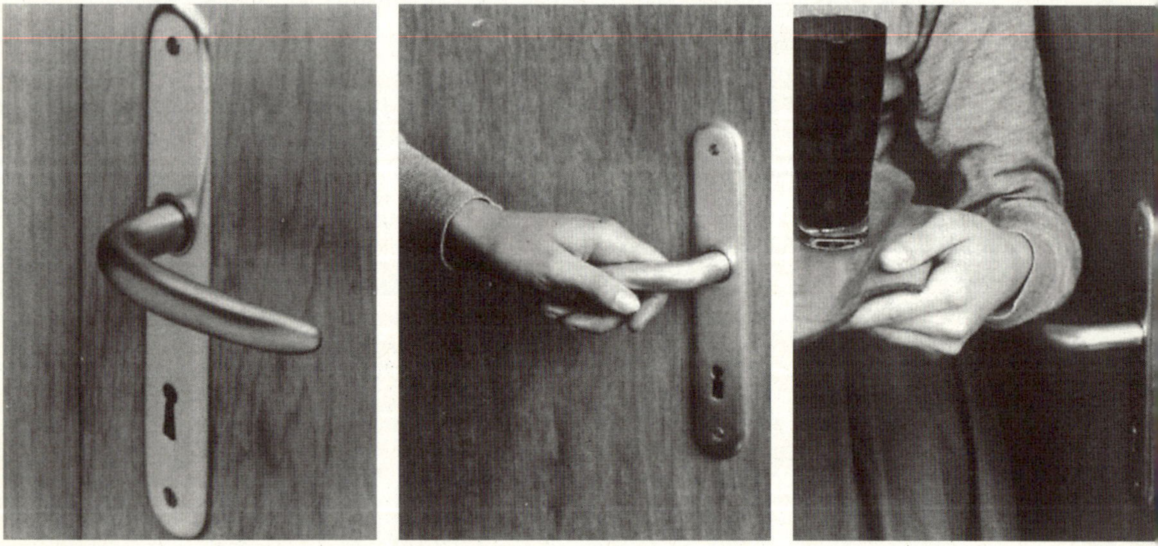

Ulm School of Design – door handle, design by Max Bill

This suggestion finds a curious coincidental echo in England: the exactly contemporary secondary school at Hunstanton designed by Alison and Peter Smithson and built between 1949 and 1954 was a similar reaction to the empty-headed attempted prettiness of much British architecture immediately after the war. Its similarly 'brutally' exposed structure and services offered its pupils Spartan surroundings without conventional architectural finishes. It differs in its simple Palladian plan and organization.

Stung by the critical reception of what was seen as the building's extreme and deliberate truculent lack of cosiness, its willed austerity, and by the distaste of some of his former teachers at the Bauhaus including Walter Gropius, Bill disingenuously replied that the budget was very tight.[5]

The building was formally opened on 2 October 1955. The curriculum devised by Bill was an idealized and generalized version of the many phases of that of the Dessau Bauhaus. A general foundation course was taught in the first year, followed in the second year by specialization in urban planning, industrial design, architecture and 'information'. *Freie Kunst* (liberal arts), which to Bill was the essence of any creative activity, was part of the curriculum. Its position, however, had always been subject to discussion. Bill regarded the arts lessons (which only the best students should be allowed to attend) as a laboratory for the creative process as such, free of the limitations usually brought about by practical needs and requirements. Aicher, who during the 1950s had started to take a more critical attitude towards the role of the arts at Ulm, strongly disagreed with Bill. A conflict about the question whether to keep the arts in the curriculum resulted in Bill's resignation as director. Only one year later he left Ulm for good. The school was subsequently run by a triumvirate of Gugelot, Maldonado and Aicher.[6]

Bill was never again challenged by the client's programme and site or the extraordinarily charged events at Ulm. He returned to Zurich where he reopened his architectural and design practice and resumed his hobbies of painting and sculpture: in 1952 he had been awarded third prize in the international competition to design a monument for the Unknown Political Prisoner. The architectural work of the office consists of one-family houses, small office buildings – mostly in economically comfortable Switzerland – and tends to be quiet and unremarkable. The largest commission of his later years in practice was an extension to the building of Radio Zurich carried out with Willi Roost from 1965.

By then an internationally known figure and Switzerland's honorary federal architect in all but name, in 1964 Bill was appointed designer for temporary buildings for the Landesausstellung (Swiss National Exhibition) in Lausanne. The loose arrangement of pavilions which nearly coalesce into a singly entity continues the theme established at Ulm, but with an orthogonal geometry, and their casually 'poor' prefabri-

5
Mies van der Rohe was the only architect of the earlier generation who was prepared publicly to admire the building as one of the best in post-war Germany. Bill wrote in 1976: 'It could not have been cheaper or more primitive. One had reached absolute rock-bottom. The only enjoyment available to me as architect was in the arrangement of the ensemble on the site; the harmonisation of the internal functions of the various parts; the choice of a sensible but primitive means of construction; the choice of robust, cheap materials whose natural qualities complemented each other and which produced the much-mocked puritan beauty. The reproach that everything was intentionally austere can be countered by replying that nothing else would have been possible: for the money available one could only today build a slightly better villa.' Max Bill, *Vom Bauhaus bis Ulm* (1976), 18-19.

6
European politics and economic circumstances had, however, changed considerably since the last remnants of the Bauhaus were extinguished in 1933, and by the mid 1960s the theoretical work of some of the teachers at Ulm, including that of Thomas Maldonado, was beginning to expose the contradictions in the role of designers and their education in an increasingly affluent economy coming to be dominated by mass consumption: were designers and architects to be the autonomous critics of industry or its servants? Along with examples of the work of staff and students, these debates were widely disseminated in the school's beautifully produced but short lived magazine *Ulm*. The increasingly eccentric and arid theoretical position of the teachers led to correspondingly shrill political criticism and agitation by both staff and students, similar to that pertaining beyond the school in Ulm, Germany, the rest of Europe and in North America, and which led to the *événements* of '68. Its hand bitten by the school it was feeding, in that year the exasperated Landtag of Baden-Wüttemberg voted to close it.

Alison and Peter Smithson, Hunstanton Secondary Modern School (1949-1954)

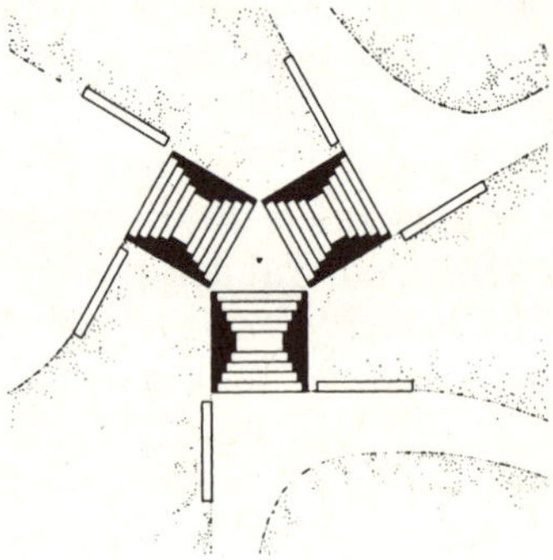

Max Bill, a monument to the unknown political prisoner, competition 1952, second prize

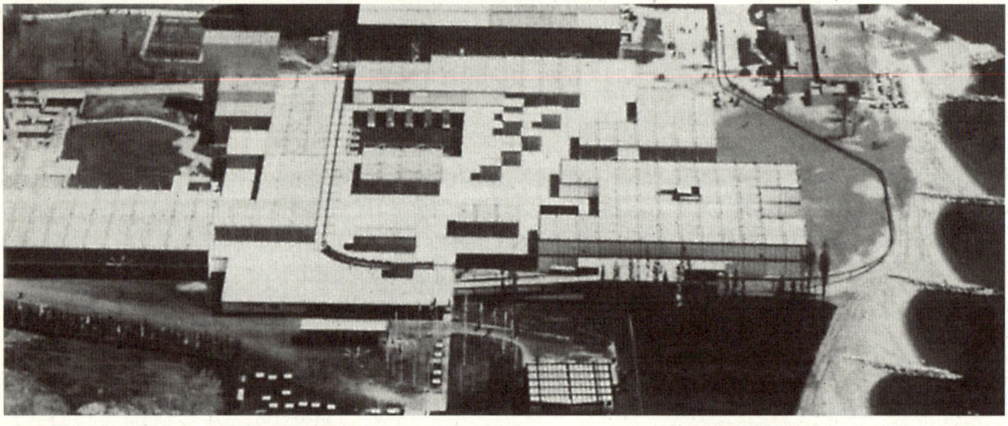

Max Bill, Swiss Regional Exhibition Lausanne 1964

Jacques Herzog and Pierre de Meuron, home for private collection in Munich, 1989-1992

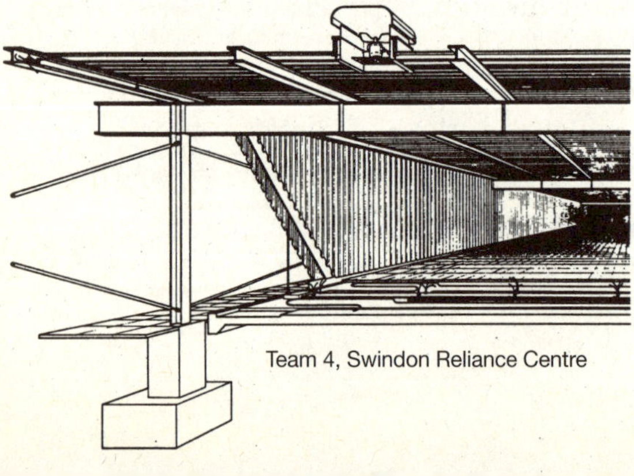

Team 4, Swindon Reliance Centre

cated materials – an exposed slim steel frame, folded metal roofs and corrugated plastic siding – continued its theme of austerity.[7] In 1967 he took up teaching again as Professor of Environmental Design at the Hochschule für Bildende Kunst in Hamburg. In the same year he was elected as federal counsellor to the Swiss Parliament. He died in 1994 aged 86.

The building for the Hochschule für Gestaltung remains an outstanding and singular achievement both in Bill's work and the architectural production of the post-war years. Outside Switzerland none of Bill's industrial designs has yet become available to be consumed as a 'classic'; his paintings and sculptures occupy a small respectable niche in the art markets but the Hochschule für Gestaltung is firmly embedded in any canon of European twentieth-century architecture. The product of very particular circumstances, its wilful layout and austerity have had no direct progeny. But as the product of what must be seen as Bill's idiosyncratic attempt to align theories of artistic, industrial and architectural practice (*produktformen*), it undoubtedly and explicitly influenced that generation of architects now in their fifties and sixties – particularly in Britain – who began their careers by attempting to wrench architecture from gentility (*Architektur*) and *art* and towards a robust employment of technique (*Bau*) and the serious consideration of the production and thoughtful assembly of materials and components: *Baukunst*.

7
Bill as exhibition designer contributed the interiors and displays of the pavilions of 'Art and Life' [*Kunst und Leben*], 'Painting and Design' [*Bilden und Gestalten*] and 'Radio and Television'.

OASE 47 presents the cladding of a building as the essence of architecture. Its underlying axiom, which takes its cue from Semper's nineteenth-century *Prinzip der Bekleidung* (The Principle of Cladding), is that rather than the architectural structure it is the architectural manifestation – its soft furnishings, shell and decoration – that communicates and provides meaning. The article by Dirk van den Heuvel takes a literal approach to the architecture of cladding, by naming architectural elements in the drapes of Petra Blaisse. The architecture of the drape is used to define the relation between the temporary and the permanent in the architecture, but a critical assessment is also made of the way in which inside and outside, architecture and interior, and structure and ornament interact.

OASE 47 offers a theoretical antidote to the moral principle of modernism and functionalism. Closely linked with Delft University of Technology, it presupposes that the essence of architecture is its structure. In the 1990s however, and especially in Mark Wigley's *White Walls, Designer Dresses*, modernist and functionalist architecture was 'unmasked': gone are the pure tectonic structure and constructive 'integrity'. The façade and interior are effectively ornaments governing the experience of the building, or 'directing the gaze' as it is sometimes called.

Following this critique a number of positions crystallised that focused attention on cladding. Hans Kollhoff believes that despite today's lack of constructive 'integrity', the façade must nonetheless represent the building's tectonics. He focuses on the *architectural readability* of the cladding. The position taken by Petra Blaisse and others focuses attention on the *sensory readability* of the cladding. The architecture of the drape is not considered as a material, but as an effect, focussed on movement and light. In this way this architecture questions the permanence, coherence and order of the space.

In retrospect, Dirk van den Heuvel's article can be seen to illuminate the work of Inside-Outside as well as that of OMA. It describes the quest for an architecture that designs spatial rather than structural elements as autonomous phenomena. It views space not as a specific site, but as an architectural situation, a moment bringing together conditions of time, space and light.

Like Bijlsma
Member of the editorial board
from *OASE* 45 to 70

Translated by Laura Vroomen

Dirk van den Heuvel

INSIDE-OUTSIDE On the Work of Petra Blaisse and the Architecture of the Drape

FIRST PUBLISHED IN *OASE* 47

ORIGINS

For a long time, the drape was unthinkable as a part of architecture. Modern architectural thinking was dominated by structure and construction. Rereadings of Gottfried Semper's theories brought about a radical change in the description of contemporary architectural production. In retrospect, this rereading has led to fundamental rewritings of the history of modern architecture. The textile, the woven material that Semper indicated as one of the original, or primal, sources of architecture, was further elaborated into a possible tectonic theory of architecture. Textile, moreover, was linked with an understanding of the outer wall as mask and signifier, and, not least, with gender theories from the field of sociology.[1] These rewritings of modern architecture history imply an evaluation and a revaluation, a shift in the hierarchy of architectural teaching, or as Henk Engel paraphrases Adolf Loos: the lining (*Wand*) comes before the wall (*Mauer*).[2]

The drape itself remained absent for the meantime, both from the architecture debate and actual architectural production. Reflection on the drape can shed light on its possible meanings for contemporary architecture. As we will see, these touch on the very position and power of architecture itself. This is not about a monumental architecture, an architecture reminiscent of Semper, who in turn reminds us of the civilizations of antiquity and their 'primal' architecture; it is about an architecture that utilizes the drape to question its own prem-

1
The most interesting publications in this connection are: Hans Kollhof (ed.), *Über Tektonik in der Baukunst* (Braunschweig/Wiesbaden, 1993); Werner Oechslin, *Stilhülse und Kern, Otto Wagner, Adolf Loos und der evolutionäre Weg zur modernen Architectur* (Zurich/Berlin, 1994); Kenneth Frampton, *Studies into Tectonic Culture. The Poetics of Construction in Nineteenth and Twentieth Century Architecture* (Cambridge/London, 1995); Mark Wigley, *White Walls, Designer Dresses. The Fashioning of Modern Architecture* (Cambridge/London, 1995); Harry Francis Mallgrave, *Gottfried Semper, Architect of the Nineteenth Century* (New Haven/London, 1996).

2
Henk Engel, 'Stijl en expressie', in: Jan de Heer (ed.), *Kleur en architecture* (Rotterdam, 1986), 63-74.

Drape at the exhibition 'OMA, the first decade' in museum Boijmans Van Beuningen in Rotterdam

ises and presuppositions, to reflect on them and formulate them anew.

Seeing the drape as a primal source of architecture undermines our conventional understanding of architecture as a stable and slow discipline. The architecture of the drape is basically an architecture of the provisional, the temporary; the tent and the tabernacle, not the patio house or the temple, are the primal types of this architecture. From this angle, the drape denotes a difference, in this case a difference in time; and in tragic terms, it denotes the temporary and transient nature of human nature itself. A second important difference that the drape denotes is a difference in space, between inside and outside.

As a metaphor, the dialectic pair of inside-outside is capable of supporting the organization of a cultural model. The interior becomes the place of the self and the subject, the exterior that of the other and the object. The interior is a space that has been cleared within the expanse of the world, a space of appropriation, colonization and occupancy by the active subject. The lining of the wall constitutes the inner horizon of this space. Window and door occupy a special place within this organization: they are the openings between inside and outside, and vice versa. This applies just as much to the spaces of the threshold, balcony and garden. They offer a view of the outside world, from the known to the unknown, from self to other, and also, to use Heidegger's words, from the earth to

ewing the hem

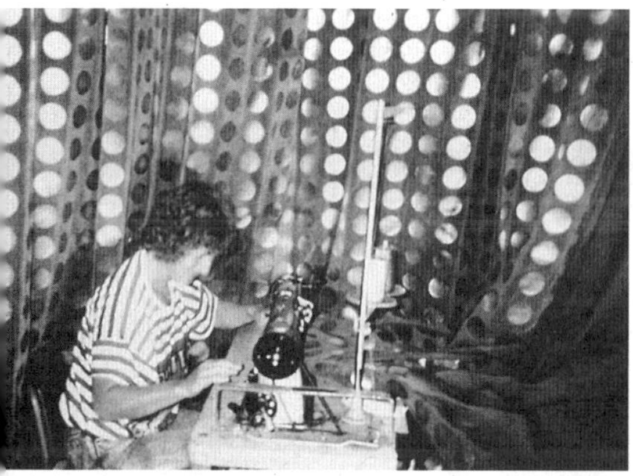

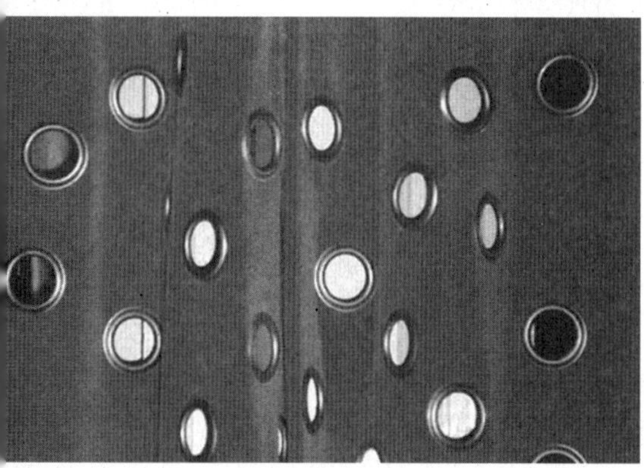

e drape for MoMA, detail

Stage curtain in the Netherlands Dance Theatre

the sky. He calls this room the 'in-between', which has been allotted to human living.[3] Here, in this 'in-between', inside and outside are simultaneously separated and brought together.[4] The exterior is interiorized, domesticated, the other is appropriated. The other way round, this is where the self mirrors itself in the other world, measures itself against it, determines its own value.

In his study *White Walls, Designer Dresses*, Mark Wigley goes a step further.[5] The drape does not just denote any difference. A mere denoting at most confirms what is already there. The radicalness of the drape lies in the fact that the drape itself puts people in a position to think in terms of inside and outside. Before the drape was there, there was no inside or outside. Like a mechanism, the drape produces the difference between inside and outside, and sets a dialectic in motion between inner and outer, between ideal and appearance, structure and ornament. The mask and the theatrical originate from the architecture of the drape.

3
Martin Heidegger, '. . . dichterlijk woont de mens . . .'; Dutch translation, in: Martin Heidegger, *Over denken, bouwen, wonen* (Nijmegen, 1991), 91-110, esp. 99-101.

4
About wall and opening, see also: Fritz Neumeyer, 'Mit dem Kopf durch die Wand: Annäherung an das Unwort "Fassade"', in: D. Kirchner, J. Kostka and C. Rothe (eds.), *Hans Kolhoff* (Berlin, 1995).

5
Wigley, *White Walls*, op. cit. (note 1); *OASE* 47 contains a translation into Dutch of the first chapter, 'The emperor's new paint', as 'De nieuwe verf van de keizer', 20-35.

ILLUSION

Although the processes in which buildings come about nowadays give every cause for an architecture of the temporary, the manifestation and materialization of buildings appeal to values of solidity and permanence. In the 1980s, the provisional featured largely in the rhetoric used by the OMA office

when describing its architecture and the use of its architecture. The Netherlands Dance Theatre by OMA is one of the realized designs in whose materialization this aspect was a guiding principle. Petra Blaisse, together with photographer Hans Werlemann, largely determined the design and dressing of the interior, particularly the furnishing of the auditorium. For instance, Blaisse was responsible for the upholstery of the chairs and designed the stage curtain.

The spatial set-up of the dance theatre auditorium was kept to a bare minimum. The auditorium, without balconies or boxes, is soberly furnished, with a black interior and chairs upholstered in a dark blue, so that maximum attention is focused on the proscenium. The curtain hangs in the traditional position between auditorium and stage. Proscenium and curtain can literally be described as an 'in-between'. This area separates auditorium and stage, audience from dancers, while at the same time bringing them together. It produces a desire in the audience and guides this desire on behind the curtain. Proscenium and curtain mark the borders, and freedom, of the theatre, in space and in time. A temporary opening offers the illusion of a glimpse into another world, which here in the theatre is above all a projective space, one that reflects the audience's own feelings and desires, intensifying them and giving them a place and a direction.

The curtain, in contrast with the sober furnishings of the blue-black auditorium, was meant to give a rather old-fashioned impression of theatrical decadence and extravagance. The incongruity of the curtain's glamorousness with the minimal, almost meager budget available for the theatre was intentionally emphasized by Blaisse. Almost automatically, illusion became the effect that the curtain had to bring about; an illusion of the theatre, of the pretensions of clients, but also of the curtain itself, an illusion of the material appearance. The most important means for this were found in changing light effects, while lamp and gold print, fold and rails constitute the composition that produces these effects.

The illusory effects of depth and transparency through light reflections and the movement of the folds were central considerations in the design and production of the curtain. These determined the nature of the cloth and the pattern printed on it. The cloth is grey velvet – the thickest, heaviest imaginable. The gold print, in a pattern of embossed discs, is made of a gold-colored plastic film. The pattern was applied with a press. First of all, the press was used to flatten the pile of the velvet, then a silk screen was used to apply the glue, after which the gold film was pressed onto the curtain. When dry, the film was pulled off, leaving the pattern behind.

The desired 'fluid' effect of the curtain when it moves determined the form and 'grain' of the printed pattern of gold discs, each about 10 cm in diameter. A rectangular or square print would have given the curtain a certain stiffness and made a fluid, falling movement of the reflections and folds impos-

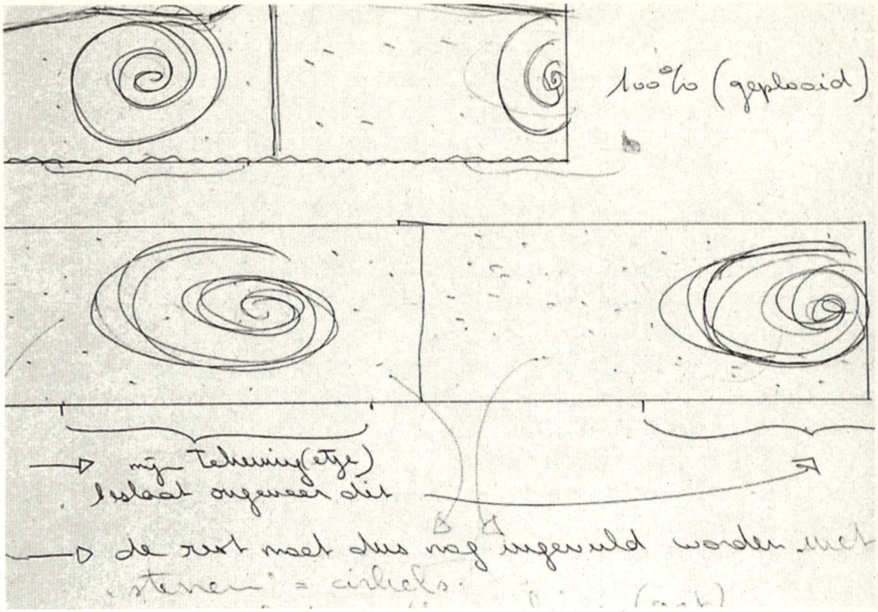

Design sketch for a drape for the Congrexpo in Lille

Drape Congrexpo, Lille, featuring starry sky pattern

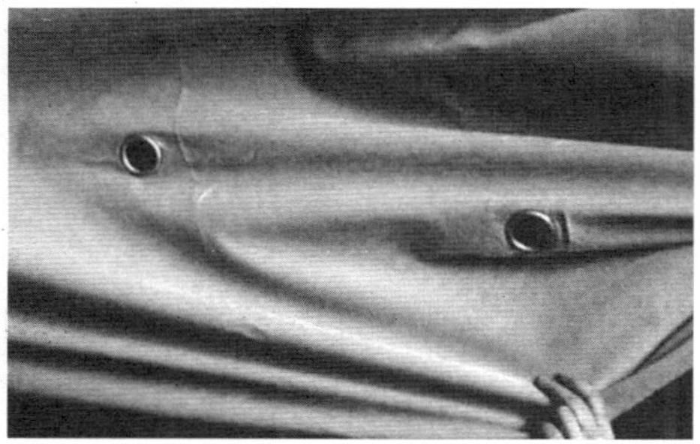

Detail of starry sky drape, Congrexpo Lille

Sample for starry sky drape

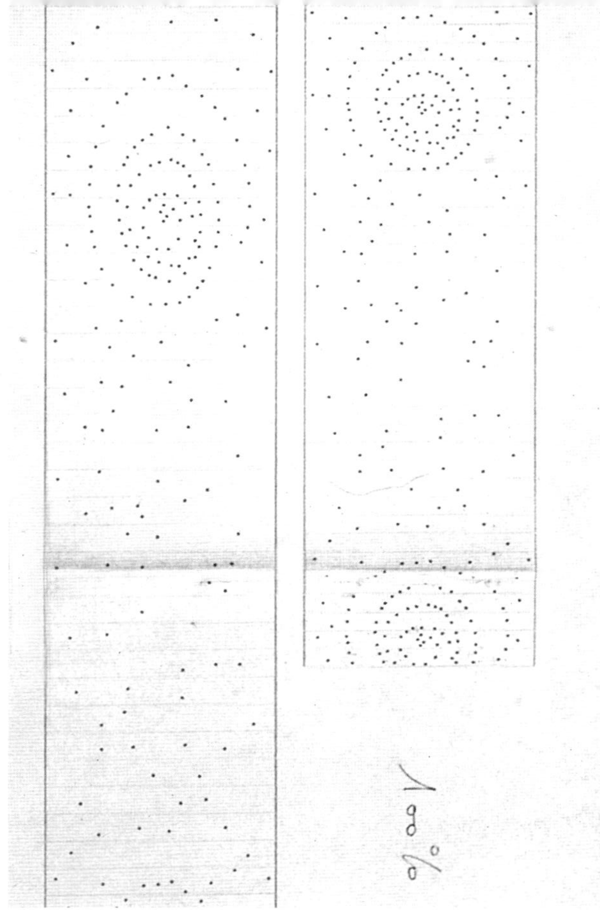

orking drawing for a drape for the Congrexpo in Lille

Drape Congrexpo, Lille, with voile

Drape Congrexpo, Lille, with voile

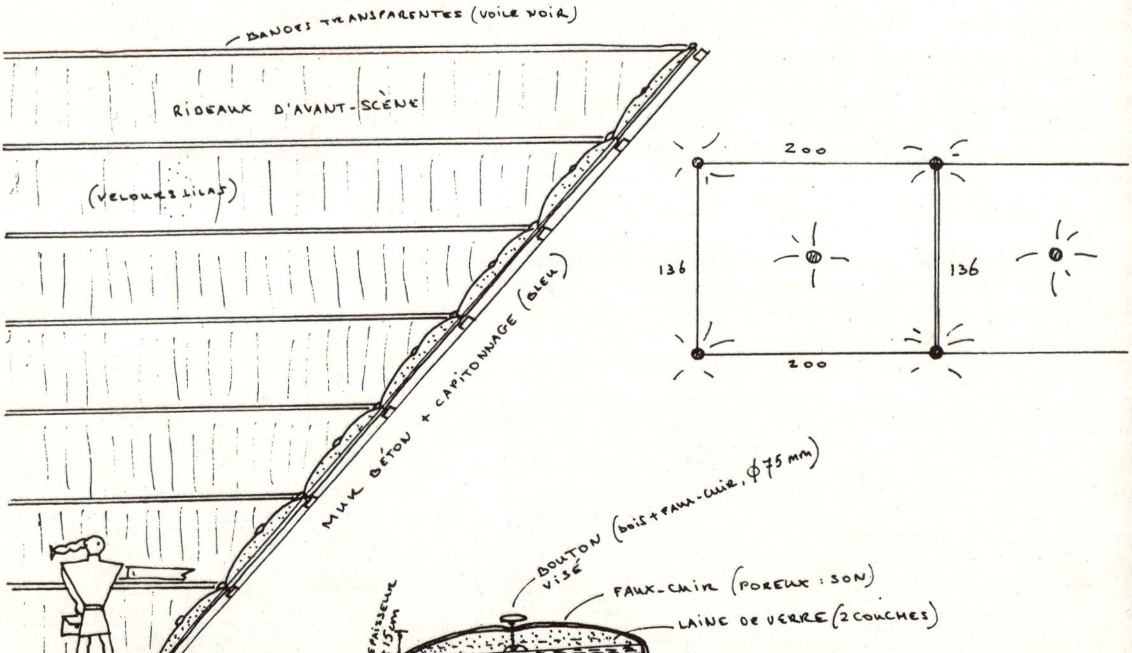

Design sketch for drape Congrexpo, Lille, with voile

MAART '94
P. BLAISSE

sible. Depending on the lighting and the movement, these gold 'discs' reflect now like the sun on the sea or seem like holes appearing in the curtain. On the theatre's ten year anniversary, Jyri Kilian, art director of the dance theatre, seized on the ritual of the opening and closing of the curtain to make a separate choreography for this tinsel waterfall. Rising and falling, closing in and yielding, the curtain itself 'danced' for a few minutes before the beginning of the anniversary performance.

EFFECT

Petra Blaisse now has an office of her own, called Inside-Outside. The office makes the widest variety of drapes, each one unique, and often for OMA projects. Blaisse made a drape to function as an acoustic and spatial partition in the Main Hall of the Kunsthal in Rotterdam. For the Congrexpo in Lille, Blaisse made two hall drapes. Smaller drapes have hung at various exhibitions. For the MoMA in New York, she designed two drapes for the restaurant, a soft green for the spring season and a bright orange for autumn. Just like with the curtain for the Netherlands Dance Theatre, the focus in the conception of these drapes was largely on their making and the position they would assume in the space. You could call the first the tectonics of the drape, the second its architectural effect.

Although the making and the material itself are of primary importance in Blaisse's working method, she is not aiming for an architecture that wants to show the materials and characteristics as such. Architecture here is not understood as pure materiality, or a pure surface that is made empty, free of meanings. Architecture is understood as an effect. Only in this effect does the material become architectural. Blaisse takes this as her starting point. She finds this effect in the material, in its processing and in the reciprocity between the two. This leads to intensive concentration on the idiosyncrasies of the available material and the specific ways of processing it. In the actual projects, the furthest limits of processing possibilities are sought, and effects considered essential are intensified.

Blaisse uses the following means to give the curtain an architectural effect: (1) light, air and movement; (2) seam, hem and fold; and (3) texture and pattern. The directly intended effects relate to volume, scale and sculptural quality, transparency and reflection and division of space and time.

At the OMA exhibition entitled *The first decade* in the Boymans-van Beuningen museum, a drape hung in front of one of the windows in the large exhibition hall that, like a sail billowing in the wind, created the impression that the window was open. In its simplicity, this drape summarized the aforementioned means and effects. A wind machine blew air into the drape and made it flutter a bit, letting it trail on the floor. The resulting volume was emphasized by horizontally stitched seams instead of the usual vertical ones. At the same time, these seams acted between the strips of material as a scale division. Artificial light behind the curtain provided the illusion of sunlight filtering through. Moreover, this light emphasized both the sculptural quality of the swelling curtain and the texture of the material.

In the design for the curtains for the two conference rooms in the Congrexpo by OMA, Blaisse mainly elaborates on aspects of lighting the curtain and the way in which the effects of transparency and depth are created. For one room, she designed a curtain with a 'starry sky'. This curtain is riddled with a holey pattern of rings that together form the spiraling geometry of a milky way. The pattern was set out and punched by hand in the various strips of cloth. The size of and distance between the holes is geared to the size of the fold and the changing speeds at which the curtain slides open and closes.

Just like at the Netherlands Dance Theatre, the pattern fulfils several functions. It provides a scale division: the metal rings, like the gold discs, are an in-between element between the large size of the curtain as a whole and the texture of the cloth. In addition, they provide different light effects. With lighting from inside the room, it seems as if holes appear in the cloth, and when lit from behind with wide-beam lights, the blue satin lining of the curtain produces a bright blue pattern of holes on the room side.

This lining, incidentally, hangs separately from the velvet drape, and flutters behind it a bit when drawn. A lead chain

sewn into the seam prevents it from flying up in a wild and uncontrolled manner.

DISPLACEMENT

The organization of looking, of the gaze, is crucial for a proper understanding of the architecture of the drape. Mark Wigley suggests that in modern architecture the architectural object is not a neutral object at which you can look in an unbiased way, but the architecture itself implies a certain way of looking.[6] The architecture is not subjected to a certain look, it presupposes and conditions a certain way of looking. In the case of the architecture of the white wall, it is about a rational look of hygiene and control, a look that detects impurity, a spiritualized look that moreover is blind, or blinded, to the physical that is behind the white screen. The white wall sets up a detached look, a subject alienated from itself.

In her discussion of Loos's architecture, Beatriz Colomina arrives at a similar conclusion: 'Architecture is not simply a platform that accommodates the viewing subject. It is a viewing mechanism that produces the subject.'[7] Wall and opening play an important role here. Colomina points out that in Loos's houses an ambiguous relationship is created between subject and object, between inside and outside. The opening in the wall is not clearly transparent and does not allow the gaze of the observing subject through without hindrance. Openings turn out to be mirrors or at most, are translucent. Transparency becomes reflection and projection. Theatrical spaces are introduced in the house. Colomina then demonstrates how the architecture of Loos's houses works like a mechanism, with the positions of subject and object constantly changing and rendered ambiguous. The looking subject knows it is being looked at by the object being looked at: '. . . when Münz describes the entrance to the social spaces of the Moller house, he writes: "Within, entering from one side, one's gaze travels in the opposite direction till it rests in the light, pleasant alcove, raised above the living room floor. Now we are really inside the house." That is, the intruder is "inside", has penetrated the house, only when his/her grace strikes this most intimate space, turning the occupant into a silhouette against the light. The "voyeur" in the "theater box" has become the object of another's gaze; she is caught in the act of seeing, entrapped in the very moment of control. In framing a view, the theater box also frames the viewer. It is impossible to abandon the space, let alone leave the house, without being seen by those over whom control is being exerted. Object and subject exchange places.'[8]

What results is the displacement of the autonomous subject. The interior in which this subject lives has suddenly changed into no more than another exterior. There remains nothing more for him/her than the difference between inside and outside. Living itself gets a fundamentally different content here. Colomina therefore speaks of *inhabiting* rather than

6
'Architecture is no longer simply a visual object with certain properties. It is actually involved in the construction of the visual before it is placed within the visual. Indeed, vision itself becomes an architectural phenomenon. The place of architecture becomes much more complicated. A building can no longer be separated from the gaze that appears to be directed at it. Before having a certain look, the building is a certain way of looking.' In: Wigley, *White Walls*, op. cit. (note 1), 2; *OASE* 47, 21.

7
Beatriz Colomina, 'The Split Wall: Domestic Voyeurism', in: Beatriz Colomina (ed.), *Sexuality and Space* (New York, 1992), 83.

8
Ibid., 82.

dwelling. This detached living is comparable with the condition of the post humanist subject described by Michael Hays, a subject that can no longer be described as a psychologically autonomous and individual person, central in the universe, but as a subject that has lost its control and authority.[9] According to Colomina, this detached subject can only still live in the wall itself.[10]

The mechanics of the wall that simultaneously separated and brought together inside and outside now produces temporary positions of inside and outside, and more often, different positions of outside and outside or inside and inside. If we try to describe inside and outside on the basis of this mechanism, we can only talk of gradual and immanent differences within the expanse of a world, where before there was still a clearly defined interior that had been cleared. The architecture of the drape at most makes these differences temporarily present, and in that sense, the architecture of the drape is an architecture of situations. The term situation can be described as an unstable, transient unity of time and space. In his dissertation, *Beweging tegen de schijn*, René Sanders described the essence of the situation as the possibility of what is immanently present to come outside, to step into the foreground. Desire and its projection are therefore guiding aspects in the construction of situations. In this context, Sanders also refers to the relationship between theatre and situation, although he does not elaborate this further into an architectural or spatial definition.[11]

9
K. Michael Hays, *Modernism and the Posthumanist Subject. The Architecture of Hannes Meyer and Ludwig Hilberseimer* (Cambridge/London, 1992), 6-7.

10
Beatriz Colomina, 'The Split Wall', op. cit. (note 7), 94-96.

11
René J. Sanders, *Beweging tegen de schijn, de situationisten, een avant-garde* (Amsterdam, 1989), esp. Chapter 4. 'Over de negatie en de negatie van de negatie van de kunst, de Situationistische Internationale in de periode 1957-1962', 101-144, and chapter 5, 'De heerschappij van en de aanval op de warenekonomie, de Situationistische Internationale in de periode 1962-1968', 145-174.

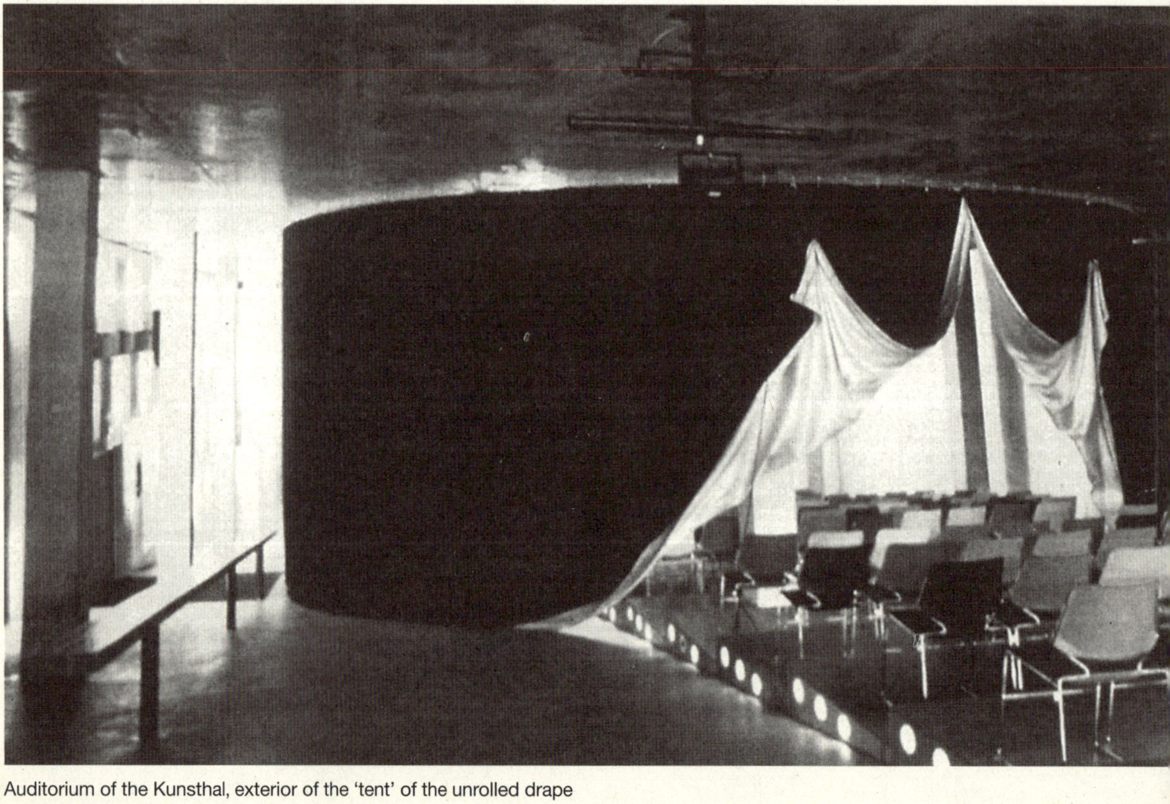

Auditorium of the Kunsthal, exterior of the 'tent' of the unrolled drape

Architectural studies based on a perspective of gender give us more to go on in this regard. Such studies, among which we can also count those by Wigley and Colomina, are capable of offering an idea of a new architectural instrumentarium and the construction of new architectural spaces. In their studies, they take as their point of departure the question of how the architectural space itself creates a subject of its own, a subject that assumes an identity along the lines of gender differences, and that complies with social conventions. The premise that architecture conditions the subject, and not the other way round, leads to a thorough investigation of the mechanisms that produce this subject and that are implied in the concrete architectures.[12] In this way, they go beyond categories of typology, iconology and construction that the discipline of architecture uses itself. In the introduction to the collection of essays entitled *Stud, architectures of masculinity*, Joel Sanders puts these mechanisms in a nutshell: 'dressing wall surfaces, demarcating boundaries, distributing objects, and organizing gazes.'[13]

SITUATION

Of the series of drapes Petra Blaisse has made, the drape in the auditorium of the Rotterdam Kunsthal is the most radical. It occupies an entirely different position in space than the others. This curtain does not hang in the traditional position between audience and stage, but is draped round one of the concrete columns in the hall. The steel rails it hangs on were cast along with the formwork of the concrete ceiling, creating the impression that the movement of the cloth has drawn a groove in the unfinished concrete, which has been left exposed. Because the floor of the hall slopes upwards, the hem of the drape does so as well. This is immediately visible when the drape is rolled up, forming a sculpture of folds and seams that spiral upwards around the concrete column.

When the drape is unfurled, it acts like a tent that makes a second interior inside the auditorium. The spatial effect of a tent is further reinforced at the back by the way in which an 'emergency exit' has been provided – at the behest of the fire brigade. The drape is simply lifted up by the hem and held up. At that moment, a view arises from outside to inside. Inner and outer drape are then simultaneously visible. The two are different. The inside one is a silvery, woven glass-fiber cloth, the outside one is made of a black cotton velvet. The black drape reaches the floor, the glass fiber hangs slightly above the floor, and is finished with a satin hem. The choice of a glass-fiber cloth was partly prompted by the permanent wall lining of the auditorium, which consists of transparent corrugated polyester panels. The woven glass-fiber cloth is a 'soft' version of this hard material, as rope is a soft, flexible version of bark. This 'metabolism' (*Stoffwechsel*) is continued in the way the glass-fiber cloth falls into folds which relate to the undulating form of the glass-fiber wall plates.

12
Letting the architecture precede the subject has far-reaching consequences for criticism itself. Colomina refers to this in the aforementioned essay about Loos, 'The split wall': 'Incapable of detachment from the object, the critic simultaneously produces a new object and is produced by it. Criticism that presents itself as a new interpretation of an existing object is in fact constructing a completely new object.' Colomina, 'The Split Wall', op. cit. (note 7), 97. Research based on gender theories (particularly those of Irigaray, Lacan and Freud) has led to a seemingly inexhaustible series of American publications, which is being added to all the time. Where architectural mechanisms and the production of a (posthumanistic) subject are concerned – apart from the above-mentioned publications *Sexuality and Space* (note 7) and *White Walls, Designer Dresses* (note 1) – the following publications are the most interesting: Beatriz Colomina, *Privacy and Publicity. Modern Architecture as Mass Media* (Cambridge/ London, 1994); Debora Fausch et al. (eds.), *Architecture and Fashion* (New York, 1994); Debra Coleman et al. (eds.) *Architecture and Feminism* (New York, 1996); Francesca Hughes (ed.), *The Architect, Reconstructing Her Practice* (Cambridge/ London, 1996); Joel Sanders (ed.), *Stud, Architectures of Masculinity* (New York, 1996).

13
Sanders, *Stud*, ibid., 13.

The position of the drape was primarily prompted by the various requirements set for the furnishing of the auditorium. For instance, the drape had to improve the acoustic quality of the hall. Apart from the fact that the drape has a muffling effect, a series of small speakers have been incorporated into it, with the particular purpose of improving the reproduction of the higher audio frequencies. These speakers are suspended between the two cloths. On the glass-fiber side, they are visible as round buttons of gauze in a rubber strip. They work like a pattern and an element of scale, comparable with the golden discs and the starry sky. A second reason to apply the drape was the wish to be able to darken the room and control the lighting independently from daylight. The softly gleaming silver inner cloth, the tent's lining, changes according to the inside lighting selected. The interior of the tent thus becomes a separate world within the auditorium, with its own light and sound.

This construction of a temporary and provisional interior seems to have been the main consideration behind the unconventional positioning of the theatre curtain. In earlier OMA designs, experiments had already been made with drapes suspended freely in space, including the design for the Netherlands Architecture Institute and the Villa Dal'Ava.[14] The limit that the drape draws in the auditorium is emphatically designed as a temporary one, not only by making the physical border out of cloth, but above all by letting the limits in space constituted by floor and ceiling continue unhindered. Photo-

14
The design for the Netherlands Architecture Institute was not carried out. For the Villa Dal'Ava, Blaisse made a number of curtains, including the golden curtain in the living room. Koolhaas's book *S,M,L,XL* (Rotterdam, 1995) contains one of the old versions of the plan of the villa, with comments by the 'master', Rem Koolhaas himself, also about the position of the curtain: 'Trajectory of yellow silk curtain to make room in the room' (177). Relevant photographs of the curtain in *S,M,L,XL* can be found on pages 153 (bottom), 154-155, 157 (top), and 158-159, 162-163 and 165. Here, the curtain is the temporary substitute of the sliding glass partition which is the – likewise temporary – substitute of an outer wall (photographs on pages 158-159 and 162-163).

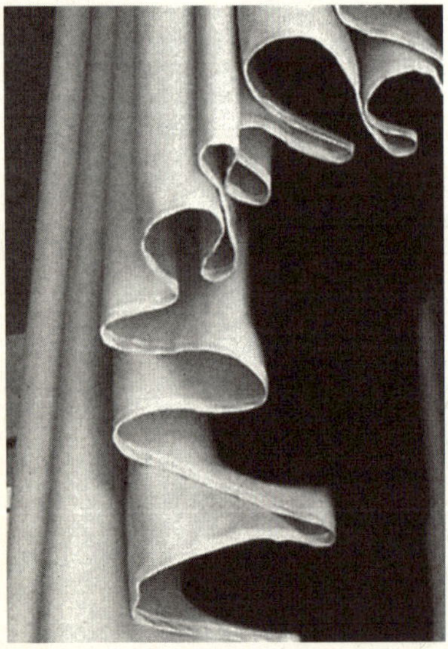

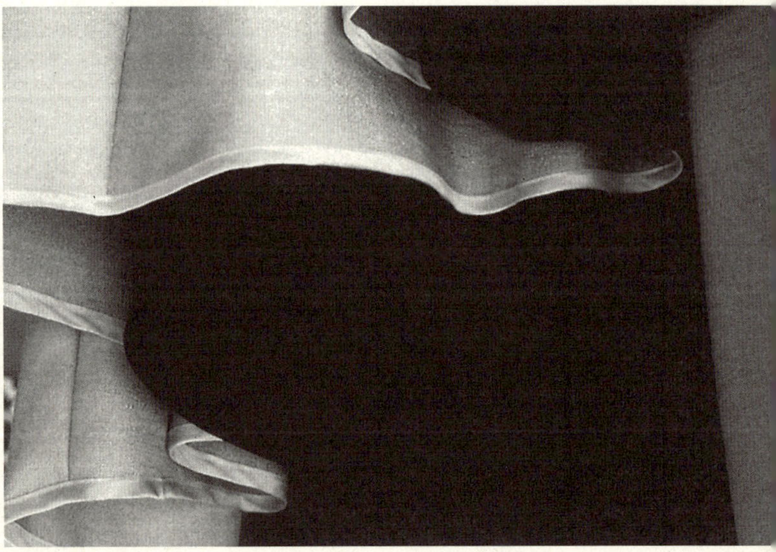

Hem detail

graphs of the auditorium with the drape unrolled show, at the opening in the cloth at the back of the room, that even the arrangement of the removable chairs continues right through the opening.[15] The drape brings out all its trumps in creating the illusion of the interior, thus paradoxically reinforcing the idea of temporariness; on the one hand by having the material of the silver inner cloth differ from that of the black outer cloth, and on the other by organizing its own light and sound effects.

15
See the photography in *S,M,L,XL*, ibid., pages 439 and 441, both at the top right-hand corners.

In addition, the drape lends the room an undeniable theatrical ambience. It directs the gaze and evokes expectations. The position of the drape and its material elaboration, however, create an ambiguous effect; it is not the 'stage' that becomes the projective room of desires and feelings, but the hall full of people.[16] To that end, the stage itself is transformed into an enormous wooden piece of furniture that takes up the entire front wall of the room. In this piece, a large window has been left open, like a black hole. It is black, or dark, because the window gives onto the darkened, covered delivery passage. Then the light from the auditorium reflects in this dark hole, this void. Where the stage was, there is now a transparent window that acts like a mirror. In the glass, the look outwards and the projective room of the theatre coincide with the mirror image of the interior. The space of the auditorium becomes a situation in which interaction between the users constantly causes the positions of subject and object to alter. Moreover, the curtain itself participates in this exchange: it is active in contributing the partition and determining positions and looks, but through its special position it is just as much an object of being looked at, a small spectacle that uses the techniques of theatre while at the same time undermining its conventions.

16
It is striking when looking at the published photographs of the auditorium that the camera is never aimed at the platform, the 'stage' at which the audience's gaze is primarily directed. Such photographs are, however, published of the halls of the dance theatre and the Congrexpo. In the case of the Kunsthal, the camera tends to be aimed at the seats (when the room is empty) or at the audience.

So the drape does not so much turn the auditorium into a house for the detached subject, it makes a displaced theatre. This displacement must be understood as a *situationistic détournement*, a reversal of the conventions that wants to make a new definition possible, one that wants to explore the limits between inside and outside anew.

Translated by Claire Jordan

OASE 54 *Re: Generic City* is a compilation of articles based on papers presented at the symposium 'The Generic City and the Old Metropolis' held at the Catholic University of Louvain in 2000. Needless to say, the symposium title referred to Rem Koolhaas's 1994 essay 'The Generic City'.

'The Generic City' was a polemic on contemporary architecture and urbanism and what Koolhaas sees as their moralistic and 'elitist view' of the urban condition. This view sees ancient centres as models for the ideal city, with the agora epitomizing the ideal public space. The public space as we knew it (or as we thought we knew it) has disappeared from the generic city. The city of 'places' has been replaced by a 'non-urban-realm'. This new urban condition is irreversible and inevitable, according to Koolhaas. But what the 'elitist view' of the city, which harks back to the restoration of the *agora*, and Koolhaas's 'realism' have in common is that both are based on the contradiction between the private and the public domains.

The sociologist Jeff Weintraub has described this contradiction as 'one of the grand dichotomies of Western thought'. This persistent dichotomy has led to an impasse in thought about the city and society. The conceptual framework of this dichotomy allows only two possible responses to the 'non-urban-realm' and the 'loss of place': either we strive for the 'restoration' of THE public domain, or we accept the loss of the public domain and embrace the urban space as a neutral, undefined (as well as dangerous) zone, in which we can only feature as autonomous individuals. In the first instance, THE public domain must be accessible to everyone. It implies major consensus on the moral values within the public domain. In the second, co-habiting within the urban space is out of the question. Because the urban space is neither owned by nor designated for any individual, it is *potentially* – and paradoxically – for everyone and therefore uninhabitable.

Thought on the public domain requires a more nuanced conceptual framework. The addition of a third domain, the collective, allows for a more complex analysis of the urban condition. In his contribution to *Re: Generic City* Kristiaan Borret offers a starting point for a possible definition of the collective domain. He does so by drawing on Weintraub's illuminating overview of the various definitions of the distinction between the public and private. With hindsight we see that the collective domain has become much more prominent in debates on the city and the practice of building.

At the same time, both the Netherlands and other Western European countries are having a fierce social debate on moral values in the public domain. The collective domain plays a negligible role in this debate. The emphasis here is on the definition of THE public domain, on questions about what binds US, on 'universal' values and (or?) on national identity. The dichotomy between the public and private domains – between the generic and the specific – is thus intensified. 'We' must play a role, as Paul Scheffer notes. But we certainly cannot work with an absolute definition of the concept of 'we'. The professional discourse on the definition of new boundaries and the relationships between private, collective and public domains will have to be linked to the broader social debate on the public domain. Without this more nuanced approach, the debate may once fail to move beyond the restoration of THE public domain. This would bring us back to square one.

Marcel Musch
Member of the editorial board
from *OASE* 41 to 64

Translated by Laura Vroomen

Kristiaan Borret

ON DOMAINS The Public, the Private and the Collective

FIRST PUBLISHED IN *OASE* 54

PROLOGUE AGORA AND ASPHALT

In the late summer of 1996, it became obvious that the psychopath Marc Dutroux and his companions had been able to kidnap, abuse, and murder a number of young girls. The spontaneous indignation about these unspeakable facts culminated in a huge protest march through the central boulevards of the Belgian capital.

Many protest actions had preceded the march through Brussels, however: two of them happened to be announced side by side in the newspaper *De Standaard*.[1] The first article describes a kind of commemorative caravan with 'thousands of motorcyclists, truck drivers, and car drivers' along the homes of four of the murdered girls in the suburban sprawl between the cities of Hasselt and Liège – a drive of some 40 km across the Belgian language border. The article concludes, 'At the point of departure in Mechelen-Bovelingen, a 20-acre parking lot will be available. The destination is the Biggs shopping mall, which has one of the largest parking lots in the whole of Limburg.'

1 'Herdenkingsrit stevent af op overrompeling' and 'Stille mars voor Loubna', *De Standaard*, 14 September 1996.

The second article deals with an expression of sympathy for the family of the disappeared girl Loubna, who lived in central Brussels. In this case a 'silent march' on foot, through the city centre, departs from the Flagey Square in Brussels. 'The destination of the march is, symbolically, the Brussels Palace of Justice.'

The contrast between two urban models in this anecdotal meeting of two newspaper articles is striking. It overflows with issues, doubts and questions that dominate the current debate about public life and public space, about city and community.

In the description of the march for the Brussels girl Loubna, we immediately recognise the traditional morphology of the European city: a compact urban fabric articulated through monumental squares and buildings. According to this paradigm, public space serves as an agora for the gathering of citizens, and public authorities are clearly represented in the cityscape. Urban space is a full and coherent whole that testifies to a glorious tradition of public life. The demonstrators are characterised as 'family members and friends'. In this view people are still part of a circle; Brussels is still a community of citizens, the ideal of the reconstruction movements that strongly inspire urban development in Brussels these days.

At the end of the pedestrian march through Brussels, demonstrators come face to face with the institution to which their reproaches are addressed: Poelaert's impressive Palais de Justice. In this sense, the journalist's use of the adjective 'symbolic' to describe the already overdeterminedly symbolic Palace of Justice is redundant. By contrast, in the other article the addition of a phrase like 'without symbolic meaning' to characterise the Biggs megamall would have been very much to the point. It might have helped to raise the question whether the spontaneous civic protest might also have been a condemnation of consumer culture.

In the megamall article, the image of a new kind of dispersed city emerges, which has been spreading in Belgium for some time now, but which has yet to find its proper paradigm. The article presents the urbanisation pattern between Hasselt and Liège as a car-scale environment: the most important feature of the assembly points for the protest drive is their size. The demonstrators are also primarily designated in terms of their mobility: they are 'motorcyclists, truck drivers and car drivers'. According to this model, the city is not a circle but a network. The final destination of the protest drive by car is the vast asphalt space of an unused parking lot on a Sunday afternoon. The building that dominates this site is a manifest sign of unbridled mass consumption, but it does not come under attack. The real target of this posturban manifestation, of course, is the waiting TV-camera, not the place. The place itself is triply empty: spatially, functionally, symbolically.[2] In this dispersed city, the familiar urban models of public space have lost their meaning, while no up-to-date alternatives seem to have been formed.

2
See for a discussion of the 'void' as a basis for public space: K. Borret, 'The "Void' as a Productive Concept for Urban Public Space', in: GUST (Ghent Urban Studies Team), *The Urban Condition. Space, Community and Self in the Contemporary Metropolis* (Rotterdam, 1999), 236-251.

MANICHEISM

The radical opposition between two models of the city and urbanity does not just lie dormant in these newspaper articles but also characterises to a considerable degree the debate on architecture and urbanism. Current theories about urban public spaces are largely like a 'literature of loss':[3] they often paint a black-and-white contrast between the authentic but lost 'good city' and the present condition of cities, between quasi-pure ideals of urban public space and the hybrid conditions of the real world. This kind of manicheism has been criticised before,[4] but remains in vogue, for example in Michael Sorkin's much-discussed book *Variations on a Theme Park. The New American City and the End of Public Space*.[5]

In his introduction to this volume of essays, Sorkin frames the discussion of contemporary urban space in a stark contrast between the new city and the traditional city. The new city, according to Sorkin, can be characterised in three ways: 'the a-geographia, the surveillance and control, the simulations without end.' These three characteristics and their parallels with other theories are a good example of the abundant literature of loss that is currently mapping the loss of urbanity and public space.

The first characteristic, that the surrogate city is a-geographic, refers to the decay of local and specific traits that traditionally distinguish cities from each other. Rem Koolhaas makes the same observation in his text on the generic city.[6] A city is no longer to be understood as a unique spatial context that varies geographically, but merely as a species, a genus, a standard infrastructure that can be deployed anywhere in the world.

Surveillance and control make up the second characteristic and refers to the obsession with security that is especially

3
M. Brill, 'Transformation, Nostalgia, and Illusion in Public Life and Public Place', in: I. Altman and E. Zube (eds.), *Public Places and Spaces* (New York, 1989).

4
For instance: Ted Kilian, 'Public and Private, Power and Space', in: A. Light and J. Smith (eds.), *The Production of Public Space* (Lanham, 1998); B. Robbins, 'The Public as Phantom,' in: B. Robbins (ed.), *The Phantom Public Sphere* (Minneapolis, 1993); R. Deutsche, 'Agoraphobia', in: R. Deutsche, *Evictions. Art and Spatial Politics* (Cambridge, MA, 1996).

5
Michael Sorkin (ed.), *Variations on a Theme Park. The New American City and the End of Public Space* (New York, 1992).

6
Rem Koolhaas, 'The Generic City', in: Rem Koolhaas and Bruce Mau, *S,M,L,XL* (Rotterdam, 1995).

prevalent in North-American cities. On the one hand, this obsession leads to extreme surveillance and security measures, on the other to an increasing segregation of different social groups. Mike Davis has described these developments to great dramatic effect in his bestseller *City of Quartz*.[7]

7
Mike Davis, *City of Quartz. Excavating the Future in Los Angeles* (New York, 1990).

The third element describes how the architecture of the surrogate city has lost all authenticity and thrives on simulations. Christine Boyer illustrates this phenomenon in her analysis of the tourist district South Street Seaport in Manhattan: maritime architecture is scenically displayed to create an absurd fictitious tableau, which satisfies the nostalgic longing of visitors and encourages consumption.[8]

8
M. Christine Boyer, 'Manhattan Montage', in: M. Christine Boyer, *The City of Collective Memory. Its Historical Imagery and Architectural Entertainment* (Cambridge, MA, 1994), 421-476.

Michael Sorkin's description of the new city involves a plea for a return to a more authentic city. However, several aspects make the model of the good city problematic. By viewing public space as a locus of political activity, Sorkin successfully challenges the mainstream discourse that would prefer to screen public space from politics to facilitate discussions of the city's shape in terms of pleasant entertainment and safe sociability. But by holding up the dazzling historical ideals of 'agora, castle, piazza, or downtown', he only succeeds in making every intimation of public space in the banal reality of the generic city pale in comparison. This merely serves to perpetuate the lament about the demise of public space.

More importantly, Sorkin's text is steeped in the conviction that the so-called urban public realm is something we all once shared but have now lost and that we should somehow regain it. This argument, however, bypasses all the different levels of exclusion on which the ideal models of urban public space relied for their functioning. Not all urban inhabitants had equal access to participation in the supposedly open debate in the agora. 'For whom was the city once more public than now? Was it ever open to the scrutiny and participation, let alone under the control, of the majority? Was there ever a time when intellectuals were really authorized to speak to the people as a whole about the interests of the people as a whole? If so, where were the workers, the women, the lesbians, the gay men, the African Americans?' asks Bruce Robbins.[9] Commentators like Sorkin mourn 'a lost state of plenitude' and chase a phantom of public space that has never really had any right to claim that title.

9
Robbins, 'The Public As Phantom', op. cit. (note 4), viii.

The manicheistic contrast that determines, in *Variations on a Theme Park*, what is to be called urban public life and what is not, ties in with the binaries that constantly crop up in theories of public space. Although the public/private dichotomy is casually applied, this pair of concepts is less obvious or monolithic than it seems. We should constantly remind ourselves that public and private are relative terms that only gain meaning through contrast, that they can't simply be consolidated spatially, and that they cover a great variety of definitions and ideologies.

THREE TRADITIONAL MODELS OF THE PUBLIC/ PRIVATE DISTINCTION[10]

The casual use of public and private obviously has to do with the fact that the distinction between the two is 'one of the grand dichotomies of Western thought'. However, for some decades now this binary has been intensely questioned within a variety of disciplines (economics, social history, feminist theory), although the different discussions can not always be easily related to each other. The distinction between public and private is not unitary but protean. It takes on different guises in different contexts. These contexts or paradigms are different but not entirely unrelated: that is precisely what makes it so difficult to separate them. Social and political theorist Jeff Weintraub has nonetheless identified three models, each of which organises the distinction between the public and the private in a distinctive way. This classification might bring some clarity and remove some of the misunderstandings and mystifications that arise by allegedly taking for granted terms such as the public or private domain.

10
For the discussion of the models of the public/private division, I made extensive use of Jeff Weintraub, 'The Theory and Politics of the Public/ Private Distinction' in: Jeff Weintraub and Krishan Kumar (eds.), *Public and Private in Thought and Practice. Perspectives on a Grand Dichotomy* (Chicago, 1997), 1-42.

The liberal-economistic model

PUBLIC	PRIVATE
– government	– market
– administrative regulation backed by coercive force	– voluntary contractual relations between individuals
– 'public sector'	– 'private sector'

The difference between public and private in the liberal-economistic model roughly comes down to the distinction between state administration and market economy. Often-used concepts such as the 'public sector' and the 'private sector' belong to this tradition. This model, dominated by economic arguments, places individuals and the organisations based on voluntary and contractual relationships between individuals over and against governmental interference and control. The boundary between these definitions of public and private is expected to be as clear as possible: what falls under public jurisdiction and what does not? When does the public interest demand government intervention and when does it not?

The citizenship model

In the citizenship model, the public side is the realm of political community based on citizenship; it corresponds neither with the free market nor with the government in the liberal-economistic model. The true distinction according to the citizenship model can therefore never be made visible in the liberal-economistic framework. Consequently, the meaning of 'public' in each model appears to be different:

liberal-economistic model		*citizenship model*	
	PUBLIC		PUBLIC
	'public sector'		'res publica'
=	administrative state	=	world of debate, collective decision making, and action in convert
		≠	market and
≠	market	≠	government

The basis here is the Aristotelian division between *oikos* (household) and the public life of political activity. The notion of public follows the tradition of republicanism (the tradition was readopted by Hannah Arendt in the twentieth century). In this context citizenship therefore means more than being part of a community, as in the communitarian definition, it implies active participation: 'Citizenship entails participation in a particular kind of community . . . one marked by, among other things, fundamental equality and the consideration and resolution of public issues through conscious collective decision making.'[11]

The 'public realm' (Arendt), the 'public sphere' (Habermas), the 'political society' (De Tocqueville) are typical concepts that belong to this model. More recently, Peter Rowe proposed his rather vague notion of 'civic realism', which fits into this framework.[12]

11
Ibid., 13.

12
Peter Rowe, *Civic Realism* (Cambridge, MA, 1997).

The sociability model

PUBLIC	PRIVATE
ancien régime polymorphous sociability	(isolated individual)
modernity Gesellschaft	(personal life)

The criterion used to distinguish the public from the private in the sociability model is the nature of social relationships. Sociability refers to spontaneous encounters and associations between heterogeneous and mutually unfamiliar individuals and groups, in a way that makes their diversity bearable and coexistence sustainable (Sennett's civility). The ideal model is the polymorphous and theatricalised public life of the *ancien régime*, when 'life was lived in public', a cosmopolitan or even

'Mediterranean' idea of street life that is more casual and promiscuous but also quite apolitical. The issues surrounding the distinction between public and private in the work of Philippe Ariès, Jane Jacobs, Richard Sennett and William H. Whyte belong to this paradigm.

This model assumes that the gap between the public and the private has widened since the onset of modernity and that sociability has been in decline ever since. Modernity causes the collapse of the original concept of sociability, with its increasing polarisation between a public domain increasingly experienced as impersonal, instrumental, individualistic (*Gesellschaft*, market, modern state, bureaucratic organisation, and so forth) and the private domain of domesticity, which is increasingly shaped by intimate and emotional relationships (modern notions of non-instrumental friendship based entirely on sympathy and affection, the ideal of romantic marriage, the position of the child in the nuclear family, and so on). The sharp distinction between, on the one hand, a private sphere of intimate relationships through the emergence of the modern family (and other relationships geared to the creation of islands of intense intimacy and privacy) and, on the other hand, a radically opposite public sphere caused the old form of sociability to fade away.

Richard Sennett has identified an additional evolution, namely that the norms for social relationships within the private sphere became so dominant that they started to manifest themselves in the public sphere as well. Sennett sees the city as the locus of tolerated heterogeneity: public space is the scene of civilised contact with the strange and the other.

Theatricality and coded expression were the rules of the game of public life during the *ancien régime*. They went into decline in the nineteenth century, according to Sennett, when notions like personality, authenticity and spontaneity made their appearance in the domain of public life. Ever since then relationships are not considered authentic unless they are sincere and spontaneously manifest the 'deeper' personalities of the parties involved. The mask should be a face. Intimacy becomes the standard for all social behaviour in the public sphere. Thus, the politician is not simply judged by his actions but also by his ability to convincingly show character and emotion in public. Sennett's well-known argument is that the ideology of 'warm' intimacy has become a tyranny that pervades society as a whole and seriously erodes the balance between the public and the private realm in the city.[13]

In discussions about urbanism we use these different models of the public/private dichotomy without really distinguishing between them: we often use them at the same time and mix them together. One example is the shifting content of critiques of the public space in the context of urban renewal.

The content of urban renewal projects in the 1970s, for example, predominantly belonged to the third model. The problem was defined in terms of sociability: the cold and

13
Especially elaborated in: Richard Sennett, *The Fall of Public Man. On the Social Psychology of Capitalism* (New York, 1978). These themes also return in Richard Sennett, *The Conscience of the Eye. The Design and Social Life of Cities* (New York, 1990), and in Richard Sennett, *Flesh and Stone. The Body and the City in Western Civilization* (New York, 1994).

deathly design of public space in accordance with the functionalist theories of late-modernist urbanism did not stimulate spontaneous, human relationships, according to this critique. Critics deplored the fact that the streets and squares of the city no longer provided obvious occasions for social contact.

One might argue that the revitalisation of the city since then has all in all been a success but has also led to the risk of the overtaking of the city centre by private businesses, as part of the boom in urban entertainment. This evolution in turn has given rise to a new kind of critique, which is formulated less in terms of sociability and more in political terms and has set its sights on urban renewal itself. It is feared that the inner city will become no more than an entertainment centre. The festivalisation of the city centre often creates commercial excesses that clash with the urban public space. Current discussions of public space precisely revolve around the concern to safeguard the fundamental statute of public space. Thus, the liberal-economistic model is foregrounded in recent critiques of the commercialisation of public space: in the eyes of critics the market is crossing its boundaries by usurping ever-larger chunks of urban life and poses a threat to the public interest.

The following scheme synthesises the three models presented so far:

	PUBLIC	PRIVATE	
liberal-economistic	government	market	*capitalism*
citizenship	political community	(oikos)	*polis*
sociability	sociability	(domesticity)	*ancient régime*

A FEMINIST MODEL

However, this scheme needs to be supplemented with a fourth model, developed through feminist criticism.

Surely the liberal-economistic model and the citizenship model – and in part the sociability model as well – have in common that they all start by filling out the public half of the dichotomy. As a result, the private half usually serves as a residual category. The feminist model reverses that order and starts by defining the private sphere as the family. In this way it makes sure that the domestic sphere is not mystified within the binary model. In the liberal-economistic model, for example, the division into public and private only relates to the part of social life that has traditionally been dominated by men, namely government and the market economy. The domestic sphere does not play a part in these environments and consequently cannot be theorised within this model.

---

public (market + government) >< *private* family

The distinction between public and private within the feminist critique is designed to reveal the asymmetry of this dichotomy in terms of gender, but does so at the cost of neglecting a very large public domain. The public sphere includes all economic and political activities outside the family and is therefore a residual category in this model. In the feminist model, the family or the domestic sphere is thematised, but market and government are relegated to the same side of the dichotomy without any distinction.

The market and the civil society[14] grafted on it, turn out to switch sides, depending on the model in which they are placed. One can offer a sociohistorical explanation for the ambivalent position of the market economy or civil society. In the Aristotelian distinction, which laid the foundations for the dichotomy of public and private, the sphere of the *oikos* or household included both family and economic life: the household was the most important institution for the organisation of production and distribution. Modernity, or the rise of the market economy, pulled these activities out of the household. Because of the increasing importance of the market economy and the development of an entire world of social relationships based on the market, the market economy could hardly be put on the same side of the binary with the family anymore. The market economy or civil society is private or public in a peculiar way, different from the way the family is private and different from the way the government is public.

14
'Civil society' is understood here as 'the social world of selfinterested individualism, competition, impersonality, and contractual relationships – centered on the market – which . . . seemed somehow able to run itself'. Weintraub, 'The Theory and Politics', op. cit. (note 10), 13.

This confusion between private and public alone, aside from any other entanglements with other divisions according to other models, shows how binary thinking about the public and the private probably poses an epistemological problem, and most definitely a terminological one as well. The binary division of public and private is not unitary and airtight. Every public/private dichotomy contains a non-reducible complexity.

THE DEFINITION OF A THIRD TERM

The distinction between public and private obviously remains an inescapable key element of Western thought. Nevertheless, it makes sense to make the limitations of the dichotomy explicit and to confront them. The political philosopher Hannah Arendt tackles the problem head-on.[15] She leaves the binary model behind and clearly defines a third domain, using a three-part model of society. She argues that the dichotomy of the public and the private is a historical model, which has been complicated since modernity through the rise of what

15
Hannah Arendt, *The Human Condition* (Chicago, 1958).

she calls the social realm. Arendt connects the social realm with the rise of mass society in the wake of a modern capitalist economy and defines it as a kind of pre-political jumbo-household.

It is tempting to introduce Arendt's three-part model into current debates on public space. But her negative qualification of the social realm makes this problematic. Because of her emphatic definition of the social realm as an apolitical area and because she cherishes the public realm like a pure hothouse flower, Arendt's tripartite model remains blind to a number of indirect power structures and political developments in the social realm and runs the risk of confirming the nostalgic litany about the loss of citizenship and public-political life.

This third term can be conceptualised in another way by considering civil society as a wider field. Rather than only centred on the market economy, civil society can be understood as a realm of several different publics, each with its own clearly defined identity. This includes neighbourhood committees, cultural organisations, environmental movements and countless other interest groups based on ethnicity, language, race, etcetera. On the one hand, they show the characteristics of a community: they share the same standards and values; they sanction their members on the basis of those standards and values; and they try to exist as a group, despite individual preferences and interests. On the other hand, their authority does not extend across society as a whole. That is why they are, in a sense, not public: they protect their members against the intervention of the government, which is on the outside, and they pursue rather more limited, particular goals than universal ones. To think about the third term in this way is closely related to the idea of micro-politics and identity-politics. Other than in Arendt's model, the third domain appears to a certain extent to be a repetition of the public domain, but within very homogeneous, independent and distinctive little reservations.

The possibility of a third term in between public and private space is also an important issue in architecture and urbanism. The Barcelona urban designer Manuel de Solà-Morales introduces a term of his own: 'Collective space is much more and much less than public space, if we limit it to public property. The wealth of a city is that of its collective spaces, of all places where everyday life takes place, presents itself, and is present as memory. And maybe they are more and more often spaces that are not public or private but both at the same time: public spaces used for private activities or private spaces that allow collective use.'[16]

Manuel de Solà-Morales gives commercial activities on public property, on the one hand, and public use of commercial spaces, on the other, a concept of their own. In one sense it resembles Arendt's social realm, because it is also a domain grafted onto the increasing importance of the market

16
Manuel de Solà-Morales, 'Openbare en collectieve ruimte: de verstedelijking van het privé-domein als nieuwe uitdaging', in: OASE no. 33 (1992), 3-8. De Solà-Morales applied these ideas convincingly in the design of the shopping mall in the building Illa in Barcelona (with R. Moneo, 1986-1994).

economy. But in De Solà-Morales's argument this domain has a positive potential as a contemporary location of public value. The pale focal points of life in the generic city, such as the supermarket, the sports centre, and the parking lot are in De Solà-Morales's eyes possible places of communal interest, as often undefined spaces where the public shape of the city is at stake. In the historic inner city of Brussels we find a classic example of both guises of collective space. The Galeries St. Hubert and the Rue des Bouchers cross each other halfway. According to a purist terminology of public space, neither would be considered as such. The Rue des Bouchers is public domain but has been completely colonised by the private activities of the restaurant business. The Galeries St. Hubert has always been open to public access, but is in fact private property. Wouldn't we put ourselves in a theoretical cul-de-sac if we were to dismiss both these marvellous urban spaces as not-public?

CLOSING

This account shows that public and private are not monolithic terms but that they vary considerably in meaning, depending on the framework within which they are used and defined. Many misunderstandings and much confusion in the current debate on public space is actually the result of the neglect of these multiple definitions of the distinction between the public and the private. Discussions in the fields of architecture and urbanism badly need more terms, more adequate terms and more specific terms to articulate and define public life. If we want to talk with some sense about an anti-Dutroux demonstration on a blue Sunday afternoon, on the parking lot of a shopping mall somewhere in the banal urban sprawl between Hasselt and Liège, we need more words than public and private.

Translated by Gert Morreel

Henk Döll	**1**	**2**	**3**	**4**	**5**	**6**	**7**	**8**	**9/10**	11	12	13	14	15	16	17	18	19	20	21	22	23	24	25	26/27	28	29	30	31	32	33	34	35	3
Peter Drijver	**1**	**2**	**3**	**4**	5	6	7	8	9/10	11	12	13	14	15	16	17	18	19	20	21	22	23	24	25	26/27	28	29	30	31	32	33	34	35	3
Miel Karthaus	**1**	**2**	**3**	**4**	5	6	7	8	9/10	11	12	13	14	15	16	17	18	19	20	21	22	23	24	25	26/27	28	29	30	31	32	33	34	35	3
Ernst Israels	**1**	**2**	**3**	**4**	5	6	7	8	9/10	11	12	13	14	15	16	17	18	19	20	21	22	23	24	25	26/27	28	29	30	31	32	33	34	35	3
Janne Hobus	**1**	**2**	**3**	**4**	**5**	6	7	8	9/10	11	12	13	14	15	16	17	18	19	20	21	22	23	24	25	26/27	28	29	30	31	32	33	34	35	3
Roy Bijhouwer	**1**	**2**	**3**	**4**	**5**	**6**	**7**	8	9/10	11	12	13	14	15	16	17	18	19	20	21	22	23	24	25	26/27	28	29	30	31	32	33	34	35	3
Dirkjan Postel	**1**	**2**	**3**	**4**	**5**	6	7	8	9/10	11	12	13	14	15	16	17	18	19	20	21	22	23	24	25	26/27	28	29	30	31	32	33	34	35	3
Karin Teunissen	**1**	2	3	4	5	6	7	8	9/10	11	12	13	14	15	16	17	18	19	20	21	22	23	24	25	26/27	28	29	30	31	32	33	34	35	3
Eric Hordijk	**1**	**2**	**3**	**4**	**5**	**6**	**7**	**8**	9/10	11	12	13	14	15	16	17	18	19	20	21	22	23	24	25	26/27	28	29	30	31	32	33	34	35	3
Paul Groenendijk	**1**	**2**	**3**	**4**	**5**	**6**	**7**	**8**	**9/10**	11	12	13	14	15	16	17	18	19	20	21	22	23	24	25	26/27	28	29	30	31	32	33	34	35	3
Reinder Nust	1	2	3	**4**	5	6	7	8	9/10	11	12	13	14	15	16	17	18	19	20	21	22	23	24	25	26/27	28	29	30	31	32	33	34	35	3
Ellen de Bruin	1	2	3	4	**5**	**6**	**7**	8	9/10	11	12	13	14	15	16	17	18	19	20	21	22	23	24	25	26/27	28	29	30	31	32	33	34	35	3
Rob van der Bijl	1	2	3	4	**5**	**6**	**7**	**8**	**9/10**	**11**	**12**	**13**	14	15	16	17	18	19	20	21	22	23	24	25	26/27	28	29	30	31	32	33	34	35	3
Arjan Hebly	1	2	3	4	**5**	**6**	**7**	**8**	**9/10**	11	12	13	14	15	16	17	18	19	20	21	22	23	24	25	26/27	28	29	30	31	32	33	34	35	3
Erik Pasveer	1	2	3	4	**5**	**6**	**7**	**8**	**9/10**	**11**	**12**	**13**	**14**	15	16	17	18	19	20	21	22	23	24	25	26/27	28	29	30	31	32	33	34	35	3
Rens Schulze	1	2	3	4	**5**	**6**	7	8	9/10	11	12	13	14	15	16	17	18	19	20	21	22	23	24	25	26/27	28	29	30	31	32	33	34	35	3
Willemijn Wilms Floet	1	2	3	4	5	6	**7**	**8**	**9/10**	**11**	**12**	13	14	15	16	17	18	19	20	21	22	23	24	25	26/27	28	29	30	31	32	33	34	35	3
Geert Hovingh	1	2	3	4	5	6	**7**	**8**	**9/10**	**11**	**12**	**13**	**14**	15	16	17	18	19	20	21	22	23	24	25	26/27	28	29	30	31	32	33	34	35	3
Dion Kooyman	1	2	3	4	5	6	**7**	**8**	**9/10**	**11**	**12**	**13**	14	15	16	17	18	19	20	21	22	23	24	25	26/27	28	29	30	31	32	33	34	35	3
Charlotte Maas	1	2	3	4	5	6	**7**	**8**	**9/10**	11	12	13	14	15	16	17	18	19	20	21	22	23	24	25	26/27	28	29	30	31	32	33	34	35	3
Dick Van Gameren	1	2	3	4	5	6	7	**8**	**9/10**	**11**	**12**	13	14	15	16	17	18	19	20	21	22	23	24	25	26/27	28	29	30	31	32	33	34	35	3
Niek Kruisheer	1	2	3	4	5	6	7	**8**	**9/10**	**11**	**12**	13	14	15	16	17	18	19	20	21	22	23	24	25	26/27	28	29	30	31	32	33	34	35	3
Niek Bisscheroux	1	2	3	4	5	6	7	8	9/10	**11**	**12**	**13**	14	15	16	17	18	19	20	21	22	23	24	25	26/27	28	29	30	31	32	33	34	35	3
Geneviève van Helden	1	2	3	4	5	6	7	8	9/10	**11**	**12**	13	14	15	16	17	18	19	20	21	22	23	24	25	26/27	28	29	30	31	32	33	34	35	3
Mark Visser	1	2	3	4	5	6	7	8	9/10	**11**	12	13	14	15	16	17	18	19	20	21	22	23	24	25	26/27	28	29	30	31	32	33	34	35	3
Ruth Visser	1	2	3	4	5	6	7	8	9/10	**11**	**12**	13	14	15	16	17	18	19	20	21	22	23	24	25	26/27	28	29	30	31	32	33	34	35	3
Erwin Zantman	1	2	3	4	5	6	7	8	9/10	**11**	**12**	**13**	**14**	**15**	**16**	**17**	**18**	**19**	**20**	**21**	**22**	**23**	**24**	**25**	**26/27**	**28**	**29**	30	31	32	33	34	35	3
Rients Dijkstra	1	2	3	4	5	6	7	8	9/10	11	12	13	**14**	**15**	**16**	17	18	19	20	21	22	23	24	25	26/27	28	29	30	31	32	33	34	35	3
Esther Gramsbergen	1	2	3	4	5	6	7	8	9/10	11	12	13	**14**	**15**	**16**	17	18	19	20	21	22	23	24	25	26/27	28	29	30	31	32	33	34	35	3
Frans Sturkenboom	1	2	3	4	5	6	7	8	9/10	11	12	13	**14**	**15**	**16**	**17**	**18**	**19**	**20**	**21**	**22**	23	24	25	26/27	**28**	**29**	**30**	**31**	**32**	**33**	**34**	35	3
Endry van Velzen	1	2	3	4	5	6	7	8	9/10	11	12	13	**14**	**15**	**16**	**17**	**18**	**19**	**20**	**21**	**22**	**23**	**24**	**25**	**26/27**	**28**	**29**	**30**	**31**	**32**	**33**	**34**	**35**	**3**
Erik Terlouw	1	2	3	4	5	6	7	8	9/10	11	12	13	14	**15**	**16**	**17**	**18**	**19**	**20**	**21**	**22**	**23**	**24**	**25**	**26/27**	**28**	**29**	**30**	**31**	**32**	**33**	**34**	**35**	**3**
Pieter van Wesemael	1	2	3	4	5	6	7	8	9/10	11	12	13	14	**15**	**16**	**17**	**18**	**19**	**20**	**21**	**22**	**23**	**24**	**25**	**26/27**	**28**	**29**	**30**	**31**	**32**	**33**	**34**	**35**	**3**
Hans Berger	1	2	3	4	5	6	7	8	9/10	11	12	13	14	15	16	17	**18**	**19**	**20**	**21**	22	23	24	25	26/27	28	29	30	31	32	33	34	35	3
Bart Goldhoorn	1	2	3	4	5	6	7	8	9/10	11	12	13	14	15	16	17	**18**	**19**	**20**	**21**	**22**	**23**	**24**	**25**	**26/27**	**28**	**29**	**30**	**31**	**32**	33	34	35	3
Jurjen Zeinstra	1	2	3	4	5	6	7	8	9/10	11	12	13	14	15	16	17	**18**	**19**	**20**	**21**	**22**	**23**	**24**	**25**	**26/27**	**28**	**29**	**30**	**31**	**32**	**33**	**34**	**35**	**3**
Michiel Riedijk	1	2	3	4	5	6	7	8	9/10	11	12	13	14	15	16	17	18	**19**	**20**	**21**	**22**	**23**	**24**	**25**	**26/27**	**28**	**29**	**30**	**31**	**32**	**33**	**34**	**35**	**3**
Lisl Edhoffer	1	2	3	4	5	6	7	8	9/10	11	12	13	14	15	16	17	18	19	20	21	**22**	**23**	**24**	**25**	**26/27**	28	29	30	31	32	33	34	35	3
Willem Sulsters	1	2	3	4	5	6	7	8	9/10	11	12	13	14	15	16	17	18	19	20	21	**22**	**23**	**24**	**25**	**26/27**	**28**	**29**	**30**	**31**	**32**	**33**	**34**	**35**	**3**
Juliëtte Bekkering	1	2	3	4	5	6	7	8	9/10	11	12	13	14	15	16	17	18	19	20	21	22	23	24	25	26/27	**28**	**29**	**30**	**31**	**32**	**33**	**34**	**35**	**3**
Wim van den Bergh	1	2	3	4	5	6	7	8	9/10	11	12	13	14	15	16	17	18	19	20	21	22	23	24	25	26/27	28	29	30	31	32	33	34	**35**	**3**
Christiaan Borret	1	2	3	4	5	6	7	8	9/10	11	12	13	14	15	16	17	18	19	20	21	22	23	24	25	26/27	28	29	30	31	32	33	34	**35**	**3**
Mikel van Gelderen	1	2	3	4	5	6	7	8	9/10	11	12	13	14	15	16	17	18	19	20	21	22	23	24	25	26/27	28	29	30	31	32	33	34	**35**	**3**
Christophe Grafe	1	2	3	4	5	6	7	8	9/10	11	12	13	14	15	16	17	18	19	20	21	22	23	24	25	26/27	28	29	30	31	32	33	34	**35**	**3**
Dirk van den Heuvel	1	2	3	4	5	6	7	8	9/10	11	12	13	14	15	16	17	18	19	20	21	22	23	24	25	26/27	28	29	30	31	32	33	34	**35**	**3**
Harm Tilman	1	2	3	4	5	6	7	8	9/10	11	12	13	14	15	16	17	18	19	20	21	22	23	24	25	26/27	28	29	30	31	32	33	34	**35**	**3**
François Claessens	1	2	3	4	5	6	7	8	9/10	11	12	13	14	15	16	17	18	19	20	21	22	23	24	25	26/27	28	29	30	31	32	33	34	35	3
Vincent Kompier	1	2	3	4	5	6	7	8	9/10	11	12	13	14	15	16	17	18	19	20	21	22	23	24	25	26/27	28	29	30	31	32	33	34	35	3
Marcel Musch	1	2	3	4	5	6	7	8	9/10	11	12	13	14	15	16	17	18	19	20	21	22	23	24	25	26/27	28	29	30	31	32	33	34	35	3
Sanna Schuiling	1	2	3	4	5	6	7	8	9/10	11	12	13	14	15	16	17	18	19	20	21	22	23	24	25	26/27	28	29	30	31	32	33	34	35	3
Udo Garritzmann	1	2	3	4	5	6	7	8	9/10	11	12	13	14	15	16	17	18	19	20	21	22	23	24	25	26/27	28	29	30	31	32	33	34	35	3
Mechthild Stuhlmacher	1	2	3	4	5	6	7	8	9/10	11	12	13	14	15	16	17	18	19	20	21	22	23	24	25	26/27	28	29	30	31	32	33	34	35	3
Like Bijlsma	1	2	3	4	5	6	7	8	9/10	11	12	13	14	15	16	17	18	19	20	21	22	23	24	25	26/27	28	29	30	31	32	33	34	35	3
Wouter Deen	1	2	3	4	5	6	7	8	9/10	11	12	13	14	15	16	17	18	19	20	21	22	23	24	25	26/27	28	29	30	31	32	33	34	35	3
Eireen Schreurs	1	2	3	4	5	6	7	8	9/10	11	12	13	14	15	16	17	18	19	20	21	22	23	24	25	26/27	28	29	30	31	32	33	34	35	3
Ivan Nio	1	2	3	4	5	6	7	8	9/10	11	12	13	14	15	16	17	18	19	20	21	22	23	24	25	26/27	28	29	30	31	32	33	34	35	3
Lara Schrijver	1	2	3	4	5	6	7	8	9/10	11	12	13	14	15	16	17	18	19	20	21	22	23	24	25	26/27	28	29	30	31	32	33	34	35	3
Marc Glaudemans	1	2	3	4	5	6	7	8	9/10	11	12	13	14	15	16	17	18	19	20	21	22	23	24	25	26/27	28	29	30	31	32	33	34	35	3
D'Laine Camp	1	2	3	4	5	6	7	8	9/10	11	12	13	14	15	16	17	18	19	20	21	22	23	24	25	26/27	28	29	30	31	32	33	34	35	3
Madeleine Maaskant	1	2	3	4	5	6	7	8	9/10	11	12	13	14	15	16	17	18	19	20	21	22	23	24	25	26/27	28	29	30	31	32	33	34	35	3
Marc Schoonderbeek	1	2	3	4	5	6	7	8	9/10	11	12	13	14	15	16	17	18	19	20	21	22	23	24	25	26/27	28	29	30	31	32	33	34	35	3
Tom Avermaete	1	2	3	4	5	6	7	8	9/10	11	12	13	14	15	16	17	18	19	20	21	22	23	24	25	26/27	28	29	30	31	32	33	34	35	3
Pnina Avidar	1	2	3	4	5	6	7	8	9/10	11	12	13	14	15	16	17	18	19	20	21	22	23	24	25	26/27	28	29	30	31	32	33	34	35	3
Filip Geerts	1	2	3	4	5	6	7	8	9/10	11	12	13	14	15	16	17	18	19	20	21	22	23	24	25	26/27	28	29	30	31	32	33	34	35	3
Johan Lagae	1	2	3	4	5	6	7	8	9/10	11	12	13	14	15	16	17	18	19	20	21	22	23	24	25	26/27	28	29	30	31	32	33	34	35	3
Willemijn Lofvers	1	2	3	4	5	6	7	8	9/10	11	12	13	14	15	16	17	18	19	20	21	22	23	24	25	26/27	28	29	30	31	32	33	34	35	3
Max Cohen de Lara	1	2	3	4	5	6	7	8	9/10	11	12	13	14	15	16	17	18	19	20	21	22	23	24	25	26/27	28	29	30	31	32	33	34	35	3
David Mulder	1	2	3	4	5	6	7	8	9/10	11	12	13	14	15	16	17	18	19	20	21	22	23	24	25	26/27	28	29	30	31	32	33	34	35	3
Klaske Havik	1	2	3	4	5	6	7	8	9/10	11	12	13	14	15	16	17	18	19	20	21	22	23	24	25	26/27	28	29	30	31	32	33	34	35	3
Véronique Patteeuw	1	2	3	4	5	6	7	8	9/10	11	12	13	14	15	16	17	18	19	20	21	22	23	24	25	26/27	28	29	30	31	32	33	34	35	3
Joachim Declerck	1	2	3	4	5	6	7	8	9/10	11	12	13	14	15	16	17	18	19	20	21	22	23	24	25	26/27	28	29	30	31	32	33	34	35	3
Anne Holtrop	1	2	3	4	5	6	7	8	9/10	11	12	13	14	15	16	17	18	19	20	21	22	23	24	25	26/27	28	29	30	31	32	33	34	35	3
Joks Janssen	1	2	3	4	5	6	7	8	9/10	11	12	13	14	15	16	17	18	19	20	21	22	23	24	25	26/27	28	29	30	31	32	33	34	35	3

OASE #75

EDITORS

Issues	Editor
39 40 41 42 43 44 45/46 47 48 49/50 51 52 53 54 55 56 57 58 59 60 61 62 63 64 65 66 67 68 69 70 71 72 73 74	**Henk Döll**
39 40 41 42 43 44 45/46 47 48 49/50 51 52 53 54 55 56 57 58 59 60 61 62 63 64 65 66 67 68 69 70 71 72 73 74	**Peter Drijver**
39 40 41 42 43 44 45/46 47 48 49/50 51 52 53 54 55 56 57 58 59 60 61 62 63 64 65 66 67 68 69 70 71 72 73 74	**Miel Karthaus**
39 40 41 42 43 44 45/46 47 48 49/50 51 52 53 54 55 56 57 58 59 60 61 62 63 64 65 66 67 68 69 70 71 72 73 74	**Ernst Israels**
39 40 41 42 43 44 45/46 47 48 49/50 51 52 53 54 55 56 57 58 59 60 61 62 63 64 65 66 67 68 69 70 71 72 73 74	**Janne Hobus**
39 40 41 42 43 44 45/46 47 48 49/50 51 52 53 54 55 56 57 58 59 60 61 62 63 64 65 66 67 68 69 70 71 72 73 74	**Roy Bijhouwer**
39 40 41 42 43 44 45/46 47 48 49/50 51 52 53 54 55 56 57 58 59 60 61 62 63 64 65 66 67 68 69 70 71 72 73 74	**Dirkjan Postel**
39 40 41 42 43 44 45/46 47 48 49/50 51 52 53 54 55 56 57 58 59 60 61 62 63 64 65 66 67 68 69 70 71 72 73 74	**Karin Teunissen**
39 40 41 42 43 44 45/46 47 48 49/50 51 52 53 54 55 56 57 58 59 60 61 62 63 64 65 66 67 68 69 70 71 72 73 74	**Eric Hordijk**
39 40 41 42 43 44 45/46 47 48 49/50 51 52 53 54 55 56 57 58 59 60 61 62 63 64 65 66 67 68 69 70 71 72 73 74	**Paul Groenendijk**
39 40 41 42 43 44 45/46 47 48 49/50 51 52 53 54 55 56 57 58 59 60 61 62 63 64 65 66 67 68 69 70 71 72 73 74	**Reinder Nust**
39 40 41 42 43 44 45/46 47 48 49/50 51 52 53 54 55 56 57 58 59 60 61 62 63 64 65 66 67 68 69 70 71 72 73 74	**Ellen de Bruin**
39 40 41 42 43 44 45/46 47 48 49/50 51 52 53 54 55 56 57 58 59 60 61 62 63 64 65 66 67 68 69 70 71 72 73 74	**Rob van der Bijl**
39 40 41 42 43 44 45/46 47 48 49/50 51 52 53 54 55 56 57 58 59 60 61 62 63 64 65 66 67 68 69 70 71 72 73 74	**Arjan Hebly**
39 40 41 42 43 44 45/46 47 48 49/50 51 52 53 54 55 56 57 58 59 60 61 62 63 64 65 66 67 68 69 70 71 72 73 74	**Erik Pasveer**
39 40 41 42 43 44 45/46 47 48 49/50 51 52 53 54 55 56 57 58 59 60 61 62 63 64 65 66 67 68 69 70 71 72 73 74	**Rens Schulze**
39 40 41 42 43 44 45/46 47 48 49/50 51 52 53 54 55 56 57 58 59 60 61 62 63 64 65 66 67 68 69 70 71 72 73 74	**Willemijn Wilms Floet**
39 40 41 42 43 44 45/46 47 48 49/50 51 52 53 54 55 56 57 58 59 60 61 62 63 64 65 66 67 68 69 70 71 72 73 74	**Geert Hovingh**
39 40 41 42 43 44 45/46 47 48 49/50 51 52 53 54 55 56 57 58 59 60 61 62 63 64 65 66 67 68 69 70 71 72 73 74	**Dion Kooyman**
39 40 41 42 43 44 45/46 47 48 49/50 51 52 53 54 55 56 57 58 59 60 61 62 63 64 65 66 67 68 69 70 71 72 73 74	**Charlotte Maas**
39 40 41 42 43 44 45/46 47 48 49/50 51 52 53 54 55 56 57 58 59 60 61 62 63 64 65 66 67 68 69 70 71 72 73 74	**Dick Van Gameren**
39 40 41 42 43 44 45/46 47 48 49/50 51 52 53 54 55 56 57 58 59 60 61 62 63 64 65 66 67 68 69 70 71 72 73 74	**Niek Kruisheer**
39 40 41 42 43 44 45/46 47 48 49/50 51 52 53 54 55 56 57 58 59 60 61 62 63 64 65 66 67 68 69 70 71 72 73 74	**Niek Bisscheroux**
39 40 41 42 43 44 45/46 47 48 49/50 51 52 53 54 55 56 57 58 59 60 61 62 63 64 65 66 67 68 69 70 71 72 73 74	**Geneviève van Helden**
39 40 41 42 43 44 45/46 47 48 49/50 51 52 53 54 55 56 57 58 59 60 61 62 63 64 65 66 67 68 69 70 71 72 73 74	**Mark Visser**
39 40 41 42 43 44 45/46 47 48 49/50 51 52 53 54 55 56 57 58 59 60 61 62 63 64 65 66 67 68 69 70 71 72 73 74	**Ruth Visser**
39 40 41 42 43 44 45/46 47 48 49/50 51 52 53 54 55 56 57 58 59 60 61 62 63 64 65 66 67 68 69 70 71 72 73 74	**Erwin Zantman**
39 40 41 42 43 44 45/46 47 48 49/50 51 52 53 54 55 56 57 58 59 60 61 62 63 64 65 66 67 68 69 70 71 72 73 74	**Rients Dijkstra**
39 40 41 42 43 44 45/46 47 48 49/50 51 52 53 54 55 56 57 58 59 60 61 62 63 64 65 66 67 68 69 70 71 72 73 74	**Esther Gramsbergen**
39 40 41 42 43 44 45/46 47 48 49/50 51 52 53 54 55 56 57 58 59 60 61 62 63 64 65 66 67 68 69 70 71 72 73 74	**Frans Sturkenboom**
39 40 41 42 43 44 45/46 47 48 49/50 51 52 53 54 55 56 57 58 59 60 61 62 63 64 65 66 67 68 69 70 71 72 73 74	**Endry van Velzen**
39 40 41 42 43 44 45/46 47 48 49/50 51 52 53 54 55 56 57 58 59 60 61 62 63 64 65 66 67 68 69 70 71 72 73 74	**Erik Terlouw**
39 40 41 42 43 44 45/46 47 48 49/50 51 52 53 54 55 56 57 58 59 60 61 62 63 64 65 66 67 68 69 70 71 72 73 74	**Pieter van Wesemael**
39 40 41 42 43 44 45/46 47 48 49/50 51 52 53 54 55 56 57 58 59 60 61 62 63 64 65 66 67 68 69 70 71 72 73 74	**Hans Berger**
39 40 41 42 43 44 45/46 47 48 49/50 51 52 53 54 55 56 57 58 59 60 61 62 63 64 65 66 67 68 69 70 71 72 73 74	**Bart Goldhoorn**
39 40 41 42 43 44 45/46 47 48 49/50 51 52 53 54 55 56 57 58 59 60 61 62 63 64 65 66 67 68 69 70 71 72 73 74	**Jurjen Zeinstra**
39 40 41 42 43 44 45/46 47 48 49/50 51 52 53 54 55 56 57 58 59 60 61 62 63 64 65 66 67 68 69 70 71 72 73 74	**Michiel Riedijk**
39 40 41 42 43 44 45/46 47 48 49/50 51 52 53 54 55 56 57 58 59 60 61 62 63 64 65 66 67 68 69 70 71 72 73 74	**Lisl Edhoffer**
39 40 41 42 43 44 45/46 47 48 49/50 51 52 53 54 55 56 57 58 59 60 61 62 63 64 65 66 67 68 69 70 71 72 73 74	**Willem Sulsters**
39 40 41 42 43 44 45/46 47 48 49/50 51 52 53 54 55 56 57 58 59 60 61 62 63 64 65 66 67 68 69 70 71 72 73 74	**Juliëtte Bekkering**
39 40 41 42 43 44 45/46 47 48 49/50 51 52 53 54 55 56 57 58 59 60 61 62 63 64 65 66 67 68 69 70 71 72 73 74	**Wim van den Bergh**
39 40 41 42 43 44 45/46 47 48 49/50 51 52 53 54 55 56 57 58 59 60 61 62 63 64 65 66 67 68 69 70 71 72 73 74	**Christiaan Borret**
39 40 41 42 43 44 45/46 47 48 49/50 51 52 53 54 55 56 57 58 59 60 61 62 63 64 65 66 67 68 69 70 71 72 73 74	**Mikel van Gelderen**
39 40 41 42 43 44 45/46 47 48 49/50 51 52 53 54 55 56 57 58 59 60 61 62 63 64 65 66 67 68 69 70 71 72 73 74	**Christophe Grafe**
39 40 41 42 43 44 45/46 47 48 49/50 51 52 53 54 55 56 57 58 59 60 61 62 63 64 65 66 67 68 69 70 71 72 73 74	**Dirk van den Heuvel**
39 40 41 42 43 44 45/46 47 48 49/50 51 52 53 54 55 56 57 58 59 60 61 62 63 64 65 66 67 68 69 70 71 72 73 74	**Harm Tilman**
39 40 41 42 43 44 45/46 47 48 49/50 51 52 53 54 55 56 57 58 59 60 61 62 63 64 65 66 67 68 69 70 71 72 73 74	**François Claessens**
39 40 41 42 43 44 45/46 47 48 49/50 51 52 53 54 55 56 57 58 59 60 61 62 63 64 65 66 67 68 69 70 71 72 73 74	**Vincent Kompier**
39 40 **41 42 43 44 45/46 47 48 49/50 51 52 53 54 55 56 57 58 59 60 61 62 63 64** 65 66 67 68 69 70 71 72 73 74	**Marcel Musch**
39 40 **41 42 43 44 45/46 47** 48 49/50 51 52 53 54 55 56 57 58 59 60 61 62 63 64 65 66 67 68 69 70 71 72 73 74	**Sanna Schuiling**
39 40 41 **42 43 44 45/46 47 48 49/50 51 52 53** 54 55 56 57 58 59 60 61 62 63 64 65 66 67 68 69 70 71 72 73 74	**Udo Garritzmann**
39 40 41 **42 43 44 45/46 47 48 49/50 51 52 53 54 55 56 57 58 59 60 61 62 63 64 65 66 67 68 69 70 71 72 73 74**	**Mechthild Stuhlmacher**
39 40 41 42 43 44 **45/46 47 48 49/50 51 52 53 54 55 56 57 58 59 60 61 62 63 64 65 66 67 68 69 70** 71 72 73 74	**Like Bijlsma**
39 40 41 42 43 44 **45/46 47 48 49/50 51 52 53** 54 55 56 57 58 59 60 61 62 63 64 65 66 67 68 69 70 71 72 73 74	**Wouter Deen**
39 40 41 42 43 44 **45/46 47 48 49/50 51** 52 53 **54 55 56 57** 58 59 60 61 62 63 64 65 66 67 68 69 70 71 72 73 74	**Eireen Schreurs**
39 40 41 42 43 44 45/46 47 **48 49/50 51 52 53** 54 55 56 57 58 59 60 61 62 63 64 65 66 67 68 69 70 71 72 73 74	**Ivan Nio**
39 40 41 42 43 44 45/46 47 **48 49/50 51 52 53 54 55 56 57 58 59 60 61 62 63 64 65 66 67 68 69 70 71 72 73 74**	**Lara Schrijver**
39 40 41 42 43 44 45/46 47 48 49/50 51 52 53 **54 55 56** 57 **58** 59 60 61 62 63 64 65 66 67 68 69 70 71 72 73 74	**Marc Glaudemans**
39 40 41 42 43 44 45/46 47 48 49/50 51 52 53 **54 55 56 57 58 59 60 61 62 63 64 65 66 67 68 69 70 71 72 73 74**	**D'Laine Camp**
39 40 41 42 43 44 45/46 47 48 49/50 51 52 53 **54 55 56 57 58 59 60 61 62 63 64 65 66 67 68 69 70** 71 72 73 74	**Madeleine Maaskant**
39 40 41 42 43 44 45/46 47 48 49/50 51 52 53 54 55 56 **57 58 59 60 61 62 63 64 65 66 67 68 69 70 71** 72 73 74	**Marc Schoonderbeek**
39 40 41 42 43 44 45/46 47 48 49/50 51 52 53 54 55 56 57 **58 59 60 61 62 63 64 65 66 67 68 69 70 71 72 73 74**	**Tom Avermaete**
39 40 41 42 43 44 45/46 47 48 49/50 51 52 53 54 55 56 57 **58 59 60 61 62 63 64 65 66 67 68 69 70 71 72 73 74**	**Pnina Avidar**
39 40 41 42 43 44 45/46 47 48 49/50 51 52 53 54 55 56 57 58 59 60 **61 62 63 64 65 66 67 68 69 70 71 72** 73 74	**Filip Geerts**
39 40 41 42 43 44 45/46 47 48 49/50 51 52 53 54 55 56 57 58 59 60 61 **62 63 64 65 66 67 68 69 70 71 72 73 74**	**Johan Lagae**
39 40 41 42 43 44 45/46 47 48 49/50 51 52 53 54 55 56 57 58 59 60 61 62 **63** 64 65 66 67 68 69 70 71 72 73 74	**Willemijn Lofvers**
39 40 41 42 43 44 45/46 47 48 49/50 51 52 53 54 55 56 57 58 59 60 61 62 63 64 65 **66 67 68** 69 70 71 72 73 74	**Max Cohen de Lara**
39 40 41 42 43 44 45/46 47 48 49/50 51 52 53 54 55 56 57 58 59 60 61 62 63 64 65 **66 67 68 69 70 71 72 73** 74	**David Mulder**
39 40 41 42 43 44 45/46 47 48 49/50 51 52 53 54 55 56 57 58 59 60 61 62 63 64 65 66 67 68 **69 70 71 72 73 74**	**Klaske Havik**
39 40 41 42 43 44 45/46 47 48 49/50 51 52 53 54 55 56 57 58 59 60 61 62 63 64 65 66 67 68 69 **70 71 72 73 74**	**Véronique Patteeuw**
39 40 41 42 43 44 45/46 47 48 49/50 51 52 53 54 55 56 57 58 59 60 61 62 63 64 65 66 67 68 69 70 71 **72 73 74**	**Joachim Declerck**
39 40 41 42 43 44 45/46 47 48 49/50 51 52 53 54 55 56 57 58 59 60 61 62 63 64 65 66 67 68 69 70 71 **72 73 74**	**Anne Holtrop**
39 40 41 42 43 44 45/46 47 48 49/50 51 52 53 54 55 56 57 58 59 60 61 62 63 64 65 66 67 68 69 70 71 **72** 73 74	**Joks Janssen**

Geert Bekaert
is professor emeritus in architecture history and theory at the KU Leuven (Flemish Catholic University of Leuven) and Eindhoven University of Technology. In 1972 he was awarded the Pierre Bayle Prize for architecture criticism and in 1978 the Rotterdam-Maaskant Prize, the *De Standaard* Prize and the Prize of the Province of Antwerp. His publications and television programmes mainly concern modern art and architecture. The majority of his writings have been collected in *Collected Essays*, the first four volumes of which (up to 1985) have been published. At the moment he is working on two volumes for the *De Standaard* Architecture Library, on Belgian architecture from 1945 to 1987 and from 2000 to 2008.

Juliette Bekkering
is president of Bekkering Adams Architects. Completed projects include the Boostergemaal-Oost pumping station in Amsterdam, the borough offices of Maashaven O.Z. de Zuidpunt and the fire station and ambulance dispatch centre of Vlissingen Middelburg. The firm is currently working on the main offices of Elektrokern Schuurman, a forensic youth psychiatry clinic in Amsterdam and an urban-design ensemble incorporating various public buildings and housing. Juliette Bekkering teaches and lectures at various architecture programmes and universities in the Netherlands and abroad. She is frequently asked to take part in competition juries (Czech National Award for Architecture, BNA-kubus, Maaskant Prize for Young Architects, Archiprix), consultation committees (Hoogvliet International Building Exhibition Professional Conclave, High-Rise Team Rotterdam), master classes and debates.

Roy Bijhouwer
is an urban designer and architect. He is co-president of the Quadrat office for urban design and landscape architecture in Rotterdam. Designs by Quadrat include the compact urban residential district of Dichterwijk in Utrecht, the 'city gardens' park in Amstelveen and the residential districts of Horsterveld in Zeewolde and Veldhuizen in Leidsche Rijn. In addition, he is a guest lecturer at Delft University of Technology and the Academy of Architecture in Amsterdam. He is a member of the editorial staff of the *Yearbook for Urban Design and Landscape Architecture* and has contributed to various publications on reconstruction in Amsterdam and Rotterdam.

Like Bijlsma
is an architect and geographer. She is the co-founder of the design firm SUB Office and also works as a researcher at the Netherlands Institute for Spatial Research. She is co-author of *The Intermediate: A Handbook for Collective Residential Buildings* and writes regularly about subjects related to typology and collectivity.

Luuk Boelens
earned a degree in urban design from Delft University of Technology and earned his doctorate in the sociogenesis of urban design, planning and philosophy with the thesis 'Urban Design and Planning – An Unfinished Project: Toward a Communicative Approach to Urban Development and Design'. Boelens is a special professor of planning at Utrecht University, a chair established by the Ministry of Housing, Spatial Planning and the Environment and dealing with mobility and spatial planning.

René Boomkens
is a professor of social and cultural philosophy at the University of Groningen and professor of popular music at the University of Amsterdam. As a philosopher and writer, Boomkens has taught and organised courses at the universities of Nijmegen and Amsterdam. He also worked as a programme organiser for De Balie in Amsterdam. He was the founding editor of the journal *Krisis* (1980-1993) and has published widely on many aspects of contemporary and popular culture. Boomkens earned his doctorate with a thesis on the philosophy of the modern city and experience and public life in modern urban environments: 'The "Middle Landscape" and the Myth of Mobility: Coming Home in Commuter Country'.

François Claessens
graduated in architecture at Delft University of Technology and in philosophy at the University of Amsterdam. He has worked for various architecture offices in the Netherlands. In 2005 he finished his doctoral research on the architectural discourse on the city in Germany around 1900. He is now an associate professor of architectural design at Delft University of Technology. In 2007 Claessens was affiliated as a research fellow with the German Institute for Art History in Paris.

Bernard Colenbrander
is a professor of architecture history and theory at Eindhoven University of Technology. He worked for many years at the Netherlands Architecture Institute in Rotterdam, ultimately as chief curator. Among his publications are *Style: Standard and Signature in Dutch Architecture* (1993), *Reference: OMA* (1995), and *De Verstrooide Stad* (The Dispersed City), his doctoral thesis (1999). Starting in 2000 he worked part time for the Ministry of Education, Culture and Science, responsible for policy concerning spatial planning. He also started his independent research practice. Since 2001 he has chronicled the planning process of the rebuilding of Roombeek, Enschede, an urban area destroyed by a fireworks-factory explosion the previous year. His recent books include a monograph on the Dutch architect Frans van Gool (2005) and, in collaboration with MUST and DaF Architects, the *Limes Atlas* (2005), describing the spatial setting of the Dutch part of the ancient Roman frontier.

Maarten Delbeke
teaches architecture history and theory at the universities of Ghent and Leiden, and is a post-doctoral fellow with the Science Foundation of Flanders. Previously a Scott Opler Research Fellow at Worcester College, Oxford, and a visiting scholar at the Canadian Centre for Architecture, he is the author of several essays and a forthcoming book on seventeenth-century art and theory. With Evonne Levy and Steven Ostrow he was a co-editor of *Bernini's Biographies: Critical Essays* (Penn State University Press, 2006). His architecture criticism has appeared in journals and books, and he co-curated the exhibition *Homeward: Contemporary Architecture in Flanders*, shown at the 2000 Venice Biennale.

Henk Döll
is an architect. He works with a team of 25 professionals on a variety of projects in the Netherlands and abroad. Recent projects include the Toneelschuur theatre and film house and the Johannes Enschedé Hof housing complex for elderly residents in Haarlem, the

New Limits apartment complex in IJsselstein en the Holland Haus in Hamburg. He frequently works with other disciplines in order to explore the limits of the field and make a contribution in addressing current social issues. This has resulted, among other things, in the book *Ground-up City – Play as a Design Tool* and the founding of the *Sustainable Dance Club.* Henk Döll was the founder of, and for over 20 years a partner in, Mecanoo Architects. In addition he has been a visiting professor at Vienna University of Technology and the University of Michigan.

Henk Engel
graduated as an architect from Delft University of Technology in 1981. He is at present co-director of the architecture office De Nijl Architects in Rotterdam, with three partners. In 1998 his office had an exhibition on their work at the Netherlands Architecture Institute, accompanied by the publication *Als we huizen bouwen, praten en schrijven we* (As we build houses, we talk and we write, NAi Publishers, 1998). Engel is an associate professor of architectural design at Delft University of Technology and teaches at several architecture academies in the Netherlands. He has been a visiting lecturer in Liverpool, Milan and Pescara. He has written extensively on various topics concerning modern and urban architecture and worked on several exhibitions.

Udo Garritzmann
is founder of Garritzmann Architects in Rotterdam and teaches and conducts research at the Faculty of Architecture of Delft University of Technology. He graduated from Delft University of Technology in 1993 and holds a Master in Design Studies from the Harvard University Graduate School of Design (2004). Before starting his own office he worked as project architect with de Architecten Cie./Frits van Dongen and OMA/Rem Koolhaas on large-scale buildings and urban-design projects. From 1995 to 2000 he was a member of the editorial board of *OASE*.

Bart Goldhoorn
was trained as an architect at Delft University of Technology. In 1995 he founded the Russian architecture journal *PROJECT RUSSIA* in Moscow, followed by *PROJECT International* in 2001 and *PROJECT Baltia* in 2007. He has been interviewed frequently in Russia by publications, radio and television. As a specialist in post-Communist architecture, he has lectured and published in various European countries as well as the USA. He is currently the curator of the first Moscow Architecture Biennale, the theme of which is housing.

Arjan Hebly
is president of Hebly Theunissen Architects in Delft. He has taught at various academic institutions, including Delft University of Technology and the Academies of Architecture in Amsterdam, Rotterdam and Tilburg. He has a variety of publications and research projects to his name, on subjects including architecture, urban design, commercial estates and contextual design. The work of his architecture firm consists mainly of renewing aging neighbourhoods and residential districts, such as the Horsten in Rotterdam, Tuindorp in Sneek and the Bomenwijk in Delft.

Jan de Heer
is the author of such publications as *Kleur en Architectuur* (Colour and Architecture) and *The Towers of Hendrick de Keyser and the Horizon of Amsterdam*, and edited the book *Carel Weeber 'ex'architect* with Umberto Barbieri and Hans Oldewarris.

Dirk van den Heuvel
is an architect, curator and assistant professor at Delft University of Technology. Together with Max Risselada, he authored *Alison and Peter Smithson – From the House of the Future to a house of today* and *Team 10 (1953-1981): In Search of a Utopia of the Present*. He was an editor for *OASE* from 1993 to 1999. He is on the editorial board of *Footprint*, the online journal of the Delft School of Design, and he is editor of *Delft Architectural Studies in Housing* (*DASH*), a new series to be published by NAi Publishers. He loves to write for the New York-based *PIN-UP* magazine and the Dutch website *ArchiNed*. Currently, he is preparing an exhibition for the Netherlands Architecture Institute-Maastricht: 'Changing Ideals – Re-inventing Domesticity'. In his spare time he runs the Institute for Ordinariness and Light.

Miel Karthaus
is co-founder of MYJ, an office for architecture, urban design and restoration. MYJ's expertise particularly lies in complex projects in which the rezoning of existing structures and new construction come together. Prior to this, he worked for Braaksma & Roos Architects.

Michel J. van Nieuwstadt
is a philosopher and writes about architecture for the newspaper *NRC Handelsblad*.

Wim Nijenhuis
is a theorist and historian of urban design. In 2003 he earned his doctorate from the Chair of Architecture History and Theory programme at Eindhoven University of Technology. He has produced radio programmes on Paul Virilio and taught at universities and academies in the Netherlands and abroad. Alone and with others he has published various works on architecture, including *Eating Brazil* (1999) and *De diabolische snelweg* (The Diabolical Highway, 2008). In 2009 the English-language commercial edition of his thesis, *The Integral City*, will be published. Nijenhuis teaches at Ghent University, de Fontys Academy for Architecture and Urban Design in Tilburg and the Artez Academy for Architecture in Arnhem.

Joost Meuwissen
graduated from Delft University of Technology and obtained a doctorate at Eindhoven University of Technology. Since 1986 he has been editor-in-chief of the *Wiederhall Architectural Serial*. Meuwissen was a partner in One Architecture in Amsterdam from 1995 to 2000 and head of the Institute of Urbanism and Environmental Design at Graz University of Technology in Austria from 2000 to 2002. He has given numerous lectures in Europe and the USA and contributed critical writings to various publications on architecture. Joost Meuwissen is currently a successor of Michael Sorkin in the Chair of Urbanism at the Vienna Academy of Fine Arts and a full partner in Grubbauer Meuwissen Architects in Graz, Austria.

Marcel Musch
is an architect and urban-design consultant. As assistant to Max Risselada, he did research on Hans Scharoun and Jean Prouvé and was involved, among other things, in the exhibition 'Functionalism 1927-1961'. He was one of the organisers of the 'Context & Modernity'

symposium (1990). He has taught at Delft University of Technology and the Academies of Architecture in Amsterdam and Rotterdam. He has written articles about private commissions and construction code-free building, land politics, rural development and the relationship between structural visions and urban design. He is currently working at the BVR consultancy, where he works on plans for urban redevelopment.

Michiel Riedijk
studied at Delft University of Technology and worked in partnership with Juliette Bekkering from 1989 to 1991. Since 1991 he has worked in partnership with Willem Jan Neutelings at Neutelings Riedijk Architects in Rotterdam. He has taught at various architecture institutions, including the Berlage Institute in Rotterdam and Delft University of Technology, and was a visiting professor at the F.W.T.H. in Achen. He has been a professor at the Faculty of Architecture at Delft University of Technology since 2007.

Frans Sturkenboom
is an architect based in Arnhem. He has taught at Eindhoven University of Technology and at various academies of architecture in the Netherlands. He has previously published articles on Frank Lloyd Wright, on Francesco Borromini and on tectonics and housing.

Willem Sulsters
studied architecture at Delft University of Technology and urban design at the Technical University of Catalonia in Spain. He has taught at Delft University of Technology, architecture academies and Ghent University. He has written about the city, research (mental mapping) and urban development in various journals. With the office WSA Stedelijke Ontwikkeling he was active for a decade in the consultancy and management of the development of inner-city residential areas in The Hague, Rotterdam and Amsterdam. As president of TCN Concepts, he is currently active in concept development for various buildings and areas.

Erik Terlouw
has served as a specially appointed researcher and lecturer for the Faculty of Architecture at Delft University of Technology. His writings include 'Een eigen huis/A House of One's Own' (*OASE* 52, 1999).

Alexander Tzonis
is a professor at Tsinghua University in China and professor emeritus at Delft University of Technology. He is the director of Design Knowledge Systems, a multi-disciplinary research centre on architectural cognition. Tzonis was educated at Yale University and taught at Harvard University from 1967 to 1981. Among his publications are *The Shape of Community* (Penguin, 1972) with Serge Chermayeff and *Towards a Non-oppressive Environment* (MIT Press, 1972), *Classical Architecture* (MIT Press, 1986) and *The Roots of Modern Architecture* (SUN, 1984) both co-authored with Liane Lefaivre. His latest books are *Santiago Calatrava's Bridges* and *Santiago Calatrava's Athens Olympics,* both published by Rizzoli in 2005.

Endry van Velzen
is an architect and partner in the firm of De Nijl Architects in Rotterdam. With his firm, he works on projects for the regeneration of various parts of the city, such as historic centres, pre-war residential districts and the post-war city. He is currently involved in urban-design plans and/or construction plans for such cities as Amsterdam, Antwerp, Apeldoorn, The Hague, Emmen, Groningen, Rotterdam and Utrecht. He frequently authors publications on the problems of urban renewal.

Pieter van Wesemael
is a partner in urban design, strategic area development and spatial policy with the Inbo consultancy in Amsterdam and a professor of architectural design and urban culture at Eindhoven University of Technology. As part of his academic chair programme, he deals with the correlation between changes in societal structures, the development of new programmatic concepts and the genesis of other spatial typologies and strategies. His current focus is on lifestyle housing concepts, multifunctional accommodations and creative factories. At Inbo, work is currently being conducted on such projects as urban-design sectional elaborations for the Zuidas in Amsterdam, spatial-programmatic area developments for Hart van Zuid in Hengelo and future projections for the red-light district in Amsterdam.

Christopher Woodward
is an architect based in London and affiliated with the Bartlett School of Architecture and Planning, University College, London. He is co-author of *A Guide to the Architecture of London* and author of such books as *The Buildings of Europe: Barcelona* and *The Buildings of Europe: Rome.*

Gerard van Zeijl
is professor emeritus in architecture history and theory at Eindhoven University of Technology. After qualifying as a structural engineer at Delft University of Technology he specialised in architecture history. As a professor at Eindhoven University of Technology he was instrumental in helping define 'the Eindhoven School'. He has also been a guest speaker at various venues in the Netherlands and abroad, including the European Association for Architectural Education. After earning his doctorate with a thesis on Durand's architectural treatises in 1993, he was appointed a professor at Eindhoven University of Technology and the Free University of Brussels. He led the doctoral research project 'Architecture for the Long Term' and, in addition to articles in various journals, has several buildings to his name. He is currently working on the book *Voorbij de zeven dagen van architectuur* (Beyond the Seven Days of Architecture).

Jurjen Zeinstra
studied at the Faculty of Architecture of Delft University of Technology. Together with Mikel van Gelderen he founded Zeinstra van Gelderen Architects. In cooperation with Ira Koers they have realised projects like the Tumble House (1998) and housing in Almere (2000) and IJburg (2006) and, with Mark Pimlott, the restaurant Puck Pip in The Hague (2007). Jurjen Zeinstra works as an assistant professor of architectural design and interiors at Delft University of Technology and has been an editor of both *OASE* and *Forum* and lectured at various architecture academies. He is currently preparing a publication on Amsterdam West.

Independent Peer-Reviewed
Journal for Architecture,
published by NAi Publishers
in collaboration with Die Keure
for the OASE Foundation

NAi Uitgevers/Publishers
T +31 (0)10 2010133
F +31 (0)10 2010130
info@naipublishers.nl
www.naipublishers.nl
www.oase.archined.nl

ISSN 0169 – 6238
ISBN 978-90-5662-063-9

OASE
p/a D'Laine Camp
Prins Frederik Hendrikstraat 107
3051 ER Rotterdam
the Netherlands

EDITORS
Tom Avermaete, Pnina Avidar, David de Bruijn, Joachim Declerck, Christoph Grafe, Klaske Havik, Anne Holtrop, Johan Lagae, Ruben Molendijk, Lara Schrijver, Mechthild Stuhlmacher

EDITORS OF THIS ISSUE
Joachim Declerck, Filip Geerts, Véronique Patteeuw, Marc Schoonderbeek

TEXT SELECTION BY
Marc Schoonderbeek, Filip Geerts

MANAGING EDITOR
D'Laine Camp

ACADEMIC EDITOR
Véronique Patteeuw

MEMBERS OF THE BOARD
Pnina Avidar, Simon Franke, Henk Hanekamp, Ton Idsinga, Dirk de Meyer, Jaap van Rijs, Max Risselada, Dirk Sijmons, Klaske Havik, Nathalie de Vries, Enno Zuidema.

ASSOCIATED UNIVERSITIES
Technische Universiteit Delft
Technische Universiteit Eindhoven
Katholieke Universiteit Leuven
Universiteit van Gent

ACADEMIC BOARD
Umberto Barbieri
Christine Boyer
Maristella Casciato
Bernard Colenbrander
Adrian Forty
Philip Goad
André Loeckx
Michael Müller
Bart Verschaffel

PHOTO CREDITS
All images were reproduced from the *OASE* issues in which the articles were originally published
For works of visual artists affiliated with a CISAC-organization the copyrights have been settled with Pictoright in Amsterdam.
© 2008, c/o Pictoright Amsterdam

It was not possible to find all the copyright holders of the illustrations used. Interested parties are requested to contact NAi Publishers, Mauritsweg 23, 3012 JR Rotterdam, The Netherlands.

DESIGN
Karel Martens & Joris Kritis, Werkplaats Typografie, Arnhem

COPY EDITING
D'Laine Camp

PRINTING
Die Keure, Bruges

PRODUCTION
Véronique Patteeuw, Barbera van Kooij, NAi Publishers

PUBLISHER
NAi Publishers in collaboration with Die Keure

SUBSCRIPTIONS AND ADMINISTRATION
Abonnementenland
P.O. Box 20
1910 AA Uitgeest
The Netherlands
Tel +31 (0)900 – ABOLAND
(0900-2265263 – € 0,10 p.m)
Fax +31 (0)251 310405
www.aboland.nl

SUBSCRIPTIONS
OASE is published three times a year. For subscriptions please contact the administration. You can fill in the card included in this issue or subscribe by email, info@naipublishers.nl. Subscriptions are renewed automatically. If you wish to cancel, please inform the administration in writing 4 weeks before the end of the subscription period. Prices are subject to change.

Subscriptions in the Netherlands and Belgium
individuals € 55
organisations € 80
students € 40
Subscriptions in Europe
individuals € 65
organisations € 85
students € 50

Subscriptions outside Europe
individuals, organisations, students € 95

This publication was made possible by the financial support of:

The Netherlands Architecture Fund, Rotterdam
HGIS Culture Fund, Rotterdam
Prins Bernhard Cultuurfonds
The Flemish Government

NAi Publishers is an internationally orientated publisher specialized in developing, producing and distributing books on architecture, visual arts and related disciplines.

www.naipublishers.nl
info@naipublishers.nl

Available in North, South and Central America through D.A.P./ Distributed Art Publishers Inc, 155 Sixth Avenue 2nd Floor, New York, NY 10013-1507, Tel 212 6271999, Fax 212 6279484.

Available in the United Kingdom and Ireland through Art Data, 12 Bell Industrial Estate, 50 Cunnington Street, London W4 5HB, Tel 208 7471061, Fax 208 7422319.

Printed and bound in Belgium

Sponsors **Arcadis Architecten** Amersfoort, www.arcadis.nl / **architecten BOB361 bvba** goedele desmet ivo vanhamme jean-michel culas, Brussel, Parijs, www.bob361.com / **BVR** adviseurs stedelijke ontwikkeling, landschap en infrastructuur, Rotterdam, www.bvr.nl / **Daad architecten** Beilen, www.daad.nl / **DaF architecten** Rotterdam, www.daf.luna.nl / **De Zwarte Hond BV** Groningen, Rotterdam, www.dezwartehond.nl / **diederendirrix** Eindhoven, www.diederendirrix.nl / **Enno Zuidema Stedebouw** Rotterdam, www.ezstedebouw.nl / **Geurst & Schulze architecten** Den Haag, www.geurst-schulze.nl / **HKB stedenbouwkundigen** Groningen, Rotterdam, www.hkbs.nl / **H+N+S Landschapsarchitecten** Utrecht, www.hnsland.nl / **Inbo Adviseurs** Stedenbouwkundigen Architecten, Amersfoort, Amsterdam, Drachten, Eindhoven, Rijswijk en Woudenberg, www.inbo.com / **Joost Meuwissen Architect** Amsterdam, www.joostmeuwissen.nl / **KCAP** Rotterdam, www.kcap.nl / **Mecanoo architecten b.v.** Delft, www.mecanoo.nl / **MVRDV** Rotterdam, www.mvrdv.nl / **Neutelings Riedijk Architecten** Rotterdam, www.neutelings-riedijk.com / **Office for Metropolitan Architecture (OMA)** Rotterdam, Beijing, New York, www.oma.nl / **Palmboom & van den Bout Stedenbouwkundigen bv** Rotterdam, www.palmbout.nl / **Rijnboutt Van der Vossen Rijnboutt** Architectuur – stedenbouw – strategie, Amsterdam, www.rvrbv.nl / **SVP Architectuur en Stedenbouw** Amersfoort, www.svp-svp.nl / **Tony Fretton Architects** London UK, www.tonyfretton.com / **West 8 urban design & landscape architecture** Rotterdam, www.west8.nl